DICTIONARY OF
S¥MßOLS

DATE DUE

DICTIONARY OF
S ¥ M ß O L S

an illustrated guide to traditional images, icons, and emblems

JACK TRESIDDER

CHRONICLE BOOKS
SAN FRANCISCO

Dictionary of Symbols

First published in the United States in 1998 by Chronicle Books

First published in Great Britain in 1997 by Helicon Publishing Ltd

Copyright © 1997 by Duncan Baird Publishers.
Commissioned artwork copyright © 1997 by Duncan Baird Publishers.
All rights reserved. No part of this book may be reproduced in any form
without written permission from the publisher.

Editors: Mike Darton, Judy Dean
Designer: John Grain
Commissioned artwork: Phillip Hood

Printed in Singapore

Library of Congress Cataloging-in-Publication Data

Tresidder, Jack.
        Dictionary of Symbols : an illustrated guide to traditional images,
    icons, and emblems / Jack Tresidder
                    p.   cm.
        Includes index.
        ISBN 0–8118–1888–8 (hc). -- ISBN 0-8118-1470-X (pb).
        1. Signs and symbols--Dictionaries.   2. Emblems--Dictionaries.
    I. Title.
    GR931.T74   1998
    302.2'223--dc21   97-27548
                                                     CIP

Distributed in Canada by Raincoast Books
8680 Cambie Street
Vancouver, B.C. V6P 6M9

10 9 8 7 6 5 4 3 2 1

Chronicle Books
85 Second Street
San Francisco, CA 94105

Web Site: www.chronbooks.com

Contents

Foreword   6

The A–Z Dictionary   9

Feature Panels
    Afterworlds   10
    Animals   14
    Beasts of Fable   23
    Cardinal Points   37
    Chastity   43
    Colours   50
    Cross   56–7
    Death   62
    Elements   74
    Fame   78
    Fidelity   80
    Fish   83
    Flowers   85
    Fortune   86
    Fruit   88
    Jewels   113
    Liberty   122
    Longevity   125
    Metals   133
    Muses   141
    Numbers   146
    Passion   153
    Peace   154
    Planets   162
    Seasons   179
    Seven Deadly Sins   180
    Truth   212
    Vanity   216
    Victory   217
    Vigilance   218
    Virtues   220
    Wisdom   229

Acknowledgments   236
Index of Supplementary Words   236

How To Use This Book

This dictionary has entries on major symbols that can be found in myth, literature and art, as well as those that have entered into the mainstream of everyday life. They are all arranged in A–Z order. Interspersed alphabetically with these entries are highlighted feature panels on both coherent symbol systems (such as Planets) and generic categories (such as Colours and Beasts of Fable); some of the most important examples mentioned in these features also have their own entries in the dictionary. Other feature panels cover the symbols used to embody abstract concepts or moral qualities (such as Peace and Chastity), which are often the subjects of works of art.

Cross-references in the margin relate to entries elsewhere in the dictionary that expand upon subjects to which reference is made in the text.

The illustrations are inspired by works of art from ancient artifacts to 19th-century painting. In all cases the artist has simplified for the sake of clarity.

The Index of Supplementary Words (p.236) covers symbols, mythological characters and works of art and literature that are discussed in the text but are not themselves the subjects of a main entry in the dictionary.

Foreword

Traditional symbols form a visual shorthand for ideas – and yet their functions and meanings extend to something much more than that. For thousands of years they have enabled sculptors, painters and craftsmen to embody and reinforce deep thoughts and beliefs about human life in single, immediate and powerful images. Like those of *haiku*, their messages are swift, simple and memorable. They are also unrestrictive because they crystallize ideas without confining them.

The essential difference between a symbol and a sign is that signs have practical, unambiguous meanings: Private, No Smoking, Danger. Symbols have greater imaginative resonance and more complex, sometimes ambiguous, meanings. Some symbols encapsulate the most ancient and fundamental beliefs that humans have had about the cosmos, their place in it, how they should behave and what they should honour or revere. Many have psychological import. Even symbols that embody simpler ideas heighten the significance of the ordinary object chosen as symbol, expanding it from the particular to the general: a heart carved in a tree is a symbol, not a sign.

In communicating large ideas, images long predated writing. Carved, painted or worked into effigies, clothing or ornaments, images that had become familiar symbols through repetition were used for magical purposes, to ward off evil or to entreat or placate gods – and also to control societies, to weld them together, to inspire loyalty, obedience, aggression, love or fear. A coherent system of living symbols could make people feel in harmony with themselves, their community and the cosmos. It could inspire collective action. People still fight and die under emblems, standards or flags that have symbolic significance.

In the beginning, the most important symbols represented attempts to give order and significance to human life in a mysterious universe. Many fundamental ideas, and the symbols for them, were remarkably similar, whether in primitive cultures or in the developed civilizations of Asia, India, the Middle East, western Europe and Central America. In the West, this symbolic language began to lose its power in the Renaissance when science, reason and increasing respect for individuality led to a loss of interest in traditional beliefs and rituals, draining many symbols of their imaginative life in civil or religious custom or in folklore.

Symbolism retains its graphic and psychological force not only in such creative fields as art, literature, music and film but also in politics and advertising. Modern symbolism, with its vast range of new imagery and transient icons, lies outside the scope of this book. Here, the aim is to provide a succinct dictionary of symbols with a longer history, many of them important to a rounded understanding of the development of human thought, art, custom, religion and mythology. Cultural reference is as wide as possible within a book intended for a Western readership. Entries first define and explain the most important and universal meanings of each symbol, and then discuss subsidiary meanings. Particular cultures are identified when the symbolic usage is more specific than general.

Myths, spoken or written, are themselves extended symbol systems, encapsulating religious, philosophical or psychological "truths", often based on tribal memories. Thus the myth of Oedipus, who killed his father and married his mother, symbolizes common human feelings of mother love and jealousy of the father. However, this book is a dictionary of individual symbols – which can be objects or graphic images standing for an idea, feeling or abstract quality, or else ritual actions standing for an inner experience.

Symbols are often iconic, imitating the form of the thing to which they refer. Their meaning is sometimes unexpected and sometimes self-evident because it is based on some quality that seems inherent in, for example, a lion (courage) or a rock (solidity). In selecting entries I have passed over subjects that have banal or entirely self-explanatory associations, such as "steel", symbolizing strength, or "curtain", symbolizing concealment. Familiar

features of the earth or the visible universe – animals, birds, fish, insects, plants or stones – are all included in the symbolic repertoire. These, like humans themselves, were once seen as reflections of a greater reality, having qualities expressive of laws and moral "truths" inherent in the cosmic order.

Alternatively, symbols may be aniconic, having a form chosen more arbitrarily. They may even be based, as often in China, on a homonym – a purely phonetic association with the name of something else. Aniconic symbols can range from graphic lines or shapes to words or ritual actions.

The entries in this book are selected to explain the meanings of visual symbols or symbolic actions, especially those that may now be puzzling, to demonstrate both the universality of many symbols and the cultural variety of others, and to show that some of the most familiar things around us have, or once had, deeper and more fascinating meanings and associations than we might now assume.

Jack Tresidder

Acacia

Immortality, especially in Judeo-Christian thought. Hardwood of an acacia species, the *shittah*, was used to build the Tabernacle and, by tradition, acacia spines formed Christ's crown of thorns. The red and white flowers suggest life–death duality. Freemasonry uses an acacia bough as an initiation symbol and funerary tribute – a reference to the branch supposedly laid on the grave of the biblical Solomon's master builder, Hiram, by fellow workers who killed him when they could not make him reveal the mysteries of his craft.

Acanthus

A Greco-Roman triumphal image of life's trials surmounted, a symbolism suggested by the plant's thorns and its vigorous growth. Stylized acanthus leaves on the Corinthian capital may refer to a Greek myth of an acanthus springing up on the grave of a hero.

Acorn

Fecundity, prosperity and the power of spiritual growth from the kernel of the truth – a symbolism that accounts for the "acorn" on the red cord of a cardinal's hat. Acorns were sacred to the rural Nordic god of thunder, Thor, as part of the cult of the oak. They may have phallic significance in some Celtic carvings.

AFTERWORLDS *see panel on p.10*

Agate

A lucky gemstone, prized since antiquity, its variously coloured bands are sometimes linked with the Moon, sometimes with Mercury. Qualities associated with agate include fortitude, happiness, prosperity and sexual success. Folklore said that the gemstone could deflect weapons.

Air

Spiritual life, freedom, purity, the primal element in most cosmogonies, equated with the soul by Stoic philosophers (followers of the Greek Zeno, 2nd century BCE). Air shares much of the symbolism of breath and wind (both of which are somewhat easier for artists to depict).

Acacia: *see*
Branch, Bough; Crown; Red; Thorn

Acanthus: *see*
Thorn

Acorn: *see*
Oak; TRUTH

Agate: *see*
PLANETS

Air: *see*
Breath, Breathing; Wind

AFTERWORLDS: *see*
Angels; Asphodel; Black;
Bones; Bridge; CARDINAL
POINTS; Cherubim;
Cremation; DEATH;
Devils; Dog; Dome;
Feathers; Fire, Flame;
Garden; Heart; Island;
Journey; Karma; Light;
Nirvana; Purgatory; Red;
River, Stream; Scales; Sea;
Seraphim; Seven; Sky; Soul;
Sphere; Stupa; Throne
(seat); Transformation;
Trumpet; Veil; Void; White

AFTERWORLDS

A theme that has created some of the richest of all symbol systems. Egyptian and Tibetan Books of the Dead lay down precise rules for conduct during and after death, and Chinese, Japanese, Mesoamerican, Buddhist, Muslim, Hindu and Christian eschatological texts similarly give guidance, but in less elaborate form. In primitive traditions the afterworld is usually non-judgmental – a happier version of the world as we know it. In ethically distinct afterworlds, the symbolism of bliss or misery is remarkably consistent: paradise lies above the vault of the sky (architecturally symbolized by the dome and stupa), sparkling with light and harmonious with music; hell lies below – dark, desolate, smoky, putrid and painful. Retribution is a common theme, symbolized by the weighing of souls. Scales were used by St Michael to weigh Christian good and evil deeds, and also in the Egyptian Hall of Judgment where hearts, symbolizing conscience, were weighed against the truth-feather of the goddess Ma'at. Judgment for Tibetan Buddhists was weighed out in black and white pebbles; for Japanese Buddhists by reference to

Egyptian figures escorting a soul into the underworld.

red and white severed heads. Other trials involved dangerous journeys – perhaps a bridge to be crossed, narrow and slippery for sinners, broad for the virtuous. The afterworld was often reached by crossing a river, like the Greek Styx with its sinister ferryman, Charon. Or it might involve a sea journey, as in Oceanic and Aboriginal traditions. Sometimes it was an exclusive place (the Scandinavian Valhalla for slain warriors), sometimes open to those whose sins were expiated in the afterworld (as in the Catholic Purgatory, a painful but not necessarily final stage for minor sinners). Hells were not necessarily final either, although medieval Christianity relished the concept of eternal hellfire. The kind of paradise depicted by artists usually represented only a transitional stage toward something ineffable, symbolized by pure light. Heaven was constructed in a series of layers or spheres (thus the Islamic Seventh Heaven in which Muhammad reached the Throne of Allah). From celestial cities or gardens the righteous soul ascended toward an abstract bliss, the contemplation of God's radiance.

Albatross: *see*
Birds

Albatross

A burden of guilt – a symbolism created by *The Rime of the Ancient Mariner*, a ballad by Samuel Taylor Coleridge (1772–1834) in which the shooting of an albatross broke a mariners' taboo. Traditionally, the bird was a good omen, its power and stamina so admired that in folklore it embodied the souls of dead sailors.

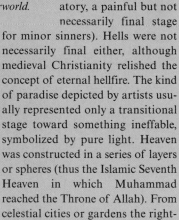

Alchemy

An ancient technological symbol for the perfectibility of the human soul. Alchemists sought initially to transmute base metals to gold and silver, and later to produce a universal solvent, curative or elixir of life made from the elements of earth, fire, air and water together with a primal fifth, the quintessence. The process was overlaid with symbolism taken from philosophy, astrology, mysticism and, in the medieval era, religion. Symbolic

An alchemist channelling stellar energy into his chemical furnace, from a German woodcut of 1519.

forms or terms were used for equipment, materials and processes, partly to borrow their force, partly to baffle the uninitiated. The colours black, white, red and gold symbolized a progression from reduction (equated with original guilt) to distillation (purity). Although charlatans abounded, serious alchemists worked with a sense of spiritual purpose, believing that divine intervention would bring success.

Alcohol

Vital energy, uniting the contradictory elements of fire (masculine) and water (feminine), the *aqua vitae* ("water of life") of alchemy. Alcohol was also linked with creativity and wisdom.

Alligator *see* Crocodile

Almond

Purity, hidden truth, virgin birth – a mythic association that has both pagan and biblical roots.

The juice of the pressed almond was equated in the ancient world with semen, leading to the story that Attis, consort of the Phrygian and Greco-Roman earth-goddess Cybele, was conceived from an almond, the pure fruit of nature. The almond was the most sacred Hebrew tree, linked with immortality. It's older links with self-generation were given biblical weight in the story of Aaron's rod (Numbers 17:8). God's sign that Aaron should have priestly status was a rod that blossomed miraculously and produced almonds. This story shares in the virgin birth symbolism of the almond-shaped aureole (mandorla) enclosing Christ and Mary in medieval iconography.

The sweet nut within its casing suggested to Arab mystics a secret reality masked by appearances. The almond is a Chinese yin symbol. The early-flowering tree is linked with rebirth, watchfulness, delicacy.

In European folklore it is said that a virgin can wake pregnant if she sleeps under an almond tree and dreams of her love.

Alpha and Omega

Totality, as represented by the first and last letters of the Greek alphabet. Used together, the letters symbolize a oneness and wholeness of space, time and spirit. On crosses, they refer to the Christ of Revelation: "I am the Alpha and Omega", and on graves to an acceptance that God is the beginning and end.

Alchemy: *see*
Alcohol; Androgyne; Bear; Caduceus; Eagle; Egg; ELEMENTS; Fire, Flame; Gold; Grail; Lion; Mercury; METALS; Oven, Furnace; Philosopher's Stone; Quintessence; Red; Salamander; Silver; Sulphur; Transformation; White; Zodiac

Alcohol: *see*
Alchemy; Fire, Flame; Intoxication; Soma; Water; Wine

Almond: *see*
Mandorla; Rod; Tree; TRUTH; Virginity; Yin-yang

Alpha and Omega: *see*
CROSS

The Greek letters alpha (above) and omega (below). For both letters the capital form is shown on the left, the lower case on the right.

Amaranth: *see*
FLOWERS; Hare, Rabbit

Amber: *see*
Amulet; Sun; Tiger

Amen: *see*
Om (Aum); Word

Amethyst: *see*
Intoxication; JEWELS;
Violet

Amulet: *see*
Ring

Anchor: *see*
CROSS; Dolphin; Phallus;
Snake; VIRTUES

Androgyne: *see*
Alchemy; Circumcision;
Man; Marriage; Woman;
Yin-yang

*A 17th-century
alchemical image
of the androgyne.*

Amaranth

A long-lasting flowering plant, depicted on Greek tombs and sculptures as a symbol of immortality. Amaranth was linked with Artemis and credited with healing properties. In China, its flowers were offered to the lunar hare at the Moon Festival as a token of immortality.

Amber

Amber is linked by its colour with solar energy. In ancient China, the word for amber literally meant "tiger soul" – resin suposedly formed from the remains of tigers, hence embodying courage. In mythology, many divinities shed tears of amber; the sisters of Phaeton were transformed into weeping pine trees as they grieved for their brother's death after he had rashly driven his father's (Helios's) sun chariot. Amber was long used as a talisman and cure for everything from rheumatism to headaches.

Amen

An affirmation (from the Hebrew meaning "truly" or "verily") which has acquired in Christianity something of the symbolic force of the sacred Hindu mantra *Om* (or *Aum*) as an embodiment in sound of the divine spirit, summoned to answer prayers.

Amethyst

A quartz gemstone symbolizing temperance, peace, humility and piety, attuned to the Age of Aquarius. Amethyst was worn by bishops because of the stone's modest violet or cool purple colour, and the Greek belief that it promoted sobriety (*amethustos*, "not intoxicated"). As talismans these stones were thought to promote wholesome dreams.

Amulet

Beneficial power. The object used as an amulet, sometimes natural, sometimes made as an inscribed medallion or locket, supposedly creates a magic connection between its wearer and the symbolic force that it represents.

Anchor

Hope, salvation, safety, firmness, fidelity, prudence. Its Christian symbolism was drawn from its form as well as its function in that the top bar could suggest a cross – its clandestine meaning in catacomb carvings. Hope of salvation is the New Testament "anchor of the soul" (Hebrews 6:19). A popular Renaissance motif combined an anchor (restraint) and dolphin (speed) with the Augustan motto *festina lente* ("hasten slowly"). As an emblem of St Nicholas, patron saint of sailors, the anchor signified safety. It appears also in Egyptian iconography as a creation image – the shape combining a boat (female) and phallic mast, snake entwined.

Androgyne

Divine wholeness – an ancient symbolism derived from widespread worship of primal gods who were simultaneously male and female. The Chinese yin-yang symbol epitomizes an androgynous perfection in which all opposites are complementary to one another. Platonic philosophy, Sufi mysticism, and Greek, Egyptian, Oriental, Aboriginal and Mesoamerican mythology all perceived the original state of being as androgynous. By implication, Adam himself contained male and female.

The androgyne was also an alchemical symbol, embodying the oneness that was the goal of Hermetic science.

Social pressures were commonly in conflict with this ideal, notably in the practice of circumcision and clitoral excision, representing efforts to clarify sexual differences. Love and marriage have been seen as more practical ways to attain oneness, symbolized in Greek mythology by the story of Hermaphroditus who was loved so fervently by a nymph of Salmacis that she became absorbed into his body. Hence "hermaphrodite" (strictly, in biology, one who has incomplete male and female organs).

Anemone

The transience of life, fragility, grief, death, virginity – symbols based on the ephemeral nature of this wild flower, its scarlet petals, and its name (meaning "of the wind"). Anemones are identified with the biblical "flowers of the field" and sometimes appear in crucifixion scenes. They were also linked with dying god symbolism from the Greek myth that they sprang up where Adonis fell dead.

Angels

Anthropomorphic winged forms personifying divine will. Possibly evolved from Semitic and Egyptian winged deities, angels appear in a number of religions as intermediaries between material and spiritual planes, but their symbolism is most elaborate in the Islamic, Jewish and especially Christian faiths. Attributes in art include trumpets, harps, swords, censers and sceptres or wands. Angels appear variously in the roles of messengers (Greek *angelos*), warriors and, in more recent thinking, guardians or protectors – as in the 1914 vision of the Angel of Mons – corresponding to the human desire for individual pro-

tection. The hierarchy of angels proposed in the 5th century by Pseudo-Dionysius the Areopagite suggests another sublimation – of the wish for order on the divine as well as the social plane. In order of closeness to God, the angelic choirs were the six-winged seraphim (red) and cherubim (blue), thrones, dominions, virtues, powers, principalities, archangels, angels. Greek philosophers thought that angels steered the stars and were formed of some ethereal substance, but in Christian iconography they were steadily dematerialized, appearing often as winged heads, or in the playfulness of baroque art, as Cupid-like infants (*putti*). Fallen angels, led by Satan, symbolized the sin of pride.

ANIMALS *see panel on p.14*

Ankh

A cross with a loop at the top, representing immortality (and corresponding to the ancient Egyptian symbol for "life" or "soul"), taken over by the Coptic Church to signify eternal life through Christ. Its geometric shape can be read as the sun rising, as the union of male and female principles or other opposites, and also as a key to esoteric knowledge and to the afterworld of the spirit.

Anointing

A rite of Middle-Eastern origin in which consecrated oil is used as a symbol of divine grace to sanctify rulers or those undergoing priestly ordination, conferring holy authority.

Ant

Diligence, patience, humility, foresight. In China, the ant symbolized order and the tireless servant. Its

Anemone: *see*
CROSS; FLOWERS; Red; Virginity

Angels: *see*
Archangels; Cherubim; Devils; Harp; Meteorite; Sceptre; Seraphim; SEVEN DEADLY SINS; Sword; Trumpet; Wand; Wings

Ankh: *see*
CROSS; Key; Sun

Anointing: *see*
Oil

An Egyptian ankh with a solar symbol superimposed, from a papyrus of the 2nd century BCE.

ANIMALS: *see*
BEASTS OF FABLE; Birds;
FISH; Totem; *and individual
names*

ANIMALS

Animals have always been the most immediate, powerful and important foundation for symbolism. No other source in the natural world has provided such a richly varied range of iconography. Few human qualities could not be personified in the animal world from close observation of animal forms, habits and characteristics.

Psychology has followed religion in attaching to animals the essential symbolism of "the instinctual", "the unconscious", the libido, and the emotions. This was by no means their original significance. The reverence paid to animals in most primitive cultures had to do with a perception that they are more in touch with unseen cosmic forces than humankind.

A detail from a decorated cloth showing shamans appeasing animal spirits.

Their frequently superior physical and sensory abilities led to the general belief that they possessed magical or spiritual powers. For shamans they were a means of access to these powers. Clans or tribes adopted them as totems for similar reasons. Their skins, furs or feathers were worn to symbolize magical alliances in which they were patrons of the wearers. Most Egyptian gods were personified by animals, and elsewhere too, the most prestigious symbolized not brute passions but spiritual qualities. Medieval bestiaries assumed that their symbolism could be strictly classified, an idea supported by a surprising degree of cross-cultural uniformity in the concepts embodied by different animals.

Antelope: *see*
Air; Deer; Wind

Antlers: *see*
Deer; Horn

industry, seen in the Bible as a virtue, was considered somewhat excessive in Hindu and Buddhist thought; thus it became an image of the ceaseless, petty activity of those blind to the transience of human life. In Mali, ants were benificent organizers, originators of the skills of building and weaving, and by sympathetic magic their nests could bring fecundity. Anteaters, conversely, symbolized harm. In Morocco, ants were fed to lethargic patients to improve their metabolism.

Antelope

Grace, speed, clarity of vision – a spiritual ideal and fit mount for gods in both African and Indian traditions. To the bushmen of southern Africa the antelope was an embodiment of the supreme creator, Cagn, and in Mali, a cult hero who brought humankind the skills of agriculture. The gazelle is an attribute of Vayu, the Persian and Indian god of air and wind. For Islamic thinkers, its soulful eyes symbolize the contemplative life.

Antlers

A benign symbol that represents spring fertility, prosperity and fecundity. Celtic antlered gods such as Cernunnos symbolized crop growth. The ten-pointed antlers of the shaman were considered to be an emblem of his supernatural powers.

Ape

An animal of sharply diverging symbolism, respected in ancient Egypt, Africa, India and China, but deeply distrusted in Christian tradition where it was equated with vice, lust, idolatry and devilish heresies. The ape's imitative skills were widely used to satirize human vanity and other follies. In Western art it appears with an apple in its mouth as a symbol of the Fall, and later more playfully as an analogue for artists themselves imitating nature. In Egyptian iconography the caped baboon is a symbol of wisdom. The Indian ape or monkey god Hanuman represents courage, strength, and self-sacrifice.

Apple

Bliss, especially sexual – a symbolism perhaps linked with the vulva shape of the core in long-section. The apple was widely used as a symbol for love, marriage, springtime, youth, fertility and longevity or immortality – and therefore suggested temptation in Christian tradition. Greek, Celtic and Nordic mythology all describe it as the miraculously sustaining fruit of the gods. The Greek hero Herakles (in Roman myth, Hercules) wins the golden apples of immortality from the Hesperides. As an object of desire, a golden apple is tossed by Eris (Discord) "to the fairest" of the goddesses, setting off a dispute arbitrated by Paris who awards the prize to Aphrodite (Venus), who fatefully rewards him with the beautiful Helen of Troy (thus causing the Trojan War).

Although the fruit that tempted Eve is unnamed in Genesis, the apple was perhaps a natural choice for later interpreters of scripture. It thus acquired both negative and positive meanings of "knowledge", in that Eve plucked it from the Tree of the Knowledge of Good and Evil. In art the apple symbolizes Original Sin when it is shown in the mouth of an ape or serpent; Christ holding or reaching for an apple is a symbol of the Redeemer.

Hermetic science, noting the "quintessential" five-fold shape of the cross-sectioned core, also used this fruit as a symbol for knowledge. In China the apple stands for peace and its blossom for beauty.

Arabesque

In Islamic art, the ultimate visual symbol of the difficult and complex journey toward sublime clarity. A decorative linear style based on intertwining flowers, leaves and stems, it brilliantly skirts the Islamic prohibition on figurative art, forming a kind of visual incantation, an infinitely varied aid to contemplation.

Arch

A triumphal feature of Roman architecture, recalling more ancient classical associations of the arch with the sky and its supreme god Zeus (in Roman myth, Jupiter). Initiates passing under an arch symbolically leave their former lives (hence the ceremonial arches formed for newlyweds).

Archangels

An order of angels with specific and personalized symbolism. Most prominently in art, Gabriel, as divine herald of the Annunciation, holds a lily or sceptre with fleur-de-lis; Michael, as warrior-guardian of the Righteous

Ape: *see*
Apple; Monkey; SEVEN DEADLY SINS; VIRTUES

Apple: *see*
Ape; Five; Snake; Tree

Arabesque: *see*
Interlacing; Journey

Arch: *see*
Marriage; Sky

Archangels: *see*
Angels; Fleur-de-lis; Lily; Scales; Sceptre; Staff; Sword

Ark: *see*
Acacia; Chest; Flood; Ship;
Whale

Arm: *see*
Rod

Arrow: *see*
Bow; Feathers; Lightning;
PEACE; Sun

Ash: *see*
Tree

and instrument of judgment, holds a
sword or scales; and Raphael, as protector of children, pilgrims and travellers, holds a staff. The other, less well
known, biblical archangel was Uriel.

Ark

Salvation, redemption, conservation,
sanctuary, regeneration. The story of
a box-like vessel preserving the continuity of life from floodwaters is found
in the mythology of many peoples all
around the world. Especially note-
worthy is the Mesopotamian *Epic of
Gilgamesh*. But Hebrew and Christian
ark symbolism is probably the richest.
The ark can stand for the Church

*A detail showing Noah's ark, from a
medieval fresco in the chapel of Saint-
Savin-sur-Gartempe, France.*

(carrying saints and sinners), for
Mary bearing her son, or for Christ as
Redeemer. The Hebrew Ark of the
Covenant, a chest of gilded acacia,
symbolized the pledge of divine protection. In more secular symbolism
the ark is the earth adrift in space; in
psychology it represents the womb.

Arm

Instrumental, protective or judgmental force. A symbol of sovereign
power and the active principle in
Egyptian, Hindu and Buddhist

iconography – and of God in the
Christian Trinity. Omnipotent gods
often have several arms and carry specific symbols of their various functions. To the Bambara of West Africa
the forearm is a symbol of the spirit, a
link between humanity and God. The
most universal symbolic gesture of
the arm is the submissive raising of
both arms, signalling both surrender
and an appeal for mercy, justice or, in
a religious context, divine grace.

Arrow

Penetration – by light, by death, by
love (human or divine), by perception.
Graphically, arrows represent energy,
directional accuracy and the annihilation of distance. They appear as sun
symbols and are the piercingly sweet
darts of Cupid and other gods of love.
Phallic symbolism, prominent in
Hinduism, is also suggested by
Bernini's sculpture of *The Ecstasy of
St Theresa* (1645–52). Arrows can
stand for the wrath of Allah, Christian martyrdom and death, especially
by lightning or by swift diseases like
the plague. Bundled or broken (as in
Native American symbolism), they
represent peace. In shamanism, feathered arrows are an ascension symbol.
Contemporary life has reduced
arrows mainly to directional signs.

Ash

The Scandinavian Cosmic Tree, linking hell, earth and heaven, and symbolizing fecundity, the union of opposites, invincibility and the continuity
of life. The ash in Greek mythology
embodies strength (and is therefore
sacred to Zeus), but in Baltic folklore
the tree is an emblem of the simple-
ton, perhaps because its leaves appear
late and are shed quickly.

Ashes

Extinction, bereavement, renunciation, penitence and, in some cultures – particularly Native American, a symbol also invoking a phoenix-like rebirth. Smearing the body with ash in some African tribal rites of passage has this meaning. In both Hebrew and Arab tradition, ashes are a mark of mourning. Indian *yogis* daub themselves with ashes to signify their renunciation of earthly vanities.

Asp *see* Cobra

Asphodel

A Greco-Roman flower of the underworld and of Persephone (in Roman myth, Proserpina) – a lily of appropriately pallid coloration with which to console the spirits of those chosen by the gods to enter the Elysian Fields. The asphodel is therefore a funerary symbol of mourning. Its roots, food for the dead, were thought to cure snakebite.

Ass

A well-entrenched symbol of foolishness, but traditionally of more varying significance. An ass was chosen by Christ for his entry into Jerusalem both to fulfil a prophecy and to signify the virtue of meekness, and thus usually stands for humility, patience and poverty in Christian thought. Chinese immortals ride white asses. By contrast, asses play harmful, even sinister, roles in both Egyptian and Indian myths, and are associated with lust or comical stupidity in Greco-Roman legends. Midas is given the ears of an ass as a symbol of his spiritual shortcomings (preferring Pan to Apollo). Ass's ears are part of the jester's cap, and Shakespeare's

Bottom (in *A Midsummer Night's Dream*, c.1595) wears the head of an ass in a satire of love. Other associated qualities are sloth and obstinacy.

Aureole

A general term for the visible radiant aura used in art to distinguish people of unusual spiritual power or holiness. More specific terms are the halo, usually shown as a ring of light; the nimbus, a cloudier form of radiance; and the mandorla, a stylized almond-shaped nimbus. The symbolism derives from radiant deities of ancient sun and fire cults. As the etymology of *aureole* indicates (from medieval Latin *aureola corona*, "crown of gold"), it is a term most aptly applied in a specific sense to radiance shown as a crown formed by spokes or beams of light, sometimes surrounding the body as well as the head.

Aurochs

A huge, extinct wild ox of Europe – a symbol in Assyrian and Sumerian iconography of the power of Enlil, the great Middle-Eastern god of the ordered cosmos, and of agriculture.

Axe

A near-universal symbol of decisive power, linked with ancient sun and storm gods, with Zeus in Greece and with Agni the Hindu god of fire. The axe is a Celtic, Nordic, African and Oceanic symbol of chiefly authority, and more generally the attribute of warriors. Its flashing, thudding, spark-striking fall explains much of its symbolic associations with fire and also with the creative, germinating force of the thunderbolt; it was used directly to invoke thunder and rain in West Africa. Axes were used to split

Ashes: *see*
Initiation; Phoenix

Asphodel: *see*
AFTERWORLDS; Lily

Ass: *see*
ANIMALS; Cap; SEVEN DEALY SINS; VIRTUES

Aureole: *see*
Almond; Crown; Halo; Mandorla; Nimbus

Aurochs: *see*
ANIMALS; Ox

Axe: *see*
Fire, Flame; Moon; Thunder

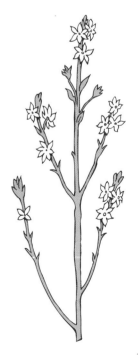

The asphodel flower, which in Greek and Roman myth was associated with the underworld.

Axis

Axis: *see*
Cave; Mountain; Omphalos;
Pillar; Tree

the skulls of sacrificial oxen in the Middle East, and are an attribute of several martyred Christian saints, notably Matthew.

More usually, an axe represents the forceful solving of a problem: it severs the round of Buddhist existence; symbolizes the union of families in Chinese marriages; and cures the headache of Zeus in the Greek legend in which Athene springs from a cleft in his head.

The double-headed axe carved into Minoan building blocks may invoke the protection of Zeus. Alternatively, its dual, half-moon curves may be a lunar symbol or may stand for the reconciliation of opposites.

Axis

A linear symbol of the centre in nearly all cosmologies of the ancient world – the supporting spine or spindle around which everything rotates.

The *axis mundi* also provided shamans and aspiring spirits with a means of moving between different layers of existence – the underworld, earth and heaven. Symbols of the axis range from rods to massive columnar structures, and from trees to sacred mountains.

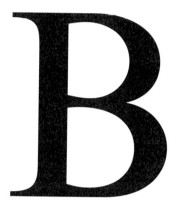

Ba

An Egyptian symbol for the soul, usually depicted as a hawk with human head. The Egyptians had a number of symbols for the individual life principle, not all of which, like the Ba, left the body at death.

Baboon *see* **Ape**

Badger

In Japan, an artful dodger with a streak of malice, the hero of many folk stories, sometimes shown outside restaurants selfishly pot-bellied. Its solitary, secretive habits have also suggested slyness in European folklore. "Badgering", meaning "harassment", relates to the controversial English sport of badger-baiting.

Baldachin

A square canopy on four poles carried in church processions and symbolizing celestial protection. The baldachin probably derived from the square or circular canopies placed above Eastern rulers denoting temporal as well as spiritual power.

Ball

A sun symbol in aerial games at ancient cultic festivals, especially in Mexico and Greece. Mesoamerican temples of sun-worship had elaborate ball courts for violent and ritualistic games. Elsewhere, the ball was one of the most popular of early playthings.

Bamboo

An Oriental symbol of resilience, longevity, happiness and spiritual truth – one of the three auspicious plants of winter. Bamboo was an attribute of the compassionate Bodhisattva Guanyin, and of the gentleman. Its ringed stem was associated with the steps to enlightenment; it can also symbolize the Buddha.

As a calligraphic tool, its pure line and hollow stem had sacred significance for Buddhist and Taoist scholars and artists. In South America, where bamboo was important as a cutting tool, blowpipe and instrument of sacred music, some tribes revered tall species of bamboo as Trees of Life. Bamboo was ritually used in Africa for circumcision.

Ba: *see*
Falcon, Hawk; Ka; Soul

Badger: *see*
ANIMALS

Baldachin: *see*
Canopy

Ball: *see*
Sun; Ziggurat

Bamboo: *see*
Circumcision;
LONGEVITY; Steps, Stairs;
Tree

The Ba, or soul, from an Egyptian painted wooden statuette of c.332–330BCE.

Banner: *see*
Air; VICTORY; Wind

Banyan: *see*
Temple; Tree

Baptism: *see*
Deer; Fire, Flame; FISH;
Initiation; Octagon; Scallop;
Shell; Water; Wind

Barley: *see*
Beer; Corn

Basilisk (Cockatrice): *see*
BEASTS OF FABLE;
Cobra; Cock (Rooster);
Dragon; SEVEN DEADLY
SINS; Snake; Toad; Wings

Basket: *see*
FLOWERS; Mother;
Woman

Bat: *see*
DEATH; Devils; Eclipse;
Light; LONGEVITY;
Night; Sun; Wings

*Indian Buddhists shown
meditating beneath the
sacred Banyan tree,
from an early 20th-
century painting.*

Banner

An emblem of ascendancy, especially in war, often thought to embody the spirit of a group or its leader. The multiple banners of Japanese warriors invoked victory, whereas Taoist banners symbolize the protective help of spirits or gods of the elements. A fluttering banner is the attribute of the Hindu god Vayu, of air and wind.

Banyan

The sacred tree of India, a probable model for the symbolism of the inverted Cosmic Tree in that it has an aerial root through which the transcendent spirit may be manifested throughout the universe. Temples were sometimes built into the main trunks.

Baptism

A spiritual rite of passage, symbolizing purification and regeneration. To psychologists, baptism by water represents dissolution of the old self and rebirth from the original waters of life. Its use in cults and religions is ancient and widespread, sometimes as a rite of initiation for either the living or the dead. Depending on the denomination, Christian baptism can symbolize entry into the Church, an adult seal of faith, rebirth in grace, atonement of past sin, or symbolic sharing in the death and resurrection of Christ. Less common are baptisms by wind, or by fire (the latter having been the fate or choice of some martyrs).

Barley

An ancient grain symbolizing fertility and life after death, especially in Middle-Eastern iconography. Barley was associated in Egypt with the resurrection of the god Osiris, and in Greece with Demeter, goddess of fecundity, and with her abducted daughter Persephone.

Basilisk (Cockatrice)

Originally a poisonous Egyptian crowned snake (perhaps a cobra); with the medieval addition of a cock's body and wings, this became a frightening personification of sins such as lust and a carrier of diseases such as syphilis. According to folklore, it was hatched by a toad from a serpent's egg laid by an aged cock on a dunghill. Unlike the dragon, which represented evil on a heroic scale, it menaced the unwary wrongdoer at the level of ordinary life.

Basket

An analogue for the protective maternal body, associated with both birth and rebirth. Basket-shaped plinths for images of Egyptian gods suggest also a symbolism of high rank; the biblical Moses and heroes of other cultures were found floating in baskets. A basket of flowers signifies hope and, in China, fruitful longevity. The Three Baskets (*Tripitaka*) divide the Buddhist canon into rules of discipline, basic doctrines and higher doctrines. Three baskets of wisdom also appear in Maori mythology, brought from heaven by the god Tane.

Bat

The enemy of light – hence widely an animal of fear and superstition, often associated with death, night and, in Judeo-Christian tradition, idolatry or Satanism. Bats can also signify madness, as in Goya's nightmarish 19th-century painting *The Sleep of Reason*. The bat is a powerful underworld divinity in Central American and

A bat, from a pre-Columbian Peruvian gold emblem. The bat was linked with sorcery in some parts of Peru.

Brazilian mythology, sometimes shown as the open-jawed devourer of light or of the sun itself. It was erroneously credited with sharp eyesight (vigilance, perspicuity) both in Africa and classical Greece. Homeric souls were bat-winged. In Europe, bats were once nailed to doors to frighten demons. This whole tradition is reversed in China where *fu* ("bat") is a homonym of "good luck". Two bats on greeting cards predict wealth, health, virtue, longevity and death with dignity.

Beads *see* **Rosary**

Bean

Fecundity, especially male, linked in Egyptian and Greco-Roman tradition with the souls of the dead (beans were an Orphic forbidden food) and the promise of life to come. They were used as love charms in India, and were popular talismans in Japan where they were customarily scattered in a house to ward off lightning and evil spirits.

Bear

Brutal primitive force – an emblem of warriors in northern regions of Europe and Asia. The bear was an incarnation of the god Odin in Scandinavia, where the fierce warrior Berserkers wore bearskins; and also of the huntress Artemis in Greece, where her cultic maidens dressed as bears. It is linked with many other warlike divinities including the Germanic Thor and the Celtic Artio of Berne (the Swiss city of "the bear"). A Native American symbol of strength, the bear is an emblem of masculine courage in China where dreams of a bear presaged the birth of sons. The bear, particularly the she-bear, also appears as a symbol of maternal strength, care and warmth (Kipling's Baloo, in *The Jungle Book*, 1894, is a male example). To the Ainu of northern Japan, and to the Algonquin Indians, the bear is an ancestral figure. It is also linked with lunar and resurrection symbolism, perhaps from its hibernation. Shamans used bear-masks to communicate with forest spirits. To Jung the bear symbolized dangerous aspects of the unconscious, and it is viewed as a dark power in Christian and Islamic traditions: cruel, lustful, vengeful, greedy – a representation of the deadly sin of gluttony in Western art. The biblical David did battle with a bear, and the formless bear cub, "licked into shape" by its mother, became an image of the heathen needing the spiritual ministrations of the Church. Similarly, the bear is the alchemical symbol for the primary state of matter.

Beard

Dignity, sovereignty, virility, courage and wisdom. Male divinities, kings, heroes and sages are commonly bearded in iconography. In Egypt, beardless rulers – including queens – were shown with false beards as a

Bean: *see*
Soul; Lightning

Bear: *see*
Alchemy; ANIMALS; Bones; Forest; Mask; Moon; SEVEN DEADLY SINS

Beard: *see*
Hair; Queen; WISDOM

Beaver: *see*
ANIMALS

Bee: *see*
Blue; Candle; CHASTITY;
Hive; Honey; Lotus; Soul;
Triangle; Virginity; Woman

Beer: *see*
Barley; Intoxication; Mead

mark of status. Semitic and Sikh traditions link beards with honour.

BEASTS OF FABLE *see panel,*
opposite

Beaver

Once common in European forests,
and a much larger species, the beaver's
busy creativity has always made it a
symbol of industry and, in Christianity, asceticism.

Bee

A remarkably rich symbol, less so in
iconography than as an exemplar of
ethical virtues, especially for writers of
homilies. Among qualities attributed
to the bee are diligence, organiza-
tional and technical skills, sociability,
purity, chastity, cleanliness, spirituality, wisdom, courage, abstinence,
sobriety, creativity, selflessness, eloquence (by association with "hon-
eyed" words) and illumination (by
association with beeswax candles).
The bee symbolized royalty or the
monarchical system in the ancient
Middle East, in Greece, and in Egypt
where, by tradition, it was born from
the tears of the solar god, Ra. In
Hittite myth, a bee saved the world
from drought by finding the lost son
of the weather god. The wild honey of
the Golden Age was linked with
ambrosia, the food of the gods.

The bee is an attribute of many
gods including the universal great
mother, the classical goddesses Cybele
and Artemis (Diana), and the Greek
fertility goddess Demeter, whose
priestesses at Eleusis were called
"bees". Essene priests were also
known as "bees", and Christianity
continued this tradition by describing
the monastic community, and the

This image, from a 15th-century
herbal, shows a young woman
collecting honey from her bees.

Church itself, as a beehive. The bee's
honey and its sting represented the
sweetness and pain of Christ. To
Bernard of Clairvaux the bee was the
Holy Spirit. In Greek, Aryan, Middle-
Eastern and Islamic tradition, the bee
was said to represent the soul.

A symbol of reincarnation, the bee
is also an attribute of Hindu gods. A
blue bee on the forehead represents
Krishna; a bee on a lotus, Vishnu; a
bee above a triangle, Shiva. The bee is
a resurrection symbol when shown on
tombs, perhaps because its winter
dormancy was misinterpreted as a
death phase. By another misinterpre-
tation it represented the Virgin Mary
because it was thought to reproduce
as chastely as the flowers on which it
fed. The Chinese associated it with the
fickle "pollination" of maidens.

Beer

To the Celts beer was a drink of tribal
rulers and warriors, believed to be the
beverage of the gods. In Egypt, it was
the gift of the god Osiris. Maize beers
in South America were used in rites of
passage to maturity.

BEASTS OF FABLE

Imaginary beasts appear worldwide in myth and folklore, as symbols of supernatural power or of the compelling projections given by the human psyche. They have vivdly provided us with images that would otherwise be hard to objectify.

Animal hybrids form the largest category of fabulous beasts. The most notable are: the Basilisk, Chimera, Dragon, Griffin, Makara, Sphinx and Unicorn. Amamet, with crocodile jaws, lion's mane and hippopotamus' body, devoured damned Egyptian souls; like the Greco-Roman hellhound Cerberus which had a mane of serpents and many heads, it personifies the fearful uncertainties of death.

Harpies (foul-smelling vultures with the heads of hags) personify guilt and retribution.

In Greek myth the Hydra, a dragon-serpent with many heads, symbolizes the difficulty in conquering vices; each time one of its heads was chopped off, it grew back. Pegasus, the winged horse that carried the hero Bellerophon to victory over the Chimera, is an opposing image of spirit over matter.

The most famous animal-human hybrids, like the classical horse-man centaur, the bull–man Minotaur and the satyrs, represent the animal-spiritual duality of human nature. The fish-tailed merman (the Triton is one of these) is a marine version of the centaur, as is the mermaid who has a gentler, wishful image in the folklore of lonely sailors. The mermaids' more dangerous mythological counterparts are the Sirens, who tempt men to destruction.

The Lamia is the snake-bodied devourer of other women's children, a Greek metaphor for jealousy. The Gorgons (with hair of snakes, boars' teeth, gold wings and bronze hands) are more straightforward embodiments of adversarial evil. The Manticore (human's head, lion's body and scorpion's tail) was a Hebrew symbol of destructiveness. Some hybrids are incarnations of divine omnipotence, such as the goat-fish Capricornus, which for the Sumerians depicted the creator-god Ea.

The elemental powers of nature called up symbolic beasts of awesome size. Leviathan had an earlier destructive counterpart in the Babylonian chaos goddess of the sea, Tiamat.

Less gigantic embodiments of the power of the sea are Scylla and Charybdis, roaring multi-jawed symbols of risky passage. The Behemoth, a hippopotamus-like land version of Leviathan, represents another image of humanity's insignificance. Giant storm birds include the Babylonian Zu and the Arabian Roc.

The phoenix and salamander belong to a further category of beasts close to natural forms but with supernatural powers. The Hindu Nagas are guardian snake symbols of instinctual powers that can be profitably mastered.

BEASTS OF FABLE: *see* ANIMALS; Basilisk; BIRDS; Boar; Bull; Centaur; Cobra; Crocodile; Dog; Dragon; Eagle; FISH; Goat; Griffin; Hippopotamus; Horse; Leviathan; Lion; Makara; Minotaur; Phoenix; Salamander; Satyrs; Scorpion; Snake; Sphinx; Unicorn; Vulture; Whale; Wings

Bell: *see*
Book; Candle; Virginity;
Word

Belly: *see*
Alchemy; Night sea
crossing; Whale

Birch: *see*
Axis; Tree; Whip, Flail;
Witchcraft

Beggar

An image of piety and otherworldliness in many Oriental and Indian traditions, especially Buddhism. In Thailand it is still customary for young men to beg their food for a period. The same symbolism is attached to mendicant Christian orders. Lazarus (at a feast) and the ascetic St Alexis appear in art as beggars. A beggar holding a heavy stone represents Poverty.

Bell

In many religions, the divine voice that proclaims the truth, especially of the Buddhist, Hindu, Islamic and Christian messages. Its sound was a repercussion of the power of the godhead in Islamic and Hindu thought, and of cosmic harmony in China where the bell also stood for respect, obedience and (by phonetic association) the passing of tests. Bells are a call to worship and, in Tibet, to hear and obey the laws of the Buddha. Small tinkling bells can represent happiness, and also sexual pleasure, as in Greek rites where they were associated with the phallic Priapus. They were conversely worn on Hebrew dresses as a sign of virginity. The bell is usually apprehended as a passive, feminine principle, its shape a link with the celestial vault, its clapper symbolizing the tongue of the preacher. It was widely regarded as protective, warding off or exorcising evil. More generally, it marks the passing of time, proclaims good news, such as weddings or victories (the United States' Liberty Bell), warns of danger and, because it tolls for death, can symbolize human mortality, as in John Donne's celebrated sermon, *Death's Duell* (1631).

A detail after a 13th-century stained-glass window showing Jonah being pulled from the belly of the whale.

Belly

The seat of life in Oriental thought, hence the significance in Japan of ritual disembowelment, *hara-kiri*. Fat-bellied Eastern images are symbols of prosperity rather than gluttony, as in depictions of Shen Yeh, the Chinese god of wealth. The biblical story of Jonah's three days and nights in the belly of a whale was used by Jesus as an analogy for his own death and resurrection. Alchemists used the belly as an analogue of the laboratory.

Belt *see* **Girdle**

Birch

The beneficial, protective tree of northern European and Asian peoples, sacred to the Germanic gods Thor or Donar and Freya or Frigg, and central in shamanistic rites much farther east as the Cosmic Tree, linking terrestial life with the spirit world. As the centre pole of circular tents (*yurts*) it had sacred meaning in initiation rites as a symbol of human ascent and of the descent of cosmic energy. In Russia it symbolized spring and young women, and was planted near houses to invoke protective spirits. Its ability to cast out evil may be the reason that witches were birched to rid them of demons. It is the emblem of Estonia in eastern Europe.

Birds

Embodiments of both the human and cosmic spirit – a symbolism suggested by their lightness and rapidity, the soaring freedom of their flight, and their mediation between earth and sky. In ancient Egypt, the soul or individual personality (Ba) was shown as a human-headed hawk leaving the body at death.

The concept of birds as souls is as widespread as the belief that they represent goodness, auguring immortality and joy – an idea delightfully expressed by the playwright Maeterlinck's *The Blue Bird of Happiness* (1908). In a few cultures, some birds are seen as ill omens, especially ravens and vultures. More usually, birds are auspicious, symbolizing in Hindu thought the love of the gods, bringing the elixir of immortality (*soma*) to humanity. In the *Upanishads*, two birds sitting in the Cosmic Tree, one eating and one watching, symbolize the individual and the universal soul. Birds play important roles in many creation myths or, like the Native American Thunderbird and the Lightning Bird of southern Africa, control elemental powers. The Mesoamerican snake-bird Quetzalcoatl combines celestial and earthly powers often separated in other myths, where birds battling snakes depict the fundamental conflict of light and darkness, spirit and flesh. Prehistoric and Egyptian paintings of bird-headed humans symbolize the spiritual side of human nature and the promise of immortality.

Another fundamental symbolism embodies the idea that birds communicate with divinities or, like the dove of the Annunciation, bore messages

Birds: *see*
Air; BEASTS OF FABLE; Feathers; Lightning; Snake; Soma; Soul; Thunder; Tree; Wings; WISDOM; *and individual names*

Birds are thought to carry messages between heaven and earth in Melanesia. This painted woodcarving was found in Papua New Guinea.

Black

Black: *see*
Alchemy; Clouds; Darkness;
Devils; Earth; Light;
Virginity; White; Yin-yang

Blindness: *see*
FORTUNE; SEVEN
DEADLY SINS; VIRTUES

from them. The Celts venerated them for this reason. Shamans equipped with feathers and bird masks could fly to higher realms of knowledge. Birds thus traditionally stood for wisdom, intelligence and the swift power of thought – far from the modern pejorative "bird-brained". Roman divination by the flight or song patterns of birds was perhaps an attempt to decode their superior knowledge. They confide useful secrets to the heroes of many fairy stories. An Aboriginal view is that songbirds can also bear information to their enemies. The expression, "A little bird told me," echoes an ancient idea. In Western art, birds can symbolize Air and Touch. The infant Christ is sometimes shown with a bird on a string.

Caged birds (which according to Plato represented the mind) appear in allegories of Spring. In China, the bird is a male symbol (a homonym of "penis"); however a "wild oriole" is a freelance whore.

Black
Black has almost inescapable symbolism as the colour of negative forces and unhappy events. It stands for the darkness of death, ignorance, despair, sorrow and evil (whose Prince of Darkness is Satan), for inferior levels, or stages (the underworld, primary dissolution in alchemy) and for ominous augury. Blackbirds are a Christian symbol for temptation. In superstition – and in modern English idiom – black is synonymous with disaster: black cats, black days, black spots, black marks, black-balling. As the colour of mourning, it dramatizes loss and absence. As the colour of Christian and Muslim clerics, it signals renunciation of life's vanities.

Black has also been an avenging colour in Islam, a tradition echoed by the Black September terrorists at the Munich Olympic games.

Yet in Egypt and some other ancient traditions, a more positive symbolism appears. The blackness of earth and of rainclouds stands for the mothering darkness of germination. (In this context, Black Virgin icons are not so puzzling.) Black is the colour of Anubis, who led Egyptian souls to the afterlife, and of Min, god of harvests. The Greek huntress Artemis (in Roman myth, Diana) of Ephesus was sometimes depicted with black hands and face. The Hindu Kali and Durga can appear as black goddesses, suggesting the light–dark duality necessary to the continuation of life, as expressed by the black-and-white Chinese yin-yang symbol.

Blindness
Ignorance, self-delusion, the heedlessness of "blind rage" or sensual love – the Roman god Cupid blindfolded. Alternatively, blindness symbolizes justice (unswayed by mere appearances) and the inner visions of seers and poets. The dichotomy can exist side by side, as in Greece, where the goddess Ate represented blind evil, whereas the blinded Tiresias had the gift of prophecy. Homer himself was, by tradition, blind – as were many bards in legend (and Milton for much of his creative life). In art blindness is a characteristic of Ignorance, Justice, Avarice and Fate or Fortune. It is a medieval Christian allegory of the Synagogue. Blinding was often the punishment of those who saw too much (as of Tiresias who saw the naked Athene) or dared too much (for example, Samson).

Blood

A ritual symbol of the life force, believed in many cultures to contain a share of divine energy or, more commonly, the spirit of an individual creature. Blood had rain-bearing or fertilizing power according to some ancient traditions, as in Middle-Eastern marriage ceremonies where the bride stepped over the sprinkled blood of a sheep. Bull's blood was used for its supposed magical power in the Roman rites of Mithras and Cybele. In the Roman *taurobolium*, initiates were led into a pit to be drenched by the blood of bull sacrifices. With the same symbolism of life force, blood is sometimes still drunk at Mexican bullfights. At the height of the Aztec empire, the blood of 20,000 victims a year was spilled to "reinvigorate" the sun after its nightly passage through the underworld. The mingling of blood is a symbol of union in many folk customs (as for example in blood brotherhood) and can mark a seal or covenant between men or between humans and God. In Roman Catholic doctrine, Christ is present in the transubstantiated wine of the Eucharist, embodying as well as symbolizing the Saviour's blood.

Blue

Infinity, eternity, truth, devotion, faith, purity, chastity, peace, spiritual and intellectual life – associations that appear in many ancient cultures and express a general feeling that blue, the colour of the sky, is the coolest, most detached and least "material" of all hues. The Virgin Mary and Christ are often shown wearing blue, and it is the attribute of many sky gods including Amun in Egypt, the Sumerian Great Mother, the Greek Zeus (Jupiter to the Romans), Hera (Juno), the Hindu Indra, Vishnu, and his blue-skinned incarnation, Krishna. Blue is linked to mercy in Hebrew tradition and to wisdom in Buddhism. In folk traditions, it stands in Europe for fidelity, in parts of China for scholarship and happy marriage. The association between blue blood and aristocracy derives from the medieval use of *bleu* as a euphemism for *Dieu* in the oath "by the blood of God" frequently sworn by French nobles, which in time led to the slang term *un sang-bleu* ("a blue-blood"). Still more recent are idiomatic links with melancholia, perhaps deriving from the twilight blues sung by African slaves in North America, and with pornography, from dimmed showings of explicit movies.

Bo Tree

The sacred fig tree (Bodhi Tree) under which Gautama Buddha meditated until he arrived at enlightenment – thus it is a Buddhist symbol for contemplation, teaching and spiritual perfection.

Boar

A primordial image of strength, fearless aggression and resolute courage, particularly across northern Europe and the Celtic world where it was the leading symbol of warriors. It also had sacred meaning elsewhere: as a sun symbol in Iran and as a moon symbol in Japan, where the white boar was taboo to hunters. The wild boar's ferocity aroused a mixture of fear, admiration and reverence. Its zoomorphic symbolism is evidenced by the discovery of small votive boars and larger stone boar sculptures as far south as Iberia. It is associated with gods of rulership, battle and fertility,

Blood: *see*
Bull; Night Sea Crossing; Ram; Sun; Water; Wine

Blue: *see*
CHASTITY; FIDELITY; Sky; VIRTUES; WISDOM

Bo Tree: *see*
Fig; Tree

Boar: *see*
ANIMALS; Black; Eye; Forest; Moon; Pig; Sun; White

A detail after a 16th-century depiction of a chalice filled with the blood of Christ.

The Bo Tree, from a 1st-century-CE stone relief at the Sanchi Bhopal temple, India.

Boat

Boat: *see*
AFTERWORLDS; Ark;
Crescent; Ship; Woman

Bonds: *see*
Chain; Cord

Bones: *see*
Bear; DEATH; Goat; Soul

Book: *see*
Grail; VIRTUES;
WISDOM; Word

such as the Teutonic Wodan, the Scandinavian Odin, Freyr and Freya, the Greek Ares (in Roman myth, Mars) and the Japanese god of war, Hachiman (a deified ruler). To the Celts it symbolized spiritual authority; its meat was eaten ritually and buried with the slain. Druids, in calling themselves "boars", identified themselves with occult forest lore. The boar helmets of Swedish warriors had protective symbolism. Respect for the boar extended into India where, as Varaha, Vishnu took on a boar's form to dive into the flood and root the earth up with his tusks after it had been captured by demons. Destructive brutality is the other side of the boar's symbolism: it was a monstrous adversary to Herakles (Hercules) and also to the Egyptian god of daylight, Horus, whose eye was torn out by his uncle Set in the form of a black boar. The boar became a Judeo-Christian symbol for tyranny and lust.

Boat

For many river and coastal peoples, small craft (as opposed to larger ones) were apprehended as the means of transition from the material to the spirit world. Symbolic cradles for the souls of those to be reborn, boats cross the perilous regions of the underworld (as in Egyptian mythology) or are cast adrift with the bodies of chiefs, as in the Amazon.

In Greek myth, a boat powered by the ferryman Charon, carries dead souls across the River Styx into the underworld.

Bonds

Beyond their obvious meaning as restraints, bonds in iconography can symbolize judicial power, especially that of divinities or rulers, and its acceptance by those bound by the law. Thus Varuna, the Vedic god of cosmic order, is shown holding cords.

Bones

Images of mortality and death – but also of what is least destructible and likeliest to form a basis for bodily resurrection. Bones were carefully protected in many ancient cultures for this reason, often under megaliths. Northern European peoples from Finland to Siberia buried the skeletons of bears and other game to ensure their rebirth. In a Scandinavian myth, Thor was angered to see one of the goats he had brought back to life after feasting on their flesh limping because his host's son had sucked the marrow from a leg bone. The concept of things bred or felt "in the bone" echoes ancient beliefs that the essence of a person – in Mali, the soul itself – was contained in the bones.

Book

A self-evident emblem of wisdom, science and scholarship, the book also

Christ Pantocrator holding a book in his left hand, from an 11th-century Greek mosaic.

appears widely in iconography as a symbol for divine revelation, especially in the Christian and Islamic faiths. To Arabic mystics it is a metaphor for life itself and the whole universe. In some legends of the Grail the quest is for a book and the missing Word. In art, books are held by prophets, apostles (John the Evangelist is seen literally swallowing the Book of Revelation), Christ, the Virgin Mary in Annunciation paintings, and the figures History, Philosophy and the Muses. A book with a cross on it represents Faith. Book-burning symbolizes the casting out of old beliefs and traditions.

Bow

Stored energy, willpower, aspiration, divine or terrestial power, and dynamic tension, especially sexual. As humanity's most effective long-range weapon for some 50,000 years, the bow is an obvious emblem of war and hunting, but the control needed to master it gave it a deeper significance. In Oriental thought, particularly, it represented spiritual discipline, the combination of force and composure extolled as a samurai virtue. A Homeric test of fitness to rule (as exemplified by the bow that only the hero/sailor Odysseus could draw), the bow is also an attribute of the Greek sun-god Apollo, a symbol of the sun's power and fecundity. A bow drawn at the sky represented spiritual aspiration. The shape of the drawn bow was linked with the crescent moon and its Roman goddess Diana. Paintings of the gods of love with bows, such as the Greek Eros, symbolize the tension of desire, the sexual life force itself.

Bowl see **Beggar**; **Pilgrimage**

Box, Boxwood

Beyond the obvious feminine symbolism of any receptacle, boxes or caskets – by enclosing and hiding their contents – represent mystery and the hazardous drama of surprise, pleasant or unpleasant. "Who chooseth me must give and hazard all he hath," says the leaden casket that wins the hand of Portia in Shakespeare's *Merchant of Venice* (c.1596). Less fortunately, in Greek myth the opening of Pandora's box, a metaphor for the unpredictable forces of the unconscious, released ills upon the world. The boxwood tree (Latin *buxus*) whose dense, fine wood was once used to make boxes, was a funerary emblem of immortality.

Branch, Bough

Branches, used for example in spring fertility rites, took on the symbolism of the trees from which they were cut. Thus, brandished branches of palm or olive were triumphal emblems in processions, and mistletoe branches were widespread symbols of resurrection, particularly in the Celtic world. In Virgil's *Aeneid* (mid-1st century BCE) Aeneas carries a mistletoe branch to ensure his safe passage through the underworld. J. G. Frazer named his great study of comparative religion after the Golden Bough used in the ritual slaying of the priest of Diana at Lake Nemi by his successor. A flowering bough stands for Logic in Western medieval iconography.

Bread

An idiom for essential sustenance in countries where it was a staple food; and, in Christianity, a metaphor for the food of the spirit and for the body of Christ himself. Bread broken and shared is a sign of union. Unleavened

Bow: *see*
Arrow; Crescent; Moon; Rainbow; Sun

Box, Boxwood: *see*
Tree; Woman; Wood

Branch, Bough: *see*
Acacia; Mistletoe; Olive; Palm; Tree; Wood

Bread: *see*
Sacrifice; Wine

Breasts: *see*
Milk; Mother; Woman

Breath, Breathing: *see*
Air; Soul

Bridge: *see*
AFTERWORLDS; Ford;
Rainbow; River, Stream

Bronze: *see*
Giant; METALS

Broom: *see*
Devils; Phallus; Sabbath;
Witchcraft; Wood

*The many-breasted
fertility goddess Diana
of Ephesus.*

bread is a symbol of purification and sacrifice at the Jewish Passover.

Breasts
Security, protection, gentleness, maternal love and nourishment. Hence in ancient times the bared breasts of the women of a defeated tribe represent an appeal for compassion. Goddesses with exaggerated or multiple breasts are fertility images.

Breath, Breathing
The life principle, spiritual as well as physical. The link between breath and spirit is part of Western and Islamic as well as Eastern tradition. Thus in Genesis (2:7), God breathes life into Adam's nostrils. Insufflation was once used in Christianity symbolically to blow the Holy Spirit into, and demons out of, troubled people. Controlled breathing, an aspect of Muslim, Buddhist and Tantric meditation, is most developed in the Hindu system of yoga where correct breathing is intended to concentrate the spirit and align individual respiration with the rhythm of the cosmos. Underlying much of the symbolism of breath/spirit is the mystical idea that breath is a divine gift, returned to its giver at death.

Bridge
Joining together. The bridge was a widespread metaphor for the difficult passage between the worlds of the living and the dead, a symbolism perhaps suggested by the hazards of crossing early narrow bridges into unfamiliar or hostile territory. The ancient Indo-Iranian religion of Zoroastrianism, still the basis of Parsee beliefs, confronted souls with Chinvat Parvatu, the Bridge of the

Separator, which could be negotiated to paradise only with the inner equilibrium of the righteous, a concept also found in some medieval Christian iconography of heaven and hell. More generally, the bridge symbolizes transition and linkage. Considered as neutral territory, it is a place of meetings, lovers' trysts, but also, like the ford, sometimes a contested place of challenge. The rainbow was often seen as a celestial bridge, a divine promise of a link from earth to heaven. The chief priesthood of ancient Rome was that of the Pontifex ("bridge-maker"). Bridge-building was apprehended as a semi-magical skill, and folklore credited some wondrous bridges (such as the Valentre at Cahors) to pacts between the architect and the Devil.

Bronze
An alloy of copper and tin (in antiquity often confused with alloys of copper with other metals) symbolizing force, power and hardness, sacred to the lame smith Hephaestus who, in Greek mythology, fashioned from it the bronze giant Talos. Cult objects made of bronze were thought to have protective power.

Broom
A modest implement invested with considerable magical power from ancient times. Essentially a symbol of removal ("the new broom sweeps clean"), it had to be used with care or it could drive out friendly spirits as well as dust. This belief explains folk prohibitions on sweeping a house at night in Brittany and, in North Africa, on sweeping a house in which someone had just died. Sacred (non-harmful) brooms were used in some rites for the same reason. The popular

belief that witches rode off to their devilish sabbats on brooms is linked to the idea that evil spirits may take possession of the magic implement used to drive them out.

Brown

Humility, renunciation, poverty – probably a symbolism deriving from the sober and lowly associations of clay soil. Hence the brown garments of Christian mendicant orders. Yet brown was also the colour of the magnificent Sung dynasty in China. Culturally there seems little ancient or modern evidence for Freud's view that associations with excrement are the predominant symbolism of brown.

Bubble

Evanescence, especially of earthly life – a symbolism that appears both in Buddhism and in Christian allegories of mortality where *putti* (boyish angels) are shown blowing bubbles, with the inscription *Homo bulla est* ("man is a bubble").

Buffalo, Bison

A symbol of formidable but peaceable power in India, Asia and North America. The bison (commonly called buffalo but a different species) symbolized to the Native American Plains Indians not only the strength of the whirlwind but also prosperity and plenty. The white buffalo was particularly sacred to them. As the sixty million-strong herds were slaughtered by white hunters, ears of corn became substitute buffalo symbols. The high status of the buffalo in India and Southeast Asia made it a sacrificial animal. Yama, the Hindu and Buddhist god of death, rode a buffalo, and a buffalo head was a death symbol in

One of the Eight Immortals, Lao-tse, riding a buffalo, from an 18th-century watercolour.

Tibet. The Chinese associated the quiet power of the domestic buffalo with the contemplative life: in legend, the sage Lao-tse left China on a green buffalo.

Bull

Power, potency, fecundity – a protean symbol of divinity, royalty and the elemental forces of nature, changing in significance between different epochs and cultures.

As the animal incarnation of many supreme Middle-Eastern gods, it was one of the most important of all sacrificial animals. In ritual and iconography, the bull has represented both moon and sun, earth and sky, rain and heat, feminine procreation and male ardour, matriarch and patriarch, death and regeneration. As a symbol of death and resurrection, it was central to Mithraism, a pre-Zoroastrian Persian cult taken up and spread through much of the Roman empire as an early rival to Christianity. Ritual sacrifices celebrated the sun-god Mithras' slaughter of a primordial bull from whose blood and semen

Brown: *see*
COLOURS

Bubble: *see*
Angels; Wind

Buffalo, Bison: *see*
ANIMALS; Bull; Corn; Ox; Sacrifice; Whirlwind; White

Bull: *see*
ANIMALS; Black; Blood; Buffalo, Bison; Calf; Cave; Crescent; DEATH; Horn; Horse; Labyrinth; Minotaur; Sacrifice; Sky; Storm; Sun; Thunder; White; Zodiac

A bull, as shown on a stone relief of c.500BCE on the Ishtar Gate in Babylon.

sprang new life, animal and vegetable. In the Roman *taurobolium*, initiates showered under bull's blood as a stream of life. Similar germination symbolism appears in much older Indo-Iranian myths. In still earlier cave art the bull is second only to the horse as the most frequently painted image of vital energy. It appears from northern Europe through to India as an emblem of divine power, especially associated with lunar, solar and sky or storm gods, including notably the Nordic gods Thor and Freya; the Greek gods Zeus (Roman: Jupiter), Dionysus (Bacchus), Poseidon (Neptune) and Cybele; the Egyptian Ra, Osiris, Ptah (incarnated as the sacred bull Apis) and Set; the Mesopotamian El (who appears with bull horns) and Baal; and the Indian Indra, Aditi, Agni, Rudra and Shiva with his bull mount, Nandi. In condemning the Golden Calf, the biblical Moses sought to change a long tradition of Semitic bull worship. In India, the first saint of the ascetic Jain sect is represented by a golden bull. Physical attributes of the bull underlie much of its symbolism – its horns are linked with the crescent moon; its sheer bulk suggests a support for the world in Vedic and Islamic traditions; its prolific semen is stored by the moon in Persian mythology; and its bellowing, stamping and horn-tossing energy is widely linked with thunder and earthquakes, especially in Crete, the home of the monstrous mythological bull–man, the Minotaur.

As the most formidable of all domesticated beasts, the bull from ancient times became an adversary as well as icon. Challenging its power was a task given to legendary heroes, such as Herakles – and a dangerous game for Minoan acrobats who somersaulted over the bull's horns. The orchestrated ritual of modern bullfighting continues a long tradition of using the bull to flirt with death. Here, the straightforward symbolism of cheating death is perhaps more fundamental than Jung's moralizing view that the defeat of the bull represents a human wish to sublimate animal passions. Sexual symbolism is certainly predominant in Greek mythology, witnessed by the link with the orgiastic rites of Dionysus and by the myth in which Zeus appears to Europa as a gentle white bull, before abducting her. Diodorus reported that Egyptian women exposed themselves to images of the Apis bull. However, death and resurrection symbolism, as found in Mithraism, is more widespread: it is very marked in Egypt and also in northern Asia, where Death rides a black bull.

Bullroarer

A wooden slat whirled on a thong to simulate the bellow of thunder, used as a sacred instrument in male initiations to invoke potency, in orgiastic rites (Greece), by Apache shamans to aid prognostication, and by the Australian Aboriginals to summon ancestral voices. It could also symbolize the voice of God.

Burning bush

A bush burning but unconsumed represents the flaming Angel of the Lord who was encountered by Moses as described in Exodus. A similar image appears in Vedic fire symbolism. In medieval Christian iconography the burning bush can also symbolize Mary's virginity.

Bustard

A large but elusive land bird, in Africa symbolizing polygamous fecundity and also the questing soul, linked to both the earth and the air.

Butterfly

Now simply a metaphor for light-mindedness, the butterfly is an ancient symbol of immortality, its life cycle providing a perfect analogy: life (the crawling caterpillar), death (the dark chrysalis) and rebirth (the soul fluttering free). Hence the Greek myth of Psyche (literally "soul"). Depicted in art with butterfly wings, she was a mortal freed from death when Zeus was touched by her love for Eros – and his love for her. Butterflies as emblems of souls are found as far apart as Zaire, central Asia, Mexico and New Zealand. They appear with this meaning on Christian tombs, and Christ is sometimes depicted holding the butterfly of resurrection. Butterflies represented the souls of slain Aztec warriors and were sacred to several Mexican deities, their flickering wings also symbolizing solar fire, an idea that recurs in Celtic tradition. In China, the butterfly is an emblem of leisure and a young male lover; through a phonetic link with the word for "seventy" it is also, when linked with the plum, a metaphor for beauty in old age. In Japan the creature stands for transient joy, female vanity and the geisha; a pair of butterflies represents conjugal bliss. In folklore illustration, fairies are often shown with butterfly wings.

Bullroarer: *see*
Thunder

Burning bush: *see*
Fire, Flame; Virginity

Bustard: *see*
Birds; Soul

Butterfly: *see*
Caterpillar; Darkness;
Fairies; Fire, Flame; Plum;
Soul; VANITY; Wings

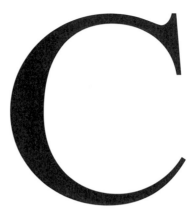

Caduceus: *see*
Alchemy; Axis; Kundalini;
Mercury; Phallus; Rod;
Snake; Spiral; Sulphur; Tree;
Wand; Wings

Calf: *see*
Bull; Lamb; Sacrifice

*The caduceus, as a
diamond-encrusted
brooch. This version is
winged.*

Caduceus

A rod entwined by two serpents, sometimes capped by wings. It is now an emblem of medicine or commerce but has enjoyed an intriguingly varied symbolism. The Greek word from which *caduceus* is derived meant "herald's staff of office" as it was the magic wand of the Greek Hermes (in Roman myth, Mercury), the messenger of the gods, which came to be used as a protective emblem by messengers on political or commercial business. In Roman myth, Hermes' counterpart, Mercury, uses a wand to reconcile two fighting snakes. This may account for the caduceus becoming a Roman emblem of balanced moral conduct – but the form of the staff has various older symbolic meanings. A stick with entwined serpents combines several fundamental elements: an axial pole suggesting phallic power and the Tree of Life (a means of communication or route for messages between earth and sky); a double spiral formed by the snakes, suggesting cosmic energy, duality and the union of opposites. The serpents themselves suggest the fertilizing forces of the earth and underworld.

Dating back at least 4,000 years, this symbol is associated with divinities (often messenger gods) in Phoenicia and Babylonia, in Egypt and in India where it became a Hindu image of *kundalini* (awakening energy). In alchemy it stood for the integration of opposites (mercury and sulphur). It could represent equilibrium and, in Western art, Peace. The association with medicine comes from the link between the snake and rejuvenation: a staff with a single snake is the attribute of Aesculapius, god of healing. Jung saw the caduceus as an emblem of homeopathic medicine – the snake that both poisons and cures.

Calf

Purity in sacrifice – hence occasionally a symbol of Christ (although more often depicted as the lamb). Calves also symbolized prosperity (killing the fatted calf). The biblical Golden Calf is usually taken as an emblem of the worship of material rather than spiritual values.

Calumet

The sacred, ceremonial pipe of Native North Americans, usually with a reed stem carrying eagle feathers, symbolizing the union of nature and spirit, earth and sky, man and god. The pipe was known as the Peace Pipe, and its smoking could signify peace (a white-feathered stem), but also war (red); more generally it was a sign of hospitality. Pipes were often used in pairs, representing male and female, and were passed east-to-west around a circle. The smoke, symbolizing vital breath, was ceremonially puffed toward the sky, the earth and the four cardinal points. Essentially, the calumet was a medium of prayer.

Camel

Sobriety and dignified obedience – associations that reflect Christian approval of the camel's ability to shoulder heavy loads uncomplainingly (as noted by St Augustine) and plod long distances without drinking. Remarkably, considering its importance as a beast of burden in North Africa, central Asia and India, the camel plays a minor role in the iconography and literature of these regions, although Zoroastrianism refers to a flying camel as a dragon-serpent image in paradise. Christ used the camel's size as an analogy of difficulty when he declared that it could pass through the eye of a needle more easily than a rich man could enter heaven (Mark 10:25). In Western art (and Roman coinage) the camel personifies Asia. It is a Christmas emblem as the Magi rode camels.

Camellia

In China, an image of health and beauty, and also of fortitude, perhaps because of the shrub's ability to bloom in autumn and winter. In Japan, the flower is associated with sudden death.

Candle

As an image of spiritual illumination in the darkness of ignorance, the candle is an important symbol in Christian ritual, standing for Christ, the Church, joy, faith and witness. At a more personal level it individualizes fire symbolism, the short-lived candle and its easily extinguished flame becoming a metaphor for the solitary, aspiring human soul. It appears with this meaning in devotional still lifes and in the more widespread custom of placing candles around a coffin. Blowing out candles on a birthday cake shifts the symbolism to the vital breath – proof of life continuing beyond all the extinguished years.

Candlestick

The general symbolism of the candle is often extended by the form of the candlestick or candelabrum, most notably in the seven-branched Jewish Menorah. The original Menorah, described in the Book of Exodus (25: 31–40) as made of gold with almond-shaped bowls for oil lamps (later, candles), alludes to the Cosmic Tree or Tree of Light, its seven branches representing the sun, moon and five ancient planets, the seven days of the week and the seven levels of heaven.

Cannibalism

Often a useful means of nourishment (Maori war parties ate prisoners on the march), cannibalism was once also a ritual custom symbolizing the absorption of the victim's vital power

Calumet: *see*
Breath, Breathing;
CARDINAL POINTS;
Circle; Eagle; Earth;
PEACE; Sky; Smoke

Camel: *see*
ANIMALS; Dragon;
Needle; Snake

Camellia: *see*
VIRTUES

Candle: *see*
Breath, Breathing;
Candlestick; Fire, Flame;
Light; Soul; VANITY;
VIRTUES

Candlestick: *see*
AFTERWORLDS;
Almond; Candle; Gold;
Light; Oil; PLANETS;
Seven; Tree

Cannibalism: *see*
Giant; Witchcraft

The Jewish Menorah candlestick, from a 12th-century Bible illustration.

Canopy: *see*
Baldachin; Circle; Parasol;
Sky; Square

Cap: *see*
Clown; Devils; Head; Horn;
Phallus; Phrygian cap; Sun;
WISDOM; Witchcraft

Cards: *see*
Tarot

Carnation: *see*
Red

Carnival: *see*
Solstice

Carp: *see*
FISH; Fire, Flame;
VIRTUES

Carpet
ANIMALS; Birds; Journey

The carp from a 19th-century Japanese painting.

and forestalling any magical vengeance. Ancient fears of being consumed appear in many folk tales of giants and witches, and in a number of early myths, notably in the story of the Greek Titan Cronos who swallowed his children at birth.

Canopy
An Asian symbol of the sky, and thus of royalty and protective power. One of the eight Chinese Buddhist emblems of good luck. Linked with the celestial symbolism of the parasol, it also alludes to the Islamic paradise. In Hindu ritual the canopy is round for kings, square for priests.

Cap
Rank, authority, power, wisdom. Caps of various kinds appear frequently in ancient iconography, and are often associated with high status, especially when tall and conical. The obvious attempt to make their wearers look more impressive may have been less significant than their solar and phallic symbolism of power. The pointed cap of the wizard symbolizes supernatural power and wisdom. The dunce's cap and the jester's cap with its flopping bells are mocking inversions of this tradition. Witches may also be shown wearing pointed caps, a reference to Satan's horns. The cap survives as a status symbol in the academic mortarboard (and in "capping" team members in some sports).

CARDINAL POINTS *see panel, opposite*

Cards
Playing cards became an allegory for the Puritan vice of idleness in baroque art, but medieval Christianty saw

card-playing as a harmless pastime, sometimes used by clerics as an educational tool, backed by suitable texts. Much of the symbolism of present-day cards is derived from the 14th-century Tarot pack.

Carnation
In Netherlandish painting a symbol of betrothal, especially when red. Pink carnations sometimes appear as emblems of maternal love in paintings of the Madonna and child.

Carnival
Traditionally the last fling for Christians on Shrove Tuesday (Mardi Gras) before Lent abstinence. The name (deriving through late Latin *carne levarium*) literally means "a deprivation of meat". The fact that carnival is sometimes held at other times, particularly just after the December solstice (December 21), suggests links with more primitive revels such as the Saturnalia (the pagan precursor to Christmas), a celebration of rebirth in nature and an opportunity for amusement, licence and mild anarchy.

Carp
An emblem of courage, virility and scholastic success in China, and of samurai fortitude in Japan – possibly from the contrast between its leaping vigour in the water and its calmness when hooked and dying. Also admired for its longevity, the carp was a symbol of good luck. Images of carp were placed on ships' masts, or roofs to ward off fire.

Carpet
An important medium for visual symbolism throughout the Arabic world

CARDINAL POINTS

The four cardinal points, East, West, North and South, graphically represented by a cross, formed an ancient symbol of the cosmos, with humankind at the centre (sometimes becoming the fifth point). Early rituals, especially in North and South America, strongly suggest that the gods dwell at these points and control human life, thus explaining the importance of the number four in mythology and in daily and religious life. From these basic directions came the rain-bearing winds to fertilize or destroy crops, personified by gods to which veneration was paid, sacrifices offered, libations poured or smoke puffed. In Chinese thought, tigers symbolizing protective forces guarded the four points and the centre. Because the symbolism of individual directions was based largely on climate and the influence of sun, cross-cultural similarities are more marked for East and West than for North and South.

East almost invariably symbolized light, the source of life, the sun and solar gods, youth, resurrection and new life. It was the key point of most natural religions, and not surprisingly, some early maps placed East, not North, at the top of the vertical axis of the cosmic cross. There lay the Chinese celestial dragon and the Aztec crocodile of creation, the Judeo-Christian Eden, the birthplace of heroes, the home of ances-

tors and, in many African traditions, the place where good souls went. Christian and Islamic prayer was directed there, and the Dakota nations, among others, buried bodies with their heads facing East, the source of the wind of paradise.

West symbolized sleep, rest, the mystery of death, the North American Happy Hunting Grounds, and the Indo-Iranian, Egyptian and Greek kingdom of the spirits. In some cultures, this symbolism was tinged with fear. Westward lay the Nordic sea of destruction, the abyss. St Jerome associated West with Satan. For some African tribes it was where bad souls went.

North symbolized belligerent power, darkness, hunger, cold, chaos and evil in most Northern-hemisphere traditions apart from those of Egypt and India, where it represented light and the masculine.principle. Associated with furious winds, it was the seat of mighty gods including Ahriman (the Iranian prince of darkness), Lucifer and Mictlanteculitli (the Aztec god of death). It is shown iconographically as the Aztec eagle of war, the Hebrew winged ox and the Chinese black tortoise.

In most parts of the world **South** symbolized fire, passion, masculinity, solar and lunar energy. Again, Egypt and India are the exceptions; South stands here for night, hell and the feminine principle.

CARDINAL POINTS: *see* AFTERWORLDS; Calumet; Centre; Crocodile; CROSS; Dawn; DEATH; Devils; Dragon; Eagle; Fire; Flame; Four; Light; Orientation; Ox; Rain; Sacrifice; Smoke; Soul; Square; Sun; Tiger; Tortoise, Turtle; Wind

and, by association, a magical means of being transported from one place to another. Animals, birds, plants and geometric motifs woven into Oriental carpets carried their symbolic meanings into the carpet itself, giving it mythic significance. In a similar way, the prayer mat took on the meaning of

Castle

Castle: *see*
Black; CHASTITY;
DEATH; Forest; Knight;
Light; Mountain; Thorn;
Virginity

Castration: *see*
Sickle, Scythe

Cat: *see*
ANIMALS; Black; Devils;
LIBERTY; Lion; SEVEN
DEADLY SINS; Snake;
Sun; Transformation;
Witchcraft

*The castle as a
stronghold of evil (the
fire-breathing dragon
within its walls), from a
medieval painting.*

a sacred space. From the idea of a carpet that elevated the worshipper to a separate plane of existence, it was perhaps a simple step to the popular legends of flying carpets such as King Solomon's, which was made only of green silk but capable of supporting his throne and his entire retinue.

Castle

A shining goal or a fearful challenge. As such, castles appear in innumerable legends and folk tales, their symbolism usually varying with their colour. The dark castle, perhaps hidden in an almost impenetrable forest and often defended by a black knight, symbolizes evil forces, the underworld and fear of death. It contains a treasure or incarcerated maiden to be wrested by courage and ingenuity from these dark powers. The bright castle, which may appear and disappear like a mirage and is usually set on a height, symbolizes spiritual quest or the City of God, difficult to attain. Castles in the air symbolize the never-accomplished goals of those who think that they can be achieved by wishing rather than through realistic effort. In art, the castle can signify chastity (because it is well defended).

Castration

Loss of power – the symbolism of the savage judicial use of castration in ritualized hangings of traitors in Elizabethan England, and in the more widespread mutilation of slain enemies perceived as significant threats. It was sometimes used in ancient fertility sacrifices. In Greek myth, the sky-god Ouranos (Uranus to the Romans) was castrated with a sickle (a frequent emblem of castration) by his youngest son, Cronos. The falling blood produced monsters; semen from the genitals formed the foam that bore Aphrodite (Venus).

Cat

Cleverness by stealth, the power of transformation and clairvoyance, agility, watchfulness, sensual beauty, and female malice. These almost universal associations had differing symbolic weight and significance in ancient cultures. In Egypt, notably in the worship of the feline-headed goddess Bastet or Bast, cats were benign and sacred creatures. Bastet, originally shown as a lioness, was a tutelary lunar goddess, popularly linked with pleasure, fertility and protective forces. In her honour, cats were venerated and often mummified, along with mice for them to eat. In iconography, the cat appeared as an ally of the sun, severing the head of the underworld serpent. Cats were also associated with other lunar goddesses, including the Greek Artemis (Diana to the Romans), and with the Nordic goddess Freya whose chariot they drew. In Rome their self-sufficient freedom also made them emblems of Liberty. Elsewhere, their night wanderings and powers of transformation (pupil dilation, sheathing and unsheathing of claws, sudden changes from indolence to ferocity) were distrusted. Black cats in particular, were linked with evil cunning in the Celtic world, with harmful *djins* in Islam, and with bad luck in Japan where folk tales described how cats could take over the bodies of women. (Misogynist symbolism surives in the epithet "catty".) In India, where cats incarnated animal beauty, Buddhists seem to have held their aloofness against them: like the serpent, they failed to mourn the

Buddha's death. The most negative view of all appears in the vast folklore of Western witchcraft where cats appear as demonic familiars associated with satanic orgies – lustful and cruel incarnations of the Devil himself.

Caterpillar
Lowly, unformed – an image of inadequacy in the Hindu doctrine of the transmigration of souls. In Native North American tradition, the caterpillar is a metaphor for sexual awakening, the first experience of sex.

Caul
The foetal membrane, sometimes partly covering the head of a baby at birth, when it is considered a good omen. More particulaly it is thought to be a charm against drowning. This superstition, dating at least from Roman times, led to some trafficking in cauls. In Slav tradition, the caul was also a sign of second-sight and metamorphosis, possibly into a werewolf.

Cauldron
Transformation, germination, plenty, rebirth, rejuvenation, magical power. At a simple level, the cauldron was the predominant ancient symbol for the transforming marvels that could be wrought by cookery, ranging from ordinary nourishment to the brewing of magic potions or hell-broths. It could also represent a means of initiation, trial or punishment. In art, several Christian saints are shown seated unhappily in cauldrons of boiling oil (which most survive), including St John the Evangelist, who is said to have emerged rejuvenated. False hope of their father's rejuvenation led the daughters of King Pelias of Iolcus in Thessaly to chop him up and throw the pieces into a cauldron on the treacherous advice of the sorceress Medea. Also in Greek myth, Thetis, the mother of Achilles, lost several earlier children when she put them in a cauldron to find out if they had inherited her immortality or were mortal like their father. A Kirghiz epic features a magic blood-drinking cauldron which the hero must recover from the bottom of the ocean. Underwater cauldrons appear in Celtic myth. The most prized possession of the Irish father-god Dagda was a life-giving cauldron (Undry) that could never be emptied. The midnight hags of Shakespeare's *Macbeth* (*c*.1605) threw "eye of newt and toe of frog" into their witch-brew, thus following a long tradition of belief in the magical properties of the cauldron.

Cave
A primal image of shelter – hence a symbol of the womb, birth and rebirth, the origin, centre and heart of being. The cave could alternatively have dark meanings: the underworld, the Celtic entrance to hell or, in psychology, regressive wishes and the unconscious. More usually, as widely expressed in myths and initiation rites, it was a place where the germinating powers of the earth were concentrated, where oracles spoke, where initiates were reborn in spiritual understanding, and where souls ascended to celestial light. Sacred caves and grottoes, usually on hills or mountains, formed earth-to-sky axial symbols, the focus of spiritual force often represented by a domed vault, pillar or lingam. Fertility symbolism associated with caves and dwarfish rain–gods appears also in Mexico. Prophets as well as gods and heroes were linked

Caterpillar: *see*
Butterfly; Soul

Caul: *see*
Transformation; Wolf

Cauldron: *see*
Initiation; Oven, Furnace; Sea; Water; Witchcraft

Cave: *see*
Axis; Dome; Dragon; Dwarf; Earth; Initiation; Labyrinth; Light; Lingam; Mother; Mountain; Pillar; River, Stream; Sea; Soul; Water; Witchcraft; Woman

Cedar: *see*
LONGEVITY; Resin;
Temple; Tree

Centaur: *see*
ANIMALS; Arrow;
BEASTS OF FABLE;
Clouds; Horse; SEVEN
DEADLY SINS; Zodiac

with caves or clefts, such as the one at Lebadea described by the Greek geographer Pausanias in the 2nd century CE. Here, those who consulted the oracle (the voice of an immured architect-king Trophonius) placed their feet in a cleft and were transported through nightmarish tunnels of inquiry to reappear enlightened but deeply shaken. The cave as a spiritual source also appears in Christian belief: a cave manger in Bethlehem was the birthplace of Christ, and John the Evangelist was granted his apocalyptic vision in a cave on Patmos. Again, in China, caves had sacred meaning, as fit burial places for emperors who would be reborn from them. In Turkic myth, a cave is the birthplace of the first man.

Mithraic rites, held in caves with streams, flowers and foliage representing the world created by Mithras, may have introduced to Greek philosophy the notion of the cave as a metaphor for the material world itself. Hence Plato's image of humanity chained in a cave and seeing illusions – reflected light from a higher reality that only mind and spirit could attain. In folklore, caves often symbolize less ethical goals – the treasures of Aladdin, for example – protected by dragons or cunning gnomes.

Cedar

The Tree of Life in Sumeria – a symbol of power and immortality. The fragrance, durability and awesome height (up to thirty metres) of this pine made the Lebanese species a biblical emblem of majesty and incorruptibility, its heartwood a later metaphor for Christ. Cedar was used to build the Temple of Solomon and for Greek and Roman busts of gods and ancestors. Its reputation for longevity may account for the use of cedar resin by Celtic embalmers.

Centaur

A symbol of man trapped by his baser impulses, especially lust, violence and drunkenness. First shown in Greek art as a man with the hindquarters of a horse, but later as a horse with human torso and head, the centaur probably mythologized lawless bands of horsemen from the mountains of Thessaly. According to one myth, the mortal Ixion ravished the cloud Nephele believing her to be the goddess Hera, wife of Zeus; Nephele duly gave birth to the monster Centaurus whose bestiality with mares in turn produced the centaurs. With this sorry lineage, the centaurs became wild, drunken rapists, often shown with anguished faces and battling unsuccessfully against the forces of law and order. As such, they represent sensual passion, adultery and heresy in Christian iconography. An alternative, humanizing myth introduced a race of morally superior centaurs which descended from Cronos, among them Chiron, wise teacher, doctor and friend to Herakles (in Roman myth,

Wild centaurs tormenting a victim, on a Greek vase dating from the 5th century BCE.

Hercules), whose poisoned arrow struck this centaur by accident. Chiron's sacrifice of his own immortality to free the hero Prometheus earned him a heavenly place as the southern constellation, Centaurus. This can be interpreted as a metaphor for the triumph of mind over instinct – forces held in tension within the dynamic image of the centaur. These hybrids appear in Vedic myth as the Gandharvas – physical virility combined with intellectual gifts.

Centre

The focal point of worship, essence of the godhead, ultimate and eternal state of being, perfection. Most of the symbolism of centrality is self-evident thanks to the fact that the centre appears or is implicit in nearly all other graphic symbols; that dynamically it is the hub, pivot or axis, the point upon which lines of force converge or from which they radiate; that it can symbolize not only divinity, the object of love or aspiration, but also rulership and administration. Less obviously, the centre is a symbol of totality in the metaphysical concept by which a central point concentrates and contains the energy and meaning of everything else.

Chain

Servitude, but also unity through bondage in friendship, communication or communal endeavour – a negative–positive symbolism nicely muddled in the famous Marxist rallying cry: "Workers unite, you have nothing to lose but your chains!" As fetters, chains are emblems of slavery and, in Christian art, of Vice (humanity shackled to worldly desires). Broken chains signify freedom and

salvation. As emblems of community linkage, chains are worn to show official status, or used in Christmas decorations as symbols of social or family cohesion. They can stand for marriage at the social level, and also for the marriage of spiritual and earthly powers, a symbolism dating back to the Greek poet Homer (c.9th century BCE), who spoke of a golden chain hung from heaven to earth by the god Zeus. It was later interpreted as a metaphor for prayer.

Chakra

The power of inner consciousness. In Tantric doctrine *chakra*s are "wheels" of vital energy, situated along the spinal column. Activated by reciting sacred words in meditation, they drive a flow of physiological and spiritual energy from the base of the spine upward to open the "thousand-petalled lotus" at the crown of the head.

The chakras *positioned along the body, from an early 19th-century Indian diagram.*

Centre: *see*
Axis; CARDINAL POINTS; Circle; Point

Chain: *see*
Bonds; Cord; Gold; LIBERTY; Marriage

Chakra: *see*
Kundalini; Lotus; Wheel

Chalice

Chalice: *see*
Blood; CROSS; Cup; Grail;
Marriage; PASSION;
VIRTUES

Chameleon: *see*
Air; ANIMALS; Lightning;
Rain; Sun; Thunder; Tree

Chariot: *see*
Black; Bull; Cat; Centaur;
CHASTITY; Cock
(Rooster); Deer; Dog;
Dolphin; Dove; Dragon;
Eagle; Elephant; FAME;
Goat; Gold; Horse;
Leopard; Lion; Moon; Ox;
Peacock; Ram; Snake;
Stork; Sun; Tarot; Thunder;
Tiger; Unicorn; Wheel;
White; Wolf

Chalice

A ceremonial goblet, associated particularly with the sacred wine of the Christian Eucharist (Christ's blood) and with the legend of the Holy Grail. It symbolizes the drinking in of spiritual illumination or knowledge, redemption, and hence immortality. The chalice appears in art as an emblem of Faith and is an attribute of several saints. In China and Japan, and in marriage ceremonies worldwide, sharing a chalice signifies fidelity. Ceremonial goblets were used in the Celtic world to denote sovereignty. Alternatively, the chalice can stand for a bitter destiny, as in the cup that Christ asked God to take from him (referring to his approaching crucifixion). The so-called poisoned chalice promises hope but delivers disaster.

Chameleon

Now simply a metaphor for changeability, this arboreal lizard has other remarkable characteristics (climbing ability, independently swivelling eyes, and a long, hunting tongue) that gave it sacred and ethical significance in many parts of Africa. Associated with thunder, lightning, rain and also with the sun, it appears widely as an intermediary between sky gods and humankind; and, in Pigmy folklore, as an agent in humanity's creation. In Western art it can personify Air.

Chariot

A dynamic image of rulership, widely used in iconography to illustrate the mastery and mobility of gods and heroes, or the spiritual authority of religious and allegorical figures. Its triumphal symbolism probably owes much to the shock force of chariot-riding warriors who spread out from central Asia from the 2nd millennium BCE. Hindu mystics (later supported by psychologists such as Jung) saw charioteering as a symbol of the Self: the charioteer (thought) uses the reins (willpower and intelligence) to master the steeds (life force) tugging the chariot (the body). In moral allegory,

The Chariots of the Gods		
Name of god *(Roman equivalents of Greek gods are given in brackets)*	**Culture**	**Chariot pulled by**
Aphrodite (Venus)	Classical	doves
Apollo	Classical	white horses
Ares (Mars)	Classical	wolves
Artemis (Diana)	Classical	stags
Cybele	Classical	lions
Dionysus (Bacchus)	Classical	tigers, panthers, leopards, centaurs or goats
Freya	Nordic	lunar cats
Galatea	Roman	dolphins
Hades (Pluto)	Classical	black horses
Hephaestus (Vulcan)	Classical	dogs
Hera (Juno)	Classical	peacocks
Hermes (Mercury)	Classical	cocks or storks
Poseidon (Neptune)	Classical	seahorses
Shiva	Indian	gazelles
Thor	Nordic	rams
Zeus (Jupiter)	Classical	eagles or bulls

CHASTITY

Personified most famously by the unicorn, Chastity also appears in Christian art as a veiled figure, often carrying a shield (against the arrows of desire) or treading on a pig (lust). Notable representatives of chastity are the Virgin Mary, the Greek Artemis (Diana to the Romans) and the nymph Daphne, who became a laurel tree as she fled from the sun-god Apollo. Traditional symbols of chastity include: the colours blue and white, bees, castles, chestnuts, crescents, crystals, diamonds, doves, elephants, enclosed gardens, ermine, girdles, hawthorns, irises, jade, laurel, lilies, mirrors, palms, pearls, the phoenix, the salamander, sapphires, sealed wells, sieves, silver, towers and violets.

CHASTITY: *see* Arrow; Bee; Blue; Castle; Crystal; Diamond; Dove; Elephant; Ermine; Garden; Girdle, Belt; Hawthorn; Iris; Jade; Laurel; Mirror; Palm; Phoenix; Pig; Salamander; Sapphire; Sieve; Silver; Tower; Unicorn; Veil; Violet; Virginity; Well; White

the chariot thus became an image of the triumphant journey of the spirit, a symbolism used by the makers of the film *Chariots of Fire*. A fiery chariot carried the prophet Elijah to heaven (2 Kings 2:11). Wheel symbolism fitted aptly to the chariots of sun gods such as Apollo or moon goddesses such as Artemis. Equally, the sound of rumbling wheels suggested the chariots of Thor and other thunder gods. Gods or allegorical figures are more often identified by the specific symbolism of the creatures that draw their chariots. Thus Chastity is drawn by unicorns, Eternity by angels, Night by black horses, Death by black oxen and Fame by elephants (see also table, left). The colour of the chariot may be significant, too – Indra's is gold. The chariot card in Tarot symbolizes self-control.

Cherry

A samurai emblem, perhaps suggested by the hard kernel within the blood-coloured skin and flesh. In China, the cherry tree is considered lucky, a symbol of spring (from its early blossom) and virginity. The vulva is a "cherry spring". In Christian iconography the cherry is an alternative to the apple as the fruit of paradise, and is sometimes an attribute held by Christ.

Cherubim

The second order of angels, whose wings formed the throne of Jehovah in the Hebrew sanctuary that Moses was commanded to build (Exodus 37). Their protective symbolism derived from earlier Persian and Mesopotamian guardian spirits who flanked temples. They usually appear in art as blue-winged heads, sometimes with a book, symbolizing divine knowledge by reason of their proximity to God, whom they are sometimes shown supporting in flight.

Chess

Now an analogy for cold, tactical foresight, chess was an ancient metaphor for the wise handling of free will and fate in a dualistic universe – or, at a more practical level, for the responsible management of war and state affairs by the ruling class of India, where the game probably originated. Chess can be seen as a simple image of warfare safely removed to the plane of an intellectual activity. However, richer accretions of symbolism, legend and allegory cling to the

Cherry: *see* Apple; FRUIT; Red; Tree; Virginity

Cherubim: *see* Angels; Blue; Seraphim; Tabernacle

Chess: *see* Castle; Chariot; Darkness; Devils; Elephant; Four; Horse; King; Light; Mandala; NUMBERS; Queen

Chest: *see*
Ark

Child: *see*
Crown; Philosopher's Stone;
WISDOM

Chimera: *see*
BEASTS OF FABLE;
Dragon; Fire, Flame; Goat;
Hero, Heroine; Lion; Snake;
Triad; Volcano

game, which dates back at least to the 6th century CE and probably earlier. Fate as well as logic intervened in ancient Indian chess, a four-handed affair in which dice were used to initiate moves. A two-handed game with some similarities existed in Persia, where the Indian version of the game (*Chaturanga*) was taken over and developed into a more strictly intellectual contest (*Shatranj*) which entered Spain, and then became hugely popular in medieval Europe. Magic chessboards in Arthurian legend became allegories of the trials of love. Folk heroes played chess with the Devil. Craftsmen produced wondrously modelled chess pieces tailored to the dramatic intrigues of politics or to moral allegories of the struggle between the forces of good and evil, light and darkness, reason and passion, life and death, tyranny and good government. The board's 64 squares derive from the fourfold (8 x 8) mandala of the Indian goddess Shiva, the field of action for the cosmic forces he controlled. Originally the key pieces were elephants (which also carried the kings), chariots, horses and foot soldiers. Their symbolism is complex, as their relative status, forms and patterns of movement changed over a long period before settling into the present values. Realization of the pawn's importance in the 18th century coincided neatly with the rising political significance of the common man.

Chest

A Roman emblem of mystical religions. Greek and Hebrew chests were receptacles for mysteries revealed only to chosen initiates, as in the chests carried in the rites of the Greek Dionysus or Demeter, or the chest holding the Hebrew Tablets of the Law. In China, chests enshrined ancient traditions or ancestral spirits.

Child

Purity, potentiality, innocence, spontaneity – a symbol of the natural, paradisal state, free of anxiety. In iconography the child can also stand for mystic knowledge, openness to faith, as in the alchemist's image of a crowned child who represented the Philosopher's Stone. Christ used child symbolism when he said that only those who humbled themselves as little children could enter the Kingdom of Heaven (Matthew 18:3).

Chimera

A monster of Greek myth, celebrated enough to become a general term for any figment of the imagination – and for hybrid animals of all kinds in architecture.

The Chimera had the mane and fire-breathing head of a lion, the body of a goat (it is often shown with a goat's head as well) and a snake-headed tail like a dragon's. Bellerophon's victory over the Chimera is an example of the much-told tale of confrontation between hero and dragon (which personified Evil).

The Chimera, a beast made up of a lion and a goat, with a serpent's tail. From an Etruscan bronze.

In medieval art the Chimera represented satanic forces. Psychologists have seen it as an image of psychic deformations. Some mythologists interpret its threefold form as the embodiment of several destructive forces in nature, including volcanic eruptions and gas flares.

Chimney

The traditional focus not only of family life but of communication with supernatural forces, its axial symbolism dating back to the open smoke-holes of nomadic tents. Hence its importance in folklore as a route out of the house for witches and into it for kindlier spirits such as Santa Claus.

Chi-Rho

The name of the wheel-like monogram formed by the combined initial Greek letters (XP) of the word *Christ*, intended to symbolize his protection and his triumph over death. For some centuries, apart from the fish, the Chi-Rho was the leading emblem of Christianity. It displaced the eagle on the Roman standard when Constantine the Great came to power by defeating Maxentius in 312CE. According to his biographer Eusebius (fl. 4th century CE), Constantine's final conversion to Christianity was linked to an auspicious dream of the Chi-Rho sign superimposed on the sun – a clue to his probable identification of Christ as the incarnated sun. The sign was not new, as the Greek word for auspicious, *chrestos*, also began with X and P, and a similar spoked-wheel emblem within a circle was earlier a Chaldean solar symbol. Both XP (Christ) and IX (Jesus Christ) appear as early Christian funerary monograms.

Christmas tree

A rebirth, more particularly the rebirth of light – a solar symbolism dating back at least to the Roman festival of Saturnalia, when evergreen decorations celebrated the death of the old year and birth of the new. Teutonic Yuletide rites in which fir trees were hung with lights and surrounded with sacrificial offerings are more direct antecedents of the modern decorated tree; Victorian ceremony took this Christmas tradition from Germany. Orbs, stars and crescents on the tree were once cosmic symbols. In the Christian era, the lights and candles came to symbolize souls.

Chrysanthemum

The imperial and solar flower of Japan, linked with longevity and joy. In China the chrysanthemum is an emblem of Taoist perfection, autumnal tranquillity and plenitude – perhaps because its blooms continue into winter.

Cicada

Immortality – a symbolism probably derived from its desiccated appearance and long lifespan. In Greece, where it was sacred to the sun-god Apollo, these aspects were combined in the myth of Tithonus, a mortal man loved by Eos (the dawn; in Roman myth, Aurora), whose ambrosia kept him alive but could not stop him from ageing. In pity, she turned him into a cicada. Chinese jade cicadas were used as amulets for the dead.

Circle

Totality, perfection, unity, eternity – a symbol of completeness that can include ideas of both permanence and dynamism. The correlation between

Chimney: *see*
Axis; Fire, Flame; Smoke; Witchcraft

Chi-Rho: *see*
Circle; CROSS; Eagle; Sun; Wheel

Christmas tree: *see*
Candle; Crescent; Globe, Orb; Light; Sacrifice; Solstice; Soul; Star; Tree; Yule log

Chrysanthemum: *see*
LONGEVITY; Sun

Cicada: *see*
Amulet; Jade; LONGEVITY

Circle: *see*
AFTERWORLDS; Alchemy; Angels; Ankh; Calumet; Centre; Chakra; Circumambulation; Clock; Dance; Disk; Dome; Fire, Flame; Globe, Orb; Mandala; Moon; Ouroboros; PLANETS; Point; Ring; Round Table; SEASONS; Sky; Sphere; Square; Sun; Trinity; Wheel; Wings; Woman; Yin-yang; Zodiac

Two forms of the Chi-Rho. On the left, the monogram is made up of X and P; on the right, the Latin cross.

the discoveries of atomic physics and mystical notions of the circle is striking. Apart from the point or centre, with which it shares much of its symbolism, the circle is the only geometric shape without divisions and alike at all points. To the Neo-Platonists, the circle embodied god, the uncircumscribed centre of the cosmos. Because the circle, which can also represent a sphere, is a form potentially without beginning or end, it is the most important and universal of all geometric symbols in mystical thought. And because it is implicit in other important symbols, including the wheel, disk, ring, clock, sun, moon, *ouroboros* and Zodiac, its general symbolism is hardly less significant.

To the ancients, the observed cosmos presented itself inescapably as circular – not only the planets themselves, including the presumed flat disk of the earth circled by waters, but also their cyclical movements and the recurring cycles of the seasons. Symbolic meaning and function were combined in the use of the circle to calculate time (the sundial) and space (directional, astrological or astronomical points of reference). Sky symbolism and belief in celestial power underlaid primitive rituals and architecture throughout the world – circular dancing or ceremonial walking around fires, altars or poles, the circular passing of the calumet in North America, the whirling of shamans, the circular form of tents and encampments, circular megalithic markings, and fortifications or ringed monuments of the Neolithic period. Circles had protective as well as celestial significance, notably in the Celtic world – and they still do have this in the folklore of fairy rings and flying saucers.

They also stand for inclusive harmony, as in the Arthurian Round Table or the "charmed circle" of acquaintanceship widely used in modern idiom. Interlocking circles (as in the modern Olympic emblem) are another symbol of union.

Dynamism is added to the circle in the many images of disks with rays, wings or flames found in religious iconography, notably Sumerian, Egyptian and Mexican. They symbolize solar power or creative and fertilizing cosmic forces. Concentric circles can stand for celestial hierarchies (as in the choirs of angels symbolizing heaven in Renaissance art), levels in the afterworld or, in Zen Buddhism, stages of spiritual development. Three circles can stand for the Christian divine Trinity but also for the divisions of time, the elements, the seasons or the movement of the sun and the phases of the moon. The circle can be masculine (as the sun) but also feminine (as the maternal womb). A circle (female) over a cross (male) is a symbol of union in Egypt, also known in northern Europe, the Middle East and China. The Chinese yin-yang symbol of male and female interdependence uses two colours within a circle, divided by an S-shaped curve, each including a smaller circle of the opposing colour. A dot within a circle is the astrological symbol for the sun and the alchemical symbol for gold.

The circle combined with the square is a Jungian archetypal symbol of the relationship between the psyche or self (circle) and the body or material reality (square). This interpretation is supported by Buddhist mandalas in which squares inside circles represent the passage from material to spiritual planes. In Western and Eastern

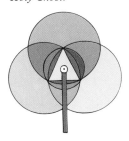

Three entwined circles from a Christian illustration representing the Father, Son and Holy Ghost.

thought, the circle enclosing a square stands for heaven enclosing earth. Circular domes, vaults or cupolas incorporate the celestial symbolism of the rounded decoration in Romanesque churches or pagan temples into architecture based on the square, cross or rectangle. "Squaring the circle" (the geometrically impossible task of forming a circle from a series of squares) was a Renaissance and alchemical allegory of the difficulty of constructing divine perfection with earthly materials. Conversely, the cabbalistic image of a circle within a square symbolizes the divine spark within a material body.

Circumambulation

The ritual of walking around a sacred object, or defining and sanctifying a space by making a circuit of it, imitates solar and astral cycles, and pays homage to celestial forces and the protective symbolism of the circle. In a celebrated example at Mecca, pilgrims make seven circuits of the Kaaba (sacred cube). Buddhist circumambulation of a temple places the worshipper in tune with cosmic rhythms and symbolizes progression toward self-knowledge and enlightenment. The direction of the Hindu and Buddhist *Pradakshina* circumambulation is clockwise (following the apparent clockwise path of the sun around the Northern hemisphere); the symbolic approach to the Seventh Heaven by Muslims at Mecca is counterclockwise (as the polar wheel of the stars).

Circumcision

An ancient ritual, widespread outside northern Europe, Mongolia and Hindu India, with both initiatory and sacrificial meanings in addition to any hygienic ones. The Hebrew commandment to circumcise males eight days after birth seems to have had both hygienic and symbolic importance, initiating children into a community chosen by God. In Christianity, the sacramental rite of baptism replaced this initiatory symbolism, and circumcision was not prescribed. Elsewhere, circumcision at puberty is a rite of passage to adulthood, often for females as well as males. An even earlier sacrificial symbolism has been suggested, with circumcision standing for a blood offering – a significant part of the body set aside in the hope of immortality. An alternative supposition is that circumcision, male and female, was an attempt to clarify sexual differences, the prepuce being seen as a feminine aspect of males, the clitoris as a masculine aspect of females.

Cloak

Power, protection, separation, metamorphosis, concealment – a diversity of symbolism related to the swiftness with which a cloak can change or hide the form. Magic cloaks appear often in Teutonic and Celtic legends, particularly Irish; they are associated with special powers, including invisibility and forgetfulness. They were an emblem of royalty, brotherhood or separation from the materialistic world, as in some monastic orders. They could also be an emblem of divine protection. Alternatively, the cloak stands for intrigue – for example, the cloak-and-dagger world of espionage.

Clock

Moderation – an attribute of Temperance in art. In devotional still lifes, clocks appear as reminders of time passing, but some portraits included

Circumambulation: *see* Circle; Kaaba; Wheel

Circumcision: *see* Androgyne; Baptism; Initiation; Sacrifice

Cloak: *see* Transformation

Clock: *see* Circle; VIRTUES; Wheel

Clouds: *see*
Darkness; Nine; Pillar

Clover: *see*
Three; Trinity

Clown: *see*
Cap; King; Sacrifice;
Scapegoat; WISDOM

Club: *see*
VIRTUES

Cobra: *see*
BEASTS OF FABLE;
Rainbow; Rod; Snake; Sun

Cock (Rooster): *see*
ANIMALS; Basilisk; Dawn;
Fire, Flame; Hen; Initiation;
Light; Phallus; Pig; Red;
SEVEN DEADLY SINS;
Snake; Sun; VIGILANCE;
White; Witchcraft

*The cobra coiled
around the sun, from an
Indian folk drawing.*

them instead to symbolize the even-tempered nature of the sitter.

Clouds
Fecundity, elemental and spiritual. Apart from their obvious fertility symbolism as harbingers of rain, clouds also stood for revelation, the presence of God, a divinity almost made manifest. Thus Jehovah guided the Israelites as a pillar of cloud, and Allah speaks from a cloud in the Koran. Clouds, especially pink ones, are symbols of happiness in China, and also emblems of ascent to heaven. "Cloud Nine" is mystical bliss.

Clover
Trefoil in shape, the clover symbolizes the Christian Trinity. Ireland's use of the shamrock as its national emblem may refer to Celtic respect for the plant's vigorous growth.

Clown
The inheritor of a tradition that includes fools (simpletons or pretended simpletons), jesters (sharp-witted pranksters) and buffoons (knockabout comedians), categories often confused. The deepest and most sinister symbolism attaches to the fool, an ancient, inverted image of the king or ruler, used as a substitute for him in early sacrificial rituals. More generally the clown or fool represents, and acts as scapegoat for human failure – the speed with which dignity and seriousness can collapse into farce, or wisdom turn into idiocy.

Club
Celtic symbol of divine force, the attribute of the supreme god Dagda, whose club could take or restore life and was heavy enough to need wheels

to shift it. This dual symbolism is analogous with the power of the thunderbolt to fertilize or to destroy. In art, the club can represent either brutality or heroism. It appears as an attribute of Fortitude.

Cobra
Apart from its general snake symbolism, the erect and hooded cobra has specific sacred significance in the iconography of India and Egypt. In Egypt, a female cobra with raised hood is the Uraeus, the burning eye of the sun-god Ra, worn on the headdresses of kings and gods, and also carved on temples, as an emblem of the power to give and take life. Aaron's rod, which turned into a snake to impress the pharaoh in the book of Exodus (7:8–12), may in fact have been the rigid body of a cobra. There is less doubt that Cleopatra's chosen instrument of suicide was the small asp cobra. The large Indian cobra is the magical Naga of Hindu mythology, guardian of treasure, corresponding also to Shesha or Ananta, the cosmic snake on which Vishnu rests between eras of creativity. In Buddhism the Naja-cobra is the mastered power of instinct. In Cambodia the miraculous seven-headed Naga is a rainbow symbol, representing the passage from earth to heaven.

Cock (Rooster)
Watchfulness, courage, virility, prescience, reliability – and, as herald of the dawn, a symbol of solar and spiritual resurrection. These positive attributes are more widespread culturally than the pride, arrogance and lust also associated with the cock. It is linked with the dawn, the sun and illumination, almost everywhere except in

Celtic and Nordic traditions. In China, where its red comb also suggested sunset and autumn, its name is a homonym of good fortune: a red cock wards off fire, a white one ghosts. The cock was sacrificed at initiations, but not eaten. It exemplified the five Chinese virtues of civil and military merit, courage, reliability and generosity (from its practice of offering food to its hens). It was also a funerary emblem, warding off evil.

Cocks were also sacred animals in Japan, hence the free run that they were given in Shinto temples. The cock calls Shinto worshippers to prayer as once it called the sun-goddess Amaterasu from the cave where she hid her light. In Buddhism, the cock, representing carnal desires, joins the pig and snake as one of the three emblematic animals that bind humanity to the round of birth and death.

The cock can also personify Lust in Western art. However, in Christianity its symbolism is generally positive. It represents light and rebirth, putting to flight the darkness of spiritual ignorance. Church weathervanes in the form of cocks are emblems of vigilance against evil. At cock crow, the ghostly apparitions of night vanish. This solar and protective symbolism is ancient throughout the Middle East. In ancient Greece, the cock was an attribute of many divinities including Zeus, Apollo, Attis and Persephone as gods and goddesses of rebirth, Ares and Athene as deities of pugnacity, Hermes as herald and Aesculapius as healer. The cock is also venerated in Islam: it was the giant bird seen by Muhammad in the First Heaven crowing, "There is no god but Allah."

The cock is a familiar messenger of the underworld in Celtic and Nordic traditions, leading souls, calling the dead to battle, or warning the gods of danger. Some African traditions associate its reputation for foresight with the idea of secret knowledge and hence witchcraft.

The cock's role as an emblem of France seems to derive from a Roman pun, the Latin *gallus* meaning both "cock" and "a Gaul". Another curious link with time is given by the three cock crows that counted off the three denials of Christ by the disciple Peter. The cock has since become one of the attributes of St Peter, who is the patron saint of watchmakers. Fables in which animals arrogantly boast to each other are the origin of the expression "cock-and-bull".

COLOURS *see panel on p.50*

Coffin

A protective womb, symbolizing the hope of rebirth. Hence the elaborate coffins for people of high rank and the reason that they are placed in sanctuaries, sepulchres or churches.

Comb

Fertility and, in Japan, spiritual power – symbolic associations that probably derive from the long-toothed ornamental combs of wood, bone or horn used by women from antiquity, suggesting rays of the sun or falling rain. A comb-like motif is the emblem of the Aztec rain-god Tlaloc.

Comet

A portent of catastrophe. Early astrologers viewed any unusual celestial event with apprehension, and the appearance of a comet augured disasters such as war, plague, drought, famine, fire or the fall of kings. Thus

Comb: *see*
Rain; Rays

Comet: *see*
Zodiac

COLOURS: *see*
Black; Blue; Brown;
DEATH; Gold; Green;
Grey; Light; Orange;
Purple; Red; Silver; Sun;
Violet; White

COLOURS

Colours have a vast and complex range of symbolic meanings. Generalizations about the specific symbolism of any one colour as if it had inherent and fixed significance psychologically or in nature are hard to sustain. Black and white (or light and dark colours) clearly stand for duality and antithesis. However, in some traditions black is the colour of death and mourning; in others white. Red, the colour of blood, is usually linked with the life principle, activity, fertility – but represented death in the Celtic world and was a menacing colour in Egypt. Experiments have shown that some colour associations apear to be true. Red is seen as strong, "heavy" and emotive. Blue is widely considered "good". People prefer colours lighter rather than darker in tone, and lighter colours seem to advance. The colours that attract our attention most are red, yellow, green and blue (those preferred by children). The red-to-yellow end of the spectrum is "warm", the blue-indigo end "cool". The range of colours thought significant is far wider than it once was, but this is a matter of growing visual sophistication.

Most fundamental colour symbolism was drawn from nature. Thus green symbolized potency in arid regions and was a sacred colour in Islam. Gold was linked almost universally with the sun, therefore suggesting illumination and rulership. Blue stood for the sky, therefore the spirit and truth ("true blue"). Religion often overlaid this with other significance. Thus yellow has a high value in Thailand not because it shares the natural symbolism of light and flame, but because the Buddha chose yellow (worn by beggars and criminals) to symbolize renunciation of the material world. In Christianity, white – by natural observation the symbolic colour of death in many cultures – came to symbolize light, purity and joy in opposition to the black of evil and mourning. Many complex systems of colour symbolism, covering everything from the planets and the elements to the cardinal points, the metals and substances of alchemy, and the organs of the body, are hardly more than arbitrary forms of identification. What does seem true is that colours generally are life-affirming symbols of illumination, as reflected in the glories of ecclesiastical stained glass.

Compasses, Dividers: *see*
Circle; VIRTUES

Calpurnia in Shakespeare's *Julius Caesar* (2:2; *c*.1600) says: "When beggars die, there are no comets seen, / The heavens themselves blaze forth the death of princes."

Compasses, Dividers

An emblem of geometry, architecture, astronomy and geography, and a symbol much used in medieval and Renaissance art as a visual shorthand for a reasoned and measured approach. A pair of compasses could also personify, by extension, associated virtues such as justice, prudence and maturity. In China, it stood for rectitude. Because the compasses were used to draft circles (celestial in symbolism), they were often linked with the set square (signifying the earth) in images representing the relationship between spirit and matter. God, as the architect of the universe, sometimes appears with compasses, setting the limits of earth or time. With the same significance, the compasses are also an attribute of Saturn, leading to an unexpected link between the compasses and Saturnian melancholy. William Blake, in his famous painting *Newton*, gives a twist to compass symbolism by using them to attack the attempt of scientists to quantify creation.

Conch
A horn-like shell, often used as a ceremonial musical instrument and symbolizing in many coastal traditions the primordial creative voice – notably in India and Polynesia. Indian mysticism links the conch to the sacred sound *Om* and to the breath of Vishnu that fills the universe. It is one of the eight Buddhist symbols of Good Augury. In Greece it is the attribute of each of the sea-god Poseidon's Tritons. Its spiral form could suggest hearing as well as sound, and in Islamic tradition it symbolized attention to the Word.

Cone
Fertility – a geometric shape suggesting both male and female sexual symbolism, circle and triangle, tower and pyramid. It was an attribute of the Semitic goddess Ashtart (Astarte).

Coral
Healing power – a symbolism based on tree, water and blood symbolism. In classical mythology, the Mediterranean red coral grew from the blood of the Gorgon Medusa. Roman amulets of coral were thought to stem

bleeding and protect children from illness or the fury of the elements, and coral necklaces were also popular medieval talismans for children. At one time, coral decorated Celtic weapons and helmets. It was prized in India where a jet-black coral was used to make sceptres.

Cord
A binding (as worn by monks bound to their vows) or union (the knotted cords of Freemasonry). In mystical thought, cords link the material and spiritual worlds and can be ascended by grace. The Silver Cord links body and spirit. Cords with fertilizing symbolism appear in Central American iconography, representing the fall of divine, fructifying seed or rain. In art, Fortune holds a cord representing mortal life, cut at whim. In Hinduism knots on cords are representative of devotional acts .

Corn
Fertility, growth, rebirth, the divine gift of life. In all regions where grain was a staple, corn seemed a miraculous and consoling image of the continuity of life through death, the grain (wheat, barley or maize) ripening in the earth and reappearing in spring. Thus Christ in the Gospel of St John (12:24): "Unless a grain of wheat falls in the earth and dies, it remains just a single grain; but if it dies it bears much fruit." An attribute of the Greek Grain Mother, Demeter, the ear of corn "reaped in silence" was the central symbol of the Eleusinian mysteries, promising new life, human and vegetable. Corn was a funerary emblem in China, Rome, the Middle East and, as the attribute of the god Osiris, Egypt. In iconography, ears of

Conch: *see*
Om (Aum); Shell; Spiral; Word

Cone: *see*
Circle; Phallus; Pyramid; Tower; Triangle

Coral: *see*
Amulet; Blood; Red; Sceptre; Tree; Water

Cord: *see*
Bonds; FORTUNE; Knot; Rain

Corn: *see*
Barley; Blue; Earth; Mother; Red; Silver

Cornucopia

Cornucopia: *see*
FLOWERS; FORTUNE;
FRUIT; Goat; PEACE;
Wine

Cow: *see*
Black; Bull; Crescent; Disk;
Earth; Giant; Milk; Moon;
Mother; Sky; Sun; White;
Wreath, Garland

Cowrie: *see*
Gold; Shell

grain appear as attributes of most earth gods and goddesses, and on the robe of the Virgin Mary in medieval and Renaissance art.

The Aztecs worshipped several corn gods, major and minor; while in Peru, fertility was represented as a woman made of maize stalks. Blue-painted maize icons in North America symbolized the fertilizing synthesis of red earth and blue sky.

In art, the Roman goddess Ceres appears crowned with ears of corn and holding a sheaf. A corn sheaf with ploughshare stands for the Age of Silver, a bound sheaf for Concord, corn and grapevines for the Christian Eucharist. Corn can also represent abundance and prosperity. It is food and seed – the cob, from which the nuggets grow, an image of ejaculation.

Cornucopia

The "Horn of Plenty", overflowing with fruits, flowers and grains, is a symbol not only of abundance, prosperity and good luck but also of divine generosity. Ancient associations between the horn and fertility lie behind the classical story that Zeus (in Roman myth, Jupiter) accidentally broke off a horn of the goat that suckled him. He gave it to his nurse, Amalthea, whereupon it provided inexhaustible food and drink.

A popular motif in art, the cornucopia appears as an attribute not only of vegetation or wine divinities such as the classical Demeter (in Roman myth, Ceres), Dionysus (Bacchus), Priapus and Flora, but also of many positive allegorical figures including Earth, Autumn, Hospitality, Peace, Fortune and Concord. *Putti* were often painted spilling nourishment (for the spirit) from a cornucopia.

Cow

An ancient symbol of maternal nourishment and, like the bull, an image of cosmic generative power. In cultures from Egypt to China the cow was a personification of Mother Earth. It was also lunar and astral, its crescent horns representing the moon, its abundant milk the countless stars of the Milky Way. Nut, the Egyptian sky goddess, sometimes appears with this symbolism in the form of a cow with stars on its belly, its legs the four quarters of the earth. Hathor, Great Mother goddess of joy and love and nourisher of living things, is also represented as a cow. As a protective emblem of royalty, she was often shown with the solar disk between her horns – a reference to the idea of a celestial, mothering cow nourishing the sinking sun with her warmth. A similar image of the cow as the nourisher of original life appears in the mythology of northern Europe where Adumla, wet nurse of the primordial giants, licks the ice to disclose the first man or, alternatively, the three creator gods. In Vedic literature, the cow is both sky and earth, its milk falling as abundant, fertilizing rain. The black cow played a part in funerary rites, the white was a symbol of illumination. To both Hindus and Buddhists, the cow's quiet, patient rhythms of life presented an image of holiness so complete that it became India's most sacred animal. Its image is everywhere one of happiness – as in Greek rites where white heifers were garlanded and led in celebratory processions with dancing and music.

Cowrie

The vulva, source of life. Among primitive peoples, the beautiful, labia-like shell of this mollusc was the most widespread natural amulet against sterility and the evil eye.

The golden cowrie was an emblem of rank in Fiji and Tonga. Cowrie necklaces were used in trade throughout the Pacific, with ritual as well as commercial significance. Associations with fecundity, sexual pleasure and good luck also made cowries prized charms in Africa and elsewhere, often far from the shores where they were gathered. As funerary or decorative emblems they can also signify life and death, their power lasting after the death of the mollusc.

Coyote
Creative or mischevious ingenuity. Among the Native North Americans, Coyote is the great trickster – a skilled and devious transformer and inventor, operating at the level sometimes of cosmic myth, sometimes of fable, and bringing benefit or disaster to humankind according to different traditions. The Navajo, who feared to kill a coyote, said that Coyote accompanied the first man and first woman into the world, but had the foresight to bring with him seeds with which to provide food; the Shoshoni and other western tribes said that he was responsible for death, along with other natural ills (winter, flood); the Sioux said that he invented the horse. The mythical Coyote is thus a resourceful animal whose blunders or successes explained the condition of life in an uncertain universe.

Crab
A lunar symbol because, like the moon with its phases, it casts off its shell for a new one – an analogy linked with rebirth symbolism in Aboriginal tradition and sometimes so used also in Christianity. Apart from its astrological significance as the Zodiacal sign Cancer, the crab appears infrequently in iconography. Greek myth tells us that Hera placed the crab in the heavens for its courage in biting the heel of Herakles while he was struggling with the Hydra, a story that contrasts oddly with its reputation for timidity. It appears in Inca tradition as a devourer, connected with the waning moon, and in Thailand and elsewhere in rain ceremonies. Again at the level of analogy, its forward and backward movements sometimes symbolized dishonesty, as in China.

Crane
Vigilance, longevity, wisdom, fidelity, honour – a symbolism particularly important in China and Japan. A contrary symbolism appears in India (where it represents treachery) and some Celtic regions (as a bird of ill-omen). The ancients were impressed by the crane's beauty and stamina, its migrations and spring reappearances, its complex mating dance, its voice and its contemplative stance at rest.

The crane was linked in China with immortality, in Africa with the gift of speech, and widely with the ability to communicate with the gods. Its cyclic return also suggested regeneration, a resurrection symbolism sometimes used in Christianity.

In ancient Greece, the cries of migrating cranes announced spring sowings and autumn reapings. The bird's role in art as the personification of Vigilance may go back to a description in the works of Aristotle of the crane's holding a stone in its mouth so that it would wake if it dropped the stone in sleep. In China, where a crane

Coyote: *see* Transformation; Trickster

Crab: *see* Moon; Rain; Zodiac

Crane: *see* Birds; Doubles; LONGEVITY; Red; VIGILANCE; White

Coyote, the trickster, from a North American plate, 11th–13th century CE.

Cremation: *see*
AFTERWORLDS; Fire,
Flame; Smoke; Soul

Crescent: *see*
Boat; Bull; CHASTITY;
CROSS; Cup; Disk; Horn;
Moon; Star

Crocodile: *see*
ANIMALS; BEASTS OF
FABLE; CARDINAL
POINTS; Circumcision;
DEATH; Dragon; Earth;
Leviathan; Makara; Sun;
Water

*The crescent and star
emblem of Islam,
signifying paradise.*

flying toward the sun symbolized social aspirations, the bird's white body represented purity, its red head the fire of life. In Egypt, the double-headed crane represented prosperity.

Cremation

Purification, sublimation and ascension. Indo-Iranian peoples often preferred cremation to burial as a result of these associations, and it was also sometimes used in western Europe from the Bronze Age, later spreading through the Roman Empire, often as a mark of high status. Near-complete dissolution of the body in fire symbolizes the freeing of the soul from the flesh and its ascension in smoke. Burial was preferred where doctrines of bodily resurrection were popular (for example, in Egypt and Christian Europe), and by the Chinese who have always been wedded to their native soil.

Crescent

The emblem of Islam, signifying divine authority, increase, resurrection and, with a star, paradise. An ancient symbol of cosmic power in western Asia, the crescent moon was taken as the barque of the great Babylonian moon-god Sin, as he navigated the vast reaches of space. The Latin etymology of "crescent" (increasing) indicates why the crescent image later developed as a symbol of Islamic expansion. It not only incorporated the idea of the constantly regenerating moon but could be read as two back-to-back horns, themselves symbols of increase. From the time of the Crusades, the crescent became a counter-emblem to the cross – and the Red Crescent is the Islamic version of the Red Cross today.

Present-day countries that fly national flags bearing crescent and one or more stars include Turkey, Libya, Tunisia and Malaysia.

Use of the crescent as an emblem long predated the Islamic empire. In Byzantium, coins were stamped with the crescent and star in 341BCE when, according to one legend, the moon-goddess Hecate intervened to save the city from Macedonian forces (their attack revealed by the sudden appearance of a crescent moon). The image of the crescent moon as a cup holding the elixir of immortality appears in Hindu and Celtic as well as Muslim traditions. In Egypt, the crescent and disk symbolized divine unity. Greek and Roman lunar goddesses wearing a crescent in their hair symbolized chastity and birth. The Virgin Mary sometimes appears with a crescent at her feet with similar chaste meaning in Christian iconography.

Crest

An emblem worn at the top of a knight's helmet, chosen to symbolize his motivating thoughts, summarize the object of his quest or proclaim his personal allegiance.

Cricket

An emblem of happiness and good luck, especially in China, where singing crickets were often kept in boxes or ornate cages. They symbolized summertime, courage (they were encouraged to fight each other) and also resurrection, probably from their metamorphosis from the larval stage.

Crocodile

Destructive voracity – an agent of divine retribution, and lord of water and earth, life and death. To

Europeans, unfamiliar with this tropical and subtropical reptile, it was a subject of uninformed awe or moralizing hostility. The author Plutarch (46–120CE) thought that it was worshipped in Egypt because it had the divine qualities of silence and the ability to see all with its eyes covered by membrane tissue. Medieval bestiaries used it as an allegory of hypocrisy, its eyes streaming as it ate its prey (crocodile tears), its lower jaw mired in mud while the upper jaw was raised in a semblance of moral elevation. Where it was known, it was treated with fearful respect as a creature of primordial and occult power over water, earth and the underworld. In India it was the Makara, the fish-crocodile steed of Vishnu. In Egyptian iconography, the dead often appear as crocodiles and the town of Crocodopolis was dedicated to the crocodile fecundity god, Sebek. In more monstrous imagery, Amamet (or Amemait), who devoured the hearts of wrongdoers, had crocodile jaws, and the god Set took the form of a crocodile to devour his brother Osiris.

In Native American iconography, the crocodile, or alligator, appears with open jaws as the nocturnal sun-swallower. Some Central American myths say that the crocodile gave birth to the earth or supports it on its back. Rebirth symbolism appears in a Liberian initiation tradition to the effect that circumcision scars are the marks of a crocodile that swallows youths and returns them as adults. In the West, the crocodile is sometimes interpreted as a form of leviathan, as an image of chaos, or as the dragon that symbolically represents evil. It appears in art with this meaning, vanquished by the Roman St Theodore.

Jungian psychology has seen it as an archetypal symbol of torpid ill-temper, an interpretation in conflict with its water and earth symbolism in many parts of Asia, including China where it appears as the inventor of the drum and song.

Crook *see* **Crozier**

CROSS *see panel on pp. 56–7*

Crossroads
The unknown – hazard, choice, destiny, supernatural powers. The importance attached to intersecting ways in most ancient cultures is remarkable. The fact that they were natural stops for wayfarers only partly accounts for the number of shrines, altars, standing stones, chapels or Calvaries sited there. In Peru and elsewhere pyramids were sometimes built up over years by travellers adding votive stones as they passed through crossroads. Spirits were thought to haunt them, hence they were sites for divination and sacrifice – and, by extension, places of the execution or burial of people or things of which society wished to be rid. Many African tribes dumped rubbish there so that any residual harm might be absorbed. Roman crossroads in the time of Augustus were protected by two *lares campitales* (tutelary deities of place). Offerings were made to them or to the god Janus and other protective divinities, who could look in all directions, such as Hermes, to whom three-headed statues were placed at Grecian crossroads. Hecate, as a death goddess, was a more sinister presence, as was the supreme Toltec god, Tezcatlipoca, who challenged warriors at crossroads. Some versions of the Oedipus myth place his fateful

Crossroads: *see* Jaguar; Pyramid; Sacrifice; Sphinx; Triad

A crocodile, from a 17th-century plaque in Benin, West Africa, where the beast's entrails were thought to have magical powers.

CROSS: *see*
Anchor; Ankh; Arrow; Axe;
Axis; Blood; CARDINAL
POINTS; Chi-Rho; Circle;
Eight; ELEMENTS; Four;
Earth; Fire; Flame; Grail;
Hammer; Lance; Man;
Moon; Nail; PASSION;
Pelican; Rain; Runes;
Sacrifice; Scapegoat; Six;
Skull; Snake; Square; Steps,
Stairs; Sun; Swastika; Ten;
Tree; Trident; VIRTUES;
Wheel; Wind

CROSS

In religion and art, the richest and most enduring of geometric symbols, taking many forms and meanings throughout history. It is both the emblem of the Christian faith and a more ancient and universal image of the cosmos reduced to its simplest terms – two intersecting lines making four points of direction. These stood for the four cardinal points and the four rain-bearing winds (notably in pre-Columbian America where the cross was often a fertility emblem of life and elemental energy), the four phases of the moon (Babylonia), and the four great gods of the elements (Syria).

The arms of the cross could be multiplied to six (as in Chaldea and Israel) or eight. In China, a cross within a square represented the earth and stability. In India, the cross was the Hindu emblem of the fire sticks of Agni; a cross within a circle, the Buddhist wheel of life; or, with arms extending beyond the circle, divine energy. The swastika – an ancient emblem of cosmic energy – was a cross given momentum by turning the ends of the arms.

The cross was also a summary of the Tree of Life, a widespread symbolism later often incorporated into Christian crucifixion iconography. The vertical axis has ascensional meaning while the horizontal axis stands for earthly life – in Hindu and Buddhist terms, an image of higher and lower states of being. In China the cross represented a heavenly ladder and also the number 10 (as a symbol of totality). Another symbol of totality is the cross formed by a

man standing with arms outstretched – the image of Man as microcosm. More generally, the cross is associated with duality and union, conjunction and, in Jungian psychology, a kindling energy.

Widespread veneration of the cross by peoples who knew nothing of Christianity puzzled early missionaries, particularly in North and Central America; in Mexico the cross was an attribute of the wind and rain gods, Quetzalcoatl and Tlaloc. Aztec images of sacrificial crucifixions have also been found. The mark of the cross in Africa could signify protection, cosmic unity, destiny or (in a circle) sovereignty. In Scandinavia, runic crosses marking boundaries and important graves may have represented the fertilizing power of the god Thor's hammer. The form of the Celtic cross, incorporating a circle at the centre of the crossbar, appears to synthesize Christian and pagan cosmic symbolism. In Egypt, the ankh – symbolizing immortality – was adopted into Christianity by the Coptic Church.

In the Roman, Persian and Jewish world, the crucifixion cross was the brutal and humiliating instrument of execution for non-citizens such as slaves, pirates and foreign political agitators or other criminals. Thus, at the time of Christ's death, it hardly seemed an emblem likely to make many converts. Fear of ridicule as well as persecution probably influenced the various forms of *crux dissimulata* (anchor, axe, swastika or trident) used by early Christians as secret cross emblems. Even after the Emperor Constantine's conversion, the cross remained for some centuries an emblem of faith secondary to Christ's Chi-Rho monogram. It became dominant as Christianity spread because it could inherit the older cross traditions and give them profound new meaning – redemption through Christ's self-sacrifice. In art, schematic representations of the crucifixion with an impassive Christ gradually gave way to powerful images of his agony, which culminate in Grünewald's Isenheim altarpiece (1515) that made the plain cross itself a consoling symbol of human suffering transcended.

The form of the cross has varied widely. The Latin *crux immissa* (its bar horizontal to and high up the upright) is traditionally the cross of Christ. Alternatively, this may have been the *crux commissa* (T-shaped Tau or St Anthony cross). The transverse *crux decussata*, signifying martyrdom, is the cross of St Andrew, said to have felt himself unworthy of crucifixion on the cross of Christ. The Greek cross, *crux quadrata* (centrally positioned bar), is that of St George. Other Christian forms include the Y-shaped cross, strongly identified with the Tree of Life; the Calvary cross with three steps at the bottom; the Papal cross with three equal bars; the patriar-

Four types of cross (clockwise from top): crux commissa, crux decussata, crux immissa and crux quadrata.

chal cross with two bars, used for archbishops and cardinals, which also appears widely in Greece and became the Cross of Anjou and Lorraine, later the emblem of the Free French; the cross of St Peter, an upside-down form of the Latin cross; the axe-bladed cross of the Templars; the eight-pointed Maltese cross of the Hospitallers; and the triangle-armed cross of the Teutonic Knights. All are images with centripetal energy. A cross tipped with arrows, was the emblem of the fascist Hungarian Nationalist Party. There are nearly 300 other forms of heraldic cross.

The cross is one of the most frequently misunderstood of all images. Crosses, particularly the transverse cross, are commonly woven into patterns with no symbolic meaning, or used simply as directional markers, signatures, or signs of dissent, assent and warning. The meanings of some ancient crosses scratched on stone or wood is therefore debatable. The symbolism of the Christian cross also created popular confusion. Superstitions that the Church found hard to eradicate included the idea that making the sign of the cross (as in benediction or prayer) could ward off any kind of bad luck. Crosses on home-baked bread, for example, were still common in Protestant England in the 17th century.

Crow: *see*
Birds; Black; DEATH; Sun

Crown: *see*
Circle; FAME; Feathers;
Gold; Horn; JEWELS;
Laurel; Lotus; METALS;
Mother; Olive; Rays; Rose;
Sacrifice; Star; Sun; Thorn;
Tiara; TRUTH; VIRTUES;
WISDOM; Wreath

encounters with his unknown father, and with the Sphinx, at crossroads – an analogy for destiny. Jung saw the crossroads as a maternal symbol of the union of opposites. More often, they seem an image of human fears and hopes at a moment of choice.

Crow

The European carrion species has been an emblem of war, death, solitude, evil and bad luck – a symbolism that appears in India also. The American species, which is gregarious and feeds mainly on grain and insects, has strikingly different symbolism – positive, even heroic, as in Tlingit myths where it appears as a solar, creative and civilizing bird, and in Navajo legends where it is the Black God, keeper of all game animals. Both American and Aboriginal myths explain the crow's black plumage as a mishap and read no ill-omen into it. More widely, the crow appears as a guide or prophetic voice – even in Greece, where it was sacred to the sun-god Apollo and the goddess Athene (Minerva in Roman myth), and in Rome, where its croak sounded like the Latin *cras* ("tomorrow"), linking it with hope.

In China, a three-legged crow on a sun disk was the imperial emblem. It also stood for filial or family love in China and Japan. Shintoism gives it the role of divine messenger. "Eating crow", the American phrase for humiliation, refers to an altercation behind British lines during a truce in the War of 1812 when a trespassing American soldier was made to eat a piece of a crow that he had just shot, but then, when his gun was returned to him, forced his British tormentor to eat a piece himself.

Crown

Victory, rank, merit or election – the supreme emblem of spiritual or temporal authority. Crowns acquired celestial, solar, spiritual or protective meaning in many cultures (through the symbolism of circularity, spoked rays, stars, thorns, turrets and so on) but are essentially forms of headdress designed to identify, glorify or consecrate chosen individuals. Crowns originated as simple wreaths, usually of woven laurel or olive leaves, herbs, reeds or other plants, used in wedding or funeral rites or conferred on victors at Greek games. Rulers awarded themselves more distinguished wreaths of gold or roses and diadems of cloth set with jewels, or ornate helmets with horns, jewels or feathers, and these various forms were gradually combined into metalled and jewelled crowns with increasingly elaborate significance.

In Christianity, Hinduism and Buddhism the crown represents spiritual illumination, the crown of everlasting life. Christ's mocking crown of thorns (which became the crown of martyrs) had ancient precedents in the crowning of sacrificial victims. Many gods wear crowns suited to their attributes (for example, the Greek Demeter with ears of corn, the Roman Bacchus with vine leaves). Others who wear crowns in Western art are poets, martyrs, saints, and allegorical figures including Faith, Hope, Wisdom, Fame, Truth and the Church – the Jewish Synagogue being shown with a toppling crown.

Crozier

A bishop's staff of pastoral authority, crook-shaped to symbolize the guardianship and management of his

The papal crown, from a façade of 1619 in Avignon, France.

flock. The crook was an emblem of rulership in Egypt, Assyria and Babylonia, and an attribute of Osiris and several of the Greek gods. The crook is also the emblem of the Apostles and some other Christian saints, and of Christ as the Good Shepherd.

Crucible

An alchemical symbol for transformation through dissolution, purification and union. The crucible could stand for the transmutation of materials or for the testing and blending of male and female in marriage.

Crystal

Clairvoyance, supernatural knowledge, spiritual perfection, chastity. The crystal, a solid that light can penetrate, struck the ancients as celestial and magical.

The crystal symbolized the notion of passing or looking beyond the material world, and was both emblem and tool of shamanistic powers. Hence the visionary crystal palaces and magical crystal (or glass) slippers of folklore. In Buddhism the crystal is the insight of the pure mind.

Cube

Perfect stability, firm ground – a symbol of the earth itself. The cube is the square in three dimensions, each face presenting the same view, hence an emblem of truth, used in art as the footrest of Faith and History.

The Mayan Tree of Life is said to grow from a cube. For both Judaism and Islam, the cube represents the centre of faith. Pilgrims in Mecca circumambulate a double cube, the Kaaba, at the centre of Islam's most sacred mosque.

Cuckoo

A parasite, hence the word *cuckold* (a duped husband), and the bird's link in Europe with jealousy and opportunism. More generally, the cuckoo was traditionally a good omen – of spring or summer, and of riches. Its repetitive call led to the superstition that it was lucky to rattle coins on hearing a cuckoo.

Cup

As the goblet, a symbol of the heart in Islamic, Egyptian and Celtic traditions – hence cups are the forerunners of the hearts suit in the Tarot. The cup also symbolizes love offered, or the blessings of revealed wisdom and everlasting life. Cups were used for making or exchanging vows, for divination (which survives in the reading of tea leaves) and for libations or offerings. In iconography, a cup on a pillar usually has both giving and receiving symbolism – for example, in Hinduism. The Buddhist begging bowl is a contrasting emblem of renunciation. An overturned cup in a still life symbolizes the emptiness of material values. Awarding cups of achievement is a more recent custom.

Cypress

An enigmatic Western symbol of death and mourning. Like other durable evergreens, in Asia and elsewhere it is an emblem of longevity, endurance and even immortality (it was the Phoenician Tree of Life). In Greece, its dual symbolism as the attribute of the gloomy god Hades as well as more cheerful deities such as Zeus, Apollo, Aphrodite and Hermes may mean no more than that its sombre form made it a suitable funerary image of life after death.

Crozier: *see*
Sheep; Shepherd; Staff

Crystal: *see*
CHASTITY; JEWELS;
Light; Star; Throne

Cube: *see*
Centre; Circumambulation;
Earth; Six; Square;
VIRTUES

Cuckoo: *see*
Birds; Clock

Cup: *see*
Chalice; Grail; Heart; Tarot;
VANITY

Cypress: *see*
DEATH; Longevity; Tree

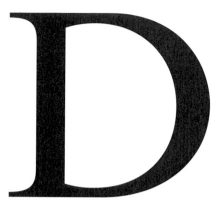

Dance: *see*
Centre; Circle; Fire, Flame;
Mask; Moon; Rain;
SEASONS; Snake; Sun;
Sword

Dagger *see* **Knife**

Dance

An ancient and instinctive expression of the life force, probably predating drawing and painting as a form of sympathetic magic. Dance is liberating and unifying. Primitive dancers, feeling themselves united with the flow of cosmic energy, believed that dance movements, patterns and gestures could influence the processes of nature or the unseen forces that control them. This belief underlies the complex symbolism of ancient dance forms intended to invoke rain or sun, crop or human fertility, military success or the healing of disease, the protection of benign spirits or the appeasement of destructive ones. Because the acting out through dance of tribal beliefs or impending events – such as a hunt – induced group support, it seemed reasonable to suppose that it encouraged the help of the gods. Dance thus became the earliest form of theatre, translating religious dogma into expressive movement, as in the religious dances of ancient

Egypt and Greece. More widely, military victory was commonly rehearsed in war dances – the symbolism behind the sword dances of the Pathans or the Scots. Round dances mimicked the apparent movements of the sun and moon, or the seasons; threading dances, the movement of the constellations. Dancing around an object concentrated its energy or had protective symbolism. Shamans whirled like planets, arms raised to draw cosmic energy downward or lowered to direct it into the earth. Dances with animal costumes, masks and miming similarly drew on the powers ascribed to different creatures. The serpentine dance of the priestess at Delphi thus drew on snake symbolism of wisdom and fertility. Union is symbolized by wedding dances and many forms of linked dancing; grief by funeral dances.

In Africa and elsewhere, shaman healers sought to invoke and reinforce curative energies by dancing. All uninhibited dancing is considered therapeutic, giving the dancer release from the tension of social rules and, particularly in trance dancing, from giving individual consciousness. This transformation symbolized the attainment of a supernatural state in which the dancer was supposedly in direct touch with cosmic energy – a link made clear in the iconography of dancing gods. Shiva, the Hindu Lord of the Dance, often shown surrounded by flames, dances as the embodiment of both creative and destructive energy. Buddha is another lord of the dance of life. In social or recreational dancing, and especially in folk dancing, which has direct links with fertility rites, the symbolism of a return to the vital centre of cosmic energy and harmony has dwindled but not disappeared.

Dandelion
An emblem of Christ's Passion – a symbolism derived from the bitterness of its leaves. It is used in Israel and elsewhere as a herb. It sometimes appears in Netherlandish crucifixion paintings.

Darkness
Like the colour black, an ambivalent symbol standing not only for death, sin, ignorance and evil but also for potential life – the dark of germination. Thus it has negative meanings only when considered within the duality of light and dark, when it becomes linked with regressive choices. In mystic thought, light and dark are equally necessary aspects of life. Darkness precedes light as death precedes resurrection. The maternal symbolism of darkness explains icons such as the Black Virgin. More obviously, darkness symbolizes mystery (a "dark horse"), concealment (keeping someone "in the dark") and the unknown (a "leap in the dark").

Date
As an important food source in northern Africa and western Asia, the date palm was linked with fertility, especially male, and also with divine bounty. Hence the date was a biblical symbol of the just, who alone would receive riches in heaven. Columnar date-palm forms in Egyptian architecture refer to the Tree of Life.

Dawn
Hope and youth – extensions of the self-evident symbolic associations surrounding dawn, illumination and new beginnings. In Buddhism the particular clarity of dawn light symbolizes ultimate enlightenmnent. The Greek goddess of the dawn Eos (in Roman myth, Aurora), is usually shown in art as a winged goddess driving a chariot, sometimes scattering flowers. Although dawn is universally linked with joy, Eos may also appear mourning her son Memnon, slain by the hero Achilles, her tears falling as dew.

DEATH *see panel on p.62*

Decapitation
Among headhunters, enemy heads were taken and preserved for the power they were thought to contain – a widespread symbolism linked with the ancient belief that the head was the seat of the soul. In Africa, particularly, the possession of soul material had fertility symbolism. Respect for the head as the essence of a dead person explains Paleolithic rituals in which it was buried separately from the body. It may also explain why in some traditions decapitation was regarded as an honourable means of execution – for example, in the Greco-Roman world, as well as in England,

Dandelion: *see*
CROSS; PASSION

Darkness: *see*
Black; DEATH; Earth; Light; Mother; Night; Shadow; Virginity; Yin-yang

Date: *see*
Palm; Tree

Dawn: *see*
CARDINAL POINTS; Deer; Dew; Light; Obelisk; Orientation; Sun

Decapitation: *see*
Head

DEATH: *see*
AFTERWORLDS; Arrow;
Asphodel; Black; Bow;
Cloak; Cypress; Dance;
Drum; Horse; Hourglass;
Poppy; Ship; Sickle, Scythe;
Skeleton; Skull; Snake;
Sword; Trident; Veil; White;
Willow; Wreath

Deer: *see*
Antlers; Arrow; Baptism;
CROSS; Dawn; Fairies;
Horn; Light;
LONGEVITY; Snake; Soul;
Sun; Transformation; Tree;
VIRTUES; Water

DEATH

Personifications of Death as an absolute are deliberately alarming. Religious symbolism modifies the image of finality, suggesting that death is a necessary stage which results in the liberation to immortality. The symbolism of fear and hope sometimes appears side by side in uneasy combination. In art, the most familiar figure of Death is the skeletal rider, cloaked and cowled, pitilessly wielding a scythe, trident, sword or bow and arrows. He holds an hour glass signifying the measured span of life. Underworld gods who ruled the dead used such grim auxiliaries to despatch souls to them but were not themselves necessarily frightening symbols. The Druids taught that the god of death

A death skeleton: a Native American shamanic statuette.

(Donn in Ireland) was the source of all life. Other symbols of Death include the skeleton, the skull, the tomb, or a black-cloaked figure with a sword, such as the Greek god Thanatos (black is associated with death in Occidental tradition, white in Oriental). Death could also appear as a drummer or dancer. Gentler symbols were a veiled woman or an Angel of Death such as the Islamic Israfil. Death ships or barges symbolized the journey to the afterworld. Death flowers include the poppy and asphodel. The cypress and weeping willow are among associated trees. Many other death symbols have strong links with notions of the afterlife, including the wreath – a sign of reward in heaven.

A white hart, from a panel in the Wilton Diptych (c.1395).

where it tended to be reserved for people of rank.

Deer

A universally benevolent symbol, associated with the East, dawn, light, purity, regeneration, creativity and spirituality. The stag or hart is a solar emblem of fertility, its branching antlers suggesting in Native American and other traditions the Tree of Life, the sun's rays and, through their shedding and regrowth, longevity and re-birth. The stag is linked with virility

and ardour, and in China with wealth and happiness – its name is a homonym of the word for "abundance".

Swiftness is a more obvious attribute, also grace and beauty – hence, perhaps, the deer's link with poetry and music. Other symbolism drawn from the observation of its habits includes solitude in both European and Japanese traditions (because the red deer stag often keeps to itself). The Celtic belief that deer were the herds of fairies or divinities, some of whom are shown with antlers, may have led to the tradition that reindeer pull the sleigh of Santa Claus. Stags were the steeds of Hittite, Sumerian-Semitic and Shinto divinities, and appear more widely as supernatural messengers or guides who show heroes the path to their goals. Curative powers were also ascribed to deer, especially the ability to discover medicinal herbs. In art, a deer pierced by an arrow and carrying herbs in its mouth was an image of lovesickness. Prudence and Hearing are also personified by the deer.

The deer's link with piety is drawn from water and serpent symbolism. Deer are shown trampling snakes underfoot – destroying evil – in Christian iconography, and the Bible makes an influential analogy between the hart panting for water and the soul yearning for God. With this meaning, deer are shown on baptismal fonts or are painted drinking at the foot of the cross. The doe appears less often, except as an attribute of lunar hunting goddesses, notably the Greek Artemis (in Roman myth, Diana). It can symbolize the female principle in rites of passage, and was a popular ancestral figure in central Asia – hence the legend that Genghis Khan's forebears were a wolf and a doe. Both does and stags appear as symbols of transformation in mythology. Alchemists took this meaning from the story of Artemis who turned the hunter Actaeon into a stag to be torn to pieces by his own dogs after he had caught sight of her bathing.

Desert

Commonly an image of sterility, the desert has deeper symbolism in both Islamic and Christian thought as a place of revelation, a furnace that gave birth to both great monotheistic religions. It was the wilderness in which Christ was tested by Satan and from which false as well as true prophets could come – as in Yeats' ominous poem *The Second Coming* (1916). The hermit (from the Greek *eremias*, "a solitary devotee") exemplifies the man who seeks the desert solitude and emptiness in which he confronts ultimate reality: God.

Devils

Adversaries of goodness personifying darkness, temptation, deceit and evil, especially within the moral context of the great monotheistic religions. Evil and misfortune were usually symbolized in the ancient world either by monsters and goblins or by the dual nature of divinities who had cruel, capricious, or destructive and demonic aspects. The Iranian prophet Zoroaster at the end of the 7th century BCE proposed a new explanation of the flaws in creation – the existence of Ahriman, a dark creator spirit who had chosen evil and then become involved inextricably in the material world of light. This concept influenced the gradual biblical development of Satan (the angel sent by God to try the patience of Job) into a fallen angel whose pride led him to choose evil and become God's adversary. Iblis is his Islamic counterpart. Other influential concepts of the devil include the Manichean notion that Adam was created by Satan with portions of light stolen from God, and the Gnostic view (more influenced by Eastern thought) that a satanic demiurge created the material world from which humanity tries to return to the godhead of which they were originally a part. Alternative names for the

Desert: *see* Oven, Furnace; Sand

Devils: *see* AFTERWORLDS; Bat; Bridge; Chess; Darkness; Dragon; Fire, Flame; Fly, Fly Whisk; Goat; Horn; JEWELS; Light; SEVEN DEADLY SINS; Snake; Tarot; Trident; Volcano; Witchcraft

The Devil, after a detail from an engraving of The Temptation of Christ *(1492).*

Dew: *see*
Dawn; Pearl; Sky; Tree;
Water

Diamond: *see*
FIDELITY; JEWELS;
Sceptre; Throne

Disk: *see*
Chakra; Circle; Crescent;
Dragon; Hole; Horn; Rays;
Snake; Sun; Swastika; Void;
Wheel; Wings

Devil are Lucifer (Satan before the Fall), Beelzebub (a name based on that of a Philistine god whom the Hebrews contemptuously called "Lord of the Flies") and Mephistopheles (the figure who in literature made a devilish pact with the German sorcerer Dr Faust). The most popular image of the Devil, taken from the pagan god Pan, shows him with horns, cloven hoofs, forked tail and sometimes bat-wings. Smaller devils follow him, armed with pitchforks or spears. A medieval Christian obsession with the sin of lust accounts for the addition of a second face on the Devil's genitals or buttocks.

As spirits of evil, devils are linked with the symbolism of the dragon (in Western tradition) and serpent (in Judeo-Christian tradition). They can stand for division, disintegration and the temptations of immorality.

Dew

Purity, spiritual illumination, rejuvenation – the nectar of the immortals. Dew is a Buddhist emblem of evanescence – a symbolism used also in Western paintings. More generally, links with the dawn and with the sky symbolism made dew the purest of waters, a metaphor for the divine word in Hinduism and for the Holy Spirit in Christianity. The Chinese "Tree of Sweet Dew" at the centre of the world symbolized immortality. In the classical world, dew was linked with goddesses of fecundity.

Diadem *see* Crown

Diamond

Solar radiance, immutability, and integrity. The diamond's combination of brilliance and hardness gave it a spiritual dimension, particularly in India, where the diamond throne of Buddha is an image of the unchanging Buddhist centre, and the diamond sceptre a Tantric symbol of divine power. In Western tradition, the diamond symbolizes incorruptibility and hence moral virtues such as sincerity and constancy – the significance of its use in engagement rings. Superstitiously, it was credited with curative and protective properties: Satan shunned its light.

Disk

A solar emblem of divinity and power. The winged disk appears in iconography throughout the Middle East as the symbol of sun gods such as Ra in Egypt, Asshur in Assyria and Ahura Mazda, the great deity of Zoroastrianism who was also called Armuzd, the creator god of light. Combining sun and eagle symbolism, the winged disk stands for the rising sun, itself an emblem of resurrection, and for cosmic energy. In Egypt, the disk with horns or a crescent is a symbol of solar and lunar unity. A rayed disk in India is the weapon of Vishnu Surya, signifying his absolute power to destroy as well as to create. As solid

A solar disk encased in wings, from a Mesopotamian bas relief dating from the 9th century BCE.

wheels (the earliest kind), disks can also represent the turning wheel of existence and the energy points of the *chakra*s. In China, a disk with a central hole is a celestial image of spiritual perfection – the cosmic circle with the unknowable essence or void at its centre. Serpents or dragons encircling a disk represent the reconciliation of opposing forces.

Dismemberment

Creation through the act of destruction. Dismemberment was a savage form of sacrifice in which humans or animals were torn apart to symbolize the process of disintegration that leads to regeneration – paralleling the hacking down and harvesting of crops. Osiris in Egypt and Dionysus in Greece are vegetation gods whose death and dismemberment symbolize this process in mythology. Dismemberment was also imitated in some shaman initiation rituals as a stage in spiritual rebirth.

Dog

Loyalty and protective vigilance – a symbolism inherited mainly from Celtic and Christian traditions. In more primitive and ancient thought, the dog was associated almost universally with the underworld in which it acted as both guide and guardian. Hence the Greek image of Cerberus, the dismaying three-headed dog at the entrance to Hades. Hell-hounds also accompanied Hecate, the death goddess who haunted tombs and crossroads and to whom dogs were sacrificed. Other aggressive dog symbols include the Scandinavian infernal dog Garm and the black dog of Satan. Usually, the symbolism linking dogs with death is more positive.

Their companionship in life and their supposed knowledge of the spirit world suggested them as suitable guides to the afterlife. They appear in this role as attributes of the Egyptian Anubis as well as in Central America where they carried souls across the river of death in Mayan myths. Xoltl, the Aztec dog god, led the sun through the nocturnal underworld and was reborn with it at dawn. Dogs were often sacrificed as companions for the dead or as intercessors with the gods, as in Iroquois sacrifices of white dogs. Souls were passed to dogs more directly in the ancient Central Asian and Persian practice of feeding dead bodies to them. Such customs may have led to the Semitic and Islamic view that dogs were unclean, vile and greedy – useful only as guards – with the exception of the greyhound, which was given higher status.

Dogs are often symbols of contempt as well as loyalty, as is evident even in modern idiom. This ambivalence is reflected in the origin of the word "cynic", from the Greek word for dog, *kuon*, abusively applied to the followers of Diogenes to illustrate their aggressive rudeness, but accepted by them as an apt description of their role as moral watchdogs. The name "Dominicans" for an order of friars – literally "dogs of the Lord" – similarly stressed the symbolism of guardianship. In Christianity the dog also fits the symbolism of the Good Shepherd, and was an emblem of the clergy. Dogs are benign symbols in Celtic iconography, the companions of many goddesses associated with healing, and of hunters and warriors. They are guardian symbols in Japan, and also in China, although less consistently because they often have

Dismemberment: *see* Initiation; Sacrifice

Dog: *see* AFTERWORLDS; BEASTS OF FABLE; Crossroads; DEATH; Eclipse; Eye; FIDELITY; Fire, Flame; River; Sacrifice; Shepherd; Soul; Sun; White

Dolphin: *see*
Anchor; Cross; Soul;
Transformation; Trident

Dome: *see*
Axis; Sky

Doubles: *see*
Soul; Twins

demonic significance, especially in the cosmic symbolism of eclipses and other destructive phenomena. They can appear as solar and wind symbols. The obedient dog is a symbol of adherence to the law, yet the Buddha said that those who lived like dogs would become them. In Hinduism, dogs again appear as attributes of a death god, Yama.

Elsewhere, the dog often appears with divinatory symbolism, especially in Africa. In Melanesian, North American and Siberian legends its intelligence made it a symbol of resourceful invention, the originator or stealer of fire. Like all such culture heroes, the dog is blamed as well as praised: in many versions of the legend, it was through a dog's failure in guardianship that humans lost the gift of immortality.

Dolphin
Salvation, transformation, speed, sea power, love – an emblem of Christ as saviour. Dolphin symbolism is drawn directly from the nature of this friendly, playful and intelligent marine mammal. Greek, Cretan and Etruscan mythology, in which the dolphin carries gods, saves heroes from drowning, or carries souls to the Islands of the Blessed, influenced its Christian symbolism. It was an attribute of the Greek deities

Hermes (Mercury in Roman myth) rides harnessed dolphins, from a mosaic floor (2nd–1st century BCE).

Poseidon (in Roman myth, Neptune), Aphrodite (Venus), Eros (Cupid) and Demeter (Ceres). Dionysus (Bacchus) was said to have turned drunken and impious sailors into dolphins, and to have turned himself into a dolphin to carry Cretan dolphin-worshippers to his shrine at Delphi.

As an emblem of the sacrificial Christ, the dolphin can appear pierced by a trident or with the secret cross symbol of an anchor. Entwining an anchor, the dolphin is a symbol of prudence (speed restrained). Heirs to the French throne were called *dauphins* (dolphins) but without dolphin symbolism – it was a personal name which became titular for the rulers of the Dauphiné province, and passed to the French crown in the 14th century.

Dome
In temple architecture, a celestial symbol of the sky curving above the world, the spirit of divine light. The crown-like Buddhist stupa extends the centre of the dome by means of a spire as an axial symbol of spiritual force.

Donkey *see* **Ass**

Dorje *see* **Sceptre**

Doubles
Animals are often duplicated in iconography to heighten their emblematic power, but doubles can also symbolize different, even opposing, characteristics. Human doubles were bad omens, signifying death – a superstition linked to the idea of body and soul as separate entities. The ghostly German *doppelgänger* is an extreme symbol of the alter ego.

Dove

Peace, purity, love, tenderness, hope – the Christian emblem of the Holy Spirit. The dove's universal importance as a peace symbol owes less to its nature (often quarrelsome) than to its iconic beauty and the influence of biblical references. The small, white bird that returned to Noah with an olive leaf plucked from the flood-waters had irresistible charm as the image of a wrathful God making peace with humanity. Here, and else-where in myth, the dove acted as a messenger. General bird symbolism, together with its white purity, also made it a pre-Christian embodiment of the divine spirit in western Asian traditions. John the Baptist saw "the Spirit of God descending like a dove" upon Christ after his baptism in John (1:32) and Matthew (3:16). The dove is therefore a symbol of baptism, and appears as the Holy Ghost, especially in scenes of the Annunciation. By extension it represented the purified soul, and is often shown flying from the mouths of martyred saints. Doves could sometimes represent souls in the classical world and in India.

The dove also appears as a Christian emblem of chastity, despite more ancient and understandable links with concupiscence. It was the attribute of the Semitic love goddess Ashtart (Astarte), assimilated into the classical world as Aphrodite (in Roman myth, Venus), and also of Adonis, Dionysus (Bacchus) and Eros (Cupid). The moan of the dove was linked with both sex and childbirth. Winged phalluses shown with doves were found in Pompeii. A pair of doves have long symbolized sexual bliss, which may be why the dove came to personify the attentive and gentle

Noah releasing the dove from the ark, from a Byzantine mosaic in St Mark's Basilica, Venice.

wife. In China the dove is one of the many symbols for longevity, as in Japan where a dove with a sword is an emblem of peace. The terminology of foreign policy involving "doves" and "hawks" is recent but relies on very ancient analogies.

Dragon

The reptilian embodiment of primor-dial power, a creature so Mesozoic that the human imagination seems to have stretched back 70 million years to give it form. Because dragons are generally beneficent symbols in the Far East, malevolent in the West, their symbolism is not as straightforward as it might appear. In myth and leg-end, the dragon and serpent were often synonymous – in China, for example, and also in Greece where large snakes were called *drakonates*, a word suggesting sharp-sightedness (from *derkomai*, "to perceive keenly"). The association between the dragon and vigilance (which it can personify in art) is evidenced by many tales in which dragons appear as guardians linked with the underworld and with oracular knowledge. In Greek myth dragons guarded the golden apples of the Hesperides and the Golden

Dove: *see*
Baptism; Birds; CHASTITY; Flood; LONGEVITY; Mouth; Olive; PEACE; Phallus;

Dragon: *see*
Air; Apple; Banner; Bat; BEASTS OF FABLE; Devils; Eagle; Earth; Fire, Flame; Golden Fleece; Horn; Knot; Pearl; Rain; Rainbow; Red; Snake; Teeth; Thunder; Turquoise; VIGILANCE; Water; WISDOM

Dragonfly

Dragonfly: *see*
Butterfly

Drum: *see*
DEATH; Thunder; Word

Fleece. The Theban hero Cadmus could reach the spring of Ares, god of war, only by killing Ares' dragon-son. The Norse hero Sigurd and the Anglo-Saxon Beowulf also slew treasure-guarding dragons. These stories have led to historicizing suggestions that in pagan legends the dragon is an unflattering image of a powerful ruler whose possessions have been seized by force. That Cadmus sowed the dragon's teeth of dissension after his victory offers some support for this theory. What is more certain is that Christianity was the primary influence behind the evolution of the dragon into a generalized symbol of adversarial evil. The Book of Revelation (12:9) identifies the dragon directly with "that old serpent, called the Devil" and goes on to link it with the sin of blasphemy. The dragons that were vanquished by many Christian saints, notably St Michael, symbolize disorder and disbelief as well as moral evils and primal bestiality. The dragon of medieval imagination combines air, fire, water and earth symbolism – a fire-breathing, horned creature with strong eagle legs, bat wings, a scaly body and a serpentine, barbed tail (sometimes shown knotted to indicate its defeat). Alternatively, it appears as a sea serpent, as in some paintings of St George, a tradition dating back to Sumerian-Semitic iconography of the chaos-goddess Tiamat. The Greek hero Perseus also battled with an aquatic monster to save the princess Andromeda. Purely as an image of terror, the dragon was a popular emblem of warriors, appearing on Parthian and Roman standards, in the carved prows of Viking ships, in the Celtic world as a symbol of sovereign force, and on banners in Anglo-Saxon England, and in Wales, where the red dragon is still a national emblem.

In Asia, and particularly in China, the dragon is a symbol of supernatural power untrammelled by moral disapproval. Undulating across robes, it symbolizes the generative rhythms of the natural elements, particularly the rain-bearing power of thunder, often shown as a pearl held in the dragon's mouth or throat. Hence the rain symbolism of the paper dragons carried in processions amid fireworks in spring festivals on the second day of the second Chinese month. The five-clawed turquoise dragon *Lung* was the motif of the Han dynasty and symbolized the active yang principle, the East, the rising sun, fertility, happiness and the gifts of spiritual knowledge and immortality. The dragon is also the three-clawed symbol of the mikado in Japan, and a leading rain symbol there and elsewhere in southeast Asia, the master of the sea and of rivers but also a celestial wingless serpent linked with the rainbow. The dragon-king is prominent in Japanese folklore.

Dragonfly
Lightness, and lightmindedness, elegance, speed. It sometimes shares the symbolism of the butterfly. The Japanese imperial ancestor-hero Jimmu-Tenno is said to have given Honshu the name Dragonfly Island.

Drum
Thunder, the voice of cosmic energy. Of all musical instruments, the drum is the most primeval means of communication, its percussive sound travelling to the heart and, by extension, suggesting the ability to communicate with supernatural forces. It symbolized the creative–destructive power of

Shiva, Kali and Indra, the Buddhist voice of the Law, the Chinese voice of heaven. Its materials – wood and hide – themselves had protective symbolism, and its rhythms were widely used to achieve states of ecstasy in which spirits were invoked or shamans could move beyond the material plane. The ancient use of the drum to inspire warriors draws on the thunder symbolism of destructive force.

Duck

Marital union, happiness and fidelity – a symbolism centred upon the mandarin duck of Asia and suggested by the synchronized swimming of the male and female birds. Sad tales of parted mandarin ducks are popular in both Japanese and Chinese folklore, and duck motifs are used as emblems of union in the decoration of bridal chambers. Young lovers are "mandarin ducks in the dew".

The duck can also appear as a mediator between sky and water – for example, in Native America – but the swan and goose are more commonly used in this symbolism.

Dwarf

A symbol of guardianship, both in mythology (the protective Bes of Egypt) and in folklore where dwarfs are almost universally credited with supernatural powers.

In Hindu and other iconography, dwarfs are sometimes demonic, suggesting a link of ideas between stunted growth and human ignorance or blind instinct. They can also be associated with the symbolism of the fool as an inversion of the king, a role sometimes played by dwarfs at court.

In folklore, they are often mischievous, miserly or malignant. They are jealous hoarders of treasures or secret knowledge, and are lovers of riddles and enigmas. According to Nordic legend, the gods ruled that dwarfs should live underground because they were born not from the vegetable world like other men but from the corpse of the giant Ymir, whose body formed the earth.

They are widely linked with subterranean life (and by extension the unconscious mind) or, in South America, with rain, forests and caves. As a result, they were thought to be skilled workers with precious stones and metals, by nature suspicious and cunning, but easily tricked. Garden gnomes refer to a kindlier aspect and to magical knowledge of the things of the earth.

Duck: *see*
Birds; FIDELITY;.Goose; Swan

Dwarf: *see*
Cave; Clown; Earth; Giant; King; JEWELS; METALS; Rain; Scapegoat

Eagle: *see*
Air; Alchemy; Baptism;
BEASTS OF FABLE; Birds;
Dragon; Feathers; Fire,
Flame; Jaguar; Light; Lion;
SEVEN DEADLY SINS;
Sky; Snake; Soul; Storm;
Sun; Thunder; VICTORY;
Wings

Eagle

The supreme all-seeing emblem of sky and sun gods, rulers and warriors – a symbol of majesty, domination, victory, valour, inspiration and spiritual aspiration. As master of the air, the eagle is one of the most unambiguous and universal of all symbols, embodying as it does the power, speed and perception of the animal world at its zenith. It is not only an attribute of the greatest gods but frequently a direct personification of them. Thus, in the Greek myth of the beautiful youth Ganymede abducted by an eagle to be the cup-bearer of the gods, Zeus, in different versions, sends the eagle as his messenger or becomes himself the eagle. The wrath of Zeus is similarly personified by the eagle that tears at the liver of Prometheus. Soaring toward the sun with open eyes, the eagle seemed a creature capable of carrying souls to heaven – the origin of the Roman custom of releasing an eagle from the pyre of emperors. The Hebrew idea that the eagle could burn its wings in the solar fire and plummet into the ocean to emerge with a new pair (Psalm 103:5) became a motif of Christian baptismal symbolism. The eagle appears not only on fonts, but on church lecterns – as the attribute of St John the Evangelist, bearer of the Christian message. In medieval iconography the eagle is associated with Christ's ascension, the wings of prayer, the descent of grace and the conquest of evil (an eagle holding a snake in its mouth).

In other traditions throughout Egypt, western Asia, India and the Far East, the link between the eagle and sky gods is ancient and consis-

An eagle fighting a snake – the symbol of evil overcome, from a medieval mosaic, Istanbul.

tent. An eagle with human arms was a Syrian emblem of sun worship. The eagle is often a storm and thunder symbol as well as a solar one, suggesting both light and fertilizing power. Garuda, the eagle–human steed of the Vedic god Vishnu, is shown battling with the serpents of evil. Alternatively, eagle and snake represent air and earth, although the lion sometimes replaces the snake, as in alchemy, which used a crowned eagle and lion to represent the dualism of volatile and fixed principles. In Native American mythology the eagle has celestial and solar symbolism. The duality of sky and earth is represented in Central America by the eagle and jaguar. Among nomads, particularly in northern Asia, the eagle was a shamanic father symbol, its feathers used in initiation and ascension rites.

The eagle is one of the most ancient and popular emblems of victory, its flight taken as an augury of military success in ancient Persia and also in Rome where, from the time of Rome's founders Romulus and Remus, it was carried on standards as "the bird of Jove". The Hittites used a double-headed eagle device, apparently still in use among the Seljuk Turks at the time of the Crusades and taken back to Europe to become the emblem of the Holy Roman Empire and later of the Austrian and Russian empires. Heraldic use of the eagle was widespread in Poland, Germany and Napoleonic France. The white-headed American eagle with outstretched wings is the emblem of the US. In art, the eagle can be an attribute of Pride.

Ear

A symbolic connection between hearing and insemination appears both in some African traditions where the ear has sexual connotations, and more curiously in the early Christian notion that Christ was conceived by the Holy Ghost's entering the Virgin Mary's ear; hence the dove at Mary's ear in some Annunciation scenes. Long ear lobes signified wisdom or status in China and India, and also in the Inca kingdom of Peru.

Earth

Maternal and protective – universally a symbol of fecundity and sustenance. On the whole, earth is personfied in mythology by mother goddesses such as the classical Ge or Gaia, the womb of life – the Egyptian earth-god Geb is an exception. In many creation myths, the first humans are formed from mud, clay or, in Polynesia, sand. The sky couples with the earth – sometimes in an embrace so close that it must be broken by a hero-god to allow life to develop – an idea common to Polynesian and Egyptian myth. Earth fertility symbolism accounts for the use of earth (and sometimes "burials") in rites of passage. Couplings in furrows were a popular feature of rural life at spring fertility festivities until fairly recently.

The earth is often represented graphically by the square, as in China. Although associated with darkness, passivity and the fixed principle, its symbolism as a source of life tended to separate it in ancient thought from the underworld of death. The Aztec goddess of the earth and of childbirth, Cihuacoatl, was perceived to feed on the dead to nourish the living, but more usually the symbolism is gentle. Hence, perhaps, the widespread ancient belief that destructive earthquakes emanated not from the

Ear: *see*
Dove; Virginity

Earth: *see*
Brown; Darkness; Elephant; Mother; Snake; Sphere; Square; Tortoise, Turtle; Woman; Worm

A jesting image of Mother Earth and her global bounty. From an engraving entitled Jocus Servens.

Eclipse: *see*
Jaguar; Light; Moon; Snake;
Star; Sun; Toad

Eel: *see*
FISH; Phallus; Snake;
Trickster

Egg: *see*
Alchemy; Birds; Dragon;
Gold; Goose; Hero,
Heroine; Lotus; Ostrich;
Phoenix; Silver; Snake;
Stupa; Sun; Virginity; White

earth but from the movements of creatures thought to support it – a giant fish (Japan), an elephant standing on a tortoise (India and southeast Asia) or a serpent (North America).

East *see* CARDINAL POINTS

Eclipse

Almost universally an ill omen – symbolically the death of light, suggesting a cosmic illness or disorder. In China, solar eclipses were interpreted as the unwelcome dominance of the feminine principle yin over the masculine yang or, at the level of the imperial household, the empress over the emperor. Other interpretations were that the sun was hiding its face in anger or that the sun, moon or stars had fallen victim to a devouring cosmic toad (China), snake or jaguar (Central America). In Peru an eclipse was said to have augured the Spanish destruction of the Inca empire.

Eel

Now a metaphor for slipperiness, the eel in Oceanic folklore sometimes appears as a trickster and more prominently as a fertility symbol, replacing this aspect of snake symbolism in countries such as New Zealand where snakes were unknown. According to a Tongan myth, an eel seduced the virgin Hine in a pool and when cut up by angry villagers produced the first coconut tree. A similar story with equally phallic symbolism appears in the Polynesian Maui cycle, a link being made between the phallic eel and the semen-like oil of the coconut.

Egg

Genesis, the perfect microcosm – a universal symbol for the mystery of original creation, life bursting from the primordial silence. Few simple natural objects have such self-explanatory yet profound meaning, and the body of myth and folklore that surrounds the egg is huge. In many creation myths, ranging from Egypt and India to Asia and Oceania, a cosmic egg (sometimes fertilized by a serpent but more often laid in the primeval waters by a giant bird) gives form to chaos, and from it hatches the sun (the golden yolk), the division of earth and sky, and life in all its forms, natural and supernatural. Creation myth carried over easily into the symbolism of re-creation: the phoenix, dying in fire, rose from its own egg; the god Dionysus was shown carrying an egg as a symbol of his eventual re-incarnation; and for both Orphics and Druids the egg was a holy, forbidden food. Also associated with the promise and hope of spring, the egg took a ready-made place in Christian Easter ceremonies as a symbol of resurrection. The egg's white purity, the miracle of life contained within its blank shell, added other connotations, as in Piero della Francesca's altarpiece *Madonna and Child* (*c.*1450) in which an egg symbolizes the Immaculate Conception (a reference also to the folklore notion that ostrich eggs hatch themselves). Eucharistic implications are suggested by the tradition of eating eggs at the end of Lent. In Jewish custom, at the Seder meal, the egg is a symbol of promise, and traditionally eggs are the first food offered to Jewish mourners.

Creation symbolism is strengthened by the egg shape of testicles and by the sexual duality of the egg's yolk and white – the yolk in the Congo standing for female warmth, the white for male sperm. In Hindu myth, the Cosmic Tree grows from the golden egg which bore Brahma. In Nepal, the cupolas of Buddhist stupas represent the cosmic egg. Alchemists took over the idea of the cosmic egg in the shape of their retorts, symbolizing transmutation. In folklore throughout the world, the egg is a propitious symbol, suggesting luck, wealth and health. Magical eggs of gold or silver are guarded by dragons. From eggs are born gods and heroes. In one story, Helen of Troy came from an egg that had fallen from the moon. Alternatively she was born from an egg laid by Leda, queen of Sparta, after she had coupled with a swan (the god Zeus in disguise). Later that night Leda also slept with her mortal husband. She laid two eggs; from one came Polydeuces and Helen and from the other Castor and Clytemnestra.

Eight
Spatially an emblem of cosmic equilibrium, and cyclically the symbol of renewal, rebirth or beatitude. The octagon was perceived as a form mediating between the square and the circle, combining stability with totality. Adding to its symbolism of totality, the number eight represented the four cardinal points together with their four intermediate points. Celtic, Hindu and other iconographic wheels were usually eight-armed – as is Vishnu in Hindu art. Octagonal baptismal fonts also incorporate the symbolism of renewal or new beginnings derived from the fact that eight follows the symbolic "complete" number, seven, and begins a new cycle. Eight was a lucky number in China, where there were eight Taoist Immortals, and also in Japanese

Shintoism. The lotus is often shown with eight petals – the number of *chakra*s and of Buddhist symbols of good augury. Eight angels support the throne of Allah.

The shape of the actual arabic numeral "8" was equated with the caduceus, and eight is the number of the Greek god Hermes (in Egyptian myth, Thoth) in Hermetic magic. The Star of Bethlehem is often shown with eight points. The octagram formed by drawing bisecting lines between each point and its opposite point, within an eight-pointed star, was an ancient symbol of the Roman goddess Venus, a Nordic protective symbol and a Gnostic sign for creation.

Elder
Thought to be a magic tree in Northern Europe, especially in Denmark where it was unlucky to use its wood for furniture. It offered protection against witchcraft on Walpurgis Night, and the credulous apologized even when picking its flowers or berries. In some accounts, Judas Iscariot hanged himself on an elder.

ELEMENTS *see panel on p.74*

Elephant
Strength, sagacity, longevity, prosperity, happiness – a symbol of sovereign power in India, China and Africa. The elephant was the stately mount not only of Indian rulers but of the thunder and rain god, Indra. The elephant-headed Ganesha was the god of wisdom and the art of writing. By association, the elephant came to symbolize not only the qualities required for good government – dignity, intelligence, prudence – but also a whole range of general benefits

Eight: *see*
Angels; Baptism; Chakras; Circle; Four; Lotus; Octagon; Square; Star; Wheel

Elder: *see*
Tree; Witchcraft

Elephant: *see*
Banyan; Chess; Earth; FAME; FIDELITY; LONGEVITY; Rain; VICTORY; VIRTUES; White; WISDOM

The Indian elephant-headed god Ganesha. From a wall-painting in Jaipur.

ELEMENTS: *see*
Air; Chameleon; Crown;
Earth; Fire; Five; Four;
METALS; Phoenix;
Quintessence; Thunder;
Water; Wood; Yin-yang

ELEMENTS

A complex system of symbolic correspondences was once attached to four – or sometimes five – substances thought to be primary constituents of the universe. In Western tradition, largely influenced by Greek philosophy, these were the elements of water, air, fire and earth, to which a fifth was sometimes added – ether, or the quintessential spirit. Fire was the agent of transformation from one state to another. Because the elements were viewed as the basis of cosmic order and harmony, early medicine sought to balance the physical and temperamental characteristics assigned to each – phlegm, the brain and the phlegmatic temperament (water); blood, the heart and the sanguine temperament (air); yellow bile, the liver and the choleric temperament (fire); black bile, the spleen and the melancholic temperament (earth). Air and fire were seen as active and masculine, water and earth as passive and feminine. Increasingly arbitrary correspondences, including colours, seasons and stages of life, were added in an attempt to create a coherent symbolic system, which began to collapse only with the arrival of scientific method. In China, a corresponding system was based on the five Taoist elements of water, fire, wood, metal and earth, balanced by the duality of the active, masculine principles of yang (air and fire) and yin (water, metal and earth). The fivefold Indian symbolic system proposed as "cosmic states of vibration" the elements of *akasha* (ether), *apas* (water), *vayu* (air), *tejas* (fire) and *prithivi* (earth). In Western art, water is personified by an overturned pitcher or by sea and river gods; air by Juno, sometimes seen flying despite attached anvils, or by a woman with a chameleon; fire by the phoenix, Vulcan, or a woman with a burning head and thunderbolt; earth by a woman with fertility symbols, or the turreted crown of Cybele.

Graphic symbols of the four elements (from top to bottom): earth, water, air and fire.

including peace, bountiful harvests and rainfall. Fertility and rainfall symbolism were particularly attached to the white elephant in Burma, Thailand and Cambodia. Although an unpopular circus attraction for P. T. Barnum (leading to the analogy between a white elephant and a costly burden), the white elephant has sacred meaning in Buddhism. The impending birth of the Buddha was announced to his mother, Queen Maya, by the dream that a charming little white elephant had entered her womb. For Buddhists the elephant is a symbol of spiritual knowledge and of the unchanging.

As an emblem of wisdom, the elephant was an attribute of Mercury in Roman myth. Its Roman association with victory (it personifies Fame in art) may account for its occasional use as a symbol of Christ's overcoming death or evil – as in depictions of an elephant trampling a snake. The medieval belief that the bull elephant refrained from sex during the long gestation period of his mate also made it a Western symbol of chastity, fidelity and love. The link with ponderous clumsiness appears to be modern, although there is a delightful Hindu legend that elephants lost their powers of flight by being cursed by a hermit whose home in a banyan tree had been crushed on their landing.

Eleven

Associated by St Augustine with sin, for the rather sophisticated reason that it suggested excess – being one more than the perfect 10 – eleven was a number also linked with danger, conflict or rebellion. It was sometimes known in Europe as the "Devil's dozen". However, African shamans used 11 as a number propitious to fecundity. Being saved at the "eleventh hour" alludes to Christ's parable of the labourers who received a day's wage even though they had been hired in the last hour of the working day.

Elf *see* Fairies

Elk *see* Deer

Emerald

Regeneration and fertility – a symbolism probably based on the vernal green colour of this beryl. It was an important stone in Aztec mythology, associated with the green-plumaged quetzal, harbinger of spring, and thus with the hero-god Quetzalcoatl. There and elsewhere it was associated with the moon, rain, water and the east. It is a Christian symbol of immortality, faith and hope, and the stone of the pope. Alchemists linked it with Hermes, astrologers with the planet Jupiter and the sign Virgo. Its extensive role in folklore as a healing amulet mingles fertility symbolism with a tradition of occult power which could be used for good or evil purposes, deriving from the story that it is an underworld stone, fallen from the crown of Lucifer. Hence it was among the most powerful talismans against illness (including epilepsy and dysentry). It was thought to speed childbirth and also to strengthen eyesight, perhaps because it was a stone used by wizards to see into the future.

Ermine

Purity and chastity – a virtue that it personifies in art. Apart from the white fur, the link with purity was reinforced by the notion that stoats died if their white winter coats (ermine) were sullied. Ermine trimming on the robes or caps of nobles, judges or teachers has the symbolism of moral or intellectual purity.

Excrement

In Africa, particularly Mali, a symbol of fertilizing power, a residue of vital force which could be purified and put to use. Hence the burning and offering of excrement to creator beings such as the Nommo among the Dogon people or the god Faro among the Bambara, and, more rarely, its ritual eating. Red copper was thought to be a form of spiritual dung which could be transformed to gold. Alchemy similarly associated the *nigredo* or state of corruption with the first stage of a process that could produce gold.

Eleven: *see*
NUMBERS; Ten

Emerald: *see*
Alchemy; Devils; Green;
Hope; JEWELS; Moon;
PLANETS; Rain;
VIRTUES; Water; Zodiac

Ermine: *see*
CHASTITY; White

Excrement: *see*
Alchemy; Gold

Eye

Eye: *see*
AFTERWORLDS; Amulet;
BEASTS OF FABLE;
Devils; Dog; Falcon, Hawk;
Fire, Flame; Hand; Heart;
Horseshoe; Jaguar; Moon;
Peacock; SEVEN DEADLY
SINS; Star; Sun; Trinity;
VIGILANCE; Witchcraft

Eye

Visually the most compelling symbol based on the human body, often used to represent the omniscience of sun gods and, in early Christianity, God the Father (a single eye) or the Trinity (an eye within a triangle). The Egyptian *wedjat*, a painted eye with a line spiralling below it (taken from the facial markings of some hawks), is the emblem of the falcon sky god, Horus, and is a symbol not only of his all-seeing power but of cosmic wholeness. In Western symbolism, the right eye is active and solar; the left passive and lunar (a system reversed in Eastern tradition). Egyptian myth said that the moon eye of Horus had been restored after its destruction in a battle with Set, a story that accounts for the popularity of the *wedjat* as a protective device on amulets. Eyes were also painted or carved on Egyptian tombs to assist the dead. Winged eyes in Egyptian iconography represent north and south.

The occult third eye, sometimes called the "eye of the heart", symbolizes the eye of spiritual perception, associated with the power of Shiva and the synthesizing element of fire in Hinduism, with inner vision in Buddhism, and with superhuman clairvoyance in Islam. Although depicted on the forehead of Shiva, it is an inner eye. Its antithesis is the "evil eye" which, in Islamic thought, is a symbol of the destructive force of envy. The Gorgon Medusa whose gaze could turn men to stone was an

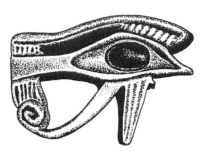

The wedjat, *or eye of Horus, the Egyptian sky god, from an ancient amulet. Many such "eyes" have been excavated from Egyptian tombs.*

earlier Greek symbol of the evil eye. Perseus used a mirror to aim the blow that killed her, and eye talismans (still hung above doorways in Turkey) serve a similar deflecting function. In medieval Europe, the horseshoe was thought to be particularly effective against the evil eye of witchcraft or Satan himself, sometimes depicted with a displaced eye on his body. Multiple eyes could also have positive symbolism, representing vigilance and the light of stars in the night sky. The peacock attribute of Amitabha, the Tibetan meditative Buddha of Infinite Light, has this symbolism (through its multi-eyed plumage). The eyes of some other animals had clairvoyant meaning. Hence the Parsee custom of bringing a dog to a deathbed so that the dying could see the afterworld in its eyes, and the belief of the Aztec shamans that they could read the mysteries of the spirit world in the eyes of the jaguar.

Fairies

Personifications of human wishes or frustrations in the form of little people with magical powers. They appear in most folk traditions under various names, usually as nature spirits enjoying their own lives at a supernatural level, sometimes meddling in human affairs. Their importance in symbolism is mainly oral and literary. As their name (derived from the Latin *fata*, "fate") suggests, they appear essentially to explain gently the workings of destiny with its unpredictable gifts or disappointments. Fairy tales are exceptionally rich in symbolism, psychological and social, portraying the challenges presented by the different stages in life.

Falcon, Hawk

Superiority, aspiration, spirit, light and liberty – like the eagle, a solar emblem of victory. As a hawk-like species (but with longer wings and a higher range) the falcon is hard to distinguish from the hawk in iconography, and their symbolism is therefore discussed together. In Peru, the falcon appears with solar significance as a companion or brother soul of the Incas, and also as a human ancestor. It was the king of birds in ancient Egypt, where many gods are shown with the body or head of a falcon, including Ra, who often has a disk in place of the crest, symbolizing the rising sun. Horus, god of the sky and of the day, is specifically a falcon god, his painted hawk-like eye a common emblem on Egyptian amulets signifying the sharpness of his protective vision. The Ba, a symbol of the individual spirit, has a hawk body and a human head. In Western tradition, the falcon is an emblem of the huntsman and is associated with the Germanic sky-gods Wodan and

Fairies: *see*
Wand; Wings

Falcon, Hawk: *see*
Amulet; Birds; Eagle; Eye; Light; Soul; Sun; Trickster; VIRTUES

A falcon, from a 3,000-year-old Egyptian sculpture. It forms a striking image of the rising sun.

FAME: *see*
BEASTS OF FABLE;
Crown; Elephant; Globe,
Orb; Palm; Trumpet; Wings

Fan: *see*
Feathers; Fire, Flame; Fly,
Fly Whisk; Moon; Wind

Fasces: *see*
Axe; Birch; Twelve; Whip,
Flail

Fasces symbolizing the power of the Roman consul Cicero, after a late-15th-century fresco.

Frigg, as well as the Nordic trickster Loki. A hooded falcon represents hope (of light and freedom). Predatory symbolism appears more rarely. As the device of the family of Anne Boleyn (Henry VIII's second wife), a white falcon aptly symbolized her aspirations and her predatory behaviour in the view of those threatened by Henry's religious reforms. The hawk is now a symbol of a warlike attitude.

FAME *see panel, right*

Fan

Large fans signify authority, especially in Asia and Africa, perhaps by association with the symbolism of wind, and with their power to kindle fire, as in the hand of the Hindu fire-god Agni. Ceremonial plumed fans, such as the *flabellum* carried in papal processions, certainly appear to have celestial symbolism. More prosaically, the use of fans to protect rulers or sacramental objects from heat and flies may have contributed to their association with status and dignity. A heart-shaped fan was used by the Taoist Immortal Chuang-li Chuan to restore life. Fan symbolism was highly developed in Japanese ritual as an analogy for the unfolding of life itself – or its closure in the case of condemned men who carried fans to their execution. The folding fan was also associated with the phases of the moon and, by extension, with the changing moods of women. Its use as an instrument of flirtation spread from Spain and Italy throughout the courts of Europe in the 18th century.

Fasces

A punitive emblem of the state's power over the individual – originally

FAME
Personified in art by a female figure with a long trumpet, sometimes winged, Fame may appear crowned or carrying a palm branch, seated on a globe or riding in a chariot drawn by elephants. Other symbols of fame include the winged horse Pegasus and the Roman god Mercury.

of Etruscan origin, it was an axe bundled in birch or elm rods from which the axe head projected, signifying the power of Roman magistrates to scourge or behead. The axe was removed from the fasces in Rome itself to acknowledge the citizen's right of appeal against capital punishment. Fasces were borne by lictors in front of Roman magistrates, the number carried increasing to 12 for consuls and 24 for dictators. The fasces had a secondary meaning of unity, which is why it sometimes appears in art as the conjugal symbol of Cupid. For Mussolini, the fasces provided a suitably coercive symbol for the political aims of Fascism, in which the interests of the individual were subordinated to the direct action of a nationalist élite. In a show of communal idealism, Italian Fascism interpreted the bundled rods as different social classes, the axe as the supreme authority of the state.

Fasting

An ancient and almost worldwide tradition of self-denial which has been used in religion to symbolize penance, purification or worship, and socially to demonstrate protest or grief. Modern protest fasting is often more a political technique than a symbolic gesture, but in the Celtic world a fast was a symbol of personal dedication to righting an injustice or settling a grievance. Of the great religious fasts, the Islamic Ramadan, the Jewish Yom Kippur and the Christian Lent all have penitential meaning. In Hinduism, Jainism and Taoism, the relevance is purification and the creation of a physical state of spiritual visions.

Father

Dominion, solar and sky power, spiritual, moral and civil authority, reason and consciousness, law, the elements of air and fire, warlike spirit, and the thunderbolt – a range of symbolism that reflects the patriarchal nature of most traditional cultures. Most, although not all, supreme gods of myth and religion are personified as fathers.

Faun *see* Satyr

Feathers

Ascension – a symbolism derived both from the weightlessness of feathers and their association with the soaring power and spiritual qualities of birds. By extension, the feathers worn by shamans, priests or rulers symbolized magical communication with the spirit world or celestial authority and protection. The feathered cloak was an attribute not only of sky gods such as the Nordic Freya but of Celtic Druids who sought by sympathetic magic to travel beyond the confines of the earth. A serpent covered by the bright green feathers of the quetzal bird was the emblem of the sky and earth power of the Aztec god Quetzalcoatl. In North America, eagle-feathered headdresses associated chiefs with the Great Spirit and with the power of air,

wind and thunder gods. The Feathered Sun (a disk with feathers pointing outward as well as inward) is a Plains Indian emblem of the cosmos and the centre. Feathers are widely an ascensional emblem of prayer; hence the symbolism of the feathered sticks used to invoke rain in Pueblo Indian solstice rituals. Feathers represent prayer and faith in Christianity, and were sometimes used as emblems of virtues, as in the Medici device of three feathers on a ring – signifying faith, hope and charity. In Egypt, feathers were the attributes of several sky gods but particularly of the goddess of justice, Ma'at, who had a single ostrich feather against which she weighed the hearts of the dead in the underworld – an allegory of the fine judgment needed to separate deserving souls from sinners. The association between white feathers and cowardice derives from cockfighting, in which white tail feathers were a sign that a bird lacked the aggression of a correctly bred gamecock.

Fennel

Perception, sharp eyesight – seemingly derived from Pliny's report that snakes improved their vision by eating this plant. Fennel wreaths were used in rites of the supreme Phrygian and Thracian god Sabazius, whose attribute was the serpent.

FIDELITY *see panel on p.80*

Fig

Abundance, maternal nourishment, procreation – the sacred tree of life in many regions (notably in Egypt, India, southeast Asia and parts of Oceania). Much of the fig's significance comes from its importance as a

Father: *see*
Air; Fire, Flame; Man; Sky; Sun; Thunder

Feather: *see*
Air; Arrow; Birds; Eagle; Fan; Ostrich; Rain; Sky; Snake; Sun; Thunder; White; Wind; VIRTUES

Fennel: *see*
Snake; Thyrsus; Wreath, Garland

Fig: *see*
Bo Tree; Olive; Phallus; Tree

An Aztec feather headdress from the Codex Mendoza.

FIDELITY: *see individual names*

Finger: *see* CROSS; Five; Three; Thumb; Trinity

Fire, Flame: *see* Alchemy; Angels; Baptism; Candle; Chimney; Cremation; ELEMENTS; Fox; Heart; Phoenix; Pillar; Red; Sacrifice; Salamander; Smoke; Solstice; Sun; Sword; Transformation; Triangle; Virginity; Volcano

The biblical Adam holding a fig leaf, after a detail from Adam, Eve and the Serpent *(12th century, Spanish School).*

food source in the ancient world. The shape of the fig leaf (famous in art for covering the male genitals), and the milky juice extracted from larger varieties of fig trees as a form of rubber, added powerful sexual aspects to its symbolism. In Genesis, Adam and Eve were the first to use fig leaves to protect their modesty when they ate the forbidden fruit and "knew that they were naked" (3:7).

The Greeks gave the fig phallic symbolism by making it an attribute of Priapus and of Dionysus. In Roman tradition, the infants Romulus and Remus, Rome's legendary founders, were suckled under the protective shade of a fig, which hence became an augury of national prosperity, a symbolism found in Judaism, too. Because Jesus laid the curse of sterility upon a barren fig tree (Matthew 21:19), a withered fig in Christian art sometimes represents heresy. Fecundity is the fig's more widespread meaning, notably in Egypt where the sycamore variety was the Tree of Life, associated with Nut and Hathor as nourishing sky goddesses; and in Chad where anyone pruning the fig was thought to risk sterility. The fig also has fecundity symbolism in India where it was linked with the procreative power of Vishnu and Shiva, and where the sacred Bo variety was the tree beneath which the Buddha achieved spiritual enlightenment. Hence its significance in Buddhism as an emblem of moral teaching and of immortality. The fig, like the olive, appears in Islamic tradition as the forbidden fruit tree in paradise.

The fig or *fico* sign (a thumb thrust between the first two fingers) was a medieval sign against the evil eye as well as an obscene gesture.

FIDELITY

Personified in art by a woman holding a key and gold seal, sometimes accompanied by a dog – one of the most common symbols of fidelity. Other attributes include the anchor, the colour blue, the chalice, cranes, diamonds, ducks, elephants, emeralds, garnet, girdles, geese, hyacinths, ivy, kingfishers, opal, pine, rosemary and topaz.

Finger

Symbolism is attached to individual fingers by some African tribes, notably in Mali where the Dogon people associated the index finger with life, the middle finger with death (this finger was left exposed for the dead to use when their bodies were enshrouded). For the Bambara, the thumb had executive power while the little finger was used to cast spells.

The positive "thumbs up" gesture originally had phallic symbolism. In Christian benediction, three raised fingers are the sign of the Trinity. Superstitious belief in the apotropaic power of the Cross accounts for the custom of crossing fingers for luck. Symbolism shades into sign language in many finger gestures, famously in the Churchillian "V" for victory.

Fir *see* **Christmas tree; Pine, Pine cone**

Fire, Flame

Divine energy, purification, revelation, transformation, regeneration, spiritual ardour, trial, ambition, inspiration, sexual passion – a masculine and active element symbolizing both creative and destructive power. Graphically, fire was represented by a triangle in alchemy, where it was the unifying element. On a domestic scale (the hearth fire), its image is protective and comforting; as a consuming force of nature it is threatening.

A duality of praise and fear underlies the rituals of fire worship. In ancient or primitive cultures, fire appears to have been revered first as an actual god, later as a symbol of divine power. A seemingly living element, growing by what it fed on, dying and reappearing, it was sometimes interpreted as a terrestrial form of the sun, with which it shares much of its symbolism. Owing to the momentous repercussions of fire-making for human development, it is seen in nearly all myth as a godlike skill. Hence the legends of fire stolen from the sky gods by culture heroes such as Prometheus, or wheedled from an infernal deity, as by the hero Maui in myths of New Zealand (where a volcanic origin of the island was plausible).

In the myth and ritual of fire worship, the most enduring and the least ominous traditions have been those of Iran (from where the Vedic god Agni ultimately originates), and the classics with their beneficial gods such as Hephaestus (in Roman myth, Vulcan). Many fire cults were horrific, as in Aztec Mexico and also in the Canaanite worship of "Moloch" to whom infants were sacrificed. Where fire was not worshipped directly, it was often a powerful symbol of divine revelation, as in the Book of Deuteronomy 12:11 when "the mountain burned with fire" and Jehovah spoke from the midst of it to the Hebrews. Again, in Christianity, fire is an incarnation of the Holy Spirit.

Fire is a manifestation of the Great Spirit in Native North American traditions, where the campfire was an image of happiness and prosperity, and the sun itself was called the Great Fire. In Buddhism, a pillar of fire is one symbol of the Buddha, and fire as illumination can be a metaphor for wisdom. In mystical thought, fire often symbolizes union with the godhead, transcendence of the human condition, the end of all things. Hence the concept of the spiritual fire that burns without consuming – the "sages standing in God's holy fire" of W. B. Yeats's poem *Sailing to Byzantium* (1927).

Fire in Christian art is the ultimate test of purity or faith, a flaming heart as the emblem of several saints including SS Augustine and Antony of Padua. The linked concept of purging evil by fire led to the cruellest atrocities of the Christian Church. Judaism has also used flame as a punitive or defensive symbol – angels with flaming swords guard a lost Eden.

The resurrection symbolism of fire is personified by the phoenix and salamander – and also by the Paschal rituals of both Roman Catholicism and Eastern Orthodox Churches in which candles are extinguished and then lit from "a new fire". New Year bonfires have their origin in forms of sympathetic magic, linking the making of new fires with the returning light and warmth of the sun. However, in Japan, Shinto fires at New Year are intended to forestall the risk of destructive fires in the year ahead. Foxes (also associated with fire) with torches tied to their tails used to be chased through grain fields in Europe with a similar objective. Apotropaic meaning is attached to Chinese firecrackers, thought to frighten demons.

The importance in primitive cul-

The Mayan god of fire, Huehueteotl, carrying a brazier on his head.

Five: *see*
CARDINAL POINTS;
Centre; ELEMENTS;
Hand; Man; NUMBERS;
Pentagram, Pentacle;
PLANETS; Quintessence;
Seven; Star; Three

Flag: *see*
Banner; Crescent; Star

tures of preserving domestic fires underlies the emblematic sacredness of an undying flame – as in the fire tended by the Vestal Virgins in Rome, or the modern Olympic tradition in which the flame carried to each new Games symbolizes the continuity of traditional sporting ideals. Similarly primal, the ancient friction technique of fire-making underlies the sexual symbolism of fire, which has often been used as a metaphor for desire.

FISH *see panel, opposite*

Five

The human number – often represented graphically by a man whose head and outstretched limbs form a five-pointed star, or geometrically by the pentagram, also called pentacle, drawn with lines crossing to the five points. Apart from its emblematic association with the human microcosm (and the hand itself), the number five was an important symbol of totality in Chinese, Japanese, Celtic and other traditions which included the centre as a fifth direction of space. Other associations are with love, health, sensuality, meditation, analysis, criticism, strength, integration, organic growth and the heart. According to Pythagorean mysticism, five, like seven, was a holistic number, marrying three (heaven) with the terrestrial two, and was fundamental both in nature and in art. It was linked generally in the classical world with Aphrodite (in Roman myth, Venus), the goddess of love and marriage. The association with love and sex may be based on the combination of the male number three with the female number two. Or it may derive from a more ancient Mesopotamian tradition in

which the five-pointed star was an emblem of Ishtar whose planet was Venus, the primary morning and evening star. Ishtar was goddess not only of love but also of war, and the five-pointed star remains prominent in modern military insignia.

In Mexico, too, the Aztec god of the morning star, Quetzalcoatl, was associated with the number 5. He rose from the underworld (also linked with five) on the fifth day, traditionally the day the first corn shoots appeared after sowing. Extending the significance of this number, the Aztecs saw their own era as that of the "Fifth Sun". In India, the five-pointed star was an emblem of Shiva, who is sometimes shown with five faces. Five was a Japanese Buddhist emblem of perfection. In China, where five was a symbol of the centre, its significance was still greater. In addition to the five regions of space and five senses, there were said to be five elements, metals, colours, tones and tastes. In Christian iconography five refers to the number of Christ's wounds. It was a beneficial and protective number in Islam, the five fundamentals of religion being faith, prayer, pilgrimage, fasting and charity. Five was a symbol of strength in Judaism, and the number of the quintessence in alchemy. The number 500 also had symbolic weight – as in St Paul's assertion that the risen Christ revealed himself to more than 500 people (1 Corinthians 15:6).

Flag

Originally an emblem of a god or a ruler borne into battle as a sacred symbol of supremacy. The flag therefore carries immense significance in terms of its triumphant advance, humiliating retreat or, worse still,

FISH

A positive symbol, widely linked with fecundity, sexual happiness and the phallus – but more famous as the earliest symbol of Christ. The letters of the Greek word for "fish", *ichthus*, form an acronym for "Jesus Christ, Son of God, Saviour" (*Iesous Christos Theou Huios Soter*). Seals and lamps in the catacombs of Rome bore this emblem as a secret sign. Gospel texts reinforced its symbolism – the miraculous draught of fishes and the analogy made by Christ between fishing and the conversion of the populace (hence the "fisherman's ring" worn by the pope); the feeding of the 5,000 with five loaves and two fishes; the baptism by water of converts. The baptismal font was in Latin called *piscina* ("the fishpond"), converts *pisciculi* ("little fishes"). Fish are shown in paintings of the Last Supper – the sacramental link with the Catholic custom of eating fish instead of other meat on Fridays. Three fishes intertwined or three fishes sharing a single head are symbols of the Trinity. Hebrew tradition prepared the way for this extensive symbolism. Fishes represented the faithful and were the food of the Sabbath and of paradise. Priests of the cult of Ea, the Mesopotamian god of the waters and of wisdom, also attached sacramental meaning to fish. As creatures of boundless liberty, not threatened by the Flood, they appear as saviours in Indian myth, avatars of Vishnu and Varuna. On the soles of the Buddha's feet, they symbolize freedom from the restraints of worldly desires. Buddha and the Greek Orpheus are called "fisher of men".

The sexual symbolism of fish is almost universal – linked with their prolific spawn, the fertility symbolism of water, and analogies of the fish with the penis. They are associated with lunar and mother goddesses and birth. In China they are emblems of plenty and good luck.

Three entwined fishes, representing the Trinity, from a stained-glass window in Wrexham Priory, England.

capture. Outside the use of flags purely for identification or signalling, the ancient link with the status, honour and spiritual values of a clan or nation continues to underly the individual symbolism of flags – an extensive but separate subject area.

Flagellation

When self-inflicted, a symbol of penance, purification, discipline or sacrificial worship. Known from ancient times in many cults and religions, flagellation became so popular among Christian sects between the 11th and 15th centuries that it was proscribed as heretical behaviour. It was believed not only to correct spiritual backsliding or exorcise personal temptations but also to drive away demons, plague, famine and sterility. Chastisement by flogging often had similar symbolism.

Fleur-de-lis

Better known as an emblem of French kings (and now of the Boy Scouts) than as a symbol, it is nevertheless notable for the diversity of association attached to it, which ranges from purity to fecundity, prosperity and glory. The heraldic fleur-de-lis is a stylized lily with three flowers (it is actually more like a bearded iris).

FISH: *see*
Baptism; BEASTS OF FABLE; Carp; Eel; Foot, Footprint; Leviathan; Liberty; Makara; Moon; Mother; Net; Octopus; Phallus; Ring; Sea; Trinity; Water

Flagellation: *see*
Whip, Flail

Fleur-de-lis: *see*
Arrow; Baptism; Iris; Lily; Phallus; Spear; Trinity

Flood: *see*
Ark; Transformation; Water

Fly, Fly whisk: *see*
Devils; Whip

Foot, Footprint: *see*
Conch; Crown; Fish; Seven;
Sceptre; Shoe; Swastika;
Vase; Washing; Wheel

Ford: *see*
Bridge; River, Stream

*The fleur-de-lis, an
emblem of French
royalty since the 12th
century.*

*The footprint of
Buddha showing the
symbols of divinity.*

The origin of the emblem is from the legend that a lily was given to Clovis, king of the Franks, on his baptism, symbolizing purity. The device was chosen as the emblem of the French king in the 12th century, and the plethora of lilies on the field was reduced to just three by Charles V in honour of the Trinity.

The lily also had ancient associations with fecundity, and versions of the fleur-de-lis appear in earlier Etruscan, Indian and Egyptian iconography, apparently with rebirth and solar symbolism. The central flower is often given an arrow or spear shape, suggesting military power, as well as masculine vigour.

Flood

Transformation by the dissolving and birthing medium of water. Stories or depictions of a great flood, which appear in the earliest mythologies, have a recurring symbolic theme of cyclic regeneration. Human sin, folly or disorder is submerged, often in a judgmental cataclysm, leading to a new, reformed or wiser human society.

FLOWERS *see panel, opposite*

Fly, Fly whisk

Flies symbolize evil and pestilence. They were such a problem in the ancient world that deities were invoked to deal with them, including Zeus under the title Apomyios (meaning "fly-preventer"). Flies were equated with demons and became Christian symbols of moral and physical corruption.

The fly whisk is a symbol of authority in Africa (where it is probably related to the Egyptian judgmental flail), China and India.

Fool *see* **Clown**

Foot, Footprint

Images of feet sometimes appear in iconography as signs that indicate contact between the earth and a divinity. In Buddhism, for example, the immanence of the Buddha is depicted by the soles of his feet, bearing seven symbols of his divine wisdom: conch, crown, diamond sceptre, fish, flower vase, swastika, and Wheel of the Law. So-called "footprints" of gods, giants or heroes (naturally formed in rock) were superstitiously venerated.

At the level of fetishism, according to Freud the foot is a phallic symbol. The binding of women's feet in China mingled fetishism with male possessiveness.

In other contexts, kissing someone's foot is a symbol of submission or abasement. Going barefoot, as in some mendicant orders, signifies humility. Christ's washing of his disciple's feet – a gesture that was imitated by English sovereigns who washed the feet of the poor to show their humility – had this meaning, although in the ancient world the washing of feet was also a gesture of hospitality or purification.

Setting foot on territory is often seen as an action invested with particular significance, famously so in recent history with Neil Armstrong's first step onto the moon.

Ford

In Celtic mythology, a place of challenge, especially in single combat. Because fords were often difficult passages, such symbolism is fairly self-evident, but Jung has drawn analogies with the transition from one state of being to another.

FLOWERS

Beauty (especially feminine), spiritual perfection, artless innocence, divine blessing, spring, youth, gentleness – but also the brevity of life, the joys of paradise. Essentially, the flower is a concise symbol of nature at its summit, condensing into a brief span of time the cycle of birth, life, death and rebirth. Ikebana, the Japanese art of flower decoration, is based upon this symbolic theme. In Eastern religions, flowers also represent the unfolding of spiritual life, symbolized specifically by the lotus. Flowers have spiritual significance in many religions. Thus Brahma and the Buddha are shown emerging from flowers; the dove-like Columbine is the flower of the Holy Spirit; and the Virgin Mary is depicted holding a lily or iris. Flowers also appear in art as attributes of Hope and the dawn, and as reminders of the fleeting nature of worldly life in still lifes. The symbolism of individual flowers is varied, ranging from allegories of virtue (the lily of purity) or wisdom (the Taoist golden blossom flowering from the head) to associations with blood sacrifice (as in Aztec Mexico) and the death of gods or humans (red or red-spotted flowers, including the anemone, poppy and violet). The colours, scents and qualities of flowers often determine their symbolism – the white lily of purity, for example; the heavily-perfumed frangipani of sexual invitation; the showy magnolia of ostentation or self-esteem. The funerary use of more delicately scented flowers as emblems of continuing life or rebirth is known from the ancient Middle East. Roses were scattered on Roman graves with this meaning. The receptive cup-like form of the flower is symbolically passive and feminine, its triadic layers signifying cosmic harmony. The flower became an effective symbol of peace for the flower children of the 1960s.

FLOWERS: *see* Amaranth; Anemone; Asphodel; Blood; Camellia; Carnation; Chrysanthemum; Dandelion; Dawn; Dove; Heliotrope; Iris; Lily; Lotus; Marigold; Mimosa; Narcissus; Orchid; Pansy; PEACE; Peony; Poppy; Primrose; Rose; SEVEN DEADLY SINS; Sacrifice; Sunflower; Violet; Virginity; VIRTUES, Wheel

Forest

A Jungian symbol of the unconscious and its threats, but in some traditions, particularly Buddhist, an image of sanctuary.

In European folklore and fairy tales, the forest is a place of mysteries, dangers, trials or initiation. Being lost in the forest or finding a way through it is a powerful metaphor for the terrors of inexperience and the achievement of knowledge – of the adult world or of the self. For settled communities, the forest is the unknown, the uncontrolled, the dwelling place of minor divinities and spirits, some of them terrifying, like the Slavic forest spirit, *leshii*.

The forest's moist, earthy, womb-like darkness was linked in the ancient world with ideas of germination and the feminine principle. To the Druids it was the female partner of the sun. Understanding the forest, its plants and its animals was a mark of shamanistic gifts, notably in Central America. In Asian traditions, the forest can parallel the desert "wilderness" of Middle-Eastern hermits as a place of retreat from the world, where it is possible to enter into contemplation and spiritual development.

Forest: *see* Bear; Boar; Earth; Initiation, Tree, Wolf; Woman

FORTUNE: *see individual names*

Forty: *see* Fasting; Flood

Fountain: *see* CARDINAL POINTS; Spring (Water); Tree; Virginity; Water

Forge *see* Smith

FORTUNE *see panel, right*

Forty

The number used ritually in Judeo-Christian and Islamic tradition to define significant periods of time – especially periods of spiritual preparation or testing, purification, penance, waiting, fasting or segregation. One explanation for the choice of the number forty is that Babylonian astronomers associated natural catastrophes, particularly storms and floods, with a forty-day period in spring when the Pleiades cluster of stars disappeared. Another is the ancient idea that the dead took forty days to entirely fade away. Roman funerary banquets were held after forty days. The idea that forty days was a suitable purification period led the port of Marseilles to impose a forty-day port ban (the *quarantine*) on ships from plague countries in the 14th century. Early historians used forty more as a symbolic number than as an accurate one. Thus, in the Bible, the Flood lasted forty days and nights; the Israelites wandered forty years in the wilderness; Moses listened to God for forty days and nights on Mount Sinai; David and Solomon each ruled for forty years; Christ spent forty days fasting in the wilderness (now Lent), forty months preaching, and forty days after Easter he ascended to heaven. In Egypt, Osiris disappeared for forty days, the period of religious fasting. Muhammad received the word of God at the age of forty. Many other Hebrew and Islamic rituals testify to the power of forty as a number symbolic of accomplishment or change.

FORTUNE

The idea that destiny is capricious is usually represented in Western art by figures based on the Roman goddess Fortuna, originally a deity of abundance but later becoming more fickle. Common attributes are a ship, rudder, prow, sail and sphere. Alternatively, Dame Fortune, who was popular in Spanish iconography, appears spinning a wheel on which some ascend while others are flung to the ground.

Fountain

The life force, and by extension rejuvenation or immortality. Also a symbol of the cosmic centre, the divine spirit, purification, inspiration and knowledge. Both Christian and Islamic traditions place a fountain or spring at the centre of paradise, at the foot of the Tree of Life, from which streams flow to the four cardinal points – an influential image for the layout of future garden and church architecture. The fountain's "pure river of water" (Revelation 22:1) was equated with the Father and Son, so that the fountain became a symbol not only of purity but of revelation and redemption. In Norse myth, the god Odin gives one of his eyes for a draught of water from the Fountain of Knowledge flowing from the world axis, the tree Yggdrasil. Greek Orphic tradition held that bypassing the Fountain of Forgetfulness and drinking from the Fountain of Memory at the entrance to Hades would ensure immortality. The Fountain of Youth, a popular theme in art, dates back at least to the Roman myth of the god Jupiter turning Juventas into a fountain. An intertwining theme is the rejuvenating effects of love, hence the frequent appearance of Cupid presiding over this fountain, and the sexual symbolism of its jetting water. The sealed fountain is a Christian image of virginity. Eastern legends located the Fountain of Life in the far north, although Florida in the US once seemed a likely site to Europeans.

Four

Comprehensiveness, ubiquity, omnipotence, solidity, organization, power, intellect, justice, stability, the earth. The symbolism of four is drawn primarily from the square and the four-armed cross. The square was the emblem of the earth in both India and China. The four-armed cross is the most common emblem of totality, the four directions of space. The significance of these four cardinal points, traditionally thought to be ruled by powerful gods of wind and weather, led to the dominance of the number four in religion and ritual throughout much of pre-Columbian America. The four heavenly gods of the Mayan pantheon, the four creator gods of the Aztecs, the four worlds of creation in the Hopi tradition of Arizona, all point to this fundamental theme. As a symbol of universality, four was hardly less important in celestial geography elsewhere. The concept of the four rivers that flow from the Tree of Life in paradise and bring the gift of spiritual nourishment or immortality is common to Babylonian, Iranian, Christian, Teutonic, Nordic, Hindu and Buddhist traditions. Four-faced gods such as Amun-Ra in Egypt and Brahma in India symbolize their rulership of all the elements. As emblematic of terrestial order and

universality, four was also the number of castes in Hindu society. The four letters YHVH outlined the unspeakable name of the Hebrew's God. The 12 Tribes of Israel were grouped under four emblems: man, lion, bull and eagle. These became the Christian emblems respectively of the four Evangelists Matthew, Mark, Luke and John. The many other fourfold symbols in the Bible, such as the horsemen of the Apocalypse, similarly express the idea of universality.

Four was, in Pythagorean terms, the first number giving a solid – the tetrahedron with a base and three sides. Symbolizing the stabilizing force of religion as well as universality, the square was the basis of much sacred architecture.

The world or heaven was thought to be supported by four pillars (Egypt) or giants (Central America). Guardianship of the directions of space was another quaternary symbol. In the process of Egyptian mummification, four guardian-headed canopic jars held the entrails of the dead. A body lying in state is still conventionally watched over by four guards. As a "rational" number, four symbolized the intellect. In ancient Western tradition there were four elements – earth, air, fire and water – and four humours. Jungian psychology has continued this tradition by envisaging the human psyche in terms of four fundamental aspects: thought, emotion, intuition and the senses. Graphic symbols of four, apart from the square and cross, include the swastika and the quatrefoil.

Fox

A representative of guile – a symbolism soundly based on its cleverness

Four: *see*
AFTERWORLDS;
CARDINAL POINTS;
CROSS; Earth;
ELEMENTS; Pillar; River,
Stream; Square; Swastika;
Tree; Wind

Fox: *see*
Devils; Fire, Flame; Red;
Rice; Transformation;
Trickster

Frog

Frog: *see*
Dew; Egg; Moon; Rain;
Water

FRUIT: *see*
Apple; Cherry; Cornucopia;
Date; Egg; Fig; Jujube Tree;
Olive; Orange; Peach; Pear;
Plum; Pomegranate;
SEVEN DEADLY SINS;
Strawberry; Tamarisk; Vine;
VIRTUES; Watermelon

but often extended, notably in European tradition, to more discreditable qualities – malice, hypocrisy, evil. As a nocturnal predator difficult to trap, the fox became a Christian analogy for the wiles of the Devil. The red fox was a fire demon in Rome. In North America the fox was a morally neutral trickster figure, not unlike the coyote. Norse mythology linked it with the trickster Loki.

Erotic associations appear in Chinese folk superstitions where "fox-women" were considered dangerous seducers and a fox's testicles were reputedly an aphrodisiac. Cunning and powers of transformation were also symbolic associations in Japan, although the white fox was the companion and messenger of the important rice god, Inari.

Frog
A foetal symbol, linked with the Egyptian frog goddess of birth,

The rice god Inari shown with two foxes, which act as his messengers and guard his rice sack.

Heket, and in other cultures also associated with the primeval state of matter, fecundity, germination, evolution, lunar phases, water and rain. Its embryonic symbolism, its amphibious transformation from egg and tadpole to a land-going creature with rudimentary human features, helps to explain the Grimm fairy tale of the frog who turned into a prince. Frogs were mocked symbols of foolish aspiration. Identified in Revelation (16:13) as an unclean spirit, and sometimes associated with heresy, the frog appears widely as a fertility and resurrection symbol, and harbinger of spring rains and the reawakening of nature – particularly in ancient Egypt and Asia.

In Vedic myth, a Great Frog, as the primordial state of undifferentiated matter, supports the earth. Frog images were used to invoke rain in ancient China where, in folklore, frogs' spawn appeared with the morning dew. Frogs signify luck in Japan, especially for voyagers. Their croaking is a common metaphor for boring instruction. Their love-play led the Greeks to associate them with Aphrodite.

FRUIT
Abundance, prosperity, earthly pleasures or desires – the food most often used to portray the paradisal state or the Golden Age of pastoral life. Various fruits (see individual entries) share some of the creative symbolism of the egg. They are attributes in art of Ceres and other agricultural deities, and of Summer, Taste, Charity and Gluttony.

Garden

In ancient traditions, an image of the perfected world, cosmic order and harmony – paradise lost and regained. For all major world cultures, gardens represented both the visible blessings of God (the divine gardener) and the ability of humans themselves to achieve spiritual harmony, a state of grace or beatitude. In the arid landscapes of Egypt and Iran, oasis-like formal gardens with their shading trees, flowers, scents, birds and flowing water, became symbols of refuge, beauty, fertility, purity and the springtime freshness of youth – a foretaste of the joys of immortality. The cross-like layout of the classic Persian garden, divided by four streams flowing from a central source or fountain, was modelled on the mythical image of paradise (a word etymologically synonymous with "garden"). In China, vast gardens with lakes and rocks and mountains created by the Han dynasty imitated the mythical Mystic Isles to which emperors hoped to go as immortals. Kyoto, the perfect example of

Japanese garden art, is imbued with spiritual symbolism. Some Indian gardens take the form of mandalas. Aztec gardens, as images of the natural world in microcosm, included wild animals as well as plants. Roman banquets held in funerary gardens symbolized the companionable nourishments of Elysium.

Psychologically, the garden is a symbol of consciousness as opposed to the wilderness of the unconscious, and also of the enclosing female principle. It is often used as a metaphor for sexual paradise constituted by the loved one – the "fountain of gardens, a well of living waters" (Song of Solomon 4:15). The sealed fruitfulness of the enclosed garden has become a Christian symbol of the Virgin Mary, who is often depicted within a garden setting, in paintings of the Annunciation.

Garlic

A superstitious emblem of protective power in southern and central Europe from classical times. Apart from anti-magnetic properties (a Roman belief),

Garden: *see*
AFTERWORLDS;
ANIMALS; Birds; CROSS;
FLOWERS; Fountain;
Island; Lake; Mandala;
Mountain; River, Stream;
Rock; Tree; Virginity; Water;
Woman

Giant: *see*
Dragon; Father; Fire,
Flame; Hero, Heroine

Gingko: *see*
Milk; Temple; Tree

Ginseng: *see*
Phallus

Girdle, Belt: *see*
CHASTITY; Circle;
FIDELITY; Knot; Ring;
Rope; Zodiac

it was said to deter snakes, lightning, the evil eye, and vampires.

The custom of hanging up bunches of garlic in the home had protective symbolism for centuries. In ancient Greece, where the smell of garlic was disliked, its chewing had more plausible value as a way for women to ensure chastity.

Gazelle *see* **Antelope**

Giant

An adversarial symbol with some similarities to the dragon in Western mythologies, probably sometimes drawn from memories of ancient tribal enemies who grew steadily more imposing as legends were woven about them. Usually portrayed as brutish, aggressive, stupid and clumsy, giants are vanquished in myth sometimes by a combination of divine and human effort, sometimes by the courage and cunning of a hero-figure. Ancient legends of giants can be seen as allegories of the struggle for social and spiritual evolution against barbarian forces or against the elemental forces of the earth. Norse giants, for example, directly personify the powers of fire and frost.

In several cosmogonies, the destruction of a race of Titans or giants is depicted as a primal stage in the process of creation – a sacrificial symbolism that may underly the burning of giant wicker figures filled with animal and human victims that were a feature of some pagan midsummer rituals. Psychologically, owing to their exaggerated physical size, giants are symbols of parental authority, particularly of the father.

Gilding *see* **Gold**

Ginkgo

A sacred tree in China, grown near temples as a symbol of immortality – aptly so in view of the extraordinarily long history of this species and the durability of individual trees. The ginkgo is particularly associated with Japan, where it is an emblem of loyalty – in legend sometimes willing to die for its owner. Because the ginkgo was said to assist the flow of maternal milk, it was also regarded as a lucky tree for nursing mothers.

Ginseng

An Oriental virility symbol, its masculine significance seemingly based on the phallic shape sometimes taken by the roots. Drugs made from ginseng have been used as reputed aphrodisiacs in China for centuries, and are also said to possess the "celestial" quality of promoting physical and mental equilibrium.

Girdle, Belt

Fidelity, chastity, strength, preparedness for action. In the older sense of a belt or sash, the girdle acquired a considerable and varied symbolism because it was used not only to hold garments together (hence an emblem of female chastity) but also to carry weapons, provisions, money, tools, and so on. Laying aside the girdle implied retirement from military service (in Rome, for example) – the opposite of warriors' or travellers' "girding up their loins". Its sexual symbolism ranged from marital fidelity (a girdle of sheep's wool given by Romans to their brides) to seductiveness (the magic girdle of the Greek goddess Aphrodite, or in Roman myth, Venus, said to make its wearer irresistible to men). Magic girdles appear in mythology as emblems of strength (the belt of Thor which doubled the power of his muscles).

Deriving from the ornate girdles of chivalry, ceremonial girdles were awarded as emblems of honour in England; hence the "belted earl". The rope girdles of monks allude to the binding and scourging of Christ; the Franciscan girdle has three knots signifying obedience to Christ and the vows of poverty and chastity. The priestly *cingulum* worn at the Roman Catholic Mass also symbolizes chastity. Circle symbolism makes the Hindu girdle an emblem of the cycles of time, and may also account for the girdles of invisibility that sometimes appear in folklore more widely.

Globe, Orb

World dominion or absolute authority – an emblem of power dating from at least the Roman Empire. Sharing with the sphere the symbolism of totality, it is a popular attribute in art of figures representing universal qualities from truth, fame, fortune and abundance to justice, philosophy and the liberal arts. The globe is also the attribute of omnipresent divinities, including the Greek deities Zeus (in Roman myth, Jupiter), Eros (Cupid), Apollo and Cybele. In Christian iconography, God often holds or stands on a globe. An orb surmounted by a cross represents the dominion of Christ and was an emblem of the Holy Roman Emperors, as it still is of British sovereigns. Emperors, kings or spiritual leaders such as the pope usually hold the globe in the left hand. A crowned globe represented the Philosopher's Stone in alchemy. A globe with stars is an attribute of Urania, the muse of astronomy.

Glove

A symbol of the executive hand itself, therefore often used as a pledge of action in days when gloves were more widely worn, especially by people of rank. The custom of throwing down a glove as a challenge (later, slapping someone in the face with a glove) goes back to medieval trials by battle. Defendants who had lost cases deposited a folded glove as security that they would carry out the court order. Gloves were also used by jousting knights as love pledges and by rulers to confer commercial rights or fiefs. In the ritual of status, removing the right glove acknowledged the superiority of an overlord or sovereign – and showed that no threat was intended. White (pontifical) gloves are used in the Roman Catholic Church as symbols of purity.

Goat

Virility, potency, lust, cunning and destructiveness in the male; fecundity and nourishing care in the female. Much of the ambiguous symbolism of the goat resolves itself along these sexual lines. The goat Amalthea was thus the revered wet-nurse of the Greek god Zeus (in Roman myth, Jupiter), her horn the cornucopia of abundance – symbolism soundly based on the quality and suitability of goat's milk for babies. The vitality of the male goat impressed the ancient world, as its connection with several Sumerian-Semitic and Greek gods shows. The goat was also the fiery mount of the Vedic Agni, drew the chariot of Thor, and was closely linked with Dionysus (Bacchus in Roman myth), as well as providing many of the physical features of Pan and the satyrs. Male goats are particu-

Globe, Orb: *see* CROSS; Crown; FAME; FORTUNE; Philosopher's Stone; Sphere; Star; TRUTH; VIRTUES

Glove: *see* Hand; Left and Right; White

Goat: *see* Chariot; Corn; Cornucopia; Devils; Horn; Milk; Satyr; SEVEN DEADLY SINS; Sheep; Spiral; Yin-yang; Zodiac

Gold: *see*
Alchemy; Fire, Flame;
Light; METALS; Sun;
TRUTH; WISDOM; Yellow

*The Vedic god Agni riding a goat,
after an 18th-century watercolour
from India.*

larly active in winter (when the female
comes on heat), which may account
for images of straw goats used in
Scandinavian corn festivals held at
yuletide – a season sometimes personified in art by the goat. However, the
goat's virility was seen by the Hebrews
as lewd. Herodotus reported bestial
sexual practices in the Mendesian cult
of the goat among the Egyptians. This
may have influenced the Christian
symbolism of the goat as a personification of impurity and vile lust. Goats
are analogous with sinners in the
gospel account of Judgment Day
when Christ is to divide them from the
sheep and consign them to everlasting
fire (Matthew 25:32; 25:41). Hence,
probably, the goatish physical characteristics of the medieval Devil, an
association strengthened by the goat's
reputation for malicious destructive-

ness. Goats can also personify folly
("acting the goat"). In China, where
"goat" and "yang" are homonyms, the
goat is a positive masculine symbol, as
it is in India where, as a sure-footed
climber, it was associated with superiority. In the Zodiac, Capricorn is a
goat-fish.

Gold
A metal of perfection, symbolically
divine through its universal association with the sun in the ancient world
and also because of its remarkable
lustre, resistance to rust, durability
and malleability. Its associated
emblematic qualities range from purity, refinement, spiritual enlightenment, truth, harmony and wisdom to
earthly power and glory, majesty,
nobility and wealth. Gold was the
alchemical Great Work, the goal of
the transformation process, and the
preferred metal for sacred objects or
for sanctified kings. In the Inca
empire, acceding rulers were covered
in resin sprayed with gold dust, the
historical origin of the El Dorado
(gilded man) legend. Gilding on the
icons of Byzantine Christianity and of
Buddhism symbolized divinity, as
does the gold-leaf work of medieval
art. In many traditions, gold was identified as the actual substance of divinity – the flesh of Ra in Egypt, the fae-
ces of the sun-god Huitzilopochtli in
Aztec Mexico – or was thought to be a
residue of the sun itself, its illumination left as threads in the earth, a mineral form of light, as in Hindu
thought. Alternatively, it was a symbol of the spirit of enlightenment, as
in Buddhism, or of Christ's message.
By association with the sun, gold is a
masculine symbol. Most of the
metal's symbolism also attaches to the

colour gold – sun, fire, glory, divinity, the light of heaven and of truth.

Golden Fleece

The famous symbol of the almost impossible goal, combining two sky or solar emblems of aspiration – the ram from which the fleece was shorn (sacred to the god Zeus) and gold, the solar metal. The epic journey of Jason and his Argonauts is often likened to the legend of the Holy Grail as an allegory of quest for the treasure of spiritual enlightenment and immortality. As an emblem of chivalrous protection, the Golden Fleece became an order of knighthood in Burgundy, Austria and Spain. (One suggested origin for the Golden Fleece tale is that wool was used to trap gold particles in early sluicing techniques.)

Goldfinch

The Christian soul or spirit – the bird most often seen in the hand of the Christ Child. Apart from its beauty and gentleness, which made it a popular children's pet, the iconography of this bird may allude to a legend that a goldfinch flew down and drew a thorn from Christ's crown on the road to Calvary, hence the blood-red splash on the front of its head.

Goose

Vigilance, loquaciousness, love, marital happiness and fidelity – a solar symbol, especially in Egypt, and also an emblem of freedom, aspiration and (through its migrations) the seasons of spring and autumn. The solar and beneficent symbolism of the wild goose is close to that of the swan, and the two are virtually interchangeable in Celtic tradition. Julius Caesar himself noted that the Gauls domesticated the goose for pleasure rather than for food. It was a masculine symbol of Celtic warriors. In Rome, too, it was linked with the war-god Mars, and became a celebrated emblem of vigilance after an incident in 390BCE when the honking of sacred geese at the temple of Juno alerted defenders of the Capitoline Hill to an attack by the Gauls. The Greeks linked the goose with Hera, Apollo, Eros and with the messenger-god Hermes. It was messenger to the gods in Egypt, too, as well as being the legendary bird that laid the cosmic egg. It became an emblem of the soul of the pharaohs (as representatives of the sun, born from the primal egg). At the accession of a new pharaoh, four geese were despatched as heralds to the cardinal points. Goose sacrifices at the December solstice symbolized the returning sun. The wild goose was a masculine solar emblem in China, but an important symbol as the lunar bird of autumn in the art of China and Japan, probably because of its migratory flights. It was the mount of Asiatic shamans, and of Brahma in India, as the soul's yearning for release from the ceaseless round of existence.

A secondary symbolic theme, widespread in fable and folklore, is based on the domestic goose, going back to its association with the Sumerian goddess of the farmyard, Bau. Here its image is of a gossipy, mothering creature, sometimes foolish (the "silly goose" of idiom). The sexual symbolism of the goose – linked with Priapus in Greece – was also widespread, and survives in the term "goosing", suggested by the nudging outstretched neck of the amorous male.

Gorgon *see* BEASTS OF FABLE

Golden Fleece: *see*
Gold; Grail; Knight; Ram; Sun

Goldfinch: *see*
Birds; Blood; Crown; Robin; Thorn

Goose: *see*
CARDINAL POINTS; Egg; FIDELITY; Sacrifice; Solstice; Soul; Sun; Swan; VIGILANCE

The Golden Fleece, seized by the hero Jason, a detail from an ancient Greek red-figure vase.

Grail

Grail: *see*
Blood; Book; Cauldron;
Centre; Chalice;
Cornucopia; CROSS; Cup;
Heart; Knight; Lance;
Philosopher's Stone; Sword;
Woman

Green: *see*
AFTERWORLDS;
Alchemy; COLOURS;
CROSS; DEATH; Dragon;
Emerald; Fairies; Grail;
Hope; Island; Jade;
LONGEVITY; Mercury;
Rain; SEVEN DEADLY
SINS; Trinity; VIRTUES;
Water

Grail

A romantic symbol of the heart's desire – for spiritual or physical nourishment, psychic wholeness or immortality. In the elaborate and charming medieval legends of the Grail, its exact physical nature is as elusive as the prize itself. Originally (in France) the Grail appears as a simple serving dish with magical properties, not unlike the classical cornucopia or the Celtic magic cauldron (the most probable pagan source for the legend). Here the Grail seems to refer to a magical restorative for the waning powers of a ruler (the Fisher King) or of Nature herself. It was also identified with the Philosopher's Stone sought by alchemists. Alternatively, it was a cup, lance, sword or book. Finally, in Christian versions, the Grail was the goblet used at Christ's Last Supper, or the cup of immortality once owned but lost by Adam, or the chalice in which Joseph of Arimathea was said to have caught Christ's blood as Christ was crucified. As such, the Grail became a symbol of the sacred heart of Christ, conferring divine grace. Jungian psychology has seen the Grail as a symbol of humanity's yearning to find its own centre, and as an essentially female symbol (the cup), both receiving and giving.

Grain *see* Corn

Grape *see* Vine; Wine

Grasshopper

A lucky emblem in China, linked with fertility. In countries where the natural balance is delicate, a symbol of cosmic disorder – notably in the Bible where a plague of locusts symbolizes the wrath of God.

Green

A generally positive symbol, as is evident even in its use as the "go" colour in modern traffic signals. Universally associated with plant life (and by extension with spring, youth, renewal, freshness, fertility and hope), green has acquired powerful new symbolic resonance as the modern emblem of ecology. Traditionally, its spiritual symbolism was most important in the Islamic world, where it was the sacred colour of the Prophet and of divine providence, and in China, where green jade symbolized perfection, immortality or longevity, strength and magical powers – a colour associated particularly with the Ming dynasty. Green is also the emblematic colour of Ireland, the "Emerald Isle", an epithet nicely linked with Celtic traditions in which good souls voyaged to the green Isle of the Blessed, the Land of Youth, *Tir nan Og*. Emerald green is a Christian emblem of faith, the reputed colour of the Holy Grail in Christianizing versions of the legend. Green appears as the colour of the Trinity, of revelation and, in early Christian art, of the Cross and sometimes of the Virgin Mary's robe.

In the pagan world, green is more widely linked with water, rain and fertility, with gods and sprites of water, and with female deities, including the Roman goddess Venus. It is a female colour in Mali and also in China. The Green Dragon of Chinese alchemy represented the yin principle, mercury and water. As the colour of germination, the Green Lion of Western alchemy symbolized the primary state of matter.

A secondary stream of symbolism is more ambivalent. Many traditions make a distinction between dark green (a Buddhist life colour) and the pale greenish tinge of death. The green of the god Osiris in Egyptian iconography symbolizes his role as god both of the dead and of new life. In English idiomatic usage, green represents immaturity but also the hues of envy and jealousy – the "green-eyed monster" of Iago's warning to Othello. It is a colour of illness, but psychologically occupies a cool, neutral position in the spectrum and is often regarded as a calming "therapeutic" colour – hence its use as the colour of pharmacy. Although green is a predominant colour of nature and of the world of the sensations, it is often linked with otherworldiness – the mystic colour of fairies and little people from outer space. Satan himself is sometimes represented as green. Perhaps this stems from the fact that green is not the skin-colour of healthy normality.

Grey

Abnegation, humility, melancholia, indifference and, in modern terminology, a simile for dull sobriety – possibly because in spite of its subtle beauties it is the hue that is most often thought of as colourless. Only in Hebrew tradition does it appear to be linked with the wisdom of age. As the colour of ash, it was sometimes associated with death, mourning and the soul. In Christian religious communities it symbolizes renunciation.

Griffin

A solar hybrid creature, combining the head, wings and claws of an eagle with the body of a lion. Because its two aspects symbolize rulership of air and land and together make a double emblem of the sun's power, the griffin was a forceful motif – popular at least from the second millennium BCE in western Asia, later in the Middle East, Greece and eventually Europe. It was a Hebrew symbol of Persia (the contending powers of Zoroastrianism), had demonic significance in Assyria, but seems in Crete to have played a protective role in palace decoration. In Greece, where the griffin was sacred to Apollo, to Athene as wisdom and to Nemesis as retribution, legend said that griffins guarded the gold of India and of the Scythians. In early Christian iconography the griffin was used to symbolize the forces of persecution, vengeance or hindrance. But from the 14th century it emerges as an emblem of the dual nature of Christ – human and divine – and of courageous vigilance, which was its usual meaning in heraldry.

The griffin, after an Islamic bronze statuette, found in Camposanto, Italy.

Grey: *see*
Ash; DEATH; Soul;
WISDOM

Griffin: *see*
BEASTS OF FABLE;
Eagle; Lion; Sun;
VIGILANCE; Wings;
WISDOM

Habit

Habit: *see*
Initiation

Hair: *see*
Black; Castration; Gold;
Head; LIBERTY; Red;
Scalp

Habit

A cowled robe symbolizing vows of poverty in Christianity and Islam. It has particular significance in Arabia: the *khirka* (a sacred woollen robe) of Sufi mystics marked the entry of the initiate after three years into the community of ascetics, judged able to follow the Law, the Way and the Truth.

Hair

Life force, strength – a deeply significant aspect of the human body both socially and personally, as can be seen from the wide range of symbolism attached to different hair styles. The power symbolism of hair growth is famously exemplified by Samson, a warrior of the ancient Hebrew Nazarite sect whose long hair was a sign both of charismatic holiness and physical strength. The Khalsa community of Sikhs let their hair and beards grow for similar symbolic reasons. In many societies long hair was a mark of royal power or of liberty and independence, as among the Gauls and other Celtic peoples. Long, loose hair in women signified the unmarried state, or virginity – as in Christian iconography of the Virgin Mary and virgin saints – compared with the braided hair of the courtesan. Alternatively, as in Russia, a single braid marked the maiden, double braids the wife. Letting down bound hair was a permissive sexual signal.

Whereas body hair was usually associated purely with physical virility

The biblical Delilah cutting Samson's hair, the source of his strength, from a woodcut of 1527.

or lower states of being (hairiness is a devilish attribute in Christian art), head hair was intimately linked with the individual spirit or vital force of a person – an idea that accounts for the custom of keeping locks of hair. In ancient Greece, taking a lock of hair from a dead person released its soul into the underworld. Scalping, in Native American warfare, removed an enemy's power, the braves daringly leaving a lock of hair on their shaven heads for this purpose. Islamic custom was to leave a tuft by which the faithful could be drawn upward into paradise. Although hermits traditionally let their hair grow, many religious orders have followed the priestly Egyptian custom of shaving the hair as a symbol of submission to God or renunciation of the material world. Submission (to the Manchus) was also the original symbolism of the Chinese pigtail. Cutting hair was close to a castration symbol in ancient China – and remains a resented symbol of conformity to military discipline in some countries. In different traditions, cutting, growing or tearing out hair has symbolized grief. Hair colour has its own symbolism, red hair once having demonic associations and golden hair standing for solar or kingly power, black for terrestrial. Dishevelled hair can symbolize asceticism – an attribute of Shiva who appears with wild locks. Nowadays, long, cropped or bizarre hair styles are fashionable symbols of protest, nonconformity or clan identification.

Halo

A circular radiance widely used in Christian art between the 5th and 15th centuries CE to symbolize the divinity or sanctity of the Trinity,

Holy Family, saints or angels. The convention, based on the nimbus surrounding the sun's disk, was adapted from pagan images of sun gods or deified rulers, particularly from the iconography of Mithraism, which Christianity supplanted in the Roman Empire. The "floating ring" image of a halo was a later form.

Hammer

A creative–destructive symbol of male strength, linked with the power of the sun and thunderbolts, with sovereign authority, gods of war and beneficent artisan gods. The hammer seldom appears as a symbol of brute force alone (although Edward I was called "The Hammer of the Scots" for his savage treatment of them). Even the mighty stone hammer of the Nordic god Thor, which he could throw unerringly to kill or use to smite valleys out of mountain chains, could be put to use as a protective emblem on gravestones or to suggest the authority by which contracts or marriages were solemnized. In the hands of the Greek god Hephaestus (Vulcan), the hammer was an instrument of divine skill, an emblem of the creative vigour that drives the chisel or shapes metal. This is the meaning of its use in Freemasonry as an attribute of the Lodge Master, symbolizing creative intelligence. The hammer and sickle emblem of Soviet Russia was likewise chosen as a forceful image of productive work. In China the hammer was a symbol of the sovereign power to shape society. There and in India, its destructiveness was linked with the conquest of evil. It was also a symbol of protection against fire. A noisy tool, it was widely linked with thunder and by extension with fecundity – the

Halo: *see*
Aureole; Mandorla; Nimbus; Ring; Sun

Hammer: *see*
Rain; Smith; Thunder

A cross form of halo, popular in Christian art of the 9th century. This example is an Eastern Orthodox image.

Hand: *see*
Eye; Five; Glove; Left and
Right; Mudras

release of rain or, in northeastern
Europe, the cracking of ice in spring.
In Japan the hammer appears as an
emblem of wealth (linked with the
recovery of gold), an attribute of the
prosperity-god Daikoku.

Hand

Power (temporal and spiritual),
action, strength, domination, protection – a general symbolism that
reflects the hand's executive role in
human life and the belief that it can
transmit spiritual as well as physical
energy. The hand was sometimes an
image forceful enough to stand alone
in iconography, as a motif in cave
paintings, for example, or in Christian
paintings of God's hand appearing
from the clouds. In Islam, the open
Hand of Fatima (the daughter of
Muhammad) proclaims the five fundamentals: faith, prayer, pilgrimage,
fasting and charity. The Hand of
Atum was a fertility emblem in Egypt,
stimulating the original life-giving
semen from the body of the
male–female creator god. Because the
number five was linked with the
underworld in ancient Mexico, a hand
with fingers spread was a death icon.
The Red Hand of Ulster became the
badge not only of the province but of
baronetcy (a title instituted to raise
money for Ulster's defence). Belief
that the hands of kings, religious leaders or miracle workers had beneficial
power existed from ancient times;
hence the laying on of hands in healing or in religious blessing, confirmation and ordination. Talismanic use of
the hands extended to the grisly practice of thieves, carrying the severed
right hand of a hanged criminal for
nefarious good luck. Except in China
and Japan, where the left hand signi-

fies honour, the right hand is widely
favoured; one Celtic ruler was deposed after he lost his right hand in
battle. Christ sits on the right hand of
God, who dispenses mercy with the
right, justice with the left. In Occidental tradition, the right hand symbolized frankness, logic, the left dup-
licity (white magic versus black).
Similarly, the right hand blesses, the
left curses. The right is sometimes
scaled up by artists, as in Michelangelo's *David* (1501).

Although the conceptual link
between hand and power (words synonymous in ancient Hebrew) is over-
whelmingly important in pictorial
symbolism, it is only one aspect of the
much more extensive and varied symbolism of hand gestures. These form
in Hindu and Buddhist *mudras* an
entire symbolic language involving
hundreds of hand and finger shapes
and positions deployed in religious
ritual, dance and theatre. Hand gestures of fairly widespread significance
(more signals than symbols) include
the following: clenched – threat,
aggressive force, secrecy, power (the
raised fist of Black Power); open and
raised with the palm outward – blessing, peace, protection, the hand of
Buddha; raised, three fingers open –
the Christian Trinity; raised, thumb
and two fingers open – pledge or oath;
both raised (orant) – adoration, recep-
tiveness to celestial grace, surrender
(now, less humbly, a victor's receptive-
ness to applause); covered or con-
cealed – respect; folded – tranquillity;
palms upward, laid on each other –
meditation (the upward palm signifying both giving and receiving); palms
together – prayer, supplication, greeting, humility; on breast – submission
(also an attitude of the sage). The left

*The Hand of Fatima,
from an Islamic
engraved pendant.*

fist placed in the right hand was a submissive signal in parts of Africa. Placing both hands in the hands of another is a more widespread gesture of trust or submission (as in feudal contracts to serve a lord). Clasping hands is an almost universal symbol of friendship, fraternity, welcome, agreement, congratulation, reconciliation or, in marriage, faithful love.

Palmists claim to be able to read more of a person's character and destiny in the hands than in the face. In iconography, an eye in a palm is a symbol of clairvoyance or, in Buddhism, of compassionate wisdom.

Hare, Rabbit

The animal most commonly linked with the moon; also a symbol of fertility, libido, procreation, cyclic rebirth, cunning, swiftness, vigilance and magical powers. To the ancients, the patches on the moon resembled leaping hares or rabbits (seldom distinguished from each other). The hare's lunar symbolism was strengthened by observation of its moonlit gambols. In African, Native American, Celtic, Buddhist, Chinese, Egyptian, Greek, Hindu and Teutonic myth, the hare was associated with the lunar and feminine cycles of regeneration. It sometimes appeared as a sacrificial or saviour figure, as in the Buddhist legend of a hare leaping into a fire to provide food for the hungry Buddha – hence the hare's elevation to a celestial place on the moon. In Taoist art, the lunar hare is depicted mixing with a pestle the elixir of longevity or immortality. The hare was an Imperial Chinese yin symbol and an augury of good fortune. (In China it could also symbolize homosexuality.)

Hares embody harmless guile in many traditions: the Brer Rabbit stories probably derive from African tales like the one in which a hare tricks a hippopotamus and elephant into a tug-of-war designed to clear land for him. Similarly, in Japan, the White Hare of Oki crosses the sea on crocodiles lined up snout-to-tail, which he pretends to be counting. Several Native North American tribes elevated the hare to the status of a culture hero – the Algonquin, for example, seeing the lunar hare as the demiurge son of the Great Manitou carrying out a creator/saviour role in shaping natural forces to man's advantage. As prolific breeders, hares or rabbits were often linked by sympathetic magic with cures for sterility or difficult labour (a talisman recommended by the Latin poet Pliny). The hare was an attribute of lunar and hunter goddesses in the classical and Celtic worlds, and also of the Greek Aphrodite (in Roman myth, Venus), Eros (as love; Cupid) and Hermes (as speedy messenger; Mercury). Ancient associations with fertility and regeneration in Teutonic and Nordic traditions underlie the symbolism of the Easter Bunny or hare (a reference to the hare-headed Eostre, the Anglo-Saxon goddess of spring). As a divine or semi-divine creature, the hare was often a forbidden food. Some Shi'ites believe it to be an incarnation of Muhammad's son-in-law Ali. The Hebrews took the view that it was unclean. Leading on from this, and from its sexual appetites, it became a Christian symbol of lust, although its ability to flee up rockfaces also made it an allegory of the believer seeking refuge in Christ. A knight fleeing from the timid hare was a medieval image of cowardice. Lewis Carroll's mad

Hare, Rabbit: *see* Knight; LONGEVITY; Moon; Sacrifice; SEVEN DEADLY SINS; VIGILANCE

Harp

Harp: *see*
Angels

Hawthorn: *see*
Tree; Virginity; Wood;
Wreath, Garland

Hazel: *see*
Fairies; Milk; Rain; Ring;
Rod; Wand; Water;
WISDOM

Head: *see*
Cap; Crown; Decapitation;
Feather; Four; Hair; Pillar;
Scalp; Sphere; Soul; Triad;
Wreath, Garland

March Hare is taken from folk observations that hares behave wildly in their spring rutting season. The folk belief that a foot of the agile rabbit or hare is good for gout or rheumatism is another example of sympathetic magic.

Harp

Purity and poetry – the instrument of the angelic choirs, of King David, and pre-eminently of the Celtic world (hence the harp emblem of Wales). Dagda, the great father god, played a magic harp. Harpstrings formed a ladder symbol of ascent to paradise in the lays of Norway and Iceland. In the Hell panel of *The Garden of Earthly Delights* (*c*.1495), Bosch used the harp as a memorable image of spiritual anguish by showing a figure crucified on the strings.

Hart *see* **Deer**

Hawk *see* **Falcon, Hawk**

Hawthorn

A tree and flower invested with magical properties in Europe from classical times when hawthorn was linked with Hymen, the god of weddings. The flowers were used for marriage garlands, the wood for marriage torches. The association between its spring flowering and virginity led to folk superstitions that it protected chastity. To others, the faintly fishy perfume of the flowers augured death if brought indoors.

Hazel

Fertility, water, supernatural powers of divination and wisdom. In northern Europe and the Celtic world, the hazel wand was the instrument of wizards and fairies, diviners and seekers of gold. A classical tradition suggested it to be the rod of Hermes, messenger of the gods. Its mystic symbolism may derive both from the deep roots of the hazel (mysterious powers of the underworld) and from the berries (secret wisdom). Apart from its use in incantation, the hazel had strong fertility and rain symbolism, was thought to bring luck to lovers, and according to Norman folklore, drew abundant milk from cows struck with a hazel ring.

Head

The ruling instrument of reason and thought, but also the manifestation of a person's spirit, power, or life force – a significance that accounts for the ancient value placed upon the severed head of an enemy. For many peoples, including Celtic warriors who wore heads as trophies, the head had fertility or phallic symbolism and was thought to transmit the strength and courage of the decapitated warrior to its new owner. In iconography, the head of a god, king or hero, mounted on a pillar, shown on a coin, or used as a funerary emblem, embodied his or her power to influence events. For Plato, the sphere of the head represented a human microcosm. In many traditions the head replaces the heart as the presumed location of the soul. In monster or animal/god symbols, it may indicate which part of the hybrid is dominant. Artists could increase the force of an image by multiplying heads or faces, sometimes to indicate different functions. Thus in Roman iconography, three-headed Hecate moved between heaven, earth and the underworld, two-faced Janus watched over entrances and exits, past and future, travellers leaving and returning. The four heads of Brahma refer to the four Hindu Vedas, the four ram heads of Amun-Ra to his rulership of all the elements. In art, the Greek twins Castor and Pollux shown one looking up and one down symbolized ascending and descending phases of heavenly bodies. Images combining male and female heads had protective symbolism in Egypt. Headdresses (crowns, wreaths or caps) and head movements – bowed in submission, raised in pride – have particular significance in human gesture.

Heart

The symbolic source of the affections – love, compassion, charity, joy or sorrow – but also of spiritual illumination, truth and intelligence. It was often equated with the soul. Many ancient traditions, did not make a sharp distinction between feelings and thought. A person who "let the heart rule the head" would once have seemed sensible rather than foolish. Symbolically, the heart was the body's sun, animating all. Ritual application of this belief led the Aztecs to sacrifice thousands of hearts to the sun each year to restore its power. As a symbol of what is most essential in a human being, the heart was left in the eviscerated bodies of Egyptian mummies. It would be weighed in the underworld to see if it was heavy with misdeeds or light enough to pass on to paradise.

The heart is an emblem of truth, conscience or moral courage in many religions – the temple or throne of God in Islamic and Judeo-Christian thought; the divine centre, or *atman*, and the Third Eye of transcendent wisdom in Hinduism; the diamond of

The weighing of a dead soul's heart against a feather, from an ancient Egyptian papyrus.

purity and essence of the Buddha; the Taoist centre of understanding. The "Sacred Heart" of Christ became a focus of Roman Catholic worship as a symbol of the Lord's redeeming love, sometimes shown pierced by nails and with a crown of thorns, in reference to the Crucifixion. A heart crowned with thorns is also the emblem of the Jesuit saint Ignatius Loyola; while a flaming heart is the attribute of SS Augustine and Antony of Padua. A heart on fire is a key symbol of the ardent Christian but also an attribute in art of Charity and of profane passion – as in Renaissance paintings of the Greek goddess Aphrodite (in Roman myth, Venus). The heart transfixed by Eros's (Cupid's) arrow was another Renaissance theme, which became the motif of St Valentine's Day – a mid-February festival with pagan rather than Christian roots. In iconography, the heart takes on a vase-like shape, or is graphically represented by an inverted triangle, symbolizing something into which love is poured or carried; in this sense it is linked with the Holy Grail.

Heaven *see* **AFTERWORLDS**

Heart: *see*
AFTERWORLDS; Arrow; Blood; Centre; Cup; Eye; Fire, Flame; Grail; Nail; Soul; Sun; Triangle; TRUTH; Vase; VIRTUES

Hedgehog: *see*
Fire, Flame; Rays; SEVEN
DEADLY SINS

Heliotrope: *see*
Sun

Helmet: *see*
BEASTS OF FABLE; Cap;
FORTUNE; Head; Hero,
Heroine

Hen: *see*
Cock (Rooster); Egg;
VIRTUES

Hero, Heroine: *see*
Dragon

Heron: *see*
Birds; Phoenix; Sun

Hexagram: *see*
Alchemy; Mandala;
Pentagram, Pentacle;
Quintessence; Six; Triangle;
Trigrams

Hedgehog

Something of a culture hero to the early nomadic peoples of central Asia and Iran, associated with the gifts of fire and agriculture. Similar links were made with the porcupine in East Africa. Rolled into a spiked ball it may have suggested an analogy with solar rays. Associations with pugnacity may account for the hedgehog, as an attribute of the Babylonian war goddess, Ishtar. Roman and early Christian writers drew approving attention to its sagacity in knocking grapes off vines, rolling on them and carrying them away on its quills. This habit seems to be the origin of its later identification with Gluttony in Christian art. The hedgehog is also an attribute of the personification Touch.

Heliotrope

Adoration – a meaning suggested by the plant's turning toward the sun. The heliotrope had solar symbolism in Roman and Asian imperial wreaths and was a Christian emblem of religious devotion, an attribute of saints and prophets. In Greek myth, the lovesick girl Clytia was transformed into a heliotrope – for ever following the object of her hopeless passion, the sun-god Helios.

Helmet

Invisible power, in particular the power of death represented by the helmet of Hades. The helmet can also symbolize thought. More obviously, it is the protective attribute of warriors or warrior divinities such as the Nordic Odin, and the Greek Ares (in Roman myth, Mars) and Athene (Minerva), and of heroes such as Perseus, whose winged helmet of invisibility enabled him to escape after slaying the Gorgon Medusa. In art the figures of Fortune and Faith are usually shown helmeted.

Hen

In Africa, a guide to the underworld, sacrificially used to call up spirits. In Europe a symbol of fussy, mothering care. A hen with chicks was a Christian image of divine providence. More rarely, the hen represents the personification Charity.

Hermaphrodite see Androgyne

Hero, Heroine

In Jungian psychology, a symbol of psychic vigour, a celebration of the human spirit. According to this interpretation, the trials of the hero represent the challenges of self-discovery. In ancient Greece, the appearance in literature and art of heroic prototypes with almost superhuman or semi-divine powers appears to have developed out of earlier forms of ancestor worship.

Heron

Inquisitiveness, but also usually a bird of good omen, symbol of the morning sun in Egypt and the model for the phoenix-like Benu bird, revered as the creator of light. The heron was an ascensional symbol in China and sometimes appeared in allegories of Christians rising above the storms of life, as the heron surmounts rain-clouds.

Hexagram

Two interlocking or overlapping triangles, one inverted, symbolizing union in duality. This is now known as the Star of David (who unified Judah

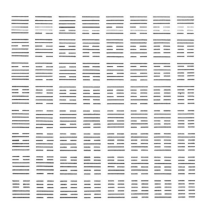

The 64 Chinese hexagrams, as used in the divinatory art of the I Ching. Each group of lines has a different meaning.

and Israel) and is the emblem of the modern state of Israel. It was earlier called Solomon's Seal or Solomon's Shield – although originally this may have been the pentacle, a five-pointed star of which there is more ancient archaeological evidence in Palestine. Hexagram shapes also appear in Indian mandalas as meditative images and, with mysterious significance, in Central American rock carvings. In alchemy, the hexagram symbolized the male/female dualities of fire and water (the inverted triangle), later the union of the four elements or the "fifth element" (the quintessence). In magic, the hexagram device was associated with exorcism.

Coded lines used in ancient Chinese divination, also called hexagrams, are groups of six broken or unbroken lines symbolizing archetypal qualities and yielding 64 possible permutations, each with different significance.

Hippopotamus

Brute strength, destructiveness, fecundity – a beast of sharply ambivalent symbolism in ancient Egypt. Theban images of the hippopotamus-goddess Tawaret – mild, human-breasted, swollen-bellied, holding the hieroglyphic rolled papyrus of protection, symbolized guardianship of women and children. But she was the consort of the destroying Set and could herself turn vengeful. The Book of Job (40:15–24) describes Behemoth as a voracious hippopotamus-like creature, symbolzing humanity's need for divine help to conquer its brutishness.

Hive

Collective work – a protective and maternal symbol of ordered industry. In Christian art, the beehive appears as an image of the monastic community, the attribute of eloquent religious leaders and of the Golden Age.

Hog *see* **Boar, Pig**

Hole

In religious artifacts and in mystic thought, less a symbol of emptiness than of an opening – to physical life at birth and to spiritual life at death. The significance of ancient pierced stones is not always explained by female sexual and fertility symbolism. In China, for example, precious jade disks were carefully perforated with a central hole as symbols of the gateway to heaven, a void leading to timelessness.

Holly

A midwinter emblem of hope and joy. Holly was among the evergreens carried at the midwinter festival of Saturnalia in Rome, but its use at Christmas is linked more directly with Teutonic customs of decorating houses with holly in December. In Christian tradition, holly is associated with

Hippopotamus: *see* BEASTS OF FABLE

Hive: *see* Bee

Hole: *see* Jade; Void

Holly: *see* PASSION; Solstice

Honey

Honey: *see*
Bee; Dew; Gold; Initiation;
Mead; Milk; Nirvana; Word

Horn: *see*
Antlers; Buffalo, Bison;
Bull; Cornucopia; Cow;
Crescent; Devils; Goat;
Helmet; Mead; Moon;
Mother; Ram; Sun

John the Baptist and with Christ's Passion (the thorn-like leaves and blood-red berries).

Honey

The food of gods and immortals, seers and poets – a symbol of purity, inspiration, eloquence, the divine Word and God-given blessings. Honey was a principal source of sugar in the ancient world, and had valued medicinal properties. It was also the basis of mead, a sacred beverage in many cultures, equated with the ambrosia of the gods. Its celestial qualities seemed borne out by its golden colour and by the idea that bees collected honey by sipping dew from flowers. Thus the mystic sweetness celebrated by Coleridge in the closing lines of *Kubla Khan* (1797–8): "For he on honey-dew hath fed, / And drunk the milk of Paradise." The biblical land of Canaan flowing with milk and honey was an image of spiritual as well as physical plenty. Honey was used not only as a votive food but also as an anointing or cleansing fluid in many ancient Middle-Eastern cultures, and in the initiatory rites of Mithraism. Kings were embalmed with it in Sparta, Scythia and Egypt. It was equated with the bliss of nirvana in India and with heavenly pleasures in China as well as in the West.

In Greece, where honey was again used in initiation rites, poets such as Homer and philosophers such as Pythagoras were reputed to have been fed on nothing else.

In addition to its use as a balm it was widely thought to be an aphrodisiac or to promote fertility (its erotic symbolism perhaps strengthened by the effects of drinking mead). Jainism forbade eating honey for this reason.

Horn

Force, strength, virility, fertility, supremacy – the potent symbol of barbaric gods, rulers, heroes or warriors. To the ancients, the horns of bulls, cows, rams, goats or bison were a crowning expression of male fighting spirit and phallic vitality, and also of female protective and reproductive power. Hence the popularity and status of horned divinities, particularly in traditions based on cattle herding or on hunting. Earliest representations of horned figures in cave paintings probably record shamanistic invocations of hunting success. Sympathetic magic may also have been conjured up by Nordic, Teutonic and Gaulish horned war helmets, designed to inspire animal ferocity as well as to terrify enemies. In the Roman army, a horned decoration, the *corniculum*, was awarded for distinguished bravery. Similarly, headdresses decorated with horns, as in Native North America, were reserved for courageous leaders.

Viewed as a container rather than weapon, the horn becomes feminine, but retains its underlying symbolism of power. Thus, the legendary Horn of Plenty (Cornucopia) could not be emptied. Drinking horns, used ritually for mead or wine, were thought to confer potency. Horns forming a crescent-moon shape often symbolize mother goddesses, such as Hathor in Egypt, shown with the head of a cow or with a horned human head. The curving horns of a bull or cow cradling the sun disk (represented in Mali by a gourd) depict both lunar and solar power. Ram horns are specifically solar – as in images of Amon who became the ruling god of Egypt and whose curling horns were adopted by Alexander the Great, "Son of Amun", as a symbol of his imperial power. In the Jewish Temple, sacred horns upon which sacrificial blood was smeared stood at the four corners of the altar as emblems of Jehovah's all-encompassing power. The Hebrew *shofar* (ram's horn), used as a warning signal by the ancient Israelites, was another symbol of protective power, and the word "horn" often appears in the Bible as a synonym for strength or, in the New Testament, for salvation. However, Christianity soon turned against pagan worship of the horn which became, in medieval art, a mark of Satan and his horned followers. Horns also identified the cuckold – possibly by association with stags losing their does to stronger males. In psychology, horns can be linked with divergence – the "horns of a dilemma".

Horse

An archetypal symbol of animal vitality, velocity and beauty. With the notable exceptions of Africa and of North and South America, where horses mysteriously disappeared for some thousands of years until the Spanish reintroduced them, the horse was linked everywhere with the rise of dominant civilizations, and with superiority. The mastered horse is a prime symbol of power – hence the popularity of the equestrian statue. In cave art, as in Romantic painting, horses flow across the surface medium like incarnations of the force of life itself. They were widely linked with the elemental powers of wind, storm, fire, waves and running water. Of all animals, their symbolism is the least limited, ranging from light to darkness, sky to earth, life to death.

Their role as emblems of the continuity of life is suggested in many rites. Each October the Romans sacrificed a horse to Mars, the god of war and agriculture, and kept its tail throughout the winter as a fertility symbol. In ancient belief, horses knew the mysteries of the underworld, the earth and its cycles of germination. This early chthonic symbolism was replaced by a more widespread association of the horse with sun and sky gods, although horses continued to play a part in funerary rites as guides or messengers in the spirit world. The riderless horse is still used as a poignant symbol in military and state funerals.

Death is usually represented by a black horse – but rides a pale horse in the book of Revelation. The white horse is almost invariably a solar symbol of light, life and spiritual illumination. It is an emblem of the Buddha (said to have left his worldly life on a white horse), of the Hindu Kalki (the last incarnation of Vishnu), of the merciful Bato Kannon in Japan, and of the Prophet in Islam (for whom horses are emblems of happiness and wealth). Christ is sometimes shown riding a white horse (Christianity thus links the horse with victory, ascension and the virtues of courage and generosity). The white horse – as delineated in the chalklands of southern England – was a Saxon standard, perhaps linked with the Celtic horse-goddess Epona, who was taken into the Roman world as the protectress of horses. The winged horse is similarly a solar or spiritual symbol. Horses draw the chariot of the sun in classical, Iranian, Babylonian, Indian and Nordic mythology, and are ridden by many other gods, including Odin,

Horse: *see*
ANIMALS; BEASTS OF FABLE; Black; Centaur; Chariot; Clouds; Darkness; DEATH; Earth; Fire, Flame; Light; SEVEN DEADLY SINS; Sky; Storm; Sun; VICTORY; White; Wind; Wings

The Nordic god Odin riding his eight-legged horse Sleipnir, from a stone carving.

Horseshoe: *see*
Crescent; Eye; Horn

Host: *see*
Bread; Sacrifice; White

Hourglass: *see*
DEATH; Drum; Father
Time; Triangle; VANITY

Hyena: *see*
Devils; Lion

Hyssop: *see*
Water

whose eight-legged mare Sleipnir represents the eight winds. Clouds are the horses of the Valkyries, Scandinavian priestesses of the goddess Freya.

Although predominantly linked with elemental or instinctual powers, horses can symbolize the speed of thought. Legend and folklore often invest them with magical powers of divination. They are associated with sexual energy, impetuous desire or lust – as in Fuseli's painting *The Nightmare* (1781), a rape fantasy in which a wild-eyed horse thrusts its head through a girl's bed curtains.

Horseshoe
An ancient talisman against the evil eye – but only if the heel pointed upward. This supports the theory that the supposed magic of the horseshoe relied on the protective symbolism of the horned moon, the iron forming a crescent shape. A more simple explanation is that the horseshoe protected the horse.

Host
The wafer of unleavened bread given in the Christian Eucharist as a symbol of Christ's sacrificial body (from the Latin *hostia*, "victim"). A text attributed to St Thomas Aquinas commends the host's symbolic roundness (perfection) and whiteness (purity).

Hourglass
Mortality and the relentless passing of time. The hourglass often appears in devotional still lifes to illustrate the brevity of human life, and is an attribute of Father Time and sometimes of Death. It can also borrow the symbolism of two triangles, one inverted, symbolizing the cycles of creation and destruction (the shape of Shiva's drum in Indian art).

Hybrid *see* BEASTS OF FABLE

Hyena
In European tradition, a symbol of cowardly greed and hypocrisy, a medieval Christian metaphor for Satan who feeds on sinners. However, the hyena had a place in West African animist rites as the acolyte of the lion; it took a guardian role in the symbolism of the Bambara people in Mali. In ancient Egypt the hyena was credited with powers of divination, perhaps from its night vision.

Hyssop
Purification, humility – a symbolism based on biblical references to the herb used with water to sprinkle the unclean in the Hebrew Temple, although this may in fact have been a caper plant with similar aromatic qualities.

Ibex *see* **Goat**

Ibis
Wisdom. The sacred ibis of ancient Egypt was revered as an incarnation of the lunar deity Thoth, patron god of scribes and lord of occult knowledge. The religious symbolism of the ibis was probably based on its habits as an inquisitive wading bird with a curving beak shaped somewhat like a sickle moon. It appears often in Egyptian iconography and was mummified in royal tombs to provide instruction in the mysteries of the afterlife.

I Ching *see* **Trigrams**

Icon
In art, a representational sacred image that is intended to be purely symbolic. Byzantine painters of religious icons held realism at arm's length by painting in pure, flat colours to rigid conventions, their aim being to maintain a strict boundary between the spiritual world and the sensory or human world. The icon is thus intended not to be "lifelike" but to reflect or symbolize a transcendent reality upon which the viewer can meditate.

IHS
Letters that by tradition form an abbreviation of the name of Jesus, symbolizing salvation or resurrection. In the pagan ancient Greek world, probably with similar meaning, the letters stood for *Iacchos*, a word used in the Eleusinian mysteries to refer to the god Dionysus. Various devices incorporating IHS (sometimes taken to mean *Iesus Hominum Salvator*, the Latin meaning "Jesus, Saviour of Mankind") are emblems of the Christian SS Ignatius Loyola, Teresa and Bernardino of Siena.

Immolation *see* **Fire, Flame**; **Sacrifice**

Incense
Purity, virtue, sweetness, ascending prayer. From the earliest times, the burning of gum and other scented resins, woods, dried plants or fruits has been one of the most universal of

Ibis: *see*
AFTERWORLDS; Moon; WISDOM

Incense: *see*
Clouds; Resin; Sacrifice; Smoke

The ibis, after a 19th-dynasty Egyptian papyrus (1295–1186 BCE).

Initiation

Initiation: *see*
Blood; Cave; Crocodile;
DEATH; Honey; Journey;
Key; Labyrinth; Pilgrimage

Intestines: *see*
AFTERWORLDS;
Labyrinth; Soul

Intoxication: *see*
Alcohol; Mead; Soma;
Wine; WISDOM

all religious rites of homage. Sacred literature and iconography suggest that incense was used originally to perfume sacrifices or funeral pyres but was later burned by itself as a purely symbolic offering, sharing the emblematic meaning of smoke as a visible link between earth and sky, humanity and divinity. Frankincense and myrrh, two of the gifts of the Magi after Christ's birth, were highly valued commodities throughout the ancient Middle East.

In the civilizations of Egypt, Persia and the Sumerian-Semitic world, and later in Greece and Rome, these and other forms of incense were burned in daily worship. Farther east, in India, China and Japan, basil and sandalwood were widely used. (Joss-sticks were a pidgin English term for sticks of sandalwood, "joss" being a probable corruption of the Portuguese *deus*, meaning "god".) In Central America, incense, often copal resin, also had fecundity symbolism, invoking rain through associations between smoke and clouds. Resin was itself a symbol of incorruption, and the Old Testament is full of references to the "savour" of scented woods, pleasing to God. The Christian Church, initially wary of the association between incense and the worship of pagan gods or the state funerals of emperors, soon joined what became a common tradition of ceremonial censing. The more recent popularity of incense in the West follows Buddhist traditions of using it as an aid to meditation.

Initiation
An attempt to dramatize the passage from one stage of life or status to another by rites in which the old self dies and a new self is born, usually after trials which may be either physical or purely symbolic. Death symbolism was often marked in ancient initiation rituals.

Interlacing
In art, interlaced motifs symbolize unity and continuity. Celtic art in Ireland is particularly rich in complex interweaving linear designs. Like similar ancient traditions of decoration, these patterns expressed the idea that divine energy was manifested by an endless cosmic vibration, seen most clearly in the motion of waves.

Intestines
A labyrinth symbol and a body organ once thought to be the source of emotion and intuitive or magical knowledge (hence expressions such as "gut feeling").

The idea that positive qualities such as courage or compassion resided in the entrails was widespread. The Egyptians kept the intestines of an eviscerated mummy in an urn, as a repository for the magical powers the soul would need on its perilous journey to the afterworld. Examining animal entrails to divine the future was an Etruscan, and later Roman, pseudo-science.

Intoxication
In ancient and primitive cultures, a symbol of communion with spirits or possession by them. Wine, mead and other intoxicants were sometimes used ritually to achieve ecstatic states in which drinkers were thought to be receptive to divine revelation. Wine-drinking was linked with both fecundity and wisdom. The Greek god Silenus is an example of the drunken sage, also found in Taoist tradition.

Inversion

The dynamics of opposites, which are sometimes interchanged in symbolism so that, for example, the fool alludes to the king, or death (sacrifice) leads to life. The idea of inversion is often symbolized by objects or shapes that form an X – for example, the hourglass or the double triangle.

Iris

Purity, protection, but also, in association with the Virgin Mary, grief – a symbolism based on the sword-shaped leaves of the gladiolus variety. The blue iris often appears in paintings of the Virgin, symbolizing the sharp sorrow of Christ's Passion. It can also refer to the Immaculate Conception. In Japanese folklore, the iris protected houses from harmful influences. The bearded iris is the probable origin of the fleur-de-lis emblem, and in Greece was sacred to the rainbow-goddess Iris.

Iron

Masculine hardness, rigidity, strength – a symbol less of civilization (historically logical though that might be) than of harsh inflexibility and the destructive brutality of war. Although meteoric iron was prized as a celestial metal, especially by the Aztecs, smelted iron was seen in the early years of the Iron Age as an instrument of evil. It was associated by the Greek author Herodotus (*c*.484–*c*.425BCE) with "the hurt of man", by the Greek poet Hesiod (fl. *c*.700BCE) with the grim hardship of contemporary life, and by the Egyptians with the bones of the destructive god Set. This symbolism suggests that iron was traditionally seen as a vulgar metal compared with copper and bronze, let alone gold, all

of which were preferred for the production of religious artifacts in particular. Iron later became a symbol of slavery, by association with fetters, although it can also appear with protective or fertility symbolism, and wrought iron became used widely in church decoration.

Island

Heaven, or haven – a symbolism that appears in countless myths and legends. In Hindu tradition the island is an image of spiritual peace in the chaos of material existence. Symbolically, it is always a magical "elsewhere", a world set apart: sometimes a spiritual goal or centre reserved for elected immortals (the Happy Isles of classical mythology and the mystic Islands of the Blessed in China), sometimes an enchanted place like Prospero's island in Shakespeare's *The Tempest* (*c*.1611) where wrongs are righted. The number of legendary islands inhabited only by women suggest that the island may also be a female symbol of a passive refuge which men both desire and reject. Thus Calypso detained Odysseus on her island for seven years until he grew bored and rejoined the struggle of life. In a similar Polynesian myth, Kae leaves the Island of Women when he discovers that he is growing older while his wife Hine renews her youth by surfing. Most paradisal islands are said to be white, although the Celtic *Tir nan Og* is green.

Ivory

Incorruptibility, purity, rank, protection. The symbolism of lofty aloofness (ivory towers) probably derives from the high status of ivory in almost all ancient cultures, where it was used

Inversion: *see*
Hourglass; Sacrifice; Scapegoat; Triangle; Yin-yang

Iris: *see*
CHASTITY; Fleur-de-lis; FLOWERS; PASSION; Sword

Iron: *see*
Bronze; Chain; Gold; METALS; Meteorite

Island: *see*
AFTERWORLDS; Green; PEACE; White

Ivory: *see*
Virginity; White

Ivy

Ivy: *see*
FIDELITY; Skull; Thyrsus;
Wreath, Garland

to produce some of the most beautiful and durable of all works of art. Walrus ivory was credited with healing powers in the Islamic world, in India and in China, where it was thought to be useful as an antidote for poison. Ranking Chinese officials wore girdle pendants or carried tablets of ivory. Its Christian association with purity and, in particular, with the Virgin Mary are linked to its whiteness.

Ivy

Immortality, and tenacity – of life and of desire. Because ivy wreaths cooled the brow, they were also thought to prevent drunkenness, hence the ivy wreaths worn by the Greek god Dionysus (in Roman myth, Bacchus) and his wine-bibbing retinue. Essentially, ivy embodied the force of plant life in the ancient Middle East and was the attribute of gods of resurrection – Osiris in Egypt, Dionysus in the Greek world and Attis in Phrygia. Ivy twining about the staff of Dionysus symbolized the protective and feminine ardour of his cult-followers. In later Christian art, ivy was a symbol of fidelity as well as eternal life (from the fact that ivy continues to grow on dead trees). Ivy-wreathed skulls in still-life paintings also refer to immortality.

Jackal

An evil-smelling scavenger, symbolizing destruction or evil in India, but in ancient Egypt worshipped as Anubis, the god of embalming, who led souls to judgment. Anubis is shown either as a black jackal or as a jackal-headed human figure.

Jade

Cosmic energy, perfection, virtue, power, authority, incorruptibility, immortality – the lapidary stone of the Chinese Lord of Heaven and of emperors. Chinese tradition associated jade with a whole spectrum of virtues: moral purity, justice, truth, courage, harmony, loyalty and benevolence. The imperial jade seal symbolized a celestial mandate. The many hues of jade, ranging from white through green, blue and red to near-black, allowed religious objects to be distinguished by colour as well as shape, the most famous being the *pi* emblem of the Gate of Heaven (a blue-green disk with a circular perforation) and the *ts'ung* emblem of the earth (a yellow cone within a

rectangular body). Although a solar and yang emblem, the lustrous smoothness of jade linked it also with the soft beauty of female flesh, mucus (jade juice) and sexual intercourse itself (jade play). The hardness and durability of nephrite (the material of most Chinese jade carving until the 18th century, when jadeite sources became more easily available) led by sympathetic magic to the belief that powdered jade could prolong life and that jade amulets could preserve the body after death – hence the number of jade objects found in Chinese tombs. Chinese alchemists believed jade to be a perfected form of stone, and in this sense it replaced gold as an emblem of ultimate purity.

Jade of green nephrite had similarly high value in ancient Mexico, where it was a symbol of the heart and of blood through its association with fertilizing waters. As in China, jade stones were sometimes placed in the mouths of the dead to ensure their resurrection. Among the New Zealand Maori, the beautiful green nephrite *pounamu*, found in the South

Jackal: *see*
AFTERWORLDS

Jade: *see*
Amulet; Blood; Earth;
Gold; Green; Heart; Hole;
VIRTUES; Water; Yin-yang

The jackal-headed god Anubis, from an ancient Egyptian papyrus.

Jaguar: *see*
Crossroads; Earth; Fire,
Flame; Mirror; Moon; Skin;
Transformation

Journey: *see*
AFTERWORLDS; Hero,
Heroine; Initiation;
Pilgrimage

Jujube Tree: *see*
FRUIT; Tree

Island, was used to make the sacred *mere*, a war club symbolizing authority, and the *hei tiki*, a pendant, in the form of a stylized ancestor figure. Nephrite (so called because of the kidney shape of many jade stones) was believed by the Spanish to be a curative for kidney disease.

Jaguar

The dominant animal in the symbolism of Central and South America, linked with divination, royalty, sorcery, the forces of the spirit world, the earth and moon, and fertility. The belief that by transforming themselves into jaguars, shamans could command occult powers, was widespread, and accounts for the many images of snarling jaguar-human hybrids in Mesoamerican art from the Olmec period (*c*.1500–*c*.400BCE) onward. The mirror-eyed jaguar was an awesome incarnation of the supreme Aztec god Tezcatlipoca, whose magic mirror revealed all things from the thoughts of humans to the mysteries of the future. Brazilian mythology made the jaguar a culture hero who brought the gifts of fire and of weaponry. More generally,

A shamanic jaguar. South American shamans believed that the beast possessed occult powers.

reverence of the jaguar was marked by fear. For some, the jaguar was the celestial swallower of the sun and moon, for others a predatory haunter of crossroads. Because the jaguar skins worn by shamans symbolized their power either to protect their own tribe or to destroy another, the jaguar was a dangerous apparition, perhaps the spirit of a dead or living shaman from a hostile village. Essentially, the jaguar is a symbol of unpredictable or capricious power.

Jar *see* **Pitcher**

Jester *see* **Clown**

JEWELS *see panel, opposite*

Journey

A universal symbol of change or evolution, expressed in countless myths and legends in which a hero undertakes a journey bristling with physical and moral trials. In psychology the journey symbolizes both aspiration or longing and the quest for self-discovery. Nearly all religious traditions envisage the soul journeying to the afterlife, and many initiation rites enact a journey that symbolizes the passage from one stage of life to the next. Pilgrimages are symbolic journeys to the spiritual centre.

Jubilee *see* **Numbers**

Jujube Tree

In Taoism, a symbol of pure nourishment, its fruit the food of immortality. The tree also appears in the Islamic paradise and is a symbol of the farthest limits of time and space. Its spiny branches had protective significance in folk superstition.

JEWELS

Minerals of luminous brilliance, embedded in the earth, were a source of wonder to ancients worldwide. In one widespread belief, they were formed from snake saliva. This link helps to explain why some jewel symbolism is similar to that of the serpent: jewels are often emblems of wisdom and, in many folk tales, jewels are found in the foreheads, eyes or mouths of serpentine guardian symbols such as dragons. A Christian parallel is the legend that jewels were scattered through the earth in the fall of the archangel Lucifer (the name given to Satan when he resided in heaven), as fragments of his celestial light. Alternatively their origin is that they are evidence of divine energy, working in the darkness of the earth to produce from dull stone perfected jewels of light. In Jungian psychology, jewels symbolize self-knowledge won from the unconscious – a not dissimilar idea.

In addition to their obvious meaning of precious things, jewels (a word derived from Latin through French for "play things") have always been symbols of spiritual illumination, purity, refinement, superiority, durability, with magical powers of healing and protection. In Eastern religion, they embody the treasures of spiritual knowledge, or divine union (the jewel in the lotus). In Buddhism the *tiratna* ("three jewels") are the Buddha, the *Dharma* (truth) and the Sangha (Buddhist saints). Jewels are linked with Vishnu in Hinduism; faith, knowledge and right conduct in Jainism; compassion and wisdom in Japan; truth in Judaism (12 jewels in the breastplate of the High Priest); and intellect and incorruptibility in Islam.

Specific virtues have been ascribed to different stones (see table). Some correspondences are based on colour – notably jet, one of very few stones that are associated with mourning, but thought also to be particularly protective against the evil eye because it reflects light. Reflective or transparent stones are associated with divination; red stones with ardour or vitality (and, in the case of the carbuncle, war).

JEWELS: *see*
Amber; Amethyst; Black; COLOURS; Coral; Crystal; Devils; Diamond; Dragon; Emerald; Jade; Lapis lazuli; Light; Lotus; Pearl; Red; Ruby; Sapphire; Snake; Turquoise; VIRTUES; WISDOM; Zodiac

Virtue/Fortune	Jewel
Courage	agate, carnelian, jade, ruby, turquoise
Fertility	jasper
Fidelity	diamond, emerald, garnet, hyacinth, opal, topaz
Friendship	carnelian, lodestone, peridot, ruby, topaz, tourmeline
Joy	chrysoprase, jasper
Longevity	amber, catseye, diamond, jade, ruby
Love, passion	carbuncle, garnet, lapis lazuli, moonstone, ruby
Purity, chastity	crystal, diamond, jade, pearl, sapphire
Royalty, power	diamond, jade, ruby, sapphire
Sobriety	amethyst
Truth, honesty, sincerity	diamond, jade, lodestone, onyx, sapphire
Wisdom	chrysolite, diamond, jade, topaz, zircon
Youth	aquamarine, beryl, emerald

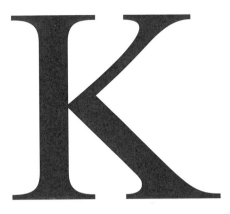

K

*St Peter holding the key
to the gates of Heaven.
A detail after* The
Dormition of the
Virgin *(13th-century
stone relief, Notre
Dame, Paris).*

Ka

The Egyptian symbol of the divine
creative energy, as it is expressed
through the personality of an individual and as it survives the person's
death. Funerary statues were believed
to embody the *ka* of the person whom
they represented.

Kaaba

The cube-shaped building at the heart
of Mecca. In Islamic faith it symbolizes the spiritual centre of the world,
the origin of civilization, stability,
totality and perfection. Pilgrims circumambulate the Kaaba seven times
and kiss the Black Stone at one corner
– a meteorite said to have been given
to Abraham by the archangel Gabriel.

Karashishi

Symbols of strength and courage, a
pair of chow-faced "lions" that guard
Buddhist temples in Japan. The male
has his mouth open, but is not terrifying. The stylized form is based on sec-
ond-hand Chinese contact with the
lion. The name "dogs of Buddha" is
an apt description.

Karma

The Vedic and Hindu term for retributive destiny; deeds or misdeeds in one
life lead inevitably to good or bad
consequences in the next. Karma,
which has been described as a moral
balance sheet, links the actions of the
individual with the forces of cause
and effect in the universe.

Key

Authority, power of choice, entry,
freedom of action, knowledge, initiation. Gold and silver keys, diagonally
crossed, are a papal emblem of
authority, the symbolic "keys of the
kingdom of heaven" which Christ
conferred on Peter. In Roman tradition, keys were similarly held in the
left hand of Janus, the guardian of
doors and gates, who was believed to
control the passage from day to night
and from winter to summer. Although
keys can lock as well as unlock, they
are nearly always visual symbols of
access, liberation or, in initiations,
progress from one stage of life to the
next (hence formerly and formally the
"key of the door" to adulthood at 21).

The Egyptian *ankh*, a key-like cross, symbolizes passage to the afterlife. Keys are often emblems of office or of the freedom of a city. They were symbols of prosperity in Japan, signifying the keys to the rice granary.

King

Often a symbol of divinely sanctioned power as well as of absolute temporal authority over a tribe, nation or region. The stronger the king's symbolic link with supernatural forces, the more crucial became his leadership qualities, intelligence and health – authority going hand in hand with responsibility for the happiness and health of his subjects. Hence ancient sacrifices of the king (or a scapegoat representing the king) when countries were overtaken by plagues or crop failures. Kings were symbols of fecundity, wisdom, military success and divine favour. The deification of emperors in Rome followed older traditions in which kings were symbolic delegates of the sun, a notion as alive in 17th-century France (when the Sun King, Louis XIV, guaranteed the eminence of his country) as it was in the empire of the Incas. Louis XVI was executed as a symbolic hostage to France's declining fortunes during the French Revolution two centuries later. In constitutional monarchies, despite ritual anointings and coronations, the ancient symbolism of kings as archetypes of human perfectibility, accountable to God rather than to the people, has been undercut, making their failings less dismaying. Traditional symbols of kingship include the sun (the queen is symbolized by the moon), gold, jade, the rod or sceptre, the throne or dais, the orb, the ruby, the sword and arrows.

Kingfisher

Fidelity, peace – a symbol of grace, nobility and conjugal devotion in China, and in Greece associated with mournful tranquillity through the myth of Alcyone (or Halcyone), in which she and her husband Ceyx were turned into kingfishers by the god Zeus. As kingfishers were thought to nest at sea, Alcyone's father, Aeolus, the god of wind, kept the waters calm for seven days each year so that his daughter could incubate her eggs.

Kiss

Beyond its obvious personal significance, the kiss is a religious symbol of spiritual union – the meaning behind the custom of kissing church images of saints.

Kissing someone's hand was a medieval sign of homage. The feet or robes of kings were kissed both in homage and in the belief that part of their sanctity might transfer itself.

Knee

Kneeling or bending the knee is a signal of submission and supplication in all cultures, or of humility and homage, as in kneeling to pray, or curtseying to royalty.

Knife

A ritual instrument of sacrifice, circumcision and martydom, the knife is usually a destructive symbol, particularly in the hands of Hindu divinities, but in Buddhism it can signify severance from the ties of materialism. The knife is the attribute of several martyred Christian saints, including St Bartholomew, who is said to have been flayed alive. Freud associated the knife with the phallus in his interpretation of dreams.

Kaaba: *see* Centaur; Circumambulation; Cube; Meteorite

Karashishi: *see* Dog; Lion

Key: *see* AFTERWORLDS; Ankh; Gold; Initiation; Silver

King: *see* Arrow; Clown; Crown; Globe, Orb; Gold; Jade; Rod; Ruby; Sacrifice; Scapegoat; Sceptre; Sun; Sword; Throne; WISDOM

Kingfisher: *see* Birds; FIDELITY

Kiss: *see* Hand

Knife: *see* Circumcision; Phallus; Sacrifice

Knight: *see*
Black; Castle; Grail; Green;
Red; White

Knot: *see*
Bonds; LONGEVITY

Kundalini: *see*
Chakra; Snake; Wheel

*Lancelot, the most
famous knight of
Arthurian legend, from
a stained-glass window
by William Morris
(1834–96).*

*The open knot – with
no beginning or end,
it represents longevity
and immortality.*

Knight

In medieval legend, a symbol of mastery of the arts of horsemanship and weaponry, the virtues of loyalty and honourable service, and the sublimation of brutish desires. Knighthood set before privileged young men a symbolic ideal and generated a vast literature of chivalry. In the colour symbolism of knighthood, the Green Knight is the questing neophyte; the White Knight the chaste, conquering hero; the Red Knight the battle-tested warrior at spiritual maturity. The Black Knight is a more ambivalent figure, representing either evil or the anonymity of the man who has austerely withdrawn to expiate his sins. The symbolism of knighthood as a mission was taken up by St Ignatius Loyola who founded the Jesuits as an order dedicated to holy chivalry. The Knight Errant, by contrast, wanders in the vague hope that a worthy mission will present itself.

Knot

Tight knots are symbols of union, fixation or blockage, whereas knots shown as a loose, interwoven pattern represent infinity or longevity (a line without beginning or end). Incorporating ideas of tying or untying, capture or release, knot symbolism is remarkably complex. Curious fishermen's superstitions in northern Europe and Scotland attach magic significance to knots tied in pocket handkerchiefs or cords, thought to influence wind and weather. The Roman prohibition on wearing knotted garments in the temple of Juno Lucina, goddess of childbirth, reflects similar belief in sympathetic magic – knots representing blockage in a context where release was crucial. "Tying

the knot", a Victorian synonym for marriage, was a popular motif in paintings of the Roman god of love Cupid. Union is also the symbolism of the knotted cord worn by Brahmins, binding them to Brahma in the same way as the thrice-knotted cord of the Franciscan friar binds him to his vows of poverty, celibacy and obedience.

Alternatively, knots often had protective symbolism, based probably on the idea of frustration. Thus, in Islam, beards were knotted to baffle demons, whereas in the presence of goodness knots were forbidden – as in the mosque at Mecca. The Gordian knot exemplified the principle of frustration. By slashing it apart, Alexander the Great found a short-term solution but never completed the conquest of Asia predicted for the man who could untie the knot. The moral lesson Buddhism drew from this famous incident was that patience, not violence, unravels knots, specifically the knots tying humanity to the round of material existence. The open-weave knot pattern is one of the eight emblems of good luck in Chinese Buddhism. Similar ornamental patterns representing continuity appear in Hindu and Celtic art.

Kundalini

The Hindu image of latent or "earth" energy, symbolically represented by a sleeping serpent coiled at the base of the spine. Through spiritual discipline, the *kundalini* is roused so that a serpentine flow of life force moves upward through the etheric body via a series of *chakras* (wheels). These elements of the self, if properly developed, pass it on in steadily purified form to the crown *chakra*, there to blaze out as enlightenment.

Labarum *see* **Chi-Rho**

Labyrinth

A structure or pattern as enigmatic as its symbolism – capable of many twists of meaning. Its ambivalence dates from the mysteries, terrors and protective advantages of the cave systems in which humans once dwelt. The earliest known artificial labyrinths, in Egypt and Etruria (central Italy), were built to keep the tombs of kings inviolate. According to the Greek author Herodotus (*c*.484–*c*.425BCE), the greatest of these architectural labyrinths, near Lake Moeris in Egypt, had a baffling 3,000 chambers and 12 courts. Early labyrinthine decorations on Greek houses seem to have taken up this protective symbolism in motifs designed to confuse evil spirits. Remarkable plumbing conduits at the Minoan palace of Knossos may have been the origin of the legendary Cretan labyrinth in which Theseus killed the Minotaur. The usual reading of this influential myth is that Theseus, who is a symbol of the saviour–hero, overcame the brutish aspects of his own character as well as the power of Minos. This meshes with the major religious and psychological meanings of passing through a labyrinth – that it represents an initiation, a symbolic return to the womb, a "death" leading to rebirth, the discovery of a spiritual centre, the laborious and often perplexing process of self-discovery.

A more obvious meaning of the labyrinth is that it symbolizes the manifold and difficult choices of life – the meaning of the labyrinth pattern used as a heraldic device by the Mantua house of Gonzaga, accompanied by the motto: "Perhaps yes, perhaps no". Labyrinths formed by garden hedges turned this problem into a game. But many labyrinths are unicursal, having no traps but leading sinuously along a single path. These were often used in early temples as initiation routes or more widely for religious dances that imitated the weaving paths of the sun or planets. They reappeared in patterns on the floors of medieval Christian churches

Labyrinth: *see*
Cave; Dance; Initiation;
Pilgrimage

Lake: *see*
Mirror; Sea; Water

Lamb: *see*
Banner; Blood; Book;
CROSS; Fire, Flame; Halo;
Lion; Sacrifice; Sheep;
Shepherd

Lameness: *see*
Smith

as "roads to Jerusalem" – paths symbolizing pilgrimage. At Chartres cathedral, France, penitents shuffled 650 feet (200 m) on their knees along such a circular maze within an area only 40 feet (12 m) in diameter.

Lake

An occult medium in mythology and legend, linked particularly in the Arthurian cycle with female powers of enchantment, through the feminine symbolism of water, and more widely with the abyss, death and the mysterious night passage of the sun (from observation of its apparent disappearances beneath the water). This was enacted in Egypt by the priests of Karnak on an artificial lake. In Greek myth, the god Dionysus descended to the underworld through a lake. In effect a two-way mirror symbol, the still water of a lake suggested both contemplation from above and observation from below by spirits thought to inhabit jewelled palaces. The Celtic custom of casting trophies to these spirits explains the connection between the Lady of the Lake and the sword Excalibur in Arthurian legend.

Lamb

Purity, sacrifice, renewal, redemption, innocence, gentleness, humility, patience – the earliest symbol of Christ. Emblematic use of the lamb in Christian iconography and scripture extended an already long tradition in which newborn lambs were sacrificed as symbols of spring renewal among the sheep-herding societies of the Middle East. The blood of the paschal lamb was, from the time of the Passover, a particular mark of Hebrew salvation, and prophets such as Isaiah described the coming

Messiah as a lamb. It was with this meaning that John the Baptist proclaimed Jesus "the Lamb of God, which taketh away the sin of the world". John can appear in art holding a lamb. Christ also sometimes carries a lamb in his role as the Good Shepherd. The *Agnus Dei* ("Lamb of God") is usually shown with a cross or cruciform halo, or with a banner (representing victory over death). In early Christian paintings, the disciples can appear as 12 sheep with the lamb in their midst. A lamb with a book or seals refers to the Christ of Revelation, also described as a lamb with seven horns and seven eyes (seven spirits of God). The judgmental lamb of the Apocalypse is capable of wrath, apparently at odds with the lamb's generally meek symbolism. In its triumphal aspect, some have seen solar symbolism, the lamb interchanging with its opposite, the solar lion. However, the lion is also a Messiah symbol. There are semantic links between the lamb and Agni, the Vedic god of fire. Iconographic representations of Christ as a lamb were eventually frowned on by the Eastern Church, perhaps to limit this kind of confusion. The lamb is also an important sacrificial and redemptive symbol in the Islamic rites of Ramadan.

Lameness

In some contexts, a warning symbol of divine power, a mark left upon the body of a demiurge or hero who has come too close to competing with a god on equal terms. Thus Jacob was made lame when he wrestled mightily with the angel of God in Genesis. The Greek smith-god Hephaestus (in Roman myth, Vulcan) was lamed in his encounter with Zeus (Jupiter).

Smith gods, masters of the creative secrets of fire, are nearly always represented in myth as men who have been maimed (again, such as Hephaestus).

Lamp, Lantern

Spirit, truth, intelligence, life itself – symbolic qualities all associated with light. The Arabian Nights tale of Aladdin who allowed his magic lamp to rust after it had brought him riches is an allegory of neglecting the spiritual side of life. In Buddhism and Hinduism, the lamp, as a symbol of life, represents continuity from one state of existence to the next. In shrines or on altars, lamps symbolize both devotion and the presence of divinity. In art, they personify Vigilance and also Night. The lamp is also a symbol of maternal care, associated with children and the sick. Florence Nightingale was called the Lady with the Lamp. The lantern (as an enclosed light) has more protective symbolism – the meaning of the Chinese magic lantern, supposedly able to ward off carp demons. The lantern was also used to cast propitious shadows. The Cynic philosopher Diogenes (4th–3rd centuries BCE) famously went about with a lantern in daylight looking for an honest man.

Lance

The shock weapon of the cavalry until the 20th century. It is associated with chivalry and Christ's Passion. Like the spear it symbolizes masculine, phallic and earthly power. Its sacrificial link with the Grail derives from a legend that the spear that was used to pierce Christ's side after his death on the Cross was a lance carried by a Roman centurion, Longinus, and that it was he who exclaimed, "Truly this man was the son of God." Longinus became the patron saint of Mantua, a city to which he was said to have returned carrying drops of holy blood. His lance, like that of the Greek Achilles, was credited with healing power. The broken lance is an attribute of St George, and symbolizes the experienced soldier. As an emblem of victory, the lance is an attribute in India of the war-god Indra. The term "freelance" came from medieval companies of knights whose lances were for hire.

Lapis lazuli

A deep blue stone with celestial symbolism, particularly in Mesopotamia where it was used in temples to depict the starry night sky, and in Mexico. Its association with divine forces helps to explain its popularity as an ornamental stone in the ancient world where it was thought to have talismanic value. It was a love emblem in Greece, an attribute of the goddess Aphrodite, and augured success in China where it was linked with clear-sightedness. Lapis lazuli was precious not only as a stone but as an early paint base for the colour ultramarine.

Larch

As one of the hardest and most durable of all pines (larch piles support much of Venice), a symbol of immortality. Larch was the World Tree of Siberia and can have funerary symbolism as an emblem of rebirth.

Laurel

Victory, peace, purification, protection, divination, secret knowledge and immortality. The aromatic bay species of laurel was the crowning emblem of the Greco-Roman world, not only for

Lamp, Lantern: *see* Candle; Fire, Flame; Light; Torch; VIGILANCE

Lance: *see* Blood; Grail; PASSION; Phallus; Spear

Lapis lazuli: *see* Blue; JEWELS; Sky

Larch: *see* Tree

Laurel: *see* Crown; Dragon; Hair; Lightning; PEACE; Tree; VICTORY; VIRTUES; Wreath, Garland

Lead: *see*
Alchemy; Chimera;
METALS

Leaf: *see*
Green

Left and Right: *see*
Black; Hand; Yin-yang

Leopard: *see*
ANIMALS; Chariot;
Devils; Eye; Lion; SEVEN
DEADLY SINS; Skin

warriors but for poets, through its association with the god Apollo. He is said to have purified himself with it in the groves of Tempe in Thessaly after slaying the Python at Delphi. The priestess of his Delphic cult, Pythia, chewed laurel before giving her prophecies. It was thought to deter pestilence and lightning, a superstition believed by the Emperor Tiberius who used to reach for his laurel wreath during thunderstorms. Associated with many deities including Dionysus (Bacchus), Zeus (Jupiter), Hera (Juno) and Artemis (Diana), laurel was an emblem of truce or peace as well as of triumph. A secondary symbolism of chastity derived from the myth that the nymph Daphne was turned into a laurel as she fled Apollo's lust. Laurel had talismanic significance in North Africa, and in China appears as the tree beneath which the lunar hare mixes the elixir of immortality. It is a Christian symbol of eternal life.

Lead

The base metal of alchemy, and therefore a metaphor for humanity at the most primitive level of spiritual development. Its more general symbolism of dull heaviness is linked not only to its physical weight but to its ancient association with the god Cronos (Saturn to the Romans). Bellerophon put lead down the throat of the monstrous Chimera, which choked when the metal was melted by the beast's fiery breath, perhaps resulting in the belief that lead had protective power.

Leaf

A Chinese emblem of happiness. Young leaves more generally share the symbolism given to green vegetation.

Leaves often symbolize countless human lives – and their brevity. The falling leaves of autumn, an ancient metaphor for mortality, became a 20th-century cinematic cliché for the passage of time.

Left and Right

Western and some other traditions assign more symbolic value to the right than to the left, probably for no better reason than that most people are right-handed. With few exceptions, the right is associated with precedence, action and the solar, male principle, the left with secondary position, weakness, passivity and the lunar, female principle. As the word *sinister* suggests, for the Romans the left was linked with bad luck. Preference for the right is particularly marked in Christian symbolism, the left often being stigmatized as the dark side of sinners and black magic. In China the concept of yin-yang harmony made for a less rigid division of symbolic values. If anything, the left is usually given precedence, as in Japan: it is associated with honour, nobility, wisdom and the male, celestial and solar principle, while the right is limited with lunar and female qualities. Attempts to explain the symbolism of left and right in relation to the movement of the sun or stars founder on this inconsistency and suggest that attitudes are based simply on custom. The modern political significance of "left-wing" and "right-wing" follows a precedent of 1789 when reformers sat on the left, reactionaries on the right in the first French National Assembly.

Leopard

Ferocity, pitiless force, courage, pride, speed – an English battle emblem, but associated with evil both in ancient Egypt and in Christian tradition. Leopard skins worn by shamans in Asia and Africa symbolized their mastery over the demonic powers of this animal. In Egypt it was equated with Set; priests dressed in leopard skins at funerary rites to demonstrate their ability to protect the dead from his malevolent influence. In the classical world, the leopard was an attribute of the god Dionysus (in Roman myth, Bacchus) as creator–destroyer, and two leopards draw the chariot of Bacchus in art. The animal's spots were associated with the legendary multi-eyed Argus. Negative Christian symbolism was based on the vision of a monstrous leopard in Daniel 7:6 and, more influentially, on Jeremiah's account of the Lord's telling him that evil-doers could change their ways no more easily than a leopard could change its spots (13:23). Hence the link between the leopard and Satan, sin and lust. The animal stood for courage in European heraldry, as well as in China where it also had lunar symbolism. The name "leopard" came from a fabled hybrid between a lion and a panther (the name now applied only to the black leopard or, in America, the puma).

Leviathan

An aquatic monster symbolizing a force of nature that only a super-human power could bring into being or control. Although often taken to mean a whale, the Hebrew word *liviatan* refers to any monster of the deep. Job 41 begins "Can you draw out leviathan with a fishhook?" and goes on to describe a creature with crocodile features. The symbolism of a creature so fierce that "none dare stir

The Greek god Dionysus riding a leopard, from a mosaic found at Delos in Greece, c.180CE.

him up" derives from Mesopotamian and Phoenician myths in which a hero god struggles to wrest order from a primordial chaos god of the deep. The English philosopher Thomas Hobbes (1588–1679), in his *Leviathan*, used the biblical monster as a symbol for the absolute state to which the individual is subordinate.

LIBERTY *see panel on p.122*

Light

A metaphor for the spirit and for divinity itself, symbolizing inner enlightenment and the presence of a cosmic power of ultimate goodness and truth. By extension, light is a symbol of immortality, eternity, paradise, pure being, revelation, wisdom, intellect, majesty, joy and life itself. Although most philosophical traditions recognize light and darkness as a necessary duality, major religions of the Near East saw them as ethically contending forces, kingdoms of good and evil, as in Zoroastrianism and Manicheanism. "Light" became synonymous with "good" or "God".

Leviathan: *see*
BEASTS OF FABLE;
Crocodile; Whale

Light: *see*
AFTERWORLDS; Aureole;
Candle; Devils; Halo; Lamp,
Lantern; Moon; Nimbus;
Star; Sun; WISDOM

Leviathan in the form of a sea snake, from a 12th-century English representation.

Lightning

LIBERTY: *see individual names*

LIBERTY

Liberty is usually represented in art by a woman holding a sceptre and wearing a Phrygian cap – a reference to the Roman custom of presenting caps to freed slaves. The cap became a popular emblem of the French Revolution, as in Delacroix's painting *Liberty Leading the People* (1830). Light itself is a symbol of liberation (from darkness), and Bartholdi's Statue of Liberty, New York, holds a torch. Other symbols of liberty or freedom include the acrobat, bell, broken chains, cat, eagle, falcon, fish, long hair and wings.

Lightning: *see* Arm; Arrow; Axe; Eye; Fire, Flame; Hammer; Phallus; Rain; Sceptre; SEASONS; Thunder; Trident; Zigzag

Thus, Christ is the Light of the World; Gautama Buddha the Light of Asia; Krishna the Lord of Light; Allah the Light of Heaven and Earth. In Judeo-Christian tradition, eternal light is the reward of the virtuous. Genesis attempts to draw a clear distinction between divine light and the more ephemeral physical light of the sun, moon or stars, created only later. Candlemas, on February 2, took over the symbolism of more ancient pagan rites in which torches or candles were lit to invoke fertility and the spring renewal of crops. In symbolism generally, the sun's light is linked with spiritual knowledge, the reflected light of the moon with rational knowledge.

Lightning

Universally a manifestation of divine wrath, power or fertilizing potency. Lightning was variously seen as the symbolic or actual weapon, arm or phallus of the supreme male sky god – or of his auxiliary. Alternatively, it was the blinding light of his eye – in Native American tradition the wink of Thunderbird, the great creator spirit; in India the flashing third eye of Shiva, the light of truth. Lightning is a rare example of a phenomenon symbolically linked with both fire and water because it often preceded rain. As both creator and destroyer, it was viewed with a mixture of fear and reverence. Places struck by lightning became sacred ground, and people it touched bore the mark of God if they survived, or were thought to be translated instantly to heaven if they died. In Mexico, for example, Tlaloc used lightning to despatch souls to the Aztec heaven. The classical master of lightning was Zeus (in Roman myth, Jupiter). Greek origin myths about Dionysus ascribe the first of his two births to a lightning flash from Zeus.

The phallic symbolism of lightning is particularly overt among the Australian Aboriginals where it symbolized a cosmic erect penis. Jewish tradition associated lightning with revelation, as in Exodus (19:16–18) where thunder and lightning announce the presence of God to Moses on Mt Sinai. Lightning was widely thought to be an augury, significant enough in Rome to cause public assemblies to close for the day. Striking from the left (the lucky east in relation to the position in which the Roman augur sat) lightning was a sign of Jupiter's favour; the Greeks took the reverse view. In iconography, lightning is represented by the flashing axe, the forked trident, the sceptre, the hammer, the arrow and graphically by the zigzag. It was sometimes personified by a giant bird of prey not only in North America, but also in southern Africa, in myths of the Lightning Bird.

Lily

One of the most ambiguous of all flower symbols – identified with Christian piety, purity and innocence, but having associations with fecundity and erotic love in older traditions through its phallic pistil and fragrance. The lily found in Christian art is the white lily named the "Madonna" in the 19th century after its association with the Virgin Mary (it was also the attribute of her husband Joseph and of many saints). It is often shown in a vase or is held by the archangel Gabriel in Annunciation paintings. The beautiful lily of the valley has the same symbolism. As a favourite garden flower of antiquity, the lily was fabled to have sprung from the milk of the Greek goddess Hera and was linked with fecundity not only in Greece but also in Egypt and the Middle East generally, where it was a popular decorative motif. Lilies symbolized prosperity and royalty in Byzantium, and this, rather than the link with purity, may have been the original reason for the choice of the fleur-de-lis as the emblem of France. Its emblematic significance for Christian saints is taken largely from the Sermon on the Mount in which Jesus used the glorious "lilies of the field" as an allegory of how God provided for those who renounced the pursuit of wealth (Matthew 6:28–30); however, these flowers are now thought to have been poppy anemones. Another biblical reference (Songs 1:2) compares the lips of the beloved to lilies, presumably red ones. The white lily can sometimes symbolize death as well as purity, and is often seen as a portent of death. The lotus, or "water lily", is a botanically different flower with a much wider symbolism.

Linden, Lime

A tree of friendship or community, a symbolism going back to the classical world but relevant particularly in Germany where the linden (or European lime) was a popular focus of village life, as it is in some French villages. Its gentle and beneficial associations may be linked with the honey made from its flowers.

Lingam

The male generative force in nature, symbolized in Hindu art and architecture by a stylized phallus representing the god Shiva as divine procreator. In the cave of Elephanta at Bombay, the lingam – a thick, smooth cone of black stone – was the focus of circumambulation rituals, indicating its role as an axial symbol as well as a phallic one, somewhat like the classical *omphalos*. In one myth, Shiva's lingam appears as a pillar of light, the upper and lower limits of which cannot be found by Brahma as a wild goose or Vishnu as a boar – proof of Shiva's power. Although essentially a virility symbol, the lingam sometimes appears with a stone circle at its base representing the *yoni* (vulva) as a symbol of the sacred marriage of male and female. The Chinese *keui*, a jade oblong with a triangular end, has similar meaning. The lingam entwined by a snake refers to the yogic *kundalini*, the serpentine flow of vital energy.

Lion

Divine solar power, royal authority, strength, courage, wisdom, justice, protection – but also cruelty, devouring ferocity and death. The lion is an image of the great and terrible in nature, a commanding personification of the sun itself. As it is actually a

Lily: *see*
Archangels; Fleur-de-lis; Iris; Lotus; Milk; Milky Way; Vase; White

Linden, Lime: *see*
Honey; Tree

Lingam: *see*
Boar; Circumambulation; Cone; Goose; Jade; Kundalini; Omphalos; Phallus; Pillar; Snake; Triangle; Vulva

The Shiva lingam, from a red sandstone sculpture in a 15th-century temple.

Lion

Lion: *see*
AFTERWORLDS; Ball;
Boar; Bull; DEATH;
Dragon; Egg; Fountain;
Gold; Griffin; Horse; Lamb;
Mask; Rays; Ring; Sea;
Skin; Snake; Sun; Torii;
VIGILANCE; VIRTUES;
Void; Wings; WISDOM;
Zodiac

shade-loving, mainly nocturnal hunter, its solar associations were based less on observation of its nature than on the iconographic splendour of its golden coat, radiant mane and sheer physical presence. It appears as both destroyer and saviour, invested with a godlike dualism and capable of representing evil and its destruction. Its aggressive–defensive symbolism is captured in a verse from the book of Joel (3:16): "The Lord roars from Zion, and utters his voice from Jerusalem, and the heavens and the earth shake. But the Lord is the refuge for his people, a stronghold for the people of Israel." The theme of the royal lion hunt, common in the early iconography of western Asia, symbolized death and resurrection – the continuation of life ensured by the killing of a godlike animal, linked both with the supreme Mesopotamian god Marduk and with the fertility goddess Ishtar. In some carvings the lion seems to offer itself for sacrifice and the king's own divinity is suggested by his fearless grasp of the animal's paws – an archetypal image of human courage matching lion courage.

In Egypt, the avenging goddess Sekhmet, represented as a lioness, symbolized the ferocious heat of the sun, but the lion was also a guide to the underworld, through which the sun was believed to pass each night. Hence the lion-footed tombs found in Egypt and images of mummies carried on lions' backs. Lions were guardians of the dead in Greece (identified with Dionysus, Phoebus, Artemis and Cybele) and of palaces, thrones, shrines, doors or gateways generally – as at Mycenae. The griffin, a lion–eagle hybrid, was an alternative guardian symbol, especially where

lions were known mainly from traveller's tales. Lion masks or ringed lion door knockers (symbols of eternity) were common on Egyptian doors. Egypt was also the origin of lion-headed water spouts or fountains, symbolizing the fertile flooding of the Nile when the sun was in the Zodiacal sign Leo (July 23–August 22).

Carvings and seals of a lion devouring a bull, horse or boar represent the complementary opposites of life and death, sun and moon, summer and winter – a symbolic theme that appears in Africa and Asia as well as the Middle East. Victory over death is symbolized by the wearing of lion skins and by myths like that in which Herakles slays the Nemean lion or Samson tears one limb from limb. Alternatively, in Judaism the lion of death is overcome by prayer (Daniel in the lion's den). The lion was the emblem of the strength of Judah and came to be linked with salvation as well as death, and therefore with the Messiah. Hence the otherwise surprising passage in Revelation (5:5–6) where the Lion of Judah becomes the redeeming Lamb (Christ). Christian calmness in the face of death is expressed in a number of symbolic stories involving lions, including the legend that St Jerome removed a thorn from a lion's paw. Links between the lion and Resurrection were strengthened by the early Christian legend that cubs (blind for the first week) were born dead and brought to life by their fathers after three days. The lion could thus appear in Christian art either as adversary or as attribute. St Mark, whose gospel stresses Christ's majesty, is identified as a winged lion (the emblem of Venice). Less ambivalently, the lion is

The biblical Samson overcoming a lion, from a 12th-century Austrian altarpiece.

widely a symbol of royal power and dominion, military victory, bravery, vigilance and fortitude, a virtue personified in art by a woman grappling with a lion. Leaders who identified with the lion include Muhammad's son-in-law Ali, the "Lion of Allah" symbolizing the destruction of evil in Islam; Richard I "the Lionheart", (lions were often used as funerary emblems of slain Crusaders); and the emperors of Ethiopia, who took the Lion of Judah as the national symbol. The lion was a royal emblem of Scotland and of England, and became a dominant symbol of British imperial power in the 19th century. The gentle Buddha is a "lion among men", because the lion in India symbolized courage and wisdom, religious zeal and defence of the law. It was a Hindu avatar of Vishnu, sometimes shown as a man–lion hybrid and the companion of the demon-slaying warrior goddess Durga. The lion was also an emblem of the great Ashoka who unified India

in the 3rd century BCE. In China and Japan the lion is protective, lion-mask dances having the same frightening purpose as dragon dances. Lions often appear in Asian art with a ball, variously a symbol of the sun, the cosmic egg or the cosmic void.

Lizard

The lizard shares some of the symbolism of its close relative the snake, especially as an emblem of resurrection (deriving from its regular skin-shedding). This may explain its use as a motif on Christian candle-holders. It was a beneficial emblem in Egypt and the classical world, sometimes linked with wisdom. It became an attribute of Logic in art. Lizards appear in Maori myth as guardian monsters. In Aboriginal, Melanesian and African folklore and decoration they are culture heroes or ancestor figures.

LONGEVITY

A preoccupation in the symbol system of the Chinese. Trees or their emblematic fruits are, not unexpectedly, the most common objects chosen to symbolize longevity, notably the apple, bamboo, cedar, citron, cypress, myrtle, oak, palm, peach, pear, pine and plum. The colour green and stones such as jade, diamond and ruby, and rock itself, also represent longevity. Other emblems include a basket of flowers, two Chinese bats, the carp, chrysanthemum, crane, deer, dove, elephant, hare, knot, marigold, mushroom, phoenix, stork, toad, tortoise and turtle. Many of these can also symbolize immortality.

Lizard: *see* Candle; Salamander; Snake; WISDOM

LONGEVITY: *see individual names*

Loom: *see*
Spider; Weaving; Web

Lotus: *see*
Blue; Chakra; Eight; Fire,
Flame; FLOWERS; Gold;
Heart; Navel; Nirvana; Soul;
Sun; Virginity; Vulva;
Water; Wheel; White;
Wreath, Garland

*The Hindu god
Brahma, seated in a
lotus flower.*

Loom

An instrument of cosmic creation and the structure upon which individual destiny is woven – an ancient symbolism encapsulated in the Greek myth of Arachne who was changed into a spider by the goddess Athene, jealous of her skill at the godlike craft of weaving. Another figure often depicted at a loom is the mythical Penelope, who, to cheat time, unpicked each night what she had woven by day to keep suitors at bay during the absence of her husband, Odysseus.

Lotus

A flower with prolific symbolic meanings, particularly in the traditions of Egypt, India, China and Japan. Its unique importance is based both on the decorative beauty of its radiating petals and on an analogy between them and an idealized form of the vulva as the divine source of life. By extension, the lotus came to symbolize, among other things, birth and rebirth, as well as the origin of cosmic life, and the creator gods or the sun and sun gods. It also represented human spiritual growth from the folded bud of the heart, and the soul's potential to attain divine perfection.

In Egypt, the lotus, rising from bottom mud as a water lily to unfold its immaculate petals to the sun, suggested the glory of the sun's own emergence from the primeval slime. A metaphor for creation, it was a votive symbol not only of solar and fecundity gods and goddesses but of the Upper Nile as the giver of life. The blue lily, more sacred than the white, was an emblem of modesty and cleanliness in Egypt and also Chinese Buddhism. Lotus wreaths for the dead took up the symbolism of rebirth.

As a decorative funerary motif symbolizing resurrection, the lotus appeared in ancient Greece and Italy, and in western Asia where decorative Egyptian lotus forms were the origin of the Ionic order of capitals in architecture. (The "lotus-eaters" of Greek myth, rapt in blissful oblivion, have nothing to do with the sacred flower: the fermented juice of a North African bush lotus is the probable source of this Homeric reference.)

In Hinduism the sacred lotus grew from the navel of Vishnu as he rested on the waters, giving birth to Brahma (a representation of spiritual growth). The lotus is a symbol of what is divine or immortal in humanity, and is almost a synonym of perfection.

Indian iconography, both Hindu and Buddhist, is full of gods (or, in Buddhism, Bodhisattvas) sitting cross-legged in the centre of flame-like lotus petals. The lotus is the attribute of sun and fire gods, and the leading symbol of Padma, the consort of the god Vishnu. It symbolizes the realization of inner potential or, in Tantric and yogic traditions, the ability to harness the flow of energy moving through the *chakra*s (often depicted as wheel-like lotuses) flowering as the thousand-petalled lotus of enlightenment at the top of the skull. A parallel concept is the "golden blossom" of Chinese Taoism, a Buddhist-inspired tradition in which the lotus is again a symbol of spiritual unfolding.

Veneration of the lotus is equally, if not more, marked in Indian, Tibetan, Chinese and Japanese Buddhism. The lotus represents the nature of the Buddha himself and is the aspirational image of the spiritual flowering of knowledge that can lead to the state of nirvana. The sexual imagery of the lotus, most marked in Tantric Buddhism, sometimes combines the male stem and female blossom as a symbol of spiritual union and harmony. This is the "jewel in the lotus", invoked in the mantra *Om mani padme hum*.

Echoing Egyptian symbolism of the birth of gods from the pure vulva of the lotus, the father of Tibetan Buddhism, Padmasambhava, was said to have been discovered at the heart of a lotus in his eighth year. Chinese Buddhism, in which the lotus is one of the Eight Auspicious Signs, added further symbolic associations – rectitude, firmness, conjugal harmony and prosperity – especially the blessing of many children, represented by a boy holding a lotus. Sacred and profane symbolism mix in Chinese tradition – a courtesan was known as a "golden lotus", although the lotus is more generally linked with purity, even virginity, and is a Japanese emblem of incorruptible morality. It appears also in Mayan iconography, apparently with rebirth symbolism.

Lozenge

Graphically, a symbol of the life matrix, the vulva, fertility and, in some contexts, innocence. It takes on dual imagery when combined with the phallic symbolism of snakes in Native American decorative art. Lozenge shapes appear with fertility symbolism on the jade skirt of the Mexican goddess of rivers and lakes, Chalchiuhtlicue, the consort of the god Tlaloc. In Mali, a half-lozenge shape with a point at the other end was a symbol for a young woman.

In Christian art, the lozenge symbol of fertility goddesses was taken as a virginity symbol in the worship of the Virgin Mary, conventionally shown within a mandorla, also known as the *vesica piscis* ("fish bladder") – a lozenge shape with aureole.

Lute

In Renaissance art, a symbol of the personifications Music and Hearing, and a popular emblem of the lover. Lutes or mandolins with broken strings appear in still lifes as symbols of discord.

In China, the lute was an attribute of the scholar and, in common with many other musical instruments, of harmony – in marriage as well as in government.

Lynx

Vigilance, a symbolism soundly based on the animal's extraordinarily acute vision, superstitiously believed to enable the lynx to see through obstacles and penetrate secrets. The lynx in art represents the sense of sight.

Lyre

Divine harmony, the music of the spheres, the vibration of the cosmos, musical and poetic inspiration, and divination. The lyre is the musical instrument most plausibly linked with classical mythology and, in particular, with Orpheus, whose music charmed wild beasts and stopped rivers in their course. A large version, called the *cithara*, was reputedly made for the god Apollo by Hermes (Mercury in Roman myth).

In art, the lyre is the attribute of Poetry personified, of Erato, the muse of lyric poetry, and of Terpischore, the muse of dance and song. The seven-stringed lyre symbolized the seven planets; a 12-stringed version represented the signs of the Zodiac.

Lozenge: *see* Almond; Aureole; Mandorla; Snake; Virginity; Vulva; Woman

Lute: *see* Music; PEACE

Lynx: *see* VIGILANCE

Lyre: *see* Music; PLANETS; Zodiac

A musician walking with a cithara *(a long lyre), from an ancient Greek vase.*

Mace: *see*
Club; Sceptre

Magpie: *see*
Birds; Marriage; Mirror;
Witchcraft; Yin-yang

Makara: *see*
Crocodile; Fish; Lotus;
Rain; Rainbow; Solstice;
Sun; Zodiac

Mace

An authority symbol. Originally a club-like weapon with flanges to penetrate armour, the mace was later carried by bodyguards and eventually became a purely ceremonial symbol of power. Because it was associated particularly with royal authority in England, the ceremonial mace acquired by the House of Commons in 1649 was a significant emblem of Cromwell's parliament's newly-won right to govern.

Magnet

To the ancients, an impressive symbol of cosmic coherence. Known mainly through the magnetic properties of lodestone, in Egypt the magnet was associated with the power of Horus, the god who regulated the movements of the heavenly bodies. Lodestone was sometimes used as a love charm.

Magpie

Joy, married bliss, sexual happiness – a happy emblem in the traditions of China where the cry of a magpie announced the arrival of friends, but in the West a bird linked with acquisitiveness, mischievous chatter and even witchcraft. The magpie's fondness for bright objects seems to be the origin of its association with a Chinese custom by which a parted husband and wife break a mirror and keep half each. If either is unfaithful, their half of the mirror will turn into a magpie and fly back to tell the other. A yang emblem and sacred bird of the Manchus, the magpie often appears on Chinese greeting cards.

Makara

A hybrid aquatic monster (shown usually as a fish-crocodile), in Hindu myth symbolizing the power of the waters. Because the makara is ridden by Varuna, lord of both physical and moral order as well as of the heavens and the deep, its image is generally beneficent, linked with the rainbow and rainfall, the water-born lotus, and the sun's return at the December solstice. In the Hindu zodiac, the makara replaces the goat-fish Capricorn, symbolizing rebirth into or release from the cycle of material existence.

Man

The paragon of animals, a symbol in most ancient cultures of what is perfectible in nature – being made in the image of God and containing both matter and spirit, earth and heaven. This mystic belief underlies the frequent depictions of humankind as a microcosm containing, at least symbolically, all the elements of the universe itself. The human body, in Pythagorean tradition a pentagram formed by arms, legs and head, was often taken as a model for temple architecture. The male principle itself is symbolized usually by sun, fire and lightning, and by phallic verticality or penetrative objects; these include the arrow, cone, lance, lingam, obelisk, pillar, or pole, plough, rod, spade, spear, sword, thunderbolt and torch.

Mandala

A design that symbolizes spiritual, cosmic or psychic order. Although Buddhist mandalas, particularly in the geometric form of the *yantra*, have become famous as aids in meditative exercises, ancient mandala forms in both Hinduism and Buddhism also had initiatory symbolism, orienting worshippers to a sacred space. They are attempts to provide an image of the supreme reality – of a spiritual wholeness that transcends the world of appearances. The Sanskrit meaning of *mandala* is "circle", and even when dominated by squares or triangles, mandalas have concentric structures. They symbolize progression toward a spiritual centre, either mentally or physically – as in the mandala structure of many temples or stupas.

The striking feature of all mandala patterns is their careful balancing of visual elements, symbolizing a divine

A sacred mandala, based on an 18th-century painting, from Rajasthan in India.

harmony beyond the confusion or disorder of the material world. To Jung, these patterns were archetypal symbols of the human longing for psychic integration. To others, the mandala represents a spiritual journey out of the self. The meaning of individual mandalas differs; some have figurative elements that invite contemplation of, for example, the specific virtues embodied by a particular Bodhisattva, often shown seated within a lotus. However, the sense of order is consistent, symbolizing a guiding intelligence, a supernatural structure, the serenity of enlightenment.

Mandorla

An almond-shaped aureole used in medieval Christian art to frame the figure of Christ at his ascension, and also to enclose the Virgin Mary, Mary Magdalen or other saints borne to heaven. As the *vesica piscis* ("fish bladder"), the mandorla was an early symbol of Christ in glory. The mystic "almond" (*mandorla* in Italian) was associated with purity and virginity, its oval shape being an ancient symbol

Man: *see* Woman; *and individual names*

Mandala: *see* Centre; Circle; Initiation; Lotus; Square; Stupa; Temple; Triangle

Mandorla: *see* Almond; Aureole; Fire, Flame; Lozenge; Transformation; Virginity

A mandorla, the almond-shaped aureole that surrounds this Eastern Orthodox image of Christ.

Mandrake: *see*
Devils; Witchcraft

Manna: *see*
Bread; Honey; Resin;
Tamarisk

Mantra: *see*
Om (Aum); Word

Marigold: *see*
FLOWERS; Heliotrope;
Sun; Virginity

Marriage: *see*
Androgyne; Bonds; Circle;
Knot; Mercury; Necklace;
Rice; Ring; Sulphur; Yin-
yang

*An anthropomorphized
mandrake, from a 16th-
century English herbal.*

of the vulva. Graphically, it also resembles a flame, a symbol of spirituality. Another view is that it represents the duality of heaven and earth – depicted as two intersecting arcs. This would explain why mandorlas usually enclose emblematically ascending figures, symbolizing not only their sanctity but also their transfiguration.

Mandrake
A Mediterranean narcotic plant of the potato family with a forked root suggesting the human form, credited with magical powers and widely associated·with sorcery and witchcraft.·It was used to cast spells by the enchantress Circe in Greek mythology; as an aphrodisiac in Egypt; as an aid to conception in Israel; and as an anti-inflammatory herbal remedy in Rome. Superstitions accumulating around the mandrake (or *mandragora*) in medieval times led to the idea that when uprooted its shrieks could kill or that, "mortals hearing them run mad" (Shakespeare's *Romeo and Juliet*, 4:3; *c.*1595).

The legend that mandrakes grew from the semen of hanged murderers illustrates a symbolic shift from the idea that a man-shaped plant could have sympathetic benefits to the fear that it represented demonic forces.

Manna
Divine grace – symbolism relating to the apparently miraculous nourishment that sustained the children of Israel for 40 years in the wilderness (Exodus 16). Its description as "honey wafers", has led to suggestions that the wafers were made up from the *Lecanora* lichen and from honey-like gum resins of the tamarisk or similar trees of the region. These are free

foods of the Bedouin, and falls of wind-blown lichen are known in North Africa. Christianity adapted the symbolism of the Jewish "food from heaven" represented by Christ as "the bread of life" (John 6:31–35).

Mantle *see* **Cloak**

Mantra
A word or syllable symbolizing an aspect of divine power in Hindu and Buddhist traditions. Whether spoken aloud, or pronounced simply in the mind of someone concentrating on it, the sonority of the sacred word has a quasi-magical value corresponding to a creative energy charge. The mantra is believed to align the worshipper with the vibration of the cosmos itself.

Marigold
A solar flower, linked in China with longevity, in India with Krishna, and in the West with the purity and perfection of the Virgin Mary, after whom it was named ("Mary-gold"). The marigold is sometimes suggested as the flower (more usually the heliotrope) in the Greek myth of Clytia, who was hopelessly in love with Apollo.

Marriage
A rite of passage invested with sacred significance in most ancient societies. It symbolized a semi-divine state of wholeness – union between the opposite principles of male and female necessary to create and protect new life. The depiction in myth and art of the "marriage" of key dualities (gods and goddesses, sun and moon, heaven and earth, king and queen or, in alchemy, sulphur and mercury) likewise symbolized the continuation of cosmic order and the fertility of nature, a

process in which human marriages were felt to be important religiously as well as socially. The idea of human–divine union was often expressed in terms of marriage, as in the description of nuns as "brides of Christ".

Wedding customs, full of symbolic meanings now largely forgotten, attempted to ensure that marriages were binding, fruitful and happy. Binding symbols still in use include the ring (a circular symbol of eternity, union and completeness); the joining of hands; and the tying of knots (as in the Hindu custom by which the bridegroom knots a ribbon around the neck of the bride).

Fertility symbols include the sprinkling of grain, rice or their substitute, confetti, over the couple; the wedding cake (food being a sexual symbol as well as a symbolic means of uniting the two families in a shared feast); the presence of small children around the bride (sympathetic fertility magic); and the breaking of glasses or other objects (successful defloration). An enormous number of other customs were devised to ward off evil influences, ensure good luck or harmlessly act out social tensions caused by the marriage or the couple's drastic change of lifestyle. A custom as peculiar as tying tin cans to the back of the couple's car may derive from the idea that bad spirits could be driven off by making a lot of noise.

Mask

Transformation, protection, identification or disguise. The primary ancient symbolism of the mask is that it embodied a supernatural force or even transformed its shaman wearer into the spirit depicted by the mask. The earliest animal masks appear to have been used to capture the spirit of a hunted animal and prevent it from harming the wearer. Later primitive masks had totemic significance, identifying the tribe with a particular ancestral spirit whose power could then be used to protect the tribe, frighten its enemies, exorcise demons or diseases, expel the lingering spirits of the dead, or provide a focus for worship. The Iroquois False Face society were professional exorcisers of disease demons, masked to symbolize the baleful twin brother of the creator god. Masks or face packs were also used in African, Native American and Oceanic initiation ceremonies to mark the transition from a childish to an adult appearance. Burial masks representing dead notables were widely used not merely to shield their decaying faces, as in the golden masks of Mycenae, but also to ensure that their souls could find their way back to their bodies, a point of concern in Egyptian and other funerary rites.

The tragic and comic masks worn to identify different characters in ancient Greek drama developed from the use of religious masks to act out myths or to symbolize the presence of divinities, particularly in the fertility cult of Dionysus. Demon-frightening masks in Asia (which survive in processional dragon and lion dances) may similarly have been the origin of the masks later used with stylized colour symbolism in the Japanese No theatre – red for virtue, white for corruption, black for villainy. The mask can also, more obviously, symbolize concealment or illusion. In Indian tradition the mask is *maya* – the world as a delusion projected by the individual who has not understood the divine *maya* or Mask of God. In Western

Mask: *see*
ANIMALS; Black; Dragon; Initiation; Lion; Night; Red; Totem; Transformation; White

Maypole: *see*
Axis; Phallus; Pillar; Pine,
Pine cone; Sacrifice; Sun;
Sun dance; Tree

Mead: *see*
Alcohol; Honey;
Intoxication

Menhir: *see*
Phallus; Man; Stone

Mercury: *see*
Alchemy; Androgyne;
Blood; Caduceus; Dragon;
METALS; PLANETS;
Sulphur; Transformation;
Water; Wings

*Mercury, carrying the
caduceus, from an
alchemical engraving
of 1666.*

art, the mask is an attribute of Deceit
personified, and of Vice and Night.

Maypole

A spring emblem of fertility and solar
renewal, linked to ancient agricultural
and resurrection rites and to the axial
symbolism of the World Tree. In England, the phallic symbolism of maypoles and wanton behaviour around
them on May Day affronted the
Puritans. Pagan sources of the maypole include the Greek and Roman
spring rites of Attis, slain consort of
the Earth Mother, Cybele. His symbol
was a stripped pine tree, wound with
woollen bands, around which dances
were performed to invoke and celebrate his resurrection. The Roman festival of Hilaria adapted this tradition,
combined with other, existing spring
rites as it spread into the Celtic world.
English maypoles emphasized the
symbolism of fecundity by attaching a
feminine disk to the male pole.
Dancers unwinding ribbons as they
circle around the pole are said to symbolize the creation of the cosmos from
the axial centre (this has similarity
with the rites of Attis, suggesting a
Roman source). More exhausting or
painful circular dances performed by
the Plains Indians in North America
used a central pole as a linking symbol
between earth and the supernatural
forces above it. These dances invoked
the power of the sun, sometimes by
offering sacrificial pieces of flesh torn
from the breasts of warriors.

Mead

The beverage of the gods in Celtic tradition, therefore making it a symbol
of immortality. Celtic legends told of
deposed kings drowned in barrels
of mead in their burning palaces. An
alcholic drink made from fermented
honey mixed with water and often
spiced, mead shares the positive symbolism of honey and may have been
the ambrosia of the Greek immortals.

Menhir

A Neolithic standing stone, often set
up near European burial sites and
thought by some to symbolize the life
force of a male divinity or hero and to
memorialize him as a durable presence protectively watching over the
living. Early standing stones appear to
be astronomical markers, but later
and smaller menhirs are sometimes
carved with figurative details supporting the idea of a more symbolic role.

Mercury

Fluidity, liaison, transformation,
volatility and the intellect – a lunar
and female metal linked by alchemists
with "cold" energy. As the only common metal liquid at ordinary temper-
atures, mercury was of great interest
to alchemists, especially because it
forms easy amalgams with other metals – and was once used to extract
gold from ore for this reason. Mercury (the metal, planet and androgynous god) has unusually consistent
and universal symbolism in mythology, astrology and alchemy. The planet
Mercury, closest of the planets to the
sun, circles the sun quickly and is elusive to observe, hence its association
with the winged messenger of the
gods (Hermes/Mecury). The metal,
also known as quicksilver or "liquid
silver", was extracted by the ancients
from roasted cinnabar and represented the second stage of alchemic purification before "conjunction" with its
symbolic opposite, sulphur. Its planetary sigil, adopted by alchemists, is at

least 3,000 years old. In China, mercury was associated with the dragon and with the liquid bodily elements – blood, water and semen. It corresponded to the yogic element in Indian tradition, associated with the internal flow of spiritual energy, and with the semen of Shiva.

METALS *see panel, below*

Meteorite

A divine spark or seed. In the ancient world, meteorites were thought to be fragments of the governing stars – virtually angels in material form, recalling humans to the existence of a higher life. Meteoric stone or metal thus had sacred value. The Kaaba, focal point of Mecca, contains a meteorite.

Midnight

In Chinese tradition, the beginning of 12 hours of solar ascent – a moment charged with power and believed to be a propitious time for conception, particularly at the December solstice. It was also, in Christian legend, the hour of Christ's birth. India's independence on the stroke of midnight had added symbolic significance because it was in Tantric tradition an hour of spiritual zenith as well as initiation.

Milk

The elixir of life, rebirth and immortality – a metaphor for kindness, care, compassion, abundance and fertility. In Indian tradition, the fundamental role of milk is expressed in a Vedic myth of the origin of the world, when gods and anti-gods churned the cosmic pail of the primeval ocean to create first milk, then butter, then the sun and moon, and finally the elixir of immortality, *soma*. A milk-giving tree grew in the Hindu paradise. Milk appears in many traditions, including Celtic, as a drink of immortality. Apart from the obvious links with nursing and motherhood or adoption, milk was an initiation or rebirth symbol in Greek Orphic rites, in Islam, and at early Christian baptisms. It was poured as a libation for the resurrection of the god Osiris in Egypt, and in spring fertility rites elsewhere. More generally, it represented the drinking

Meteorite: *see*
Kaaba; Iron; Spark; Star

Midnight: *see*
Initiation; Solstice

Milk: *see*
Baptism; Cow; Gingko; Goat; Initiation; Milky Way; Mother; Tree; White

METALS

Cosmic energy trapped in solid form – a symbolism that explains some puzzling aspects of ancient attitudes toward metals. Early extraction, purification and smelting techniques and, still more, the efforts of alchemists to transmute base metals to gold, made metallurgy an allegory of spiritual testing and purification. Metals, like humans, were earthly things with celestial potential. Hence the development of a cosmic hierarchy in which metals were paired with the seven known planets. In ascending order, least precious to the most precious, these were: lead with Saturn; tin with Jupiter; iron with Mars; copper with Venus; mercury with Mercury; silver with the moon; gold with the sun. In psychology, metals represented the human's sensuality, transcended only by spiritual development. In some initiation rites, metallic possessions were discarded to signify the shedding of impurities.

METALS: *see*
Alchemy; Bronze; Gold; Initiation; Iron; Lead; Mercury; PLANETS; Silver

Milky Way: *see* AFTERWORLDS; Lily; Milk; Serpent; Thunder

Mimosa: *see* FLOWERS; Gold; Light

Minotaur: *see* BEASTS OF FABLE; Bull; Centaur; Labyrinth; Sacrifice; SEVEN DEADLY SINS

Mirror: *see* AFTERWORLDS; CHASTITY; Heart; Karma; Lake; Light; Magpie; Marriage; Moon; SEVEN DEADLY SINS; TRUTH; Twins; VANITY

The bull–man Minotaur, from an ancient Greek black-figure vase.

in of knowledge or spiritual nourishment. Its colour also made it a symbol of purity – milk rather than blood was said to have spurted from the decapitated St Catherine of Alexandria.

Milky Way

Our Galaxy, so called from the classical myth that it was created when Herakles, suckled by Hera, tugged so hard at her breast that milk showered the heavens (the milk that fell to earth became lilies). The Milky Way appears as a celestial serpent in Central American myth; the path travelled by souls to the afterlife in North America; a celestial river from which the thunder god draws rain in Peru; and as a symbolic boundary or bridge between the known world and the divine.

Mimosa

The certainty of resurrection – a religious symbolism based on the solar colour of its golden flowers and on the idea that it was a mimic of sentient life, its leaves responding to stimuli and unfolding to the light everlasting.

Minotaur

A fabled Cretan monster with the head of a bull and the body of a man, symbolizing tyranny – and, in a psychological sense, the destructiveness of hidden or repressed lusts. In Greek myth, Pasiphaë, wife of King Minos, gave birth to the Minotaur after coupling with a white bull – an act of revenge arranged by the sea-god Poseidon (in Roman myth, Neptune), who was angry that Minos had not sacrificed the bull to him. Minos hid the Minotaur in a labyrinth and fed it regular tributes of young Athenians until the hero Theseus beat it to death.

The bull head on a human body symbolized the complete dominance of animal instinct.

Mirror

Veracity, self-knowledge, sincerity, purity, enlightenment, divination – a predominantly positive symbol because of its ancient association with light, especially the light of the mirror-like disks of the sun and moon, thought to reflect divinity to earth. Hence the belief that evil spirits could not abide mirrors and, as spirits of darkness, had no reflection. Although mirrors sometimes appear in Western art as disapproving attributes of Pride, Vanity or Lust, they more often symbolize Truth – the folk wisdom that the mirror never lies: "You may not go," Hamlet rages at his mother, "until I set you up a glass where you may see the inmost part of you." (Shakespeare's *Hamlet*, 3:4; *c.*1600). The Virgin Mary is sometimes shown holding a mirror – a reference to her untainted chastity and to the Christ Child as the mirror of God. The mirror (until the late Middle Ages usually a round disk of bronze or silver, polished on one side) was an emblem of the Greek goddess Aphrodite (Venus to the Romans) and of mother goddesses in the Middle East.

The philosophical significance of the mirror as a symbol of the self-examined life is widespread in Asian traditions and particularly important in Japanese myth and religion: the creator-god Izanagi gave his children a mirror, telling them to kneel and look into it morning and evening until they had shed evil thoughts and passions. In the Shinto hell, a giant mirror reflects the sins of new arrivals and determines the region of their punishment in ice or fire. The bronze mirror Yatano-Kagami, kept at Ise in Japan's most important Shinto shrine, symbolizes the sun-goddess Amaterasu, who was tempted by a magic mirror to emerge from the cave in which she had hidden her divine light. The mirror was an imperial solar emblem handed from emperor to emperor. In both Hinduism and Buddhism it symbolizes the enlightened realization that the phenomenal world is an illusion, a mere reflection. Yama, the Hindu guardian of the underworld, also uses a mirror to judge the state of a soul's karma. The mirror is one of the Eight Precious Things of Buddhism. It is a Chinese emblem of sincerity, harmony and marital happiness linked with the magpie.

Almost everywhere, mirrors have been linked with magic and especially with divination because they can reflect past or future events as well as present ones. Shamans in central Asia aimed mirrors at the sun or moon in order to read the future. The mirror can also symbolize a mystic door into a parallel world, as in *Alice in Wonderland*. The widespread superstition that breaking a mirror brings bad luck is linked with primitive ideas that a person's reflection contains part of his or her life force, or a twin "soul". Equally widely, the brightness or dullness of a mirror is an allegory for the state of a person's soul. In both Islamic and Christian thought, the human heart is likened to a mirror that reflects God.

Mist

A transition, evolution or supernatural intervention – the significance of mist in some Oriental paintings and in traditional symbolism generally. Mist

stood for the indeterminate, a prelude to revelation or to the emergence of new forms, as in initiation rites.

Mistletoe

Fertility, protection, healing, rebirth, immortality – the magical "golden bough" of the Celtic world. As an evergreen parasite that produces yellow flowers, and white berries in midwinter, mistletoe symbolized the continuing potency of the deciduous trees on which it was found. Mistletoe clinging to an oak (a rare event) was a female fertility symbol to the Druids who, according to the Roman author Pliny (*c*.24–79CE), cut it with a golden sickle on the sixth day of the new moon (probably at the Celtic New Year in November) and sacrificed a young white bull beneath the tree. The berry juice (which was equated with the tree's semen and its connotations of power and wisdom) supposedly prevented sterility or disease in cattle and was credited with other healing properties.

Celtic reverence for mistletoe – thought to be produced by lightning – may have influenced the account in Virgil's *Aeneid* (*c*.29–19BCE) of Aeneas travelling safely through the underworld carrying a bough of it. The golden bough of life appears more unexpectedly as an instrument of death in the Nordic and Germanic myth of Balder, god of light, who was killed by an innocent dart made from mistletoe. This apparent inversion of its talismanic symbolism may signify the passage from mortal to immortal status through the agency of a sacred plant. Celtic tradition seems to account for Christmas kisses under a bunch of mistletoe, an augury of fruitful union.

Mist: *see*
Air; Initiation; Water

Mistletoe; *see*
AFTERWORLDS; Branch, Bough; Bull; Gold; Kiss; Light; Lightning; Oak; Sacrifice; Sickle, Scythe; White

Monkey

Monkey: *see*
Ape; Apple; SEVEN
DEADLY SINS; WISDOM

Moon: *see*
AFTERWORLDS;
Alchemy; Bear; Boat; Bull;
Cat; CHASTITY; Circle;
Cow; Crescent; Cup;
Darkness; Disk;
Dismemberment; Eye; Fox;
Frog; Hare, Rabbit; Horn;
Light; Mirror; Mother;
Otter; PLANETS; Rain;
Sabbath; Silver; Snail; Sun;
Tarot; Toad; Tree; Virginity;
Water; Week; Witchcraft;
Woman; Year; Zodiac

*The monkey-god
Hanuman playing with
the peaches of
immortality, from a
Chinese plate*

Monkey

Like the ape, the monkey is an animal
with a higher symbolic status in the
East than in the West. Its imitative
skills and wide behavioural range
make its symbolism inconsistent, and
enable it to be used variously to personify virtuous or foolish aspects of
human behaviour. In Tibetan tradition, the Bodhisattva Avalokiteshvara
(incarnated by the Dalai Lama) originally entered the country in the guise
of a saintly monkey, took pity on an
ogress who had fallen in love with
him, and with her fathered the six
ancestors of the Tibetan race. Stories
of monkey-kings appear also in
Chinese and Indian myth where they
play agile and intelligent hero roles.
Hanuman, the Hindu monkey god,
was a fertility symbol as well as healer,
warrior and loyal follower of the god
Rama. The gibbon monkey symbolized maternal protection in Chinese
art, and monkey dolls had similar protective symbolism in Japan. The
famous *koshin* – three monkeys who
see, hear and speak no evil, carved in
wood on the shrine of the first
Tokugawa shogun at Nikko – unexpectedly signify the wisdom of discretion, an inversion of the Western view
of the monkey as inquisitive and chat-
tering. The carving has been explained as a talisman against slander.
Malice, lust and greed are attributes of
the monkey in Christian art: monkeys
often caricature the venial faults of
human nature or represent the imitative arts.

Monolith *see* **Menhir; Pillar**

Moon

Fertility, cyclic regeneration, resurrection, immortality, occult power, muta-

bility, intuition and the emotions –
ancient regulator of time, the waters,
crop growth and the lives of women.
The moon's appearances and disappearances and its startling changes of
form presented an impressive cosmic
image of the earthly cycles of animal
and vegetable birth, growth, decline,
death and rebirth. The extent and
power of lunar worship and lunar
symbolism are partly explained by the
moon's enormous importance as a
source of light for night hunting and
as the earliest measure of time – its
phases forming the basis of the first
known calendars. Beyond its influence
on the tides, the moon was widely
believed to control human destiny as
well as rainfall, snow, floods, and the
rhythms of plant and animal life in
general and of women, through the
lunar rhythms of the menstrual cycle.

Although primarily a symbol of the
female principle, the moon was sometimes personified by male gods, especially among nomadic or hunting cultures. The great Sumerian-Semitic
moon-god Sin, whose sign was a boat-
shaped crescent, was Lord of Months,
and of destiny. The moon was male in
Japan, Oceania and the Teutonic
countries as well, and also among
some African and Native American
tribes. Female moon deities vary in
character, ranging from protective
great mother goddesses to fierce, sil-
very defenders of their virginity such
as the horned Greek hunter-goddess
Artemis. Chastity, mutability, fickle-
ness or "cold" indifference are all
qualities associated with the moon. Its
best-known classical personification,
Diana, was a minor Italian woodland
goddess, later identified with Artemis,
who had absorbed elements of the
Greek moon cults of Selene, lover of

Endymion, and Hecate, representing the moon in its funerary aspect. The "dark of the moon" (its three-day absence) made the moon a symbol of the passage from life to death as well as from death to life. In some traditions, the moon is the way to the afterlife or the abode of the honoured dead. Although generally a benevolent symbol, the moon can sometimes appear as an evil eye, a witching presence, by association with death and with sinister aspects of the night. Both the Egyptian god Thoth and the Greek goddess Hecate combined lunar and occult symbolism.

Graphically, the moon often appears in iconography as a waxing crescent (with tips to the left), a propitious sign for the sowing of crops. The Turkish crescent, with tips right, was the ancient protective symbol of Byzantium, chosen in honour of Hecate. Combined with the star of Ishtar (Venus in Roman myth), it later became the symbol not only of Turkey but of Islam in general, signifying sovereignty and the power of Allah as well as growth and prosperity. The crescent with tips upward combines lunar and bull or cow fertility symbolism. The sliver of the new moon symbolizes chaste birth, as in Christian depictions of the Virgin Mary with the new moon at her feet (Revelation 12:1). The full moon shares the symbolism of the circle as an image of wholeness or perfection. It is a Buddhist symbol of beauty and serenity, and, in China, of the completed family. The harvest moon (a full moon near the September equinox) is, for agricultural reasons, a fertility symbol, widely associated with love and marriage. The Chinese moon festival, held at the September

equinox with fruits, sweetcakes and lanterns, also has fertility symbolism. The idea that the full moon brings on forms of madness other than love is of Roman origin (hence "lunatic"). Born idiots may be called "mooncalves" for the same reason, but also because the moon, presiding over dreams, is linked with fantasy or bemusement.

The moon's changes of form determine much of its symbolism and are linked by some with myths and rituals of dismembered and resurrected gods such as the Egyptian Osiris. It is a dissolving, mediating and unifying symbol, an emblem of eternal youth in Oceanic tradition, and almost universally of immortality – hence its association with trees, as on some Islamic graves where the crescent appears above the Tree of Life. In Oriental iconography, the lunar hare mixes the elixir of immortality beneath the Tree of Life. (Elsewhere, the crescent moon sometimes appears as a cup bearing this elixir.) Apart from major fertility symbols like the hare or rabbit, lunar animals include the hibernating bear, amphibians such as the frog and toad, other nocturnal animals such as the cat and fox – and the snail with its appearing and disappearing antennae (the "horns" on the crescent moon). The hare or rabbit and the toad were most often identified with the patches on the moon (alternatively thought to be an old man gathering sticks, a water-carrier or – in Africa – mud slung by the jealous sun). More often in myth (and alchemy), the sun and moon form a necessary duality as husband and wife, brother and sister, hot and cold, fire and water, male and female – notably symbolized by the Egyptian headdress which shows the sun disk enclosed by the horns of the

The Moon card from a Tarot pack.

Mother

Mother: *see*
Basket; Bear; Black; Boat;
Breasts; Cornucopia; Cow;
Crescent; Cup; Darkness;
Dismemberment; Dove;
Earth; Fountain; Goat;
Goose; Labyrinth; Lion;
Lozenge; Moon; Partridge;
Pear; Sea; Sphinx; Spiral;
Swallow; Tree; Triad;
Virginity; Vulture; Water

moon. Astrology stressed the passive aspects of the moon as a mere reflector of the sun's light, hence its association with conceptual or rational thought rather than direct knowledge (although Taoism saw it as the eye of spiritual knowledge in the darkness of ignorance).

Psychology links it with subjectivity, intuition and the emotions – and with shifts of mood, which is a recurring symbolism.

Mother

Nature, the earth and its waters, fertility, nourishment, warmth, shelter, protection, devotion – but sometimes also an image of stifling love, mortal destiny and the grave. Paleolithic carvings, perhaps 30,000 years old, suggest that swollen-breasted maternal figures were the earliest of all fertility symbols. And although many cosmogonies identify male or dual-sex creator divinities as the original source of life, it is possible that they were predated by worship of mother goddesses personifying Nature, the Earth or the Creative Force itself. Hesiod (fl. *c.*700BCE), the poet who systematized Greek mythology, placed Ge or Gaia (the earth) first in his genealogy of the gods as the "universal mother, firmly founded, the oldest of divinities". She bore the gods and, according to Attic myth, the first human, Erichthonius. In the Greco-Roman world, worship of maternal nature symbols including Rhea and Demeter culminated in the Phrygian Great Mother, Cybele, whose cult was an early rival to Christianity.

The Christian cult of the Virgin Mary is unique, not only because Mary was a young woman (the human element in Christ), and not a goddess, but also because she represented a complete break with the long tradition of venerated mothers who were essentially nature symbols. Her symbolic link with earlier mother goddesses is that her son was killed. The death, emasculation or dismemberment of the mother goddess's loved ones is a great recurring theme in the mythic symbolism of the mother – representing the death–rebirth cycle that is the iron rule of nature.

Mothering–devouring symbolism is attached to both earth (the darkness of germination and of the grave) and sea (the primeval waters of life, represented by the great Sumerian goddess Nammu, and the dread abyss). Kali, the "Dark Mother" of Hindu mythology, is the most alarming image of the creator–destroyer. The "terrible mother" of psychology is a symbol of possessive love and the danger of an infantile fixation persisting and blocking development of the self. Mother–witch symbolism can reflect this tyranny as well as ancient ties between the mother and secret earthly lore. The mother is linked psychologically with instinct, emotions, sentiment, tenderness and moodiness. Multiple aspects of the mother were sometimes represented in iconography by triform or triple goddesses, as with Hecate and in Celtic carvings. Celtic mother goddesses were usually protective, especially of animals, including wild beasts. Their attributes included boats or rudders, as well as more familiar emblems of fertility and prosperity such as baskets of fruit, sheaves of corn or cornucopias. Other mother symbols include the bear (especially in dreams), cow, dove, goose, partridge and swallow in addition to other productive animals and

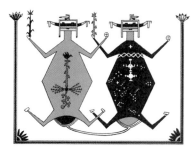

Mother Earth (left) and Father Sky (right), after a Navajo sand painting.

some wild beasts, especially the lioness; fountains, lakes, oceans, rivers and the moon; gardens, gates, houses and ships; containers, especially baskets and cups; the crescent of the waxing moon; the labyrinth sign known as the "mother and child" pattern; or, in graphic representation the lozenge or the spiral; and founding or nurturing entities such as Church, university, or country of birth.

Mound

In Egyptian tradition, the intermediate state of matter. According to Egypt's creation mythology, the first form to arise from the primeval state of chaos (Nun) was a mound providing a perch for the Benu bird, personifying the creator sun god. Mounds also had sacred axial symbolism for lowland peoples as mediating places between the natural and supernatural worlds.

Mountain

The spiritual peak and centre of the world, the meeting place of earth and heaven – a symbol of transcendence, eternity, purity, stability, ascent, ambition and challenge. The belief that

deities inhabited mountains or manifested their presence there was universal in countries with peaks high enough to be veiled by clouds. Such mountains were often feared as well as venerated – as in Africa. They were associated with immortals, heroes, sanctified prophets and gods. The Bible is full of references to sacred mountains. God's revelations to Moses on Mt Sinai were paralleled in Christianity by Christ's Sermon on the Mount. It was on Mt Carmel that Elijah triumphed over the priests of Baal, on Mt Horeb that he heard the word of God, and on the Mount of Olives that Christ ascended into heaven according to the Acts of the Apostles. In medieval legends of the Grail, the elixir of life is guarded in a castle on Montsalvat. In China, the World Mountain, Kunlun, thought to be the source of the Yellow River, was a symbol of order and harmony, the dwelling-place of immortals and of the Supreme Being. Fujiyama, almost an emblem of Japan itself, was and is a sacred place of Shinto pilgrimage. In Central Mexico, Mt Tlaloc was a personification of the great fertility and rain god. From Mt Olympus, the Greeks were subject to the whims of their quarrelsome gods. Sacred mountains could be figurative as well as real, as in the Celtic White Mountain, the emerald-based Qaf of Islam, or Mt Meru, the Hindu World Mountain at the North Pole. In Hindu cosmogony, Mt Mandara is used as a pivot to churn the cosmic waters.

The polar mountain is both centre and axis of the world, spreading out from its peak like a great inverted World Tree. The peak could be seen both as a navel and as a hole or point of departure from terrestrial life.

Mound: *see*
Axis; Heron; Sun

Mountain: *see*
Axis; Castle; Cave; Centre; Clouds; CROSS; Crown; Emerald; Grail; Hole; Pagoda; Pyramid; Star; Steps, Stairs; Stupa; Tree; Triangle; White; Ziggurat

Mouse

Mouse: *see*
Dove; Rat; Soul

Mouth: *see*
AFTERWORLDS; Breath,
Breathing; Cicada; Disk;
Dragon; Fire, Flame; Jade;
Ka; Mask; Red; Vulva;
Whale

Mudras: *see*
Dance; Hand

Mushroom: *see*
Fairies; Phallus;
LONGEVITY; Ring; Soul;
Witchcraft

Sometimes the mountain was hollow, and contained sleeping immortals. Figurative mountains were usually envisaged as layered, representing the progressive stages of spiritual ascent. (The risks of scaling mountains unprepared were well understood.) Mountain-shaped temples express the same idea in the great ziggurats of Mesopotamia or Central America and in the stupas and pagodas of Asia. Psychologically, climbing the mountain symbolizes a great challenge, the stages toward self-knowledge. Verticality makes the mountain a masculine symbol, although the great mother Cybele was specifically a mountain deity. In art, twin-peaked mountains symbolize dual powers. Other mountain symbols include the triangle, the cross, the crown, the star and steps or ladders. Muhammad reputedly used the immutability of mountains as an allegory of the need for humility when he ordered Mt Safa to move: when it refused to budge he went to the mountain to thank God that it had stayed put.

Mouse

Timidity – an ancient symbolism, judging from the legendary insult of the Egyptian king Tachos, disappointed by the puny appearance of a Spartan ally: "The mountain laboured, Jupiter stood aghast, and a mouse ran out." The secret depredations of mice made them a Jewish symbol of hypocrisy and a Christian symbol of wicked destructiveness. In folk superstition, mice were souls that had slipped from the mouths of the dead (red if good, black if corrupted) – rather as doves were said to fly from the mouths of saints as their souls departed. Mice were used for divina-

tion in Africa because they were believed to understand the mysteries of the underworld.

Mouth

Open mouths in iconography may be symbols of devouring (as in the many images of gaping-jawed monsters representing the gates of hell) or of spirits speaking (as in primitive masks or carvings). They can also symbolize the breath of life.

In Egyptian funerary rites, the mouths of the dead were opened to enable their *ka* to give evidence in the judgment hall of the afterlife – and to receive the gift of new life. Solar disks were placed in the mouths of the dead, as were jade objects (symbolizing immortality) in China and Mexico. Jung saw a symbolic link between the mouth – as red and consuming – and fire, expressed in fire-breathing dragon legends. More commonly, the mouth is associated with the vulva, as in Chinese symbolism.

Mudras

An extensive system of subtle and symbolic hand gestures used in Hindu and Buddhist iconography, in ritual religious dancing and also, with adaptations, in dance and the theatre generally throughout much of Asia.

Mule *see* Ass

MUSES *see panel, opposite*

Mushroom

Life from death – an important symbol of longevity and happiness in China, and the legendary food of the immortals in Taoist tradition. Mushrooms personify souls of the reborn in some parts of central

MUSES

The patron goddesses of epic poetry (Calliope), lyric poetry (Erato), history (Clio), music (Enterpe), tragic drama (Melpomene), mime (Polyhymnia), comic drama (Thalia), dance (Terpsichore) and astronomy (Urania). Their symbolism was based on the association between springs or fountains and inspiration. Hence their origin as Greek nymphs of mountain streams, the daughters of the god Zeus and his adultery with Mnemosyne. They appear in art as companions of Apollo or alone with a variety of attributes including books, scrolls, tablets, flutes, viols, tambourines, trumpets, lyres, harps, horns, crowns, laurel wreaths, masks, or, in the case of Melpomene a sword or dagger.

Melpomene and Calliope either side of Virgil, from a mosaic.

Europe, and Africa. Their magical sudden appearance, and possibly the use of some varieties as hallucinogens, may account for folklore associations with the supernatural, leading to the notion of pixie houses or witches' rings. The shape of the mushroom, once linked with phallic potency, has become the most powerful apocalyptic symbol of the nuclear age.

Music

A mystical order. Music was linked with the origin of life itself in some traditions, notably in India where sound is regarded in Hindu doctrine as the primordial vibration of divine energy. From this comes the legend of Krishna's flute, which brought the world into existence.

Primitive music, based on rhythm and imitations of the sounds of animals and the natural world, was essentially an attempt to communicate with the spirit world. With the development of more sophisticated instruments and harmonics, music became a symbol of cosmic order and was associated in China and in Greece with number symbolism and with the planets ("the harmony of the spheres"). Plato believed that the cosmos formed a musical scale and number, and that the planets would create a divine harmony by moving at different speeds to one another, just as musical pitch changed when strings were vibrated at differing rates.

Yin or yang qualities were allocated to the semitones of the earliest Chinese octave, music thus becoming a symbol of the vital duality holding together disparate things. In art, musicians or musical instruments often symbolize peace or love.

Myrrh *see* **Incense**

Myrtle

Sensual love, marital happiness, longevity and harmony. Perhaps because of its purple berries, this fragrant evergreen shrub, growing wild in the Mediterranean and sometimes used for victors' wreaths, was widely associated with love goddesses, especially the Greek Aphrodite (in Roman myth, Venus), and with rituals surrounding marriage and childbirth. Myrtle was revered by the Mandaean sect as a life symbol. It was a Chinese emblem of success. The crackling of its leaves was thought to show whether a lover would be faithful.

MUSES: *see*
Book; Crown; Fountain; Harp; Laurel; Lyre; Mask; Music; Scroll; Spring; Sword; Tablet; Tambourine; Trumpet; Wreath, Garland

Music: *see*
Drum; Flute; Harp; Lyre; MUSES; NUMBERS; PEACE; PLANETS; Tambourine; Trumpet; Yin-yang

Myrtle: *see*
VICTORY; Wreath

Nail: *see*
CROSS; PASSION

Nakedness: *see*
Initiation; LIBERTY; Sky;
Witchcraft

Nail

Protection – as in the Chinese custom of hammering superfluous nails into houses to ward off demons, or the annual ceremonial hammering of a nail into the temple of Jupiter in ancient Rome.

A binding or fastening symbolism is thought to explain nails driven into some African fetishes (to keep their resident spirits fixed on the task for which their help was invoked). In art, three nails symbolize the Crucifixion. They also appear as the attributes of figures associated with legends about Christ or the Cross – notably Helena, mother of Constantine the Great, who was said to have discovered the True Cross and the nails themselves, a claim disputed by others interested in possessing the relic.

Nakedness

Innocence, freedom, vulnerability, truth and, in the idealizations of Greek art, divinity itself. Although nakedness can also symbolize carnality, shame or wickedness – as in the huddled naked figures of a Bosch painting depicting hell (*c*.1490) – the unadorned human body was, in most traditions, a symbol of openness, simplicity and the purity of the new born. Hence the disrobing of initiates and sometimes of priests in some ancient religious rites.

The Bible's depiction of Adam and Eve as naked before the Fall associated nakedness with the primal state of innocence. Ascetics have sometimes gone naked for this reason. The 18th-century Russian peasant Christian sect of Dukhobors ("spirit wrestlers") – most of whose members later emigrated to Canada – used nudity as a symbolic protest against materialism and the authority of the Church and state. In medieval art, naked witches symbolized the fleshly temptations of Satan, but modern witch covens use the term "sky-clad" (naked) to suggest their openness to supernatural forces. Similarly, naked Indian ascetics are "clothed in air".

In civilizations where nudity was frowned upon, such as China, nakedness symbolized primitiveness or poverty, as it did for the Romans.

The beautiful youth Narcissus of Greek myth, after a painting of 1711, by Nicolas-Bernard Lécuver.

Narcissus

A flower of spring, but also a symbol of youthful death, sleep and rebirth. The range of plants belonging to this genus (which include daffodils and jonquils) may account for its wide variety of symbolism. The Narcissus of Greek mythology was a beautiful youth who fell in love with his own reflection in a pool and pined away gazing at it. The story is usually taken to be an allegory of vanity, self-love or, in psychological terms, morbid introspection, but its original symbolism may have been more straightforward. The narcissus blooms and dies early, and, as the anthropologist J. G. Frazer states, self-reflections were feared in the ancient world as omens of death. The narcissus was the flower that Persephone was gathering when the chariot of Hades erupted from the earth and the king of the underworld carried her off to his realm. It was used in the rites of Demeter and planted on graves to symbolize the idea that death was only a sleep (the Greek name for the flower has the same root as "narcosis": *narké*, "numbness"). The fragrance of the narcissus symbolized youth in Persia. Its upright stem also made it an Islamic emblem of the faithful servant or believer. As it bloomed at the Chinese New Year, it was a symbol of joy, good luck or a happy marriage in Oriental tradition. A white narcissus was the sacred lily of China, and sometimes replaces the lily in Christian art as the attribute of the Virgin Mary.

Navel

Creative force, origin of life and spiritual centre, a focus of yogic concentration as a centre of psychic energy. In Vedic tradition, the lotus of creation grew from the navel of Vishnu as he rested on the cosmic waters, giving birth to Brahma. In Norse myth, the Pole Star was the cosmic navel. As a life symbol, the navel is sometimes exaggerated in African statuary. A prominent navel was also a Chinese emblem of strength and beauty.

Necklace

Linking and binding. A symbol with sexual significance in cultures where the neck had erotic associations. In parts of Africa, extravagant neck ornaments were status symbols.

Needle

A yin-yang symbol in China: the eye female, the point male. Needle pricks were often associated with bad luck in folk tales, leading to superstitions against sewing on certain days, as in the Chinese notion that a needle could pierce the Buddha's eye if used in the first five days of New Year.

Net

Magical capture – a symbolism based on the ability of an apparently flimsy device (composed largely of spaces) to ensnare. As described in Luke's gospel, Christ used a net to catch both a miraculous draught of fishes and, through this demonstration of his

Narcissus: *see* DEATH; FLOWERS; Lily

Navel: *see* Lingam; Omphalos; Pole Star

Necklace: *see* Bonds; Chain; Marriage

Needle: *see* Yin-yang

Net: *see* Devils; Fish; Sea

Niche: *see*
Candle; Cave; Lamp,
Lantern; Word

Night: *see*
Chariot; Crescent;
Darkness; DEATH; Mask;
Mother; Owl; Ox; PEACE;
Poppy; Rat; Witchcraft

Night sea crossing: *see*
Belly; Soul; Sun; Whale

Nightingale: *see*
Birds

power, to capture the disciples Simon Peter, James and John, who were themselves to become "fishers of men". As a stealthy snarer of souls, Satan was popularly believed to possess a great net. An earlier mythic symbol of the net's power was its use by the Babylonian hero-god Marduk to subdue Tiamat, chaos goddess of the primeval ocean. Islamic tradition deriving from Iran envisaged a mystic net as the means by which men could apprehend God. Still more poetic is the Taoist image of the stars as the "net of heaven", arranged in a wide mesh through which nothing can escape – in effect a symbol of cosmic unity. In art, nets are usually attributes of sea gods, including the Norse goddess Ran, who gathers drowned souls in her net. The Greek goddess Aphrodite (in Roman myth, Venus) and the god Ares (Mars) are sometimes shown under a net, in reference to the myth that Hephaestus (Vulcan) caught them with a net of bronze wire when he found his consort Aphrodite cuckolding him with the god of war.

Niche

In Christian, Islamic and Hindu architecture, a symbolic cavern formed by a horizontal (earth) beneath an arch (sky) – the dwelling-place of God. A lamp or candle in a niche signifies the divine presence or Word.

Night

Night is personified in Western art by a maternal figure with a white child (sleep) and a black one (death), an image that conveys the ambivalent symbolism of night. As darkness, it is associated with primeval fears of the unknown, concealment, evil and the Powers of Darkness, witchcraft and haunting spirits, despair, madness and death – but also with germination, the passive, female principle, sexuality, rest, peace, sleep, dreams and renewal. The positive symbolism of "silent night, holy night" is as universal as the negativity of "the dark night of the soul". Night was depicted usually as a calm figure with folded wings, although the Greek Nyx, who wore a robe of stars and rode in a chariot pulled by black horses, was associated with inflexible destiny. Her children included not only Thanatos (death) and Hypnos (sleep) but also the Fates. In Renaissance illustration, Night and Day are depicted as black and white rats gnawing at time symbolizing remorselessness. Associated symbols are the crescent moon, the stars, nocturnal creatures (especially the owl), poppies and masks.

Night sea crossing

The influential image of solar death and resurrection expressed in ancient beliefs that the sinking sun plunged into the waters of the underworld, there to voyage eastward throughout the night and be reborn. Jung saw parallels between this primitive notion and myths such as Jonah's reappearance from the belly of a whale or the hellish journeys often depicted in accounts of the soul's passage from death to rebirth.

Nightingale

The anguish and ecstasy of love – a symbolism based on the beauty of the song poured forth by the nightingale cock during its spring mating season. The "immortal Bird" of Keats' *Ode to a Nightingale* (1819) is a metaphor for both singers and poets. Its song has often been linked with pain as well as joy, as in the horrific Greek myth of Philomela whose tongue was cut out in order that she would not reveal that her brother-in-law Tereus had raped her; she was turned into a nightingale by the pitying gods. Usually a good omen, the nightingale was variously said to sing of love, loss, yearning for paradise or, in Japan, holy writ. It was once eaten in the superstitious belief that its meat would promote a musical or eloquent voice.

Nimbus

A cloudy radiance surrounding the head or figure, symbolizing divine energy, sanctity or power. Stylized forms of radiance used in Christian iconography include the arched or circular halo, the rayed aureole and the almond-shaped mandorla. Other conventions were the use of a triangular nimbus for God or the Trinity, cruciform for Christ, square for a living person and hexagonal for allegorical figures. Pagan personifications of sun gods were sometimes surrounded by a nimbus which, in Eastern art, could symbolize power as well as divinity. In paintings, the nimbus is usually gold in Christian art, red in Indian art and blue for the classical sky gods.

Nine

As the triple triad, a supremely powerful number in most traditions, notably in China, in Buddhism and in the Celtic world. The most auspicious Chinese number and most potent yang number, it was the basis of much Taoist ceremonial and of ritual divisions in architecture and property. In mysticism, it represented the triple synthesis of mind, body and spirit, or of the underworld, earth and heaven. Early mathematicians were impressed by the way that multiplication by nine always produced digits that added up to nine. The number was a Hebrew symbol of truth and a Christian symbol of order within order – hence, perhaps, the organization of angels into nine choirs. There were nine heavens or celestial spheres in many traditions and, in Central America, nine underworlds. Often associated with male courage or endurance, nine was a key number in the shamanistic rituals of northern and central Asia. The nine days and nights during which the Nordic god Odin (Wodan in Teutonic tradition) hanged himself on the World Tree Yggdrasil symbolized the ritual period required for his magical resurrection or rejuvenation.

Nirvana

The symbol of transcendence in Hindu and Buddhist thought – a state in which the individual is finally released from cyclic reincarnation, extinguished as "self" but absorbed into the ultimate reality. This blissful state of undifferentiated being or pure illumination lies beyond objective description. Its clarity has been likened in Buddhism to the brilliance of the full moon revealed by parting clouds.

Noon

The hour of revelation in Jewish and Islamic tradition and, more generally, the moment of naked confrontation. The positive spiritual significance of midday comes from the absence of shadows (which, symbolically, are considered harmful) and from ancient rituals of sun worship at the zenith when the sun appeared in its full power and glory.

North see CARDINAL POINTS

Nimbus: *see* Almond; Aureole; Blue; Circle; Gold; Halo; Mandorla; Rays; Red; Sun; Triangle; Trinity

Nine: *see* AFTERWORLDS; Angels; NUMBERS; Three; VIRTUES

Nirvana: *see* Karma; Transformation; Wheel

Noon: *see* Shadow; Sun; Twelve

NUMBERS: *see*
Darkness; Devils; Eight;
Eleven; Five; Forty; Four;
Light; Moon; Music; Nine;
One; Seven; Six; Sun; Ten;
Three; Twelve; Yin-yang;
Zero

NUMBERS

Divine order, the cryptic keys to cosmic harmony. The greatest mathematical philosophers of ancient Babylonia and Greece, and later, India, believed that numbers could reveal the principles of creation and the laws of space and time. In the interplay of odd and even numbers the Greek philosopher Pythagoras (*c*.580–*c*.500BCE) saw the workings of a dualistic universe of opposites – limit and unlimited, straight and curved, square and oblong. "All things are numbers," he said. In Hinduism numbers were the basis of the material universe. The Aztecs assigned to each fundamental number a god, a quality, a direction and a colour. Because numbers were used by gods to regulate the world, they were thought to have particular symbolic significance. Numbers were seen as fundamental in music, poetry, architecture and art.

Jewish Cabbalists allocated number values to letters of the Hebrew alphabet and used the system to re-interpret the Old Testament, a forerunner to numerology. Number superstition is often based on the traditional symbolism of numbers (sacred seven, unlucky 13). The sequence 1, 2, 3 almost universally represented unity, duality and synthesis. In Pythagorean terms, 1, 2, 3, 4 symbolized the flow from point to line to surface to solid. In Greece, odd numbers were masculine and active, even numbers feminine and passive. In China, odd numbers were yang, celestial, immutable and auspicious; even were yin, terrestrial, mutable and sometimes less auspi-

cious. Numbers with archetypal significance ran from one to ten (or one to 12 in duodecimal systems). Higher numbers in which important archetypes reappear (17 in Islamic tradition; 40 in the Semitic world) often reinforce number symbolism.

In many traditions **13** was considered unlucky, possibly because early lunar-based calendars needed the intercalation of a 13th "month", thought to be unfavourable; advice not to sow on the 13th of any month at least goes back to Hesiod (8th century BCE); Satan was the "13th figure" at witch's rites. In the Tarot, Death is the 13th card of the major arcana. In Central America, 13 was sacred (13-day weeks in the religious calendar). The "leftover" five days of the Mayan 20-month solar calendar were unlucky.

Twenty was a sacred number in Central America, associated with the sun god. **21** was associated with wisdom in Hebrew tradition. **Fifty**, the year of jubilee, was hallowed in Jewish tradition because it followed 49 years (sacred 7x7), and so was when debts should be forgiven, slaves freed and property returned. Shabuoth, the Feast of Weeks (on the Pentecostal 50th day) is similarly linked with seven because it follows the end of the seventh week after Passover. **Sixty** was used as the basis for the Chinese calendar. **Seventy**, the biblical life span, represented totality or universality. For many, **10,000** symbolized infinite numbers or infinite time (such as in China). The Greeks called the 10,000 élite warriors of Persia, the "Immortals".

Oak

Might, endurance, longevity, nobility. The oak was sacred to the thunder gods of Greece, Germany, Scandinavia and the Slavic countries, possibly because it was thought to bear the brunt of lightning strikes.

In Druidic rites it served as an axial symbol and natural temple, associated with male potency and wisdom. Although predominantly a male emblem (the acorn was equated by the Celts with the glans penis) Cybele, Juno and other Great Mother Goddesses were also linked with the oak, and the Dryads were oak nymphs. In Greek legend, Herakles' (for the Romans, Hercules') club was of oak, and according to some traditions Christ died on an oaken cross. Oak-leaf clusters are used as military insignia in the US.

Oar

For some seafaring peoples, a rod-like symbol of royal power, executive action or skill, probably by association with its propulsive and guiding force. According to the Roman poet Virgil (70–19BCE), an oar was ceremonially carried around the site of the city of Troy to dedicate its rebuilding. River gods sometimes carry oars in iconography.

Obelisk

An Egyptian symbol of the sun-god Ra in the form of a rectangular, tapering pillar topped by a reflective pyramid designed to catch and concentrate the light. Obelisks were used as funerary pillars or memorials, perhaps emblematic of the penetrative potency of sunbeams and of immortal power. They were also erected as temple pylons, often in pairs.

Ocean see Sea

Octagon

In religious architecture, and particularly in baptisteries, a symbol of rebirth to eternal life. Eight is a number emblematic of renewal, and eight-sided forms were felt to mediate between the symbolism of the square (earthly existence) and the circle (heaven or eternity). In temples, a

Oak: *see*
Acorn; Axis; Club; CROSS; Lightning; LONGEVITY; Mistletoe; Temple; Tree; WISDOM

Oar: *see*
Rod

Obelisk: *see*
Phallus; Pillar; Pyramid; Sun

Octagon: *see*
Baptism; Eight

Octopus: *see*
Amulet; Spiral; Zodiac

Oil: *see*
Anointing; Olive

Olive: *see*
Anointing; Dove; Oil;
PEACE; Tree; WISDOM;
Wreath, Garland

Om (Aum): *see*
Mantra; Triad; Word

*An octopus on a
Minoan vase.*

*The Om sign: the sound
is used in Hindu
meditation.*

dome supported by eight pillars in square plan – representing the cardinal and intercardinal points – was a similar image of totality.

Octopus

A vortex and underworld symbol, linked with the spiral, whirlpool, spider and sea serpent. The octopus shown on Mycenaean medallions with decoratively coiled arms may have been a seafarer's amulet against the dangers of the deep or the evil eye. There are intriguing similarities with the round-faced, snake-haired, paralyzing-eyed Medusa of Greek legend (so close that the similarly tentacled jellyfish is called the "medusa"). A sinister or ,infernal symbolism may also have been suggested by the inky cloud ejected by a frightened octopus. The Zodiac sign Cancer, which is linked with the moon, the waters and the June solstice, was sometimes represented by the octopus rather than the crab.

Oil

Spiritual grace, illumination and benediction – associations traditional in the Middle East where olive oil was used for light and nourishment, and was also a medicinal balm. Anointing kings symbolized their consecration as rulers with divine authority. In many parts of the world, oil was given protective and fertility symbolism.

Olive

A blessed tree in Judeo-Christian, classical and Islamic traditions, famously associated with peace but also with victory, joy, plenty, purity, immortality and virginity. As an early, important and exceptionally durable crop in the Mediterranean world, the olive was sacred in Greece to the warlike goddess Athene, who is said to have invented the tree for Athens, thereby winning a contest with Poseidon for the patronage of the city. The tree was associated also with Zeus, Apollo, Hera and Cybele.

Brides wore or carried olive leaves (signifying virginity), and olive wreaths crowned victors at the Olympic Games. The peace symbolism of the olive became dominant under the *Pax Romana* when olive branches were presented by envoys submitting to the imperial power. For Jewish and Christian symbolists, the olive twig brought back to Noah by the dove (initially signifying nothing more than this tree's hardiness) acquired the Roman emblematic meaning as a sign of peace between God and humanity. The olive tree is an attribute of Peace, Concord and Wisdom in Western art.

In Islamic tradition it is a Tree of Life, associated with the Prophet and also Abraham – one of the two forbidden trees of Paradise. In Japan it is an emblem of friendship and success, in China of calmness.

Om (Aum)

The sacred Hindu syllable representing the primordial sound that created the existential world – the divine Word or mantra of mantras. Its three phonetic elements (*ah-oo-mm*) symbolize fundamental triads, including Brahma, Vishnu and Shiva as creating, sustaining and destroying principles in the cycle of being.

Omphalos

A sacred zone or object symbolizing the cosmic navel or centre of creation – a focus of spiritual and physical forces and a link between the underworld, the earth and the heavens. The omphalos at Delphi – a white standing-stone with a tracery of carving – was sacred to Apollo and may originally have been a focus of Earth Mother worship and divination. In one myth, Rhea (the earth) wrapped the stone in a swaddling cloth and, in place of her newborn son Zeus, gave it to her husband Cronos, who was devouring his children at birth.

Omphalos symbols ranged from stones of phallic shape or ovoids with serpentine carving symbolizing generative forces to sacred trees or mountains. The holes in sacred Chinese jade disks have somewhat similar significance.

One

A number symbolizing primordial unity, the deity or creative essence, the sun or light, and the origin of life.

In Western tradition, the Arabic numeral itself had phallic, axial, aggressive and active symbolism. It was the symbol of God in all the great monotheistic religions, and particularly in Islam.

In Pythagorean thought, the number one was the point, the common basis for all calculation. It was the Confucian perfect entity, the indivisible, the mystic centre from which everything else radiated. More obviously, one is an emblem of the beginning, of the self, and of loneliness.

Orange

Fertility, splendour, love. Orange blossom was an ancient token of fertility, used in bridal wreaths – a custom continued in Christian countries but with the symbolism shifted toward purity.

Oranges were possibly the "golden apples" of the Hesperides, a link with the setting sun. The colour is associated with fire and luxury, except in Buddhist countries where the saffron robes of monks symbolize humility. In art, the Christ Child sometimes holds an orange, a redemption symbol because the orange was thought by some to be the forbidden fruit of the Tree of Knowledge. Oranges are eaten as emblems of good fortune on the second day of the Chinese New Year.

Orb *see* Globe, Orb

Orchid

A Chinese fecundity symbol and charm against sterility, but also an emblem of beauty, scholarship, refinement and friendship. In Chinese paintings, orchids in a vase symbolize concord.

Orgy

A symbol of primeval chaos and the supremacy of instinct and passion as elemental creative forces. Apart from specific orgiastic cults, many ancient cultures institutionalized periods of licence in which social norms were rejected or reversed. In Babylonia, 12 days of anarchy acted out a mythic struggle against the chaos goddess to establish cosmic order.

The Roman Saturnalia was similarly an authorized 12-day carnival at the December solstice to celebrate the rebirth of the vegetation god. The symbolism of the religious orgy, as in the frenzied pagan rites of the Greek god Dionysus, was the annihilation of the difference between the human state – limited by time, morality, social convention or physical stamina – and the timeless, unlimited, ever-energized state of divinity.

Omphalos: *see*
Axis; Centre; Hole; Lingam; Mother; Navel; Phallus; Stone

One: *see*
Axis; NUMBERS; Phallus; Point

Orange: *see*
Apple; COLOURS; Fire, Flame; Yellow

Orchid: *see*
FLOWERS; Vase

Orgy: *see*
Carnival; Solstice; Wine

Orientation: *see*
CARDINAL POINTS;
Light; Sun; Temple

Ostrich: *see*
Birds; Egg; Feathers; Heart

Ouroborus: *see*
Circle; Egg; Snake; Wheel

Oven, Furnace: *see*
Alchemy; Fire, Flame;
Woman

Orientation

The orientation of mosques, temples and churches toward the east is almost universally linked with the symbolism of light as divine illumination. In many Christian churches the eastern window was precisely aligned with the east to allow the rising sun to strike the altar. Alternatively, it faced the direction of the rising sun on the day of the saint to whom the church was dedicated. Islamic worshippers face east to signify that their spirits are turned to the divine source.

Ostrich

An ostrich feather was the attribute of Ma'at, the Egyptian goddess of justice and truth: the mythological feather against which the hearts of the dead were weighed to ascertain if they were heavy with sin. The even length of ostrich feathers is given as a reason for this symbolism of equity. More probably, the feathers had special status because they came from Africa's largest bird. The decorative impact of large ostrich eggs may also explain why they (rather than other eggs) were hung in Eastern Orthodox churches as resurrection symbols.

The idea that the ostrich hides its head in the sand (giving us the modern idiom meaning "not facing facts") seems to have come from its habit of stretching its neck out close to the ground when threatened.

Otter

A lunar animal, linked with fertility and cult initiations in both Africa and North America. The Chinese associated the friendly and playful otter with a high sexual drive, and there are folk tales of otters disguising themselves as women to seduce men.

Ouroboros

The circular image of a snake swallowing its own tail – an emblem of the eternal and indivisible, and of cyclic time. The image has been variously interpreted, combining the creation symbolism of the egg (the space within the circle), the terrestial symbolism of the serpent and the celestial symbolism of the circle. In its original Egyptian religious form, the *ouroboros* is thought to have symbolized the sun's daily return to its point of departure, passing through sky and underworld. In Greece, death and rebirth symbolism seems indicated by its use in Orphic iconography. Gnostics saw it as an image of self-sustaining Nature, endlessly recreating itself, and of unity in duality, the essential oneness of life, the universal serpent moving through all things. The maxim "One is all" sometimes accompanies the symbol. As an emblem of eternity, it was associated in the Roman Empire with Saturn, as the god of time, and Janus, the god of the New Year.

Oval *see* **Lozenge**

Oven, Furnace

A matrix or womb – an instrument of spiritual purification or regeneration. The "burning fiery furnace" into which Nebuchadnezzar cast the Jewish administrators of Babylon, Shadrach, Meshach and Abednego is a biblical symbol of spiritual trial. To the king's astonishment, they came out unscathed, proving the superiority of their God over the golden idol that they had been asked to worship. The purification symbolism of the oven or furnace derives from the processes of metallurgy and alchemy.

The ouroboros*, from an illustration found in a medieval Greek manuscript on alchemy.*

Owl

Now an emblem of sagacity and bookish erudition, the owl had sinister, even ferocious symbolism in some ancient cultures, particularly in China. Its silent, predatory night flights, staring eyes and eerie cry linked it widely with death and with occult powers, particularly of prophecy – perhaps from its ability to see in the dark. It was the bird of death in ancient Egypt, India, Central and North America, China and Japan, but in some traditions it appears as a guardian of the night or guide to the afterlife – among the Native American Plains' Indians, for example, where owl images or ritually worn feathers had protective significance.

In China, young owls were fabled to peck out their mother's eyes. It was an ancient emblem of destructive yang forces, linked with thunder and the June solstice. As a creature of the dark, the owl was a Christian symbol of the Devil or witchcraft, and an image of the blindness of non-belief. Its association with intelligence comes from the Athenians who made the owl sacred to their goddess of wisdom and learning, Athene Pronoia ("the foreseeing"). Greek coins of Athene show an owl on the reverse side. It is from this that the wise owl of European fables is derived, hence the common motif of owls perching on books, and the use of the term "owlish" to describe scholars blinking behind their bifocals. The owl also appears as an attribute of the personifications Night and Sleep.

Ox

Strength, patience, submissiveness, steady toil – a universally benevolent symbol. As the power that drove the ancient plough, the ox was a valuable animal, often used as a sacrifice, especially in cultic rituals connected with agricultural fertility.

The ox is a Christian symbol of the sacrificial Christ and also the emblem of St Luke and of the priesthood generally. With the ass, it is the beast most often shown at the Nativity, and sometimes appears supporting baptismal fonts. Now identified with slow-witted brawn, the epithet "dumb ox" was once applied by Albertus Magnus to his bulky but formidably intelligent student Thomas Aquinas (1225–74): "One day the dumb ox will fill the world with his lowing."

As an image of humanity's animal nature mastered, the ox is a Taoist and Buddhist attribute of the sage and of contemplative learning in China. The white ox was a forbidden food in several traditions. In the classical world, white oxen were sacrificed to the Greek god Zeus (in Roman myth, Jupiter) and black to Hades (Pluto). Black oxen pull the chariot of Death in art and are also an attribute of Night. Lunar associations often distinguish the ox from the solar bull.

Oyster

Female sexuality and reproduction – a symbolism taken both from the general fertility symbolism of water and from the association between bivalves and the vulva. Pistol's famous boast, "Why then the world's mine oyster, which I with sword shall open" (Shakepeare's *The Merry Wives of Windsor*, 2:2; *c*.1600) refers not to this symbolism but to the idea that wealth can be found anywhere, like pearls in oysters – a misconception, as the mollusc that produces true pearls is not the edible oyster.

Owl: *see*
AFTERWORLDS; Birds;
DEATH; Devils; Moon;
Night; WISDOM;
Witchcraft

Ox: *see*
Ass; Baptism; Black; Cow;
DEATH; Night; Sacrifice;
White

Oyster: *see*
Pearl

The wise owl, an attribute of the goddess Athene, from an ancient Greek coin.

Pagoda: *see*
Axis; Mountain; Steps,
Stairs

Palm: *see*
Branch, Bough; Date;
LONGEVITY; Pilgrimage;
Tree; Victory; VIRTUES

Pa Kua *see* **Trigram**

Pagoda
An architectural symbol of the Buddha and of heavenly ascent through progressive stages of spiritual enlightenment. The tiered pagoda, widely found in southeast Asia, China and Japan, was based on an Indian temple near Peshawar. It was the prototype for the conical stupa or sacred funeral mound which is an architectural diagram of the cosmos.

The tiers rising in diminishing scale represent the steps up the World Mountain or the axis linking earth and sky. The word *pagoda* is thought to be a Portugese corruption of the Sanskrit word *bhagavati* (meaning "of the divine").

Pairs *see* **Doubles; Twins**

Palm
Victory, supremacy, fame, longevity, resurrection and immortality. The majestic palm with its huge, radiant leaves was a solar and triumphal symbol in the ancient Middle East; it was equated with the Tree of Life in both Egypt and Arabia. As a food source, one species, the date palm, also had feminine, fecundity symbolism both in western Asia and China. Thus, palm motifs are associated not only with the sun cult of Apollo but also with the goddesses Astarte and Ishtar – and later with the Virgin Mary (Song of Solomon 7:7: "you are stately as a palm tree").

The emblematic use of palm fronds in victory processions (and as awards to winning gladiators) was adapted by Christianity to mean victory over death through Christ, whose entry into Jerusalem is celebrated on Palm Sunday. The palm, already a symbol of longevity or immortality, thus became the attribute in art of many Christian saints and martyrs as well as of Victory, Fame and (through the Virgin Mary) Chastity. St Paul the Hermit (*c*.249–341CE) wears a loincloth of woven palm leaves. Pilgrims who had visited the Holy Land were "palmers". Palm forms on lamps or other funerary objects symbolize resurrection.

Pansy

Fond remembrance, hence its common name "heartsease". The word *pansy* comes from the French *pensée* ("thought"). Some symbologists have proposed a tortuous link between this and the number five, the number of petals that the flower has. The symbolism of the petals is more plausibly based on their heart-like shape and the "thoughts" of the heart.

Panther *see* Leopard

Paradise *see* AFTERWORLDS

Parasol

Sovereignty, spiritual dominion, ascension, dignity, wealth, protection – a solar and royal emblem throughout India and Asia. In India the parasol was an attribute of Vishnu and of the Buddha. On a terrestrial level, it both protected dignitaries from the sun and acted as an elaborate symbol of their high status, its domed top representing the sky, its radiating struts the sun's rays acting as a solar nimbus, its shaft the world axis. The same symbolism appears in the parasol-like disks surmounting pagodas, representing heavenly spheres. The struts of the parasol also symbolized wheels of energy (*chakras*) in Tantric Buddhism.

Parrot

A messenger or link between humanity and the spirit world, an obvious symbolism in view of its talkativeness. Parrots were therefore associated with prophecy and thought to be useful rain-makers, both in India and Central America. The parrot also appears as an attribute of the Hindu god of love, Kama. In Chinese folk tales, parrots inform on adulterous

---

PASSION
In Christian symbolism, the suffering and Crucifixion of Christ, in particular the period from the Agony in the Garden to the Descent from the Cross, forming a major theme in world art. Symbols of the Passion include the chalice, cock, cross, crown of thorns, dice, the goldfinch, a hammer and nails, a ladder, lamb, pelican, silver coins, purple or red robe, red poppy, red rose, reeds, rope, skull, spear, sponge, sword, vinegar and whip.

The deposition of Christ – the last event of the Passion when he was taken from the Cross. A detail after a painting by Petrus Christus, c.1450.

---

wives. As a gaudy chatterer, a parrot is a Chinese slang term for a bar-girl.

Partridge

Fecundity, love, feminine beauty. The partridge was associated with the goddess Aphrodite in Greece and with grace and beauty in Indo-Iranian tradition; folk superstition crediting its flesh with aphrodisiac qualities. Adverse analogies by some early Christian writers, particularly St Jerome, led to the bird being linked in Romanesque iconography with ill-gotten gains, and its cry with the temptations of Satan.

PASSION *see panel, above*

PEACE *see panel on p.154*

Peach

One of the most favourable of all Chinese and Japanese symbols, its wood, blossom and fruit linked with immortality, longevity, spring, youth, marriage and protective magic. In Chinese myth, the peach Tree of Immortality, tended by the Queen of

Pansy: *see*
Five; FLOWERS; Heart

Parasol: *see*
Axis; Chakras; Disk; Dome; Nimbus; Rays; Sun; Wheel

Parrot: *see*
Birds

Partridge: *see*
Birds

PASSION: *see individual names*

Peach: *see*
Bow; FRUIT; Heart; LONGEVITY; Rod; Tongue; Tree; VIRTUES; Wood

PEACE: *see individual names*

Peacock: *see* Birds; Chalice; Dance; Eye; Pheasant; SEVEN DEADLY SINS; Snake; Sun; Throne; Tree; Wheel

A peacock, after a medieval Persian painting.

Heaven, Xi Wang Mu, fruits every 3,000 years. Shou Lao, god of longevity, holds a peach or is depicted within the fruit. Peachwood was used to make miraculous bows, exorcism rods, talismans, oracular figures and effigies of tutelary gods; and peach boughs were laid outside houses at New Year. This apotropaic significance appears in Japan too, as in the story that Izanagi routed eight pursuing thunder gods by hurling three peaches at them. In both countries, peach blossom is an emblem of purity and virginity. The peach is one of the Three Blessed Fruits of Oriental Buddhism. In Western Renaissance art, a peach with a leaf attached was an emblem of truthfulness – a reference to an ancient use of this image as a symbol of the tongue speaking from the heart.

Peacock
Solar glory, immortality, royalty, incorruptibility, pride. The shimmering majesty of the male peacock's display is the origin of its association with immortality. In the ancient traditions of India and later in Iran, the wheel-like radiance of this display was a symbol of the "all-seeing" sun and of the eternal cycles of the cosmos. Because snakes were enemies of the sun in Iranian symbolism, the peacock was said to kill them and use their saliva to create the iridescent bronze–greens and blue–gold "eyes" of its tail feathers. To this legend was added the idea that the peacock's flesh was incorruptible. As the fame of the bird spread and it was put on show in the Mediterranean world, it became an emblem not only of rebirth (as in early Christian symbolism) but also of the starry firmament, and therefore of cosmic totality and unity. Unity in duality (the sun at zenith and the full moon) is depicted by the Islamic motif of two facing peacocks beside the Cosmic Tree.

In classical tradition, the peacock became sacred to the Greek goddess Hera (in Roman myth, Juno), who was said to have bestowed on it the 100 eyes of the slain Argus Panoptes ("all-seeing"). Peacocks were widely held as emblems of royalty, spiritual power and apotheosis. In Rome, the peacock was the soul-bird of the empress and her princesses, as the eagle was of the emperor. The Persian court was the "Peacock Throne", and peacocks are also associated with the thrones of the Hindu god Indra, Amitabha (who presides over the Chinese Buddhist paradise) and the wings of the cherubim who support the throne of Jehovah. The peacock is the escort or mount of several Hindu deities, notably Sarasvati (of wisdom, music and poetry), Kama (of sexual desire) and the war-god Skanda (who could also transform poisons into the elixir of immortality). As a Buddhist emblem of Avalokiteshvara (Guanyin in China) the peacock represents compassionate watchfulness – and had similar meaning in the Christian Church. Peacocks sometimes appear in Christian art at the Nativity or drinking from a chalice – both motifs of eternal life. However, Christian doctrines of humility led to an analogy between the peacock and the sins of pride, luxury and vanity (associations instigated by the 2nd-century-CE scientific text *Physiologus*). Although the peacock thus chiefly personifies Pride in Western art, most other traditions saw it as a wholly positive symbol of rank and dignity, especially in China where it was an emblem of the Ming dynasty. Peacock dances of southeast Asia draw on the original idea of the bird as a solar emblem, its enacted "death" bringing rain.

Pear

A mother or love symbol, its erotic associations probably taken from the swelling shape of the fruit, suggesting the female pelvis or breast. Linked in classical mythology with the Greek goddesses Hera (in Roman myth, Juno) and Aphrodite (Venus), the pear was also a longevity symbol in China, because the tree itself is long-lived. However, white symbolized mourning in China, and so pear blossom was a funerary token.

Pearl

Among jewels, the quintessential symbol both of light and of femininity – its pale iridescence associated with the luminous moon, its watery origins with fertility, its secret life in the shell with miraculous birth or rebirth.

Hidden light also made the pearl a symbol of spiritual wisdom or esoteric knowledge. The pearl is an emblem both of fecundity and of purity, virginity and perfection. To the ancients, the jewel in the mollusc – an image of fire and water unified – was a marvel and a mystery, conjuring up theories of celestial impregnation by rain or dew falling into the open shell, by thunder and lightning, or by trapped moonlight or starlight. Hence the appearance in Chinese art of the pearl (lightning) in the throat of the dragon (thunder). As a form of celestial light, the pearl is the third eye (spiritual illumination) of Shiva and of the Buddha. It is the Islamic word of God, the Taoist mystic centre, the Christian "pearl of great price" from the waters of baptism. It is also a metaphor for Christ in the womb of the Virgin Mary. Spiritual symbolism persisted even after the Chinese found a non-celestial explanation for the production of pearls. They formed nacreous Buddhas by placing small metal images inside the freshwater molluscs used to produce cultured blister pearls.

The transfiguration of matter into a "spiritual" jewel made the pearl a widespread symbol of rebirth and led to the expensive Asian funerary custom of placing a pearl in the mouth of the dead, and of pearl-decorated tombs in Egypt. In the afterlife, pearls formed the individual spheres enclosing the Islamic blessed – and the gates of the new Jerusalem (in Revelation). They were thought to be medicinal as well as sacred. The Romans, who wore pearls in homage to Isis, used them as talismans against everything from shark attacks to lunacy, and powdered pearl is still an Indian panacea.

Pear: *see* Breasts; FRUIT; LONGEVITY; Mother; White

Pearl: *see* AFTERWORLDS; Dew; Dragon; Eye; Fire, Flame; JEWELS; Light; Lightning; Moon; Oyster; Thunder; Virginity; Water

Pelican: *see*
Birds; Blood; CROSS;
Phoenix; VIRTUES

Pentagram, Pentacle: *see*
Circle; Five; Hexagram;
Horn; NUMBERS; Star;
Three; Two

*A pelican: a detail from
a wood-carving on a
tabernacle.*

The sexual symbolism of the pearl is ambivalent. In classical tradition it was worn by the foam-born love-goddess Aphrodite (in Roman myth, Venus). Yet it is also a symbol of purity and innocence. Its association with tears (of sorrow and of joy) made it an unlucky bridal jewel – a broken pearl necklace was particularly ominous. Yet it was a propitious jewel in the East – one of the Eight Jewels of China and Three Imperial Insignia of Japan. In the ancient world, pearls were also, of course, straightforward symbols of wealth (the richest of all merchandise, according to the Latin writer Pliny, *c*.24–79CE), fished from the Persian Gulf centuries before the birth of Christ. Cleopatra reputedly dropped a pearl earring in her wine and drank it to show Antony how rich she was.

Pelican
Self-sacrificial love – a symbolism based on the legend that pelicans tear their breasts (rather than empty their bills) to feed their young. The earliest Christian bestiary drew an analogy between the male pelican's reviving its young with its blood and Christ's shedding his blood for humankind. The pelican sometimes appears in Crucifixion paintings with this meaning, and can represent Charity in still lifes and filial devotion in heraldry. It represents Christ's human nature when paired with the phoenix.

Pentagram, Pentacle
A geometric symbol of harmony, health and mystic powers – a five-pointed star with lines that cross to each point. When used in magic rituals, this sign is usually called the pentacle. The pentagram seems to have

The pentagram or pentacle – a five pointed star, thought to be the seal of Solomon and used in divination.

originated in Mesopotamia 4,000 years ago, probably as an astronomical plot of the movements of the planet Venus. It became a Sumerian and Egyptian stellar sign, is thought to have been the figure used on the Seal of Solomon (although the hexagram is also proposed), and was the official seal of Jerusalem *c*.300–*c*.150BCE. In Greece, the Pythagoreans adopted it as an emblem of health and mystic harmony, the marriage of heaven and earth, combining the number two (terrestrial and feminine) with three (heavenly and masculine). The resulting number five symbolized the microcosm of the human body and mind. From this point on, the pentagram steadily acquired occult meaning. Gnostics and alchemists associated it with the five elements, Christians with the protective five wounds of Christ, medieval sorcerers with Solomon's reputed powers over nature and the spirit world.

Magicians sometimes wore pentacle caps of fine linen to conjure up supernatural help. In casting spells, special powers were credited to pentacles drawn on virgin calfskin, but they were also protectively inscribed in wood, on rocks and on amulets or rings. Goethe's *Faust* (1808) draws a pentacle to prevent Mephistopheles from crossing his doorway. With one point upward and two down, the pentacle was the sign of white magic, the "Druid's foot". With one down and two up, it represented the "Goat's foot" and horns of the Devil – a characteristic symbolic inversion. Latin or Cabbalistic Hebrew lettering often appears on talismanic pentacles drawn within protective circles. The pentacle was also a Masonic aspirational symbol, the "flaming star".

Peony

An imperial flower of China, associated with wealth, glory and dignity because of its showy beauty. It was a Japanese fertility symbol, linked with joy and marriage. In the West its roots, seeds and flowers had an ancient medicinal reputation, hence its name, taken from the Greek word for "physician" and from the Paeon who healed the gods who had been wounded at Troy. The peony is sometimes identified as the "rose without a thorn".

Phallus

Creation, generative force, the source of life – a solar and active fertility symbol widely believed to be protective and lucky. Overscale erect phalluses in art were often more symbolic than erotic. Figures of Priapus, the hideous but enormously well-endowed son of the god Dionysus (Bacchus, in Roman myth) and goddess Aphrodite (Venus) were placed in Greek and Roman gardens, vineyards and orchards to encourage growth

and scare off thieves as well as crows with his red-painted phallus. Many upright or penetrative objects used as symbols in the ancient world had phallic significance. Phallic funerary objects symbolized the continuity of life after death. Phallic-shaped talismans were popular with farmers and fishermen, and were also used as charms against sterility.

Pheasant

An imperial and yang emblem in China, associated by its beauty and colour with the sun, light, virtue and the organizing ability of high-ranking civil servants. The Chinese also linked it with thunder, presumably from its clapping wings. In Japan it was a messenger of the great sun-goddess Amaterasu. The Chinese pheasant and Indian peacock (members of the same family) were exotic birds in ancient Europe, and their shining plumage may have influenced artistic depictions of the fabled phoenix.

Philosopher's stone

The key to spiritual enlightenment. In the physical processes of alchemy, the "stone" was a mysterious substance which, once created, could be used as a powder or tincture at the final stage of the Great Work to turn base metals into gold. Symbolism based on this belief made the Philosopher's Stone the elixir of life, the Grail itself – the spiritual wholeness that human beings strive to find.

Phoenix

The most famous of all rebirth symbols – a legendary bird that endessly renews itself in fire. The phoenix legend had its origin in the city of Heliopolis, ancient centre of Egyptian

Peony: *see*
FLOWERS; Rose

Phallus: *see*
Head; Lingam; Man;
Omphalos; Pillar; Rod

Pheasant: *see*
Birds; Peacock; Phoenix;
Sun; Thunder

Philosopher's stone: *see*
Alchemy; Gold; Grail

Phoenix: *see*
Alchemy; BEASTS OF
FABLE; Birds; Eagle; Fire;
Flame; Heron;
LONGEVITY; Palm;
Pelican; Pheasant; Red;
Salamander; Sulphur; Sun

A representation of the Philosopher's stone, from a 17th-century alchemist's book.

Phrygian cap: *see*
Cap; Horn; LIBERTY; Red;
Sacrifice

*A phoenix rising from the ashes,
from an illustration in a 14th-
century herbal.*

sun worship, where sacrifices were
made to the heron-like Benu as the
creative spirit of the sun. Based on
these fire rituals and on descriptions
of more gorgeous exotic birds such as
the golden pheasant, Greek writers
wove stories which vary in detail but
have an overall coherence. The
phoenix (a word applied to the solar
palm tree as well as to the bird) was a
unique male bird of miraculous
longevity – 500 years, or more by
some accounts. At the end of this
period, the phoenix built an aromatic
nest, immolated itself, was reborn
after three days, and carried the nest
and ashes of its previous incarnation
to the altar of the sun in Heliopolis.

Initially a symbol of the cyclic dis-
appearance and reappearance of the
sun, the phoenix soon became an
emblem of human resurrection – and
eventually of the indomitable human
spirit in overcoming trials. Because
artists were never quite sure what it
looked like, its iconography is easily
confused with the general solar (and
soul) symbolism of other birds –

especially with the eagle released from
the pyre of a Roman emperor.

On Roman coins the phoenix symbolized the undying empire. It appears
in early Christian funerary sculpture
as a symbol of Christ's resurrection
and the hope of victory over death. In
medieval paintings it represents the
divine nature of Christ when paired
with the pelican (a symbol of his
human nature). The phoenix can also
appear as an attribute of Charity. A
common motif in alchemy, it symbolizes the purifying and transforming
fire, the chemical element sulphur,
and the colour red. A Jewish legend
attributed the bird's longevity to its
refusal to eat the forbidden fruit of
paradise.

Analogies are sometimes made
between the phoenix and other fabled
birds. These include the Persian
Simurgh, the Chinese Feng-huang (a
symbol of conjugal interdependence)
and the Central American Quetzal
bird. Only the Simurgh shares enough
of the phoenix's symbolism to suggest
that the two myths might have
enriched one another. There are closer
links with Arabic legends of the salamander that lives in fire.

Phrygian cap

A conical cap of soft felt which
became an emblem of liberty during
the French Revolution – as in
Delacroix's painting *Liberty Leading
the People* (1830). This style of cap
was worn by the freemen of Phrygia in
Asia Minor under the reign of Midas.

In art, the youth Paris can be shown
wearing it – perhaps a reference to the
phallic significance of its pointed
cone. Traditionally the cap was red,
suggesting sacrificial symbolism,
aptly so in the French Revolution.

Pig

Gluttony, selfishness, lust, obstinacy and ignorance – but also motherhood, fertility, prosperity and happiness. The affectionate view of pigs in much myth contrasts with their generally negative symbolism in world religious traditions. In earlier cultures, sows were venerated as Great Mother emblems of fecundity. The Egyptian sky-goddess Nut was sometimes depicted as a sow suckling her piglets (the stars). The sow was linked also with Isis and with mother goddesses in Mesopotamia, Scandinavia and the Celtic world, where Ceridwen was a sow goddess. The Celtic legend of Manannan, who had a herd of miraculously self-renewing pigs, expressed a general symbolism of abundance.

In some accounts of Greek myth a sow nourished the infant Zeus (in Roman myth, Jupiter), and pigs were prestigious fertility sacrifices, offered to the agricultural deities Demeter (Ceres), Ares (Mars) and Gaia. The pig was also a fertility (and virility) symbol in China.

Jewish and Islamic distrust of eating scavengers' meat, together with more general associations between pigs and animal passions (as in the Greek myth of Circe who turned her suitors into pigs) changed all this. In Western art the pig symbolizes Gluttony and Lust (spurned by the figure of Chastity) as well as Sloth. The story of how Christ cast out demons into the Gadarene swine (Matthew 8:28–34) symbolized the need for humanity to sublimate its sensual greed. A similar theme appears in Buddhism where the pig, symbolizing ignorance, is one of the three animals that tie humankind to the endless wheel of existence.

Pigeon see Dove

Pilgrimage

A journey to a spiritual centre, symbolizing trial, expiation or purification, and the achievement of a goal or ascension to a new plane of existence. In an emblematic sense, the pilgrimage is as much an initiation as an act of devotion. Its rationale is the ancient belief that supernatural forces manifest themselves most powerfully at particular localities. In the Islamic faith, the location is Mecca, birthplace of the Prophet. In Hinduism it is Benares on the Ganges. For Buddhists and Christians it is key sites in the life of Gautama Buddha and Christ. When the Holy Land fell under Islamic rule, the focus of huge Christian pilgrimages shifted to the shrines of saints, notably in Rome (associated with Peter and Paul) and in Santiago de Compostela (James, the son of Zebedee). More recently the cult of the Virgin Mary has again shifted Roman Catholic pilgrimages to places where she is said to have appeared and where miraculous cures are therefore expected. Traditional symbols of the Western pilgrim include the bowl, broad-brimmed hat, cowl (sometimes bearing a red cross), gourd or flask, palm leaves (signifying a visit to Palestine), sack, scallop shell (the attribute of St James) and staff.

Pillar

An obvious general symbol of support, but also a sacred axis and emblem of divine power, vital energy, ascension, steadfastness, strength and stability – terrestrial and cosmic. A broken pillar or pole was a symbol of death or chaos not only in Western art but for the Aboriginals of Australia.

Pig: *see*
Animals; Mother; Sacrifice; SEVEN DEADLY SINS; Sky; VIRTUES; Wheel

Pilgrimage: *see*
Centre; Initiation; *and individual names*

Pillar: *see*
Axis; Crown; Eagle; Fire, Flame; Liberty; Maypole; Moon; Obelisk; Ram; Sun; Thyrsus; Tree; VIRTUES

Pine, Pine cone

Pine, Pine cone: *see*
Bamboo; Cedar; Christmas
tree; Deer; FIDELITY; Fire,
Flame; Maypole;
Mushroom; Plum; Stork;
Tree; Yule log

Freestanding pillars in the ancient world often had specific emblematic meanings, and architectural columns sometimes did also. At a primitive level, pillars of wood or stone often represented either World Trees (like the German Irmensul) or supreme gods. Two pillars engraved with eagles were a focus of the worship of Zeus on Mt Lycaeon in Arcadia. In Egypt the *djed* pole (a pillar eventually embellished with four capitals) was said to represent the spinal column of the god Osiris, symbolically canalizing his flow of immortal life. Mesopotamian and Phoenician gods were similarly represented by pillars, sometimes topped by emblems such as the ram's head of the great Ea. At Carthage, three pillars symbolized the moon and its phases. The role of the pillar as a symbol of communication with supernatural forces is also clear in pre-Columbian cultures, as at Machu Picchu where Inca priests ritually "tied" their sun god to a pillar.

In the Book of Exodus, the God of the Israelites guides his people through Sinai as a pillar of fire. The fiery pillar is likewise a symbol of the Buddha. In Hinduism a pillar with a crown symbolizes the Way. Wisdom has seven pillars according to the Book of Proverbs. Five devotional pillars mark the true follower of Islam. Two giant pillars, called Jachin and Boaz, flanked the porch of Solomon's Temple, a symbol of stability in duality – later taken as a Masonic emblem of justice and benevolence. In art, the pillar is the attribute of Fortitude and Constancy, and it is with this symbolism that Christ appears tied to a pillar in scenes of his flagellation.

Heroes of legendary strength and courage are associated with pillars –

the Irish Cúchulainn belts himself to one so that he can die upright; Samson dies wrenching down the pillars of the Philistine temple; Herakles sets up the rock of Gibraltar and the citadel of Ceuta as pillars of the civilized world, keeping monsters out of the Mediterranean and prudent men in. The boastful heraldic device of Charles V showed the Pillars of Herakles with the words *plus ultra* ("farther beyond"), a reference to Spanish dominions in the Americas.

Pine, Pine cone
In Oriental symbolism, the most important of all resinous evergreens, representing immortality or longevity. Like the cedar, it was linked with incorruptibility and was planted around Chinese graves with this symbolism. Its resin was fabled to produce the mushrooms on which the Taoist immortals fed. The Scots pine is a favourite motif in Chinese and Japanese art, either singly representing longevity or in pairs representing married fidelity. It appears often with other emblems of longevity or renewal including the plum, bamboo, mushroom, stork and white stag. The pine is also an emblem of courage, resolution and good luck – the tree of the Shinto New Year. As the fir, it is similarly propitious in Nordic tradition, sacred to Odin (Wodan), and the centre of the Yuletide rites that led to its adoption as the Christmas tree of Western Europe. Its general symbolism in the West was linked to agricultural fertility, particularly in the Roman spring rebirth rites of Cybele and Attis (represented by a pine wound around with wool), the probable origin of the maypole. The pine was sacred also to the Greek gods

Zeus (Jupiter in Roman myth). The emblem of the god Dionysus (Bacchus), is the *thyrsus* (rod) tipped with a pine cone. The cone itself is a phallic and flame symbol of masculine generative force. Surmounting a column (and sometimes mistaken for the pineapple), it was an emblem of the Mesopotamian hero-god Marduk.

Pitcher

Like other vessels, a maternal womb symbol, associated in iconography with the source of life or (in Egypt where it is an attribute of Isis and Osiris) the fertilizing waters. In art, Temperance pours water from one pitcher to another. Hebe, handmaiden of the gods, carries a pitcher. It is the attribute of Aquarius and of the Star in the Tarot pack.

PLANETS *see panel on p.162*

Plants *see* Vegetation

Plough

An Old Testament symbol of the peaceful arts of agriculture, and more generally a male fertility symbol – the phallic plough entering the female earth. Ritual ploughing by a new Chinese emperor symbolized his responsibility for the fertility of his country. The plough is an emblem of the Silver Age, the descent into labour. Nomadic peoples both in western Asia and in America, where the plough was unknown before Europeanization, once saw ploughing as an affront to the integrity of Mother Earth. The Plough asterism (a group of seven bright stars in the constellation Ursa Major) was taken as a symbol of the celestial energy that created diversity from primal unity.

Plum

In China, where the hardy Oriental plum blossoms early, an important symbol both of longevity and of virginity or nuptial happiness. Because its flowers appeared in late winter, it joined the pine and bamboo as one of the Three Friends of Winter. Legend said that the great sage Lao-tse was born under a plum, and the tree was a samurai emblem in Japan.

Point

In mystical thought, the centre and origin of life – a symbol of primordial creative power, sometimes conceived as being so concentrated that it could be represented only in a non-material way – as a hole. This ancient symbolism of infinitely compressed energy, widespread in mystical writing, comes close to the central theories of modern astronomy and physics.

Pole Star

Constancy, the axis of the wheeling firmament. Polaris, visible as the bright unmoving North Star in the constellation Ursa Minor, was of enormous importance in navigation. Many traditions revered it as the zenith of a supernatural pole or pillar linking the terrestrial and celestial spheres. It was sometimes thought to be the shining Gate of Heaven. The ancient Egyptians associated the pole star of their era (Thuban in Draco) with the souls of their pharaohs, the Chinese with a supreme being. The North Pole itself – sometimes depicted as a plumbline, as in Masonic symbolism – was connected to a spiritual centre individual to each culture, often a sacred mountain or World Tree. The globe surmounted by a cross is a polar emblem.

Pitcher: *see*
Tarot; Water; Woman; VIRTUES; Zodiac

Plough: *see*
Earth; PEACE

Plum: *see*
Bamboo; FRUIT; LONGEVITY; Pine, Pine cone; Virginity

Point: *see*
Centre; Hole

Pole Star: *see*
CROSS; Globe, Orb; Mountain; Soul; Tree; Wheel

PLANETS

The ancient belief that the planets were powerful living gods has profoundly influenced the evolution of symbolism. For more than two thousand years after the Greeks incorporated this belief into their myths, leading thinkers in the fields of science, philosophy and religion accepted the principle that all the planets presided over events on earth – as the sun and moon unarguably do. Although astrology and science had parted company by the 18th century, planetary symbolism had by then become an inextricable part of human life. The days of the week are themselves based on the seven "planets" which the ancients could see moving busily against the vast backcloth of the stars. Taking the earth as the unmoving centre, these seven (a mystic number in consequence) were the moon, Mercury, the sun, Venus, Mars, Jupiter and Saturn (the other three planets were as yet unknown). To each were assigned characteristics based partly on their colour and motion, and a system of "correspondences" linking them to specific directions of space, colours, metals, bodily organs, jewels, flowers and so on. The theory underlying this complex symbol system was that the "planets" and all aspects of terrestrial nature, including humankind, were interconnected. Of the seven "planets", the moon, Mars and Saturn had potential for evil, the others were perceived as generally beneficial.

Set out below are the distinguishing features that identify the planets in the cosmology and myth of Western tradition.

Mercury Personified by an androgynous, lissom youth: Mercury (Roman), Hermes (Greek) or Nabu (Mesopotamian). He has a caduceus, a winged cap and sandals, and is associated with mobility, mediation, reason, eloquence, free will, adaptation, commerce, Wednesday, quicksilver, purple or grey-blue, the centre, Virgo and Gemini.

Venus Personified by a beautiful woman: Venus (Roman), Aphrodite (Greek), Ishtar (Mesopotamian). Attributes include laurel, myrtle and rose, the shell or dolphin, the torch or flaming heart and a chariot drawn by doves or swans. Associated with love (sacred or profane), desire, sexuality, pleasure, rebirth, imagination, harmony and happiness as the evening star (in Mesopotamia, war as

Left to right: Jupiter, Mars, sun, Saturn, moon, Mercury, Venus (from the Dijon Bible).

morning star), Friday, copper, green/pale yellow, west as the evening star, Libra and Taurus.

Mars Personified by an aggressive man: Mars (Roman), Ares (Greek), Nergal (Mesopotamian). Helmeted with a shield and sword or spear, perhaps mounted, sometimes with a wolf. Energy, violence, courage, ardour, tension, fire, Tuesday, iron, red, south, Aries and Scorpio.

Jupiter Personified by an imposing, godlike man: Jupiter (Roman), Zeus (Greek), Marduk (Mesopotamian), often bearded. Attributes include the eagle, sceptre and thunderbolt. Power, equilibrium, justice, optimism, organizing ability, Thursday, tin, blue, east, Sagittarius and Pisces.

Saturn Usually personified by a man with a grey beard: Saturn (Roman), Cronos (Greek), Ninib (Mesopotamian). He has a sickle and often a crutch. Once associated with agriculture but generally with pessimism, rigidity, morality, religion, chastity, contemplation, inertia, death, melancholy, Saturday, lead, black, north, Capricorn and Aquarius.

In **Chinese astrology**, Mercury was linked with north, water and black; Venus (male) west, metal and white; Mars south, fire and red; Jupiter east, wood and blue; Saturn the centre, earth and yellow.

Pomegranate

Fecundity, abundance, generosity, sexual temptation. The multicellular structure of the pomegranate with its many seeds bedded in juicy pulp within a leathery casing also led to subsidiary emblematic meanings – the oneness of the diverse cosmos, the manifold blessings of God, the Christian Church protecting its many members. An ancient Persian fruit, known to the Romans as the "apple of Carthage", the pomegranate was predominantly a fertility symbol linked with love, marriage and many children both in the Mediterranean world and in China, where it was one of the Three Blessed Fruits of Buddhism. It was sacred to love goddesses such as Astarte and Aphrodite (Venus in Roman myth), and also to the maternal and agricultural goddesses Hera (Juno), who holds a pomegranate as a marriage symbol, and Demeter (Ceres) or her daughter Persephone (Proserpine). Hades gave a pomegranate (symbolizing indissoluble wedlock) to Persephone when she asked permission to return to the earth's surface. By eating it, she condemned herself to spend four months each year with her underworld lord – a sexual symbolism exploited in Rossetti's pre-Raphaelite painting of her holding a bitten pomegranate (*Proserpina*, 1874). The fruit was said to have sprung from the blood of Dionysus (a spring fertility god). This tradition accounts for paintings in which Christ holds a pomegranate as a resurrection symbol. Muhammad recommended the fruit to purge envy and hatred.

Poplar

A duality symbol in China because the leaves of the white poplar are dark green on the upper (solar) side but appear white on the lower (moon) side where they are covered with down.

The Greeks explained this colour change in the myth of Herakles (Hercules to the Romans) who bound a poplar branch around his head for his descent into the underworld. Smoke darkened the top of the leaves while his sweat blanched their lower surfaces. The poplar was sacred to Sabazius and to Zeus (Jupiter), but is usually funerary in its symbolism.

Poppy

In art, an emblem of the Greek gods of sleep (Hypnos) and dreams (Morpheus); and in allegory, of Night personified – a symbolism based on the properties of the opium poppy which grew as a wild flower in Greece and the eastern Mediterranean, and was used for herbal infusions from ancient times. The poppy was linked also with the Greek agricultural-goddess Demeter (Ceres in Roman myth) and her daughter Persephone (Proserpine) as a symbol of the winter "sleep" of vegetation. Christianity borrowed aspects of this older tradition, making the red poppy an emblem of Christ's sacrifice and "sleep of death". The battlefields of Flanders gave fresh poignancy to the sacrificial symbolism of the red poppy.

Precious stones *see* Jewels

Primrose

Wanton pleasure – as in Ophelia's warning to her brother not to tread "the primrose path of dalliance" (Shakespeare's *Hamlet*, 1:3; *c*.1600). This early budding perennial was a European emblem of youth, linked to the "little people" of Celtic folklore.

PLANETS: *see*
Androgyne; Black; Blue; Caduceus; CARDINAL POINTS; COLOURS; Dolphin; Dove; Eagle; Green; Heart; Iron; JEWELS; Laurel; Lead; Mercury; METALS; Moon; Music; Myrtle; NUMBERS; Red; Rose; Sceptre; Seven; Shell; Sickle, Scythe; Spear; Star; Sun; Swan; Sword; Thumb; Thunder; Torch; VIRTUES; Week; White; Wolf; Wood; Yellow; Ziggurat; Zodiac

Pomegranate: *see*
Apple; Blood; FRUIT; Marriage; Vulva

Poplar: *see*
Branch; Tree

Poppy: *see*
FLOWERS; Night; Sacrifice

Primrose: *see*
FLOWERS

A detail showing the Christ Child fed from a pomegranate, from Madonna Della Melagrana *by Sandro Botticelli (1480s).*

Prince, Princess: *see* Frog

Procession: *see* Ark; Dragon; Sacrifice

Purgatory: *see* AFTERWORLDS; Alchemy; Fire, Flame

Purple: *see* COLOURS

Pyramid: *see* Light; Mound; Obelisk; Sun; Ziggurat

Prince, Princess

The ideal young man or woman – a persistent symbol of all that is most beautiful, gentle or heroic. The prince, in particular, was a hopeful emblem of renewed national vigour or fertility. Public disappointment with the visible defects of princes may help to account for the popular fairy stories of frog princes transformed by love into something closer to the ideal.

Procession

A purification ritual or demonstration of power in many early traditions. Sacred objects or sacrificial animals were carried in processions around newly sown fields to protect crops from disease or to ensure successful growth. The paper dragons still carried in Chinese processions invoked rain. Processional marching around an enemy symbolically bound and weakened them, as when the Israelites marched around the walls of Jericho with the sacred ark. Roman triumphal processions not only displayed military heroes to the public but asserted their power over the captives they led.

Purgatory

Spiritual refinement or purification – a symbolism suggested by the processes of metallurgy and alchemy but transferred to early Christian concepts of the afterlife. In the Roman Catholic faith, the souls of those with venial (less than mortal) sins may need to pass through the fiery (but temporary) state of Purgatory on their way to heaven.

Purple

The colour of royalty and dignity in the ancient world. Its emblematic meaning was based on the high value of cloth dyed purple by the secretions of two species of molluscs, which was an expensive process. Purple was worn by high priests, magistrates and military leaders in the Roman world but was associated particularly with emperors. The children of Byzantine emperors were born in a room with purple drapes, hence the phrase "born in the purple". Cardinals are still said to be "raised to the purple" although their robes are actually red.

Pyramid

In Egypt, a "hill of light" – symbol of the creative power of the sun and the immortality of the pharaoh whose tomb it was. Pyramidal constructions elsewhere, notably Babylonian ziggurats rising to temple sanctuaries, had different symbolic aims. The Egyptian pyramid was developed from the conventional flat-topped *mastaba* tomb by Imhotep, the high priest of the sungod Ra. Although his pyramid for the pharoah Zoser at Saqqara was stepped, later architects perfected the form of the true pyramid, facing it with limestone to reflect the light, clarifying its symbolism. It represented the primal mound which, in Egyptian cosmogony, first caught the light of the creator sun. The mass and power of the structure were "material for eternity" – a building whose permanence negated death and whose height and reflective surfaces symbolized the perfect union between the buried pharaoh and the sun god. Apart from concentrating the light, the sloping triangular sides have more structural than symbolic purpose, providing the stability that made these stupendous monuments possible.

Python *see* **Snake**

Quail

Warmth, ardour and courage – a symbolism based on the bird's reddish-brown colour, its combativeness, and its migratory appearance in early summer. Quail were linked with the Greek island of Delos, mythical birthplace of the sun-god Apollo and the huntress Artemis. The quail was an emblem of military valour in both China and Rome. The Chinese linked it with the south, fire and summer. Its association with light seems confirmed by the Hindu myth of the twin Ashvin deities who released a quail (symbolizing spring) from the mouth of a wolf (winter). As a night flyer the quail has been linked with witchcraft in Europe, but in general it was a good augury, notably for the Israelites for whom it provided food in the desert during the Exodus.

Queen

Like the king, a celestially ordained archetype of her sex, a human symbol of the moon. The two were linked in a duality seen as necessary for the prosperity and happiness of the realm. In alchemy, the sacred marriage of the white queen (mercury) and red king (sulphur) symbolized the union of male and female principles to produce the Philosopher's Stone. As consorts, queens were subordinate to the dynastic male, but as sovereigns they could quickly acquire symbolic importance, as did Elizabeth I (on whom Edmund Spenser based his *Faerie Queene* Gloriana; 1596). In the ancient world, mother goddesses (including the Virgin Mary) were Queens of Heaven, lunar goddesses Queens of the Night. Symbolic attributes included the blue robe, chalice, turreted or starry crown, orb and sceptre, and the metal silver.

Quintessence

Perfected matter. Western alchemists said that the four elements (earth, air, fire and water) were surrounded by a purer fifth essence, similar to the Eastern notion of *prana*, the energizing etheric spirit. The animal symbols eagle (air), phoenix (fire), dolphin (water), man (earth), were grouped to represent the quintessence.

Quail: *see*
Fire, Flame; Light; Red;
SEASONS; Wolf

Queen: *see*
Alchemy; Blue; Globe, Orb;
King; Mercury; Moon;
Philosopher's stone; Sceptre;
Silver; Sulphur; Tower;
White

Quintessence: *see*
Air; Alchemy; Dolphin;
Eagle; Earth; Fire, Flame;
Man; Phoenix; Water

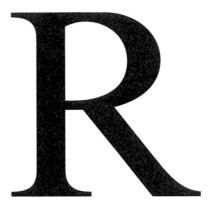

Rain: *see*
Axe; Black; Blood; Bull;
Cat; Chameleon; Clouds;
Comb; Cord; Cow; Crab;
Dance; Dog; Dragon;
Dwarf; Elephant; Emerald;
Feathers; Frog; Green;
Hammer; Hazel; Incense;
Lightning; Makara; Moon;
Parrot; Rainbow; Snake;
Spider; Storm; Tamarisk;
Tambourine; Thunder;
Toad; Tongue; Triangle;
Turkey; Water; Yin-yang

*The Aztec rain-god
Tlaloc, from a
Mesoamerican codex.*

Rabbit *see* **Hare, Rabbit**

Rain

A vital symbol of fecundity, often
linked in primitive agricultural societies with divine semen, as in the
Greek myth in which the god Zeus
impregnated Danaë, the mother of
Perseus, in the form of a golden show-
er. The traditional belief that the gods
determine whether to withhold rain,
unleash it with punishing force, or
sprinkle it sweetly like a blessing, has
never entirely disappeared. Gentle
rain (likened to mercy by Portia in
Shakespeare's *The Merchant of
Venice*; *c.*1596) was widely seen as a
sign of divine approval or, in China,
yin-yang harmony in the celestial
sphere. The supreme fertility god of
the Aztecs, Tlaloc (or Chac in the
Mayan pantheon), was a rain god
whose motif was a bar with comb-like
teeth representing falling rain. To him,
children were sacrificed on mountain
tops, their blood and tears propitious
signs of coming rainfall.

A similar link between blood and
rain appears in Iranian mythology
where the rain-god Tishtrya, as a
white horse, is sustained by sacrifices
as he fights the black horse of
drought. The heavenly origin of rain
made it an emblem of purity, and
purification rituals were often carried
out to invoke its fall. In the straightforward sympathetic magic of rain
dancing, stamping feet imitated the
patter of drops striking the earth.
Apart from the axe, hammer and
thunderbolt (a rain of fire or light),
symbols of rain include the snake or
horned serpent, the dragon in China,
frogs and other amphibians, lunar
creatures such as the crab and spider,
dogs (associated with wind gods) and,
more unexpectedly, the cat, chameleon, cow, elephant, parrot and turkey.

Rainbow

A bridging symbol between the supernatural and natural worlds, usually
optimistic (as meteorologically the
rainbow often is). In Judeo-Christian
tradition, a rainbow was the sign of
God's reconcilement with terrestrial
life after the Flood: "I have set my
bow in the clouds, and it shall be a

sign of the covenant between me and the earth" (Genesis 9:13). In Greece, the rainbow-goddess Iris, robed in iridescent dew, carried messages to earth from the supreme god Zeus and his wife Hera. In India the rainbow was the bow of the hero-god Indra (a tradition paralleled in the Pacific where the rainbow is the emblem of Kahukara, the Maori war god). In Tibetan Tantric Buddhism the "rainbow body" is the penultimate transitional state of meditation in which matter begins to be transformed into pure light. The beneficial symbolism underlying all these traditions was not universal. As a solar and water emblem, the arc of the rainbow touching the earth usually suggested fertility and treasure – the folklore "pot of gold". But in some early cultures, an underworld symbolism appears. The rainbow was associated with a serpent in parts of Africa, India, Asia and Native North America, as well as in Australia, and its powers were unpredictable. In some central African myths, Nkongolo, the Rainbow King, is a cruel tyrant. Hence, perhaps the African and Asian superstition that it was provocative and risky to point at a rainbow. In central Asia, rainbow-coloured ribbons were a shamanistic aid to sky travel, but there were folklore warnings against treading on the end of a rainbow and being whirled upward. More often, the ladder symbolism of the rainbow is positive. It is the seven-coloured ladder of the Buddha, and in many traditions the path to paradise.

In Western art, Christ sometimes sits in judgment on top of a rainbow, which can also appear as an attribute of the Virgin Mary and (with three bands) the Trinity.

Ram

Solar energy, impetuous ardour, virility, hot-headedness, obstinacy – a symbol of fire as both a creative and a consuming, or sacrificial, force. Its spiral horns were an emblem of the increasing solar power of Amun-Ra in Egypt who took over the symbolism of the ram-headed creator god Khnum. In iconography the ram was a popular symbol of potent gods including Ea and Baal in the Middle East, Zeus and Apollo in Greece, Indra and Agni in India, and, by association with its battering power, thunder gods such as the Scandinavian Thor whose chariot is drawn by rams. A ram-headed serpent (virility and renewal) is the companion of the Celtic god Cernunnos. As the first sign of the Zodiac, Aries the ram symbolizes the renewal of fertility and returning warmth of the sun at the March equinox. It is an astrological sign of the choleric temperament and the fiery planet Mars. As a fire and solar emblem the ram was also an important• sacrificial animal – in Hebrew tradition it was the last-minute replacement for Isaac when God tempted Abraham to sacrifice his son (Genesis 22). Christian iconography sometimes makes Christ the sacrificial ram. More often, Christ with a ram has protective significance. As protector of flocks, the ram was an attribute of the Greek god Hermes (in Roman myth, Mercury). The Golden Fleece came from the marvellous ram of Hermes, which was sacrificed to Zeus. The *shofar*, or Hebrew sacred ram's horn, is a protective emblem.

Rat

Destructiveness, avarice, foresight and fecundity. As nocturnal raiders of

Rainbow: *see*
Bridge; Dew; Flood; Ladder; Light; Rain; Seven; Snake; Trinity

Ram: *see*
Chariot; Fire, Flame; Golden Fleece; Horn; PLANETS; Sacrifice; Snake; Spring; Sun; Thunder; Zodiac

Rat: *see*
Devils; Mouse; SEVEN DEADLY SINS; WISDOM; Zodiac

Raven

Raven: *see*
Ark; Black; Crow; DEATH;
Sun

Rays: *see*
Aureole; Nimbus; Seven

Red: *see*
Alchemy; Blood;
COLOURS; DEATH; Fire,
Flame; JEWELS; Phallus;
Sulphur; Tarot

granaries, rats were usually perceived as harmful in the ancient Middle East. They were linked with the underworld and, in Christianity, with the Devil. But a different symbolism based on their knowingness, fecundity and bread-winning abilities is evident not only in folklore (their legendary foreknowledge of doomed ships) but also in their association with Asian gods of wisdom, success or prosperity (including the "riches" that comprise many children). A rat is the steed of the elephant-headed god Ganesha in Indian myth, and the companion of the Japanese god of wealth Daikoku. In the mythology of southern China, a rat brought rice to humankind. The rat is the first sign of the Chinese Zodiac. Some Renaissance paintings show a black and white rat, representing night and day gnawing at time.

Raven

Like its close relative the crow, a bird associated with death, loss and war in western Europe but widely venerated elsewhere. Its Western reputation was influenced by its association as a soothsayer with Celtic battle goddesses such as the Morrigan and Badb and with the predatory Vikings whose war god, Odin, was accompanied by two ravens, Hugin and Munin. However, these two, apart from reporting events on earth, symbolized the constructive principles of mind and memory. Hebrew symbolism is also ambivalent. As a scavenger, the raven was unclean. But it was the astute bird released from the ark by Noah which flew to and fro until the earth dried. Ravens also fed Elijah and several Christian hermit saints. In general, the raven is a solar and oracular symbol, its glistening black plumage

perhaps suggesting an ability to survive a close relationship with the sun. It was the messenger bird of Apollo as well as of the goddess Athene in Greece and was linked with the sun cult of Mithras. In China, it was the three-legged emblem of the Chou dynasty, symbolizing the rising, zenith and sinking of the sun (in which a legendary raven was said to live). In both China and Japan, ravens are emblems of family love. The raven appears in Africa and elsewhere as a guide, warning of dangers, and in Native North America as a culture hero and trickster. For the Inuit it is Raven Father, a creator god whose killing would bring foul weather.

Rays

Fertilizing power, sacredness, spiritual illumination and creative energy. Rays can represent the hair of the sun god, a manifestation of divinity or the emanations of sanctified individuals. In solar symbolism, the seventh ray is the central path to heaven.

Red

The active and masculine colour of life, fire, war, energy, aggression, danger, political revolution, impulse, emotion, passion, love, joy, festivity, vitality, health, strength and youth. Red was the emblematic colour of sun and war gods, and of power generally. In its destructive aspect it was sometimes linked with evil, notably in Egyptian myth where it was the colour of Set and of the chaos serpent, Apep. Death was a red horseman in Celtic tradition. As the colour of arousal, it was also linked with sexuality – with the phallic god, Priapus, in Greece and with the "scarlet woman" of prostitution. More often, however, its symbolism was positive. In China, where it was the emblem of the Chou dynasty and of the south, it was the luckiest of all colours, associated with life, wealth, energy, and summer. Red on white could symbolize lost blood and the pallor of death, but the Asian red beauty spot is protective. In the Chinese theatre, red paint on an actor's face marks them out as holy. Red ochre was used in early burials to "paint life" into the dead. Even in Christianity, where the main symbolism of red is sacrificial (Christ's Passion and the martyrdom of saints), it was also an emblem of God's soldiers – crusaders, cardinals and pilgrims. Calendars marking feasts and saints' days in red are the origin of the "red-letter" day. Red is also traditionally linked with the occult arts and is a dominant colour in the Tarot. In alchemy it symbolizes sulphur and the fire of purification.

Reed

A Japanese emblem of purification in the creation myth of Izanagi, perhaps by association with water. "The Reed Plain" is a Japanese metaphor for the mortal world, and the reed for manifestation. The reed also had purification symbolism in the Celtic world and was superstitiously thought effective against witches. It had fertility symbolism in Mesoamerica and was an emblem of the god Pan (from his invention of the reed "pan pipes") and music in Greece. More generally, the reed is a symbol of weakness, as in the biblical reference to Egypt as a weak ally, a "broken reed" (Isaiah 36:6). The reed cross is an emblem of John the Baptist who, Christ said, was not a reed shaken in the wind. The reed is also a symbol of Christ's Passion

because a sponge, soaked in vinegar, was put on the end of a reed to reach Christ's mouth as he was crucified.

Reindeer see Deer

Resin

Immortality – a symbolism based on the belief that resin was an incorruptible substance of long-lived trees such as the cypress, and that it could ensure life after death. Resin was used in embalming and was mixed with incense.

Rhinoceros

A lucky emblem in China, curiously linked with scholarship. Folklore said its horn could detect poison. Superstitiously, powdered rhinoceros horn is thought to improve virility, and its medicinal use in India may have contributed to the legend of the unicorn.

Rice

A fecundity symbol at weddings – a custom taken from India. In Asia, rice is the emblematic equivalent of corn, a symbol of divine nourishment, both bodily and spiritually.

In myth, either it was the gift of a culture hero or it appeared in the primeval gourd with human life itself. Rice wine was drunk ritually in China as a form of ambrosia, and rice grains, which had protective symbolism, were placed in the mouths of the dead. Balinese veneration of the Rice Mother, a figure made from a long (male) and shorter (female) corn sheaf, expressed southeast Asian folk beliefs that rice plants, like humans, contained within them a vital spirit. In Japan, Inari was a god not only of rice but also of prosperity.

Right see **Left and Right**

Reed: see
CROSS; PASSION; Water; Witchcraft

Resin: see
Cypress; Incense; Tree

Rhinoceros: see
Horn; Unicorn

Rice: see
Corn; Fox; Marriage

Ring: *see*
Amulet; Circle; Marriage;
Scarab; Wreath, Garland

River, Stream: *see*
Axis; CARDINAL
POINTS; Ford; Sacrifice;
Tree; Water

Robin: *see*
Birds; Goldfinch; Thorn

Rock: *see*
LONGEVITY; Rod; Stone

Ring

Eternity, unity, wholeness, commitment, authority. The circular symbolism of the ring makes it an emblem of completion, strength and protection as well as of continuity – all of which help to give significance to engagement and wedding rings. The oldest surviving rings (from Egypt) are signets bearing either personal seals or amulets, usually in the form of a scarab beetle symbolizing eternal life. Thus from the earliest times the ring has been an emblem of authority or delegated authority, of occult protective power and of a personal pledge. Roman betrothal rings were tokens of legal vows. The later custom of giving a wedding ring was based probably on ecclesiastical use of signet rings. Wedding rings were originally worn, like episcopal rings, on the third finger of the right hand. The Pope's Fisherman's Ring (showing Peter drawing in a net), broken at his death, is the supreme Roman Catholic seal. The plain gold nun's ring is a binding symbol of her marriage to Christ. The Doge's ring, thrown into the Adriatic at Venice on Ascension Day, was a token of perpetual Venetian sea power, a mystic ceremony initiated by Pope Alexander III after the city helped him to humiliate Emperor Frederick Barbarossa in 1176. Rings are associated with magical force or hidden treasure in many legends – a theme which goes back to the belief that Solomon's ring was the source of his supernatural powers and wisdom.

River, Stream

The flowing away of all things – a powerful natural symbol of the passage of time and life. For the many great civilizations dependent on their irrigating fertility, rivers were important symbols of supply as well as purification and removal. The common image of four streams in paradise flowing from the Tree of Life to the cardinal points was a metaphor for divine energy and spiritual nourishment coursing through the whole universe. In Hinduism, the Ganges, personified by the supreme river goddess Ganga, was an axial symbol, depicted in myth as falling from heaven to cleanse the earth (cushioned by Shiva) and penetrating also to the underworld. Purification in the Ganges is a central ritual in Hinduism. A cruder example of purification symbolism appears in the Greek myth of Herakles (in Roman myth, Hercules) who diverted a river through the Augean stables. Because they were unpredictable, rivers were propitiated with sacrifices to local gods or, more usually, goddesses. They often appear as boundaries, particularly dividing the worlds of the living and the dead. The Celts thought that confluences of rivers were particularly sacred. In China, the drowned were thought to haunt rivers, hoping to find living bodies that they could inhabit.

Robin

An alternative to the goldfinch in the legendary story of a bird that plucked a thorn from Christ's crown and was splashed with his blood. This may have led to European superstitions that the robin announces death by tapping at a window pane, and that it is bad luck to kill one.

Rock

Dependability, integrity, steadfastness, stability, permanence, strength and, in China, longevity. Rock, the most common biblical metaphor for reliability, is often equated with the living force of God, manifested by water springing from the rock struck by the rod of Moses. Christ is the "Rock of Ages", the source of eternal life. The Church itself was founded by the Disciple that Christ renamed Peter (Greek *petros* "a stone", *petra* "a rock"). In Chinese painting, rock is a yang (male and active) symbol. Rock sculptures, notably on Easter Island, in Egypt, and more recently in Borglum's monumental presidential carvings at Mt Rushmore in the US, convey the same emblematic meaning of timeless power. Gods were reputedly born from living rock in several Middle-Eastern religions, notably Mithraism.

Rod

An ancient emblem of supernatural power, symbolically associated with the potency of the tree or branch, the phallus, the snake and the hand or pointing finger. The creative and fertility symbolism of the rod is clear in the biblical story of Aaron's rod, which flowered and produced almonds as a sign of divine blessing on the house of Levi – endorsing the authority of Aaron (the brother of Moses) as the founder of the Jewish priesthood (Numbers 17). In religion, myth, legend and folklore, the rod, especially from particular trees such as the hazel, is an emblem of personal authority or gives its holder power over the natural world – to transform, prophesy, arbitrate, heal wounds, find water and summon or dismiss spirits.

Rood screen

A carved and decorated partition of wood or stone between the chancel and the main body of the medieval Christian church, originally carrying a Crucifixion cross (rood). Like the veil of the Hebrew temple, it symbolized the division between material and spiritual spheres, earth and heaven.

Rope

Bondage, but also ascension – the spiritual symbolism of the Indian rope trick. The idea of a rope or cord forming a ladder from earth to heaven was widespread in the ancient world and was sometimes linked with the umbilical cord – specifically among the Australian Aboriginals. In Hindu mysticism, the rope is an emblem of the inner path to spiritual illumination. Ropes and serpents were often linked, as in the Vedic myth of the cosmic serpent acting as a rope to twirl the mountain that churned creation from the sea of milk. In art, looped rope is a sinister attribute of Nemesis, the goddess of retribution, and of St Andrew, who was bound to the cross. Medieval penitents wore ropes around their necks as emblems of submission and remorse.

Rosary

Literally, a "rose garden", the name given by Christian mystics in the 13th century to a sequence of prayers, counted off on a string of beads and addressed to the Virgin Mary as the Rose of Heaven. Prayer beads were used much earlier in India – and with more specific symbolism. The fifty beads of the Hindu rosary are the number of letters in the Sanskrit alphabet and the rosary is linked with the creative power of sound, and in particular with Brahma and his consort Sarasvati, as well as with Shiva. In Buddhism, the beads number 108

Rod: *see*
Almond; Branch, Bough; Caduceus; Crozier; Hand; Hazel; Phallus; Sceptre; Snake; Staff; Wand

Rood screen: *see*
CROSS; Veil

Rope: *see*
Bonds; Cord; Snake

Rosary: *see*
Rose; Wheel

Rose: *see*
Centre; CROSS; Crown;
Cup; Dawn; FLOWERS;
Heart; Initiation; Lotus;
Red; Sun; Thorn; Wheel;
White; Wreath, Garland

Rosemary: *see*
Dew; FIDELITY; Marriage

(12 x 9) – a number referring to the legend that 108 Brahmins were present at the Buddha's birth. The circle of beads symbolizes the Wheel of Life and Time. The Islamic rosary, the *mala*, has 99 beads representing all the names of God. A mystic 100th bead, unsounded and non-existent, symbolizes the name that is known only in paradise. Rosaries are superstitiously thought to have talismanic power.

Rose

The paragon of flowers in Western tradition – a mystic symbol of the heart, the centre and the cosmic wheel, and also of sacred, romantic and sensual love. The white rose is an emblem of innocence, purity and virginity; the red symbolizes passion and desire, voluptuous beauty. Both are symbols of perfection and images of the cup of eternal life. With this meaning, rose petals were scattered on graves at the Roman festival of Rosaria, and Roman emperors wore rose wreaths as crowns. Mortality is symbolized by the blown rose, and the red rose can signify spilt blood, martyrdom, death and resurrection. Roman myth linked the red rose through its colour with the war-god Mars and his consort Venus (in Greek myth, Aphrodite), and with her slain lover Adonis. According to a Greek version of the myth, Adonis was fatally attacked by a wild boar. As Aphrodite ran to her wounded lover's side, she tore her foot on the thorns of a white rose, the drops of her blood turning it red. The rose was also a sun and dawn emblem and was linked with the Greek god Dionysus, the goddess Hecate, the Graces and the Muses.

For Christianity, the blood-red rose

with its thorns was a poignant symbol of the suffering of Christ and of his love for humanity. This became the focal image of the occult and Cabbalistic Rosicrucian society in the 17th century, whose emblem was a cross formed by a rose itself or a wooden cross with a central rose or roses at the intersections of the arms. Multilayered petals symbolized stages of initiation, the central rose representing the point of unity, the heart of Christ, divine light, the sun at the centre of the wheel of life. The rosette (the flower seen from above) and the Gothic rose also have wheel symbolism, connoting the unfolding of generative power – a Western equivalent of the emblematic lotus. In the related symbolism of Freemasonry, three St John's roses represent light, love and life. The Virgin Mary is the Rose of Heaven and the sinless Rose Without Thorns, a reference to her faultless purity. Rose garlands were also a symbol of virginity in Rome. A gold rose is an emblem of the pope. An important secondary symbolism of the rose is discretion. Various tales account for this. In a Roman myth, Cupid stops rumours about the infidelities of Venus by bribing the god of silence with a rose. Another explanation is that rose garlands were worn at Dionysian (Bacchanalian for the Romans) revels in the belief that they would moderate drunkenness and loose talk. Roses were later hung or painted above council or banqueting tables as signs that conversation was *sub rosa* – private not public.

Rosemary

"There's rosemary, that's for remembrance," says Ophelia in Shakespeare's *Hamlet* (4:5; *c.*1600). This aromatic

herb was chosen as an ancient marriage token, perhaps for its lingering fragrance. Its Latin name literally meant "sea dew", and it was therefore connected with the foam-born goddess Aphrodite (in Roman myth, Venus) and with fidelity in love.

Round of Existence *see* Wheel

Round Table

Unity, coherence, and completeness. According to Arthurian legend, the famous table with an empty place for the Holy Grail was designed by Merlin to seat 150 knights without wrangling over precedence. The magical power of the Round Table derives from Celtic reverence for the circle, probably based on earlier worship of sky gods. Cosmic significance is similarly suggested by the Hindu round table constructed in 12 segments and linked with the Zodiac and the months of the year.

Ruby

Ardent love, vitality, royalty, courage – the stone of fortune and happiness (including longevity) in India, Burma, China and Japan. Its colour, ranging from red to the purplish "pigeon's blood" hue of the most valuable rubies, linked it in the classical world with the fiery Ares (in Roman myth, Mars), but also with Cronos (Saturn), who controlled passion. It was said to inflame lovers and was believed to glow in the dark. Its habit of looking paler under some lights was read as a warning – of poison or other dangers. (Catherine of Aragon's ruby reputedly lost colour as she lost favour with Henry VIII.) Homeopathically, the ruby was a medicinal jewel, thought to be effective for loss of blood as well

as low spirits. Fire is the symbolism of its appearance on the foreheads of legendary dragons.

Rudder

As the instrument of guidance, an emblem of responsible authority, sometimes shown on official medallions. In Western art it is an attribute of Fortune, as well as Abundance.

Rue

A bitter herb sometimes used in church to sprinkle holy water, and in Hebrew tradition associated with repentance. Thus it became the "herb of grace" mentioned by Ophelia in Shakespeare's *Hamlet* (4:5; *c.*1600). As a homonym in English, it is also a symbol of sorrow.

Runes

Early Gothic lettering which acquired quasi-magic symbolism as this form of alphabet spread from southern Europe north to Scandinavia and Britain. The linking of specific runes to the sun, moon and other sky gods, and the art of funerary rune carving, led to the belief that runes embodied supernatural powers – to protect, to avenge and particularly to foretell the future. Runes inscribed on stone, wood or leather were shamanistically used to cast spells or convey oracular messages. Intriguingly, the forked lines inside the circular emblem of the Campaign for Nuclear Disarmament closely resemble the Germanic Todesrune (death rune). The zigzag sign of Adolf Hitler's SS, based on the Sigrune (associated with the sun, victory and the yew from which bows were cut), was a notorious example of Nazi and neo-Nazi attempts to use runic letters as "Aryan" symbols.

Round Table: *see* Circle; Grail; Twelve; Wheel; Zodiac

Ruby: *see* Blood; Dragon; Fire, Flame; JEWELS; LONGEVITY; Purple; Red

Rudder: *see* FORTUNE

Rue: *see* Water

RUNES: *see* Sun; Swastika; VICTORY; Yew; Zigzag

Rune symbols inscribed on a wooden stick, from a medieval engraving.

Sabbath: *see*
Moon; Seven; Week;
Witchcraft

Sacrifice: *see*
Blood; Bull; CROSS; Lamb;
Ox; Ram

Saddle: *see*
AFTERWORLDS

Sabbath

The Jewish symbol of God's Creation and of the covenant between God and the Israelites, commemorated in a festive day of rest on Saturday. Mainstream Christianity followed the established tradition of resting on the seventh day (Saturday), but with less strict prohibitions, and on a Sunday – the emblematic day of Christ's resurrection. The Islamic holy day of rest is Friday. Behind these common Semitic customs lies an earlier seventh-day tradition based on the four quarterly phases of the moon. The Babylonian seventh day was dedicated to the moon-god Sin, and was a time at which important state functions were suspended. This has suggested to some scholars the symbolism of an unpropitious "day out of time". The "witches' sabbath" of medieval imagination was an inversion of the Christian Sunday, suggesting that while God rested, demons were abroad.

Sacrifice

A means of communion between a god and a person or persons in which something prized is sanctified and then destroyed as a symbolic offering. The high status and value of domestic animals in the ancient world made them the most common sacrifice.

Forms of sacrifice are extensive and varied, ranging from rituals of atonement or purification to offerings made in propitiation or gratitude – and even to funerary customs in which human victims were killed to become tutelary spirits or to provide companionship or services in the afterlife. At its deepest level, sacrifice was a creative act mimicking the death of all living things, particularly vegetative life in winter, as a necessary prelude to rebirth or the renewal of fertility.

Saddle

An emblem of family life in ancient China where the word for "saddle" was a homonym of "peace". Hence the custom by which a bride steps over a saddle at the gateway of her husband's parental home. On the steppes of central Asia, dying shamans were pillowed on their saddles – symbols of their journey to a celestial afterlife.

Sails

In art, an attribute of Fortune (because she was inconstant) and of the Greek goddess Athene (to the Romans, Minerva). More generally, sails were sometimes used by artists to depict what could not otherwise be shown – the element of air, wind, vital breath and the soul, as in medieval paintings where sails represented the advent of the Holy Spirit.

Salamander

A legendary lizard which lived in the heart of fire, therefore taken as an emblem of fire itself. Pliny reported the belief that the salamander survived fire by quenching it with its cold body, a story perhaps based on the damp-loving amphibians called fire salamanders because of their bright yellow-and-black markings. The salamander, said to be born in fire, is a

The legendary salamander surviving flames, which led to its symbolic association with fire itself.

common symbol in alchemical drawings, symbolizing the purifying agents of fire and sulphur. It is a Christian symbol of the pure-spirited believer who resists the flames of temptation, and sometimes a symbol of chastity. As the device of Francis I of France, the salamander symbolized the patronage of good things, the destruc-

tion of bad. More usually, in heraldry, it symbolizes courage.

Salmon

Virility, fecundity, courage, wisdom and foresight – a symbolism common to coastal peoples of northern Europe and of the American northwest. Salmon battling their way upstream became totemic images of nature's bounty and wisdom. For the Celts, transformation and phallic symbolism mingle in the story of Tuan mac Cairill who, in salmon form, was said to have impregnated an Irish queen to whom he was served after being caught. The Irish hero Finn scalded his thumb as he cooked the Salmon of Knowledge. He sucked his thumb to ease the pain, and in tasting the salmon's juice acquired powers of prophecy and wisdom.

Salt

A key symbol of hospitality and friendship in the ancient Middle East, where salt was an important and valuable commodity. Because it was used as a preservative as well as for its savour, sharing salt and bread also implied a lasting relationship. The association between salt and incorruptibility made it a covenanted offering in Hebrew sacrifices and an emblem of purification in religious rituals from Greece to Japan. The Christian elect were the "salt of the earth" according to Christ's Sermon on the Mount.

Greeks and Romans both credited salt with protective qualities. Hence the superstition that it is bad luck to spill it and that a pinch should be thrown over the left shoulder to avert this. (Judas Iscariot has ominously spilt the salt in Leonardo da Vinci's

Sails: *see*
Air; Breath, Breathing; FORTUNE; Soul; Wind

Salamander: *see*
Alchemy; Fire, Flame; Sulphur; VIRTUES

Salmon: *see*
Fish; Thumb

Salt: *see*
Salt; WISDOM

Sand

Sand: *see*
Hourglass; Washing

Sap: *see*
Soma; Vine; Wine

Sapphire: *see*
Blue; JEWELS; Sky;
VIRTUES

Satyr: *see*
Dance; Devils; Goat; Snake;
Wreath, Garland

Scales: *see*
AFTERWORLDS;
VIRTUES; Zodiac

Satyrs drinking from a wineskin, a detail from a 5th-century-CE wine cooler.

Venus in her scallop, after The Birth of Venus *(1484–6), by Sandro Botticelli.*

painting *The Last Supper*, *c.*1495). Salt is also associated with the bite of sharp wit and wisdom.

Sand

A symbol of multiplicity because of its countless grains. In arid regions, particularly in North Africa and the Middle East, sand was a substitute for water as a cleansing medium and was associated with purification. More generally, it symbolizes instability, obliteration and the erosion of time (through its use in hour glasses).

Sap

The vital force that permeates all life – symbolically an agent of renewal, spiritualization and immortality. Plant juice was widely equated with the cyclic storing and flow of semen, with the death and renewal of vegetative life, and with growth toward divine light. The Dionysian cult of the grape and the Vedic cult of *soma* (with which it was possibly connected) are the most significant expressions of these ideas.

Sapphire

A jewel of heaven (from its cerulean colour) and, in stone lore, an emblem of celestial harmony, peace, truth and serenity. The sapphire was sacred to the planet Saturn in Hindu tradition and was therefore associated with self-control.

Satyr

A goatish symbol of male lust and the life of sensual pleasure. In classical mythology satyrs accompany nature gods such as the Roman Silvanus, the Greek Dionysus (in Roman myth, Bacchus) and Pan (Faunus). They ravish nymphs and naiads, drink copiously, play pipes, and pour their unbridled energy into ecstatic dancing. Attributes include ivy wreaths, bunches of grapes, fruit, cornucopias and snakes – a reference to the legend in which Faunus turned himself into a snake to violate his own daughter. Medieval Christianity took a stern view of satyrs, associating them not with the Golden Age of carnal delights but with evil.

They remained favourite subjects for erotic art, usually depicted as semi-human with a goat's beard, hairy legs and hoofs, and sometimes a horse's tail.

Scales

Justice, impartiality, equilibrium, harmony, truth, divine judgment. Scales represent the Zodiac sign of Libra at the balancing point of the year when the sun crosses the equator southward. They are the most common emblem not only of Justice but of the causal link between sin and punishment in the afterlife. In Western art, scales are the attribute of Themis, the Greek goddess of law and order; the messenger-god Hermes (in Roman myth, Mercury); the archangel Michael; and Logic and Opportunity personified. Empty scales may be carried by Famine. Judgmental scales are associated with Christ and, in Egypt, with Osiris and the truth goddess, Ma'at. In Tibetan art, good deeds and bad were symbolized by white and black stones in the balancing pans.

Scallop

Like other bivalves, a symbol of the vulva, but particularly significant through its association with the birth of the Greek goddess Aphrodite (in Roman myth, Venus). The painter

Sandro Botticelli famously shows her coming ashore in a scallop shell blown by the West wind (*The Birth of Venus*, *c*.1484–6).

Christianity took over this pagan sexuality and fertility myth to make the scallop shell a symbol of the hope of resurrection and rebirth. The scallop is the particular symbol of the Apostle James, son of Zebedee, reputed to have voyaged to Spain; his shrine at Santiago de Compostela was a focus of medieval pilgrimage. The scallop shell became an emblem first of this pilgrimage and then of pilgrims in general, thirsty for the waters of the spirit.

Scalp

Among Native North Americans a symbol of life force. Scalping was equivalent to head-hunting as a means of capturing the power or vital energy of an enemy. Among some tribes, warriors left a scalp lock as a sign of confidence and a challenge to men of other tribes.

Scapegoat

The symbolic discharger of other people's sins or shortcomings. A scapegoat or "goat for Azazel" (a desert demon) was sent into the wilderness by the Hebrews on the Day of Atonement, Yom Kippur, emblematically bearing away the transgressions of the Israelites. In Christianity, Christ made himself a scapegoat by taking on himself the sins of the world. According to J. G. Frazer in *The Golden Bough* (1890), earlier traditions in Asia Minor involved the beating and burning of a human victim as a scapegoat for the ruler in countries afflicted by drought, plague or crop failure.

Scarab

A solar and male emblem of genesis, rebirth and the eternal life force – the most popular amulet of Egypt and later of the ancient Middle East. This little dung beetle was strongly associated with Khepri, the Egyptian god of the rising sun. All scarabs were thought to be male and to produce larvae by incubating their semen in balls of dung which they rolled in microcosmic imitation of the sun's passage through the sky. Protective scarab amulets or signet rings, funerary pendants and seals symbolized generative energy, cyclic renewal and, in early Christianity, resurrection. In China, the scarab was thought to be a model of autogenesis.

Sceptre

Like the rod, a fertility emblem of creative power and authority, but more ornately decorated and associated with supreme gods or rulers. The sceptre often implies royal or spiritual power to administer justice, including punishment. Thus the pharaonic sceptre of Egypt was topped by the head of the violent god Set. Other sceptres are specifically linked with the creative–destructive force of the thunderbolt – in particular the "diamond sceptre" or *vajra* of Hindu and Buddhist tradition and the Tibetan *dorje*. They symbolize both indestructible spiritual dominion and compassionate wisdom or illumination. The ivory sceptre of Rome was surmounted by the eagle of supremacy and immortality. Spherical tops symbolized universal authority, as in the sceptre of British monarchs with orb and cross. In China, the Buddhist sceptre, the *ju-i*, was taken as a symbol of heavenly blessings – the meaning of

Scallop: *see*
Pilgrimage; Shell; Vulva; Water

Scalp: *see*
Hair; Head

Scapegoat: *see*
Clown; CROSS; Goat; Sacrifice; Witchcraft

Scarab: *see*
Amulet; Ring; Sun

Sceptre: *see*
CROSS; Eagle; Globe, Orb; Rod; Thunder

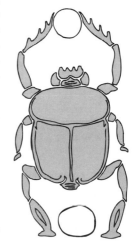

The scarab, from an ancient Egyptian pendant. The circle between its front claws represents the sun.

Scissors

Scorpion: *see*
Snake; Zodiac

Scroll: *see*
Book; WISDOM

Sea: *see*
Flood; Snake; Water;
WISDOM

Seal: *see*
BEASTS OF FABLE

Sephiroth: *see*
NUMBERS; Tree

its presentation to a bride's family – or of the honour due to elders.

Scissors *see* **Shears**

Scorpion
Death, chastisement, retribution, vindictiveness, treachery. In Greek mythology, the hunter Orion was stung to death by a scorpion, either for his boastfulness or for forcing his attentions on the huntress Artemis.

Like the serpent, the scorpion was sometimes a guardian emblem: in Egypt it was sacred to Selket, protector of the dead. Because it was thought to secrete a medicinal oil against its own sting, it had an ambivalent wounding/healing symbolism in Africa.

The scorpion is a demonic creature in the Bible, and appears in medieval art as an emblem of deadly treachery and sometimes of envy or hatred. In art it is an attribute of Africa and also of Logic, perhaps as a symbol of conclusive argument.

Scroll
In iconography, usually an emblem of ancient wisdom, prophecy or canonical law. In Judeo-Christian tradition, scrolls are attributes not only of great prophets such as Isaiah and Jeremiah but also of the Apostles, especially James, son of Zebedee.

Sea
In many traditions, the primeval source of life – formless, limitless, inexhaustible and full of possibility. In Mesopotamian myth, life arose from the mingling of Apsu, the sweet waters on which the earth floated, and the salt waters, personified by the chaos-goddess Tiamat who gave birth

to all things and whose destruction led to the organized world. In Genesis, God moves upon the face of the primordial sea. The Hindu creator-god Vishnu sleeps on a serpent coiled upon the sea.

The sea is a maternal image even more primary than the earth, but implies also transformation and rebirth. It is also a symbol of infinite wisdom and, in psychology, of the unconscious.

Seal
Associated by the Greeks with transformation. Virginal nymphs, turned into seals to escape importunate men, formed part of the train of the sea-god Proteus (who could himself change shape at will). Hence, perhaps, mermaid legends and fairy tales of seals who shed their skins and wander the shore as alluring women.

SEASONS *see panel, opposite*

Sephiroth
A Hebrew symbol system, usually depicted as a Tree of Life with 10 branches, through which medieval Cabbalists hoped to understand the mysteries of creation and the inner life of God. Although the symbolism of the *sephiroth* is complex and esoteric, its underlying idea is that the whole of Creation reveals the nature of God who sought to behold in it His own attributes.

Cabbalists believed that these attributes were set out in coded form in the scriptures. Spiritual illumination could be achieved by understanding their precise relationships, charted in a sinuous path from *keter* (meaning "crown") to *malkhut* (which means "kingdom").

SEASONS

Like the phases of the moon, the seasons were universal symbols of birth, growth, death and rebirth, the orderly cycles of nature and of human life. Most traditions recognized four seasons. Native American myths held that these were caused by the struggle of contending gods who controlled the four directions of space. Egypt and some other cultures recognized only three seasons – winter, spring and summer.

In Western art and astrology, **spring** is represented by a child or young woman with sprigs of blossom. It is linked with the Greek goddess Aphrodite (Venus in Roman myth), the god Hermes (Mercury), the Roman Flora, the lamb or kid, and the Zodiac signs Aries, Taurus and Gemini.

Summer is shown by a woman crowned with ears of corn, carrying a sickle. It is linked with the goddess Demeter (Ceres) or the god Apollo, the lion or dragon belching flame, and the signs Cancer, Leo and Virgo.

Autumn is a woman with vine leaves, grapes and other fruit, perhaps in a cornucopia. It is linked with Dionysus (Bacchus), the hare, and Libra, Scorpio and Sagittarius.

Winter may appear as an old man by a fire or a bare-headed woman in a winter landscape. It is linked with Hephaestus (Vulcan) or Boreas, the salamander or wild duck, and Capricorn, Aquarius and Pisces.

SEASONS: *see*
Corn; Cornucopia; Dragon; Fire, Flame; FLOWERS; Hare, Rabbit; Lion; Salamander; Sickle, Scythe; Vine; Zodiac

Seraphim

The highest of the nine orders of Judeo-Christian angels, symbolizing the purifying fire of the spirit. Isaiah (6:2–6) described the seraphim as six-winged creatures standing above the throne of God and singing his praises. One brought Isaiah a live coal to purge his lips of sin.

Serpent *see* Snake

Seven

A sacred, mystical and magic number, especially in the traditions of western Asia, symbolizing cosmic and spiritual order and the completion of a natural cycle.

The importance of the number seven is based on early astronomy – in particular the seven wandering stars or dynamic celestial bodies (the sun and moon, Mars, Mercury, Jupiter, Venus and Saturn) after which the days of the week in many cultures were named. Another influence was the four seven-day phases of the moon that made up the 28 days of the lunar calendar. Arithmeticians further noted that the first seven digits added together came to 28.

Seven was fundamental in the Mesopotamian world, which divided both the earth and heaven into seven zones and depicted the Tree of Life with seven branches.

In the Bible, God's blessing on the seventh day is followed by scores of other references to seven. It was the number of Jewish feasts, festivals, purifications and years between sabbaticals. Seven was also the number of the Pillars of Wisdom and in other cultures it was often linked with intellectual mastery .

Seven was sacred to the god Osiris

Seraphim: *see*
Angels; Cherubim; Fire, Flame

Seven: *see*
AFTERWORLDS; COLOURS; Dragon; Initiation; Kaaba; Lyre; Moon; Mountain; Music; NUMBERS; PLANETS; Pillar; Rays; Sabbath; Square; Tree; Triangle; Week

SEVEN DEADLY SINS:
see
Angels; BEASTS OF
FABLE; Green; Mirror;
Ziggurat; *and names of
individual animals*

SEVEN DEADLY SINS

In art, particularly Renaissance and baroque painting, the Seven Deadly Sins represent the "moral" lesson of good against evil.

Anger The vice that in Renaissance art is often represented as a woman tearing up her clothes.

Avarice A favourite subject of medieval sculptors, and later of painters. Avarice is usually symbolized by a sinner holding or wearing a purse or by a harpy whose claws tormented misers, who might be shown hoarding money or golden apples. Among the other symbols of avarice are the rat and toad.

The deadly sin Lust, after a detail from Pallas Expelling the Vices from the Garden of Virtue *by Andrea Mantegna (*c.*1500).*

Envy A sin usually portrayed as a woman eating the heart torn from her own breast (the origin of the colloquialism "eat your heart out") or sometimes her entrails. Her familiar attribute is a snake, sometimes shown as her protruded, poisonous tongue. Other symbols of envy include the scorpion, the "evil eye" and the colour green (hence "green with envy").

Gluttony Personified in art either by corpulent and voracious figures or by the animals most commonly linked with this fleshly vice – the pig, bear, fox, wolf or hedgehog.

Lust This vice was a popular subject for medieval artists. Lust is usually represented in Western art by snakes or toads that are shown feeding on the breasts or genitals of women (whose sexual urges seemed more shocking to the Church than those of men).

Other emblems of lust include the ape, ass, basilisk, bear, boar, cat, centaur, cock, Devil, goat, hare, horse, leopard, Minotaur, mirror, monkey, pig, rabbit, satyr, torch and witch.

Pride This sin is usually personified in Western art by a woman with a peacock, She may also be shown with a lion and an eagle as dominant emblems of earthly and celestial nature. The biblical saying "pride goes before destruction and an haughty spirit before a fall" (Proverbs 16:18) led to medieval allegories of pride as an unseated horseman. This symbolism influenced Carravaggio's masterpiece *The Conversion of St Paul* (*c.*1600) showing Saul thrown from a horse on the road to Damascus. Other symbols of pride are the cock, fallen angel, leopard, mirror and ziggurat.

Sloth A sin that is usually personified in Western art by an overweight man or a pig. Sloth often rides or is accompanied by a beast of burden such as the ass or ox. The snail was also a Christian emblem of sloth.

in Egypt (a symbol of immortality); to the god Apollo in Greece (the number of strings on his lyre); to Mithras, the Persian god of light (the number of initiatory stages in his cult); and to the Buddha (his seven emblems).

In Hindu tradition, the world mountain has seven faces, the sun seven rays. The seventh ray is a symbol of the centre, the power of God. In Islam, where the number seven symbolizes perfection, there are seven heavens, earths, seas, hells and doors to paradise. Pilgrims walk around the sacred Kaaba at Mecca seven times.

In Arabic and other folklore customs, seven had protective power, associated particularly with childbirth. Legends are full of sevens, as in the widespread tales of seven-headed dragons or the story of the Seven Sleepers of Ephesus – young Christians, reputedly walled up in a cave during the reign of Diocletian, who were resurrected 200 years later.

Shadow
In primitive traditions, the soul or alter ego, associated particularly with the spirits of the dead. In China, the Immortals, as beings wholly penetrated by light, had no shadows, whereas in Western folklore people who cast no shadow were suspected of having sold their souls to the Devil and of being, in a sense, "unreal" (shadows being proof of material reality). As the antithesis of light, the Devil was himself a shadow. In psychology, the shadow symbolizes the intuitive, selfish side of the psyche, often repressed.

Shears, Scissors
Mortality, the unpredictability of life. With this symbolism, shears or scissors are the attribute in art of Atropos, one of the three Fates, who in Greek lore severs the thread of human life.

Sheep
Meekness – a Christian symbol of the laity, needing spiritual leadership and easily led astray. "Feed my sheep" were among the last words said by Christ to his disciple Peter before his ascension, according to the Gospel of St John (21:15). The "lost sheep" is a misled sinner, the "black sheep" an incorrigible one. Although sheep are generally associated with dimwittedness, the Mongols believed that the breastbone of a sheep had divinatory power.

Shell
Auspicious, erotic, lunar and feminine symbol, linked with conception, regeneration, baptism and, in many traditions, prosperity – probably through fecundity symbolism based on its association with the vulva. Prized shells were a form of currency in Oceania. The shell is one of the eight symbols of good luck in Chinese Buddhism. As underworld and resurrection symbols, shells were sometimes funerary tokens. More recently, the shell has become a symbol of introspection or withdrawal.

Shepherd
In pastoral communities, a symbol of spiritual leadership – a common personification of Christ in early Christian art. Depictions of Christ with a ram or lamb on his shoulders were based on classical images of the Greek god Hermes (in Roman myth, Mercury) carrying one as the protector of flocks. Hermes also shepherded the souls of the dead. Other symbols

Shadow: *see*
Black; Devils; Light; Soul

Shears, Scissors: *see*
Sickle, Scythe; Weaving

Sheep: *see*
Black; Crozier; Lamb; Shepherd

Shell: *see*
Baptism; Conch; Cowrie; Oyster; Scallop; Vulva

Shepherd: *see*
Lamb; Ram; Sheep

Ship: *see* Anchor; Ark; Boat; Crescent; CROSS; Spire; Woman

Sickle, Scythe: *see* Castration; DEATH

Sieve: *see* CHASTITY; Net

Silver: *see* CHASTITY; METALS; Moon; Queen

Six: *see* Androgyne; Cube; Devils; Kaaba; Hexagram; Triangle; Trigrams

of the Good Shepherd include Ra and the crook-carrying pharaohs of Egypt; the Iranian protective god Yima; and, in Tibet, the Dalai Lama.

Ship

A symbol of security, representing a female (or lunar) womb or cradle. Also a symbol of quest and passage to other states of being. In the ancient world, ships often symbolized the voyaging of heavenly bodies – the crescent of the Babylonian moon god navigating space, or the Egyptian barque of the sun on its nightly passage through the underworld. Funerary ships were provided for the dead in Egypt, and other traditions, notably in the Viking custom of immolating chieftains in longships. The ship with mast and anchor as a cryptic sign of the Cross was an early Christian symbol of Christ, and of the Church as an image of security amid the storms of life. Churches themselves were symbolic ships, with the nave (Latin *navis*: "ship") carrying passengers, buttresses as oars and a spire as a mast. In art, the ship is an attribute of St Peter and of Fortune, ships being emblems of uncertain prosperity – as in the expression, "when my ship comes in".

The Ship of Fools, a theme of both literature and art, is an allegory of voyaging toward material rather than spiritual goals.

Sickle, Scythe

Death, but also fertility. The curved sickle was a lunar harvest symbol of the agricultural-god Cronos (in Roman myth, Saturn). With this meaning the sickle was also an attribute of the fertility-god Priapus and of summer. In early Greek myth, Cronos used a sickle to castrate his father, Ouranos (Uranus) – symbolizing the separation of earthly creation from the sky. In art, Death (sometimes personified as Father Time or the Grim Reaper) carries a scythe.

Sieve

Discernment, conscience, purification – a biblical emblem of God's coming judgment. Because of its ancient associations with purification (sifting out dross), in art the sieve is an attribute of Chastity.

Silver

Purity, chastity and eloquence. In the symbolism of metals, silver was lunar, feminine and cold, and is the attribute of moon-goddesses, in particular the Greek Artemis (in Roman myth, Diana), and of queens. Through its link with the moon it was equated also with the light of hope and with wisdom – orators are silver-tongued. Hence the Oriental proverb: "Speech is silver, silence golden." The Silver Age was emblematic of lost innocence, perhaps because, as the malleable metal of much ancient coinage, silver had some negative associations – famously so as a symbol of Christ's betrayal for "thirty pieces of silver".

Six

The number of union and equilibrium, graphically expressed by the hexagram combining two triangles, one pointing up (male, fire, heaven), one pointing down (female, water, earth). This figure, now known as the Star of David, symbolized the union of Israel and Judah and is sometimes also taken as an ideogram for the human soul. It was a Greek symbol of the androgyne.

The Chinese oracular Book of

Changes, the *I Ching*, is based on the unifying symbolism of six broken or unbroken lines making up an overall system of 64 linear "hexagrams".

In the Pythagorean system, six represented chance or luck – as it does in modern dice. As the cube with six surfaces, the number six represents stability and truth.

In Genesis, and in earlier Sumerian-Semitic tradition, the world was created in six days. According to the book of Revelation (13:18), the number of the Beast (Satan) was "666". One theory is that this number was chosen because it falls repeatedly short of the sacred number seven. Numerological theories explain it as a coded version of the name of various oppressive Roman emperors. Alternatively, it is suggested as a monastic number that identifies Simon Magus, a forerunner of Gnosticism, whom the writer of Revelation may have regarded as a dangerous influence in early Christianity.

Skeleton

Like the skull, a symbol of the death of the flesh, often used as a *memento mori* in art (and, according to the 1st-century CE Greek author Plutarch, at Egyptian banquets).

Death personified often appears as a skeleton with a scythe, the Grim Reaper. So do some gods of death, as in Mayan iconography. Skeletons are often shown dancing or making love, often as a satire on carnal pleasures but sometimes as a symbol of life to come, the skeleton (like the spirit) outlasting death.

Skin

A husk enclosing fresh life – the grim meaning of Aztec rites in which the priests of the vegetation-god Xipe Totec wore the skins of flayed victims to symbolize the shell, pod or husk enclosing spring plants. The snake shedding its skin was a similar emblem of regeneration. Similarly, shamans put on animal skins to acquire their powers.

Skull

In its most self-evident form, a symbol of mortality, hence a frequent attribute of saints in medieval and Renaissance art, calling attention to the vanity of earthly things. The skull had richer significance in many traditions as the seat of intelligence, the spirit, vital energy, and the part of the body most resistant to decay – the symbolism underlying pagan cults of the skull in Europe.

Renunciation of life is symbolized in Hindu iconography by a skull filled with blood. The piratical skull with crossed thighbones was designed to terrify and is now a universally understood warning signal.

Sky

Universally associated with supernatural forces, a symbol of superiority, dominion, spiritual ascension and aspiration. The fertilizing influence of sun and rain, the eternal presence of the stars, the tidal pull of the moon, the destructive forces of storms, all helped to establish the sky as the source of cosmic power. With few exceptions, notably in Egyptian myth, the sky was a masculine or yang symbol, often thought to have separated from the female earth in order to allow terrestrial life to develop. Heaven (usually but not always imagined as being located above the earth) was in most traditions a region of the

Skeleton: *see* Bones; DEATH; Skull

Skin: *see* Corn; Snake

Skull: *see* Bones; Head; SEVEN DEADLY SINS; Skeleton

Sky: *see* AFTERWORLDS; Arch; Birds; Blue; Clouds; Dome; Light; Moon; Rain; Sapphire; Soul; Star; Storm; Sun; Zodiac

A shamanic depiction of the skeleton, from an image found in Canada.

Smith: *see*
Fire, Flame; Lameness; Thunder; Volcano

Smoke: *see*
Calumet; Incense

Snail: *see*
Horn; Moon; SEVEN DEADLY SINS; Spiral

Snake: *see*
Apple; Basilisk (Cockatrice); BEASTS OF FABLE; Caduceus; Chimera; Cobra; CROSS; Devils; Dragon; Eagle; Earth; Eclipse; Egg; Golden Fleece; Initiation; JEWELS; Kundalini; Lightning; Lion; Ouroboros; Pearl; Phallus; Rainbow; Seven; Spiral; Sun; Teeth; Tree; Vine; VIRTUES; Water; WISDOM

A Naga, one of the mystical snakes probably based on the cobra, from an Indian bronze.

sky arranged in layers through which the soul could ascend toward ultimate light and peace.

Smith

A symbol of divine or magical creative skills in most early traditions, linked with the natural forces of thunder, lightning, fire and volcanic activity, and with initiations into earth mysteries. In Greek myth the smith is the lame god Hephaestus (in Roman myth, Vulcan). Typically, he acts as demiurge or technician to the creator god and is benevolent despite his links with the underworld.

Smoke

An ascension symbol – of prayers or of purified souls. In Native North America, smoke was a means of communication on a cosmic as well as a mundane level. Less often, it appears as a symbol of concealment or of the transitory nature of life.

Snail

Now simply a metaphor for slowness, but in older traditions – especially in Africa and Central America – a lunar and fertility symbol. Periodically showing and hiding its horns like the moon, the snail also suggested by its helical shell the spiralling processes of cyclic continuity. It thus became an emblem of rebirth or resurrection, and of fecundity generally, as in Aztec iconography. The shell and uncoiling body also combined female and male sexual symbolism.

Snake

The most significant and complex of all animal symbols, and perhaps the oldest. Snakes carved on Paleolithic antlers in Africa or drawn on rock faces were primarily fertility or rain symbols, and sexual or agricultural fertility symbolism remained a basic element in most later snake cults. But obvious analogies between the snake and the penis, the umbilical cord or the humid processes of birth (for the snake combines male and female symbolism) do not explain the almost universal importance of the serpent in mythology. The snake was above all a magico-religious symbol of primeval life force, sometimes an image of the creator divinity itself. The *ouroboros* motif of a snake swallowing its own tail symbolizes not only eternity but a divine self-sufficiency.

Emblematically, the snake was in touch with the mysteries of the earth, the waters, darkness and the underworld – self-contained, cold-blooded, secretive, sometimes venomous, able to glide swiftly without feet, magically swallow large creatures, and rejuvenate itself by shedding its own skin. Its serpentine form was as allusive as its other characteristics, suggesting undulating waves and landscapes, winding rivers, vines and tree roots, and in the sky the rainbow, the lightning strike, the spiralling motion of the cosmos. As a result, the snake became one of the most widespread of all animist symbols – depicted on a gigantic scale in the 400-metre-long Great Serpent Mound in Ohio.

The snake coiled around its eggs suggested the analogy of a great serpent coiled around the world, supporting it or holding together the waters surrounding it. Thus the Hindu creator-god Vishnu rests on the coils of a great snake, Ananta (Shesha); Indra slays a chaos snake, Vritra, to release the fertilizing waters it enclosed; and the great earthquake snake, Vasuki, is used to churn the sea of creation. In African and other myths, a rainbow snake reaches from the watery underworld into the heavens. In Nordic myth, the great tempest serpent of Midgard holds the world in his unpredictable coils. (The snake-shaped prow of Viking ships had protective as well as aggressive symbolism.) In South America, eclipses were explained as the swallowing of the sun or moon by a giant serpent. In Egypt, the barque of the sun that travels through the underworld waters at night is threatened by the serpent Apep, and has to enter another great serpent to be reborn each morning. In Mexico, Quetzalcoatl, the Aztec version of the bird-snake divinities known throughout Central America, unites the powers of earth and heaven.

The protective–destructive symbolism that runs through these and other serpent myths illustrates the degree to which the snake is a dualistic force, a source of strength when mastered but potentially dangerous and often emblematic of death or chaos as well as of life. A positive symbol of serpentine inner strength, psychic energy and latent spiritual power is the yogic *kundalini* coiled at the base of the spine. Mastery of the snake in its more dangerous aspect is symbolized in both India and Egypt by the erect, hooded cobra. In Egypt, this forms the uraeus or diadem of the pharaohs, a protective serpent emblem of royal power to strike down enemies. Images of the uraeus enclosing a sun disk or of a lion-headed snake were similarly emblems of solar guardianship. In India, cobra divinities (Nagas) were guardian symbols, generally benevolent, as in the image of the seven-hooded cobra that shields the

Buddha. Snakes often appear there and elsewhere as guardians of shrines, of sources of water or of treasure. These traditions are linked both with serpent fecundity symbolism and with the superstition that precious stones were formed underground from snake saliva. The Hindu cobra is often shown with a jewel in its hood, symbolizing spiritual treasure. In Chinese folklore, snakes rewarded human benefactors with pearls.

Paradoxically, the snake was often used as a curative symbol. Entwined snakes on the caduceus – the staff of Hermes (Mercury) symbolizing mediation between opposing forces – was interpreted by psychologist Carl Jung as an emblem of homeopathic medicine. The brass serpent set up by Moses at God's suggestion to heal snakebites (Numbers 21:9) was a similar homeopathic emblem and was later taken to prefigure Christ on the cross, healing the sins of the world. A snake nailed to the cross in medieval Christian art is thus a symbol of resurrection and of spiritual sublimation of the physical life force. In the ancient world, the snake's rejuvenation symbolism linked it specifically with the classical god of healing, Aesculapius. On the other hand, the snake was blamed for humanity's losing the gift of immortal life – not only in the story of Adam and Eve but also in the Babylonian *Epic of Gilgamesh*, who went to superhuman lengths to find the magic plant of rejuvenation only to have it stolen by a snake.

The snake's duality, the balance between fear and veneration in its symbolism, accounts for its appearance as either progenitor or aggressor, culture hero or monster. In its fearful aspect, it gave birth to the dragons and sea serpents of Western tradition and to snake hybrids that symbolized the multiple perils of human existence, typified by the children of Echidna in Greek legend – the Hydra, the Chimera and the snake-backed hell-hound Cerberus. A snakebite carried Eurydice, wife of Orpheus, off to the underworld where the snake-tailed Minos judged the dead. At the level of Western folklore, the snake's symbolism is usually negative, its forked tongue suggesting hypocrisy or deceit, its venom bringing sudden and treacherous death. In Tibetan Buddhism the green snake of hatred is one of the three base instincts. The snake is one of the five noxious animals of China, although it appears in more positive roles too. The snake as Satan was foreshadowed in the dualistic Iranian religion of Zoroastrianism, for which the serpent symbolized the darkness of evil.

Birds associated with light, such as the eagle, falcon and the legendary Garuda in India, are often shown killing snakes, as do many gods and heroes. In Germanic lore both Thor and Beowulf slay and are slain by dragon-serpents. It is tempting to see snake-slaying as a symbol of the destruction of a paternal or older power – as in the legend in which the Greek hero Herakles (Hercules) strangled two snakes in his cradle. To establish his cult at Delphi, Apollo had to kill Python, dragon nurse of the terrible monster Typhon – a myth that suggests the replacement of an older, maternal serpent cult. This may be the meaning of Baal's destruction of the seven-headed serpent Lotan in Phoenician myth. In its positive mythological aspect, the snake fathers gods or heroes (including Alexander the Great, reputedly sired by Zeus – Jupiter – in snake guise). Amun and Atum, progenitor divinities of Egypt, were both snake gods. In Greek legend, Cadmus, the founder of Thebes, sows the teeth of a serpent-dragon from which then spring the Theban nobility.

Snakes appear widely as ancestor figures in African and Native American legends, and in China, where Na Gua and Fu Xi were snake-bodied progenitor gods and house snakes were thought to bring luck as forefather spirits. Ancestral symbolism, together with the belief that snakes understood earth mysteries and could see in the dark, help to account for the strong link between the serpent and wisdom or prophecy. Be wise as serpents, and innocent as doves, Christ told his disciples (Matthew 10:16). The Greek word *drakon* ("dragon" or "beady-eyed snake") was linked etymologically with vision, and in art the serpent is an attribute of the Greek goddess Athene (Minerva) as wisdom, and of Prudence in the sense of foresight. The Trojan Cassandra was said to owe her prophetic gifts to the sacred snakes of Apollo who licked her ears as she lay in his temple.

In a context where too much knowledge was impious, the snake's wisdom was turned against it – as in the biblical story of how Eve was beguiled by a serpent "more crafty than any other wild animal that the Lord God had made" (Genesis 3:1). The snake wound around the forbidden tree in Eden has many parallels in the Middle East. In Greek myth a snake guards the golden apples of the Hesperides and also the tree on which the Golden Fleece hangs. A snake-entwined tree was a specific emblem of the Near-Eastern fertility goddess Ishtar. As shown by the many other earth goddesses who are depicted holding phallic snakes, serpents played important roles in vegetation fertility cults of the Mediterranean and Near East. Initiation rites of the Asia Minor fertility god Sabazius mimed the passage of a snake through the body of the acolyte. The snakes wound around the limbs of satyrs in paintings of Bacchanalian revels refer to classical fertility rites based on such earlier models and especially associated with the sinuous vine. Snakes also featured in Semitic fertility cults which used sexual rites to approach the godhead. Eve's offer to Adam of the forbidden fruit (a symbol of a sacrilegious attempt to acquire divine powers) has been read as a Hebrew warning against the seductions of such rival cults. Hence – according to this exegesis – the Judeo-Christian symbolism of the serpent as the enemy of humankind and its later identification with Satan himself: "that old serpent called the Devil" (Revelation 12:9). In Western art, the snake thus became a dominant symbol of evil, sin, temptation or deceit. It appears at the foot of the cross as an emblem of the Fall, redeemed by Christ, and is shown being trampled by the Virgin Mary.

Solstice

Significant in solar rituals, particularly those marking the Northern winter solstice on December 22, the shortest day in the Northern hemisphere, after which the sun was symbolically "reborn". In 274CE, the Emperor Aurelian sought to unite the Roman Empire around the cult of the "Unconquered Sun" (the Persian god

of light, Mithras) and fixed December 25 as the sun's birthday. Some 60 years later, the Christian Church borrowed this date to commemorate the birth of Christ as the new prince of light. The December solstice was the birthday of several other gods who died, such as Osiris in Egypt and Balder in northern Europe. It is the origin of the Saturnalia and Yuletide festivals as well as of the 12 days of Christmas.

Soma

The fermented juice of a desert plant, symbolizing in Vedic and Hindu ritual the divine life force. There are close affinities with the symbolism of ambrosia, sap, semen and wine. *Soma* was personified by a Vedic god, identified in later Hindu tradition with the moon, from whose cup the gods drank *soma* (replenished each month from solar sources). In mystic rites, *soma* was drunk as a symbol of communion with divine power. In Hindu iconography, emblems of the exhilarating strength of *soma* include the bull, eagle and giant.

Soul

A symbol of the spiritual or non-bodily aspects of individual human existence. Most traditions envisaged one or more souls inhabiting the body, sometimes wandering from it during dreams and persisting in some form after death. In Egypt the soul that left the body was depicted as a human-headed hawk. In Greece it was shown as a butterfly leaving the mouth, or sometimes a snake. The Greek personification of the soul as the beautiful Psyche may have influenced the Christian iconography of souls as little winged figures. Doves flew from the mouths of saints, eagles from the

Solstice: *see*
SEASONS; Sun; Wheel

Soma: *see*
Sap; Wine

Soul: *see*
Ba; Butterfly; Dove; Eagle; Falcon, Hawk; Ka; Spark; Wings

Spark: *see*
Fire, Flame; Light; Soul

Sparrow: *see*
Birds

Spear: *see*
Lance; Lightning; Phallus;
Weapons; Zig-zag

Sphere: *see*
Circle; CROSS; Globe, Orb

Sphinx: *see*
Lion; Mother; Ram; Sun;
Wings; WISDOM

pyres of emperors. In later Western art, souls often appear as naked children. In Semitic and other mystic traditions, souls were sparks of light.

South *see* **CARDINAL POINTS**

Spark
A soul symbol in Orphic, Gnostic, Cabbalistic and other mystic traditions, conceived as a fragment of divine light separated from the Godhead in the dualistic universe of light and darkness, but able to rejoin it once freed from the material world.

Sparrow
A perky and prolific bird linked in China with the penis and sometimes eaten for its supposed potency. Sexual symbolism appears in Greece too, where the bird was an attribute of the goddess Aphrodite, and in Western art, where a woman holding a sparrow represents a wanton.

Spear
Male potency. The spear's phallic symbolism is clear in the Japanese myth in which the creator-god Izanagi stirs the ocean with a jewelled spear, drops from which form the first solid land. Fertility symbolism also linked the spear with lightning, as in Phoenician iconography of the storm-god Hadad who thrusts a spear with a zig-zag shaft into the earth.

Sphere
The sphere shares the symbolism of perfection with the circle and totality with the globe. The Greek symbol for the sphere was the gamma cross (a cross in a circle), an ancient emblem of power. The armillary sphere, a skeletal globe composed of metal

rings demonstrating the earth-centred Ptolemaic theory of the cosmos, was an old emblem of astronomy.

Sphinx
Originally, in Egypt, a monumental human-headed lion symbolizing the power and majesty of the sun and the eternal glory of the ruler whom it commemorated. The archetype is the Great Sphinx of Giza, which displays the head of Khafre facing the rising sun – an ancient and serene image that has nothing to do with the "riddle of the Sphinx", an invention of Greek myth-making genius.

Egyptian funerary sphinxes such as the ram-headed guardians at Karnak evolved into the winged protective sphinxes of the Near East and eventually to the monstrous Greek hybrid with wings and a female head and breasts which waylaid Oedipus on the road to Thebes and asked him (at peril of his life) what went on four legs in the morning, two at midday and three at night – the answer being a man. This entirely Greek sphinx (seen by the psychologist Carl Jung as an

A sphinx, after an Egyptian relief.
This image of the creature shows signs
of transition into the Greek form.

image of the devouring female or "terrible mother") led to the popular symbolism of the sphinx as an enigma or source of ancient wisdom.

Spider

A lunar and female symbol associated with the weaving of human destiny and therefore with divination. In India, the spider's web is a symbol of *maya* ("illusion") – the fragile and mortal world of appearances. Spiders often appear elsewhere in mythology as attributes of moon goddesses, and as culture heroines or demiurge creators of the world.

They can symbolize either ensnarement (by the Devil in Christian symbolism) or protection from storms, as among some Native North Americans. Folklore associations of the spider with good luck, wealth or coming rain are widespread, a symbolism that may be suggested by the spider descending its thread, emblematically bringing heavenly gifts.

Spindle

Like the spider's web, a lunar symbol of the transitory nature of human life, but with more positive creative aspects, particularly in folklore. The spindle is an attribute of the mother goddess and of women generally. In art it is held by Clotho, the Greek Fate who spins destiny.

Spiral

From the earliest times a dynamic symbol of life force, cosmic and microcosmic. Spiral forms are seen in nature from celestial galaxies to whirlwinds and whirlpools, from coiled serpents or conical shells to human fingertips – and (as science has discovered) to the double helix structure of DNA at the heart of every cell.

In art, spirals are one of the most common of all decorative motifs, ranging from Celtic double spirals in northern Europe or the volutes on Roman capitals, to the whorls in Maori carving and tattooing in the South Pacific. Maori whorls, based on fern forms, show the close link between spiral motifs and natural phenomena. Although this sometimes provides a key to their symbolism, spirals are so allusive that other clues are needed before specific meanings can be read into them. The symbolism of decorative spiral motifs is more often unconscious than conscious.

Carved on megaliths, spirals suggest a labyrinthine journey to the afterlife, and perhaps a return. The spiralling snakes on the caduceus – and double spirals in general – suggest a balance of opposing principles – the meaning of the yin-yang motif, which is itself a form of double spiral. Vortex forces in wind, water or fire suggest ascent, descent or the rotating energy that drives the cosmos.

By adding wheeling momentum to a circular form, the spiral also symbolizes time, the cyclic rhythms of the seasons and of birth and death, the waning and waxing of the moon, and the sun (often symbolized by the spiral). Like the yogic "serpent" at the base of the spine, the spring-like coil of a spiral suggests latent power. The uncoiling spiral is phallic and male, the involuted spiral is female, making the double spiral also a fertility symbol.

The spiral as an open and flowing line suggests extension, evolution and continuity, uninterrupted concentric and centripetal movement, the very rhythm of breathing and of life itself.

Spider: *see*
Loom; Moon; Rain; Spindle; Weaving; Web

Spindle: *see*
Spider; Weaving; Web

Spiral: *see*
Caduceus; Kundalini; Labyrinth; Moon; Shell; Snake; Sun; Wheel; Whirlpool; Whirlwind; Yin-yang

A spider, from a 1,000-year-old shell disk from Illinois, USA. In some parts of Native North America the spider was a protection against storms.

Spire: *see*
Tower

Spleen: *see*
Yin-yang

Spring (water): *see*
Fountain; Tree; Water;
Well; WISDOM

Square: *see*
CARDINAL POINTS;
Circle; Earth; Four;
Mandala; Temple

Square (carpentry): *see*
VIRTUES

Squirrel: *see*
Rat

Spire

A symbolic expression of the aim of Gothic architects to create churches that appeared to soar toward heaven. Gothic cathedrals sought to "render immaterial all that is material".

Spittle

A bodily fluid often thought to have special power to harm or heal, depending on the way it was used. Thus St John (9:6) reports that Christ healed a blind man by mixing spittle with clay to anoint his lids. The habit of spitting for good luck uses the old offensive symbolism of spitting in the face of demons or witches.

Spleen

Once thought to be the ruling organ of emotion, but symbolizing ill humour in the West, good humour and laughter in the East. In ancient China, the spleen was one of the Eight Treasures, associated with yin energy.

Spring *see* Seasons

Spring (water)

Purity and fertility – a source of spiritual wisdom, salvation or healing. In myth, folklore and religion, springs are magical or spiritually significant places, an idea based partly on the general symbolism of water and partly on the spring as the unpolluted origin of water.

In pagan cults, springs were linked with the wisdom or gifts of benevolent underworld spirits. The healing properties of mineral springs may have added to the curative symbolism of springs in general. A spring flowing from the Tree of Life fed the four rivers of paradise – a Christian symbol of salvation.

Square

The ancient sign for the earth, particularly important in the symbol systems of India and China. Based on the order implied by the four directions of space, and on the stabilizing "female" symbolism of the number four, the square symbolized permanence, security, balance, the rational organization of space, correct proportion, limitation, moral rectitude and good faith (the "square deal"). As opposed to the dynamism of the circle, spiral, cross and triangle, the square is the most static of the graphic shapes frequently used as symbols. Combined with the circle, as in many Hindu mandalas, it stands for the union of earth with heaven – the symbolic basis of domed temples built on square ground plans. In many traditions, the square was an emblem of the perfect city, built for eternity – an extension of the symbolic difference between the "permanent" four walls of the house and the circular base of the nomadic tent.

Square (carpentry)

Once an emblem of the Chinese emperor as Lord of the Earth, and later of the Lodge Master in Freemasonry, its right-angle symbolizing a Freemason's duty to uphold moral rightness, justice and truth.

Squirrel

A fertility symbol in Japan. In Europe an animal that shares the destructive, voracious symbolism of other rodents. Its darting journeys up and down trees suggested the Scandinavian myth of a squirrel go-between fostering enmity between the eagle at the top of the World Tree, Yggdrasil, and the serpent at the bottom.

Staff

Like the rod and sceptre, a male symbol of power and authority, often held as an emblem of office or carried ahead of high priests in ecclesiastical processions. The shepherd's staff, or crook, was, with the flail, the main emblem of the god Osiris as shepherd and judge of Egyptian souls. As a weapon, the staff can have punitive meaning, but usually appears in art as the attribute of pilgrims and saints.

Stag *see* **Deer**

Star

Supremacy, constancy, guidance, guardianship, vigilance and aspiration. Ancient beliefs that the stars ruled or influenced human life, either as divinities or agents of divinity, account for much of the symbolism of the star, as well as underlying the hugely influential symbol system of astrology. Greek stellar myth peopled the sky with starry gods and heroes. In religion, stars formed the crowns of great mother goddesses, notably Ishtar in the Near East, and the Virgin Mary. Stars were cosmic windows or points of entry to heaven. They were the eyes of Mithras, Persian god of light. In the Old Testament, the "star out of Jacob" is a Messianic symbol, recalled in the New Testament description of Christ as "the bright and shining morning star".

Moving or shooting stars presaged the death of great men or the birth of gods, as in the Christmas story of the birth of Christ or Indian myths of Agni and the Buddha. In general symbolism, the most significant stars are the Pole Star, symbolic pivot of the universe, and the "star" of Venus – the aggressively bright, emblem of warfare and life-energy as the morning star, and of sexual pleasure and fertility as the evening star.

Among star images, the five-pointed pentagram and six-pointed hexagram (drawn with internal lines connecting each point) have major symbolism, discussed in their individual entries. The four-pointed star is the sun star of Shamash, the Mesopotamian solar god. The five-pointed star was the Sumerian emblem of Ishtar in her warrior aspect as the morning star. As an emblem of ascendancy, it is the star with the Islamic crescent, and the star most widely used on flags and in military and police insignia today. It is also the most common form of Bethlehem star or birth star. In Freemasonry, the five-pointed "blazing star" symbolizes the mystic centre and regeneration. The six-pointed star is the Star of David, the Pole Star, and sometimes appears as a birth star. The Gnostic mystic star has seven points. The eight-pointed star, linked with creation, fertility and sex, was the emblem of Ishtar in later Near-Eastern symbolism, and of Venus as the evening star. This is an alternative form of Bethlehem star.

Steps, Stairs

Symbols of progress toward enlightenment, esoteric understanding or heaven itself. Steps and terraces were often used in religious architecture and altar design, or in the rites of mystery cults, to symbolize the marked difference between earthly and spiritual planes, the gradually ascending stages of initiation, and the slow and difficult process of spiritual transformation. The number of steps often had specific meaning, as in the nine steps leading to the god Osiris

Staff: *see*
Caduceus; Crozier;
Pilgrimage; Rod; Sceptre;
Wand

Star: *see*
Crescent; Crown; Eight;
Eye; Hexagram; Meteorite;
Pentagram, Pentacle;
PLANETS; Pole Star;
Zodiac

Steps, Stairs: *see*
Initiation; Mountain;
PLANETS; Ziggurat

An eight-pointed star representing the great Near-Eastern goddess Ishtar, from a carved stela.

Stone: *see*
Altar; Amulet; Beggar; Bones; JEWELS; Ka; Lingam; Menhir; Meteorite; Mother; Omphalos; Pillar; Rock

Stork: *see*
Fire, Flame; LONGEVITY; Mother; Red; Sun

Storm: *see*
Axe; Bull; Hammer; Thunder

(the completed cycle) in Egyptian tradition or the seven steps (the planets represented as diferent metals) in Mithraic initiations.

Stomach *see* Belly

Stone

Once a compelling animist symbol of magical powers thought to exist within inanimate matter. In nearly all ancient cultures, the general symbolic qualities of rock – permanence, strength, integrity – were heightened and given sacred significance in individual standing stones, sacrificial stone axes or knives, and stone objects such as amulets. Stones stored heat, coldness, water and (as jewels) light. They could appear as giant, lifelike presences. In Native North America, they were the metaphoric bones of Mother Earth, as also in Greece and in Asia Minor where the great mother goddess Cybele was worshipped in the form of a stone later carried to Rome. Stones could come from the sky as meteorites, like the sacred black stone of the Kaaba at Mecca. Thus they were linked with both earth and sky. As durable symbols of life force, they were used to mark sacred places and to act, like the altar, *omphalos* or lingam, as a focus of worship, or sacrifice or an invocation of fertility. Sacrificial victims were bound to them or (in Fiji) had their brains dashed out on them.

In funerary memorials, stone symbolized eternal life. In coronation rituals, it signified authority hallowed by tradition. To symbolize his claim to suzerainty over Scotland, Edward I stole the Stone of Scone on which Scots kings were crowned until 1296 and installed it at Westminster (it was

returned to Scotland in 1996). The tradition of kissing a stone at Blarney Castle to acquire "the gift of the gab" is based on the oracular symbolism of stone not only in Celtic tradition but also elsewhere. Thrown stones are associated both with death (especially in Hebrew tradition) and with life. In Greek myth, Deucalion and his sister restore the human race after the Deluge by throwing over their shoulders stones which become men and women. Stone fights were superstitiously thought to promote fertility and bring rain in China. Stone chimes were Chinese fertility emblems. The use of stones and stone objects as phallic cures for sterility was widespread. With the decline of animist beliefs, stone became primarily a symbol of unfeeling coldness.

Stork

In the Orient, a popular emblem of longevity and, in Taoism, of immortality. There and elsewhere, the stork symbolizes filial devotion because it was thought to feed its elderly parents as well as its own children. Its nursing care and association with new life as a migratory bird of spring made it sacred to the Greek goddess Hera (in Roman myth, Juno) as a protective divinity of nursing mothers – the basis of the Western fable that storks bring babies. In art, storks draw the chariot of the god Hermes (Mercury) and are often shown killing snakes. Christian iconography links the stork with purity, piety and resurrection.

Storm

Although associated with divine anger or punishment in most parts of the world, the storm was a symbol of creative energy and fecundity. Hence

A detail from a carving of the great Amarvati stupa *(from the Sanskrit word meaning "mound").*

the name "house of abundance" for the temple of the great rain-bringing Mesopotamian storm-god Hadad. Most storm gods depicted wielding axes, hammers or thunderbolts have dual creative–destructive symbolism.

Stranger
In most primitive traditions, an enigmatic symbol of impending change – perhaps a god, perhaps a dangerous rival. In Greek legend, one of the enemies of Herakles (Hercules) is Busiris, an Egyptian king who sacrificed strangers, beginning with the prophet who told him that this practice would end famine in the land.

Strawberry
A symbol of carnal pleasure in the paintings of Bosch, who shows giant strawberries growing in *The Garden of Earthly Delights* (*c.*1495). Fruits eaten

in the afterlife can symbolize the end of any chance of returning to the living, as in a Native Canadian myth of the temptation of strawberries.

Stupa
A domed reliquary built as a symbol of the Buddha's teaching – the renunciation of earthly desires. In its classic form based on the simple tumulus grave, a square base symbolizes the terrestial plane, a dome the cosmic egg, surmounted by a balcony representing the 33 heavens ruled by Shiva. The whole is penetrated by an axial mast with rings or parasols symbolizing the Buddha's ascent and escape from the round of existence.

Sulphur
In the symbolism of alchemy, the active, fiery, male generative principle. Sulphur in reaction with the female principle of mercury would, it was thought, steadily purify base metals. Chinese superstition credited sulphur with magical powers against evil, whereas in Christian tradition Satan is himself a sulphuric figure controlling an infernal world of brimstone.

Summer *see* Seasons

Sun
The dominant symbol of creative energy in most traditions, often worshipped as the supreme god or a manifestation of his all-seeing power. In spite of the geocentric (earth-centred) basis of ancient astronomy, some of the earliest graphic signs for the sun show it as the symbolic centre or heart of the cosmos. As the source of heat, the sun represents vitality, passion, courage and eternally renewed youth. As the source of light out of darkness,

Stupa: *see*
Axis; Dome; Egg; Parasol; Ring; Square

Sulphur: *see*
Alchemy; Devils; Fire, Flame; Mercury

Sun: *see*
Ankh; Aureole; Ball; Bull; Centaur; Chariot; Chi-Rho; Chrysanthemum; Circle; Cock (Rooster); CROSS; Dawn; Diamond; Disk; Eagle; Eclipse; Eye; Falcon, Hawk; Fire, Flame; Globe, Orb; Gold; Halo; Heart; Heliotrope; Horse; Light; Lion; Lotus; Moon; Noon; Phoenix; PLANETS; Ram; Raven; Rays; Red; Ring; Rose; Ruby; Scarab; Snake; Solstice; Spiral; Star; Sun dance; Sunflower; Swan; Swastika; TRUTH; Wheel; Yellow; Yin-yang; Zodiac

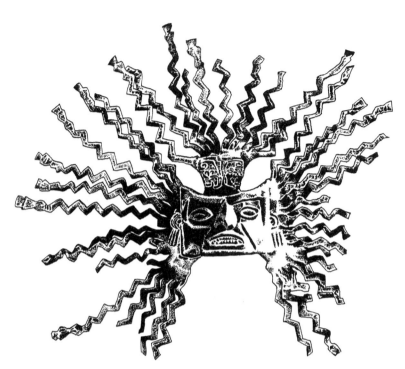

The sun with zigzagging rays, after a golden Inca mask.

it symbolizes knowledge, intellect and Truth personified, who, in Western art, sometimes holds a sun in her hand. And as the most brilliant of the celestial bodies, it is the emblem of royalty and imperial splendour.

The sun represents the male principle in most traditions, but was female in Germany and Japan and for many tribes in the Celtic world, Africa, Native America, Oceania and New Zealand. It was an imperial yang emblem in China but was never seen as supreme in the Chinese pantheon of gods. Like a number of other peoples, the Chinese symbolized the destructive aspects of solar power in a myth about how multiple suns made the world too hot. The ten original

suns refused to share their solar duties on a rota basis and entered the sky together. The divine archer Yi had then to kill nine of them to restore cosmic balance. A distinctive solar emblem in China is a red disk with a three-legged black raven or crow symbolizing the three phases of the sun (rising, zenith, setting).

The most elaborate sun cults were those of Peru, Mexico and Egypt. Emphasizing the Inca claim to be "children of the sun", the Peruvian sun deity was depicted in human form with a disk-like golden face. In the Aztec cult of the Fifth Sun, the war god Huitzilopochtli required continuing human sacrifices to sustain the strength of the sun as guardian of the contemporary era. This charmless story, masking Aztec blood lust, is a pole away from the Nordic legend of the death of the handsome young Nordic god of light, Balder, but is one of countless myths and rites based on the symbolic theme of the sun's eclipse, nightly disappearances or seasonally waxing and waning power. Thus Egyptian solar myth depicts the barque of the sun travelling each night through underworld perils before emerging triumphantly from the mouth of a serpent each morning. In a farcical treatment of the theme, the Japanese sun-goddess Amaterasu hides herself in a cave and has to be tricked to come out again. Personifications of the sun are multiple in some cultures, as in Egypt where Khepri is the scarab god of the rising sun, Horus the eye of day, Ra the zenith and Osiris the setting sun. In Greece, Helios personified the sun, whereas the Roman Sol was desultorily displaced by Apollo, representing the brilliance of its light.

Alternatively, the sun is the son of the supreme god or symbolizes his vision or radiant love. It was the eye of Zeus in Greece, of Odin in Scandinavia, of Ahura Mazda (alternatively called Ormuzd) in Iran, of Varuna in India and of Allah to Muhammad. It was the light of the Buddha, of the Great Spirit in Native North America, of God the Father in Christianity. Christ, the Sun of Righteousness, replaced Mithras in the Roman Empire as a resurrection symbol of the Unconquered Sun.

In iconography the sun is represented by a vast range of emblems. These include the gold disk, the rayed or winged disk (most common in the Middle East), the half-disk with rays (Nihon, meaning "sun-source", the emblem of Japan), the circle with central point (a symbol of the conscious self in astrology), and a star, spiral, ring, wheel, swastika (or other turning cross forms), heart, rosette, lotus, sunflower and chrysanthemum. It could be further represented by bronze, gold, yellow, red, diamond, ruby, topaz, a winged or feathered serpent, an eagle or an eagle with a serpent, or a falcon, phoenix, swan, lion, ram, cock or bull. Golden or white horses or swans draw the solar chariot. The "black sun" was an alchemical symbol of unworked primal matter.

Sun dance

The most important ritual of the Native North American Plains, symbolizing the power of the sun as a manifestation of the Great Spirit. To become shamans, to avenge insults or for other reasons, "pledgers" drew on this power by dancing in a circle around a forked world axis pole, staring at the sun and tearing from their chests cords binding them to the pole to symbolize release from ignorance.

Sunflower

Solar adoration – a symbolism used by Anton van Dyck (1599–1641), who painted himself with a sunflower to ingratiate himself with Charles I of England, his royal "sun". The sunflower, a plant brought to Europe from North America, is sometimes confused with the heliotrope, source of a Greek myth of solar infatuation.

Swallow

The traditional messenger of spring and so a renewal or resurrection symbol in many traditions. An emblem of childbirth. In China, where its arrival coincided with fecundity rites at the March equinox, swallows nesting in a house presaged early marriage with

Sun dance: *see* Axis; Circle

Sunflower: *see* Heliotrope

Swallow: *see* Birds; Marriage; SEASONS

Swan: *see*
AFTERWORLDS; Birds;
DEATH; Goose; Harp;
Knight; Light;
Transformation; Sun

Swastika: *see*
Axis; CARDINAL
POINTS; Centre; Circle;
CROSS; Foot, Footprint;
Four; Hammer; Light;
Lightning; NUMBERS;
Sky; Sun; Wheel

many children. The swallow was
sacred to Isis in Egypt and to mother
goddesses elsewhere.

Swan

A romantic and ambiguous symbol of
light, death, transformation, poetry,
beauty and melancholy passion, especially influential in Western literature,
music and ballet. As a solar and male
emblem of light, the white swan
became the shining hero of Wagner's
opera *Lohengrin* (1848) and other
tales of the swan knight. As an
emblem of female softness, beauty
and grace, it became the heroine of
Tchaikovsky's ballet *Swan Lake*
(1876). Similarly, in classical myth, the
swan was the attribute both of the
beautiful Greek goddess Aphrodite
(in Roman myth, Venus) and of
Apollo as god of poetry, prophecy
and music. The Greek fable that
swans sing a last song of unearthly
beauty as they die reinforced the
swan's association with poetry and
linked it also with death, as in the
Finnish legend of the Swan of
Tuonela in which it personifies the
waters of the underworld.

The persistent theme of transformation in swan symbolism is prefig-
ured in the myth in which the Greek
god Zeus (Jupiter) disguised himself
as a swan to ravish Leda. Through
such myths the swan evolved into a
symbol of achieved passion and the
ebbing or loss of love. The swan is
linked with bardic inspiration in
Celtic tradition (where it is almost
interchangeable with the goose) and is
often associated in iconography with
the harp and the otherworld of spiritual beings. A pair of swans, linked by
a gold or silver chain, draw the Celtic
barque of the sun.

Leda and the Swan, *with the Dioscuri
on the ground beside them, after a
16th-century copy of a lost painting by
Leonardo da Vinci.*

Swastika

An ideogram representing cosmic
dynamism and creative energy, one of
the most ancient and widespread of
all linear symbols. Named from the
Sanscrit *su* "well", and *asti* "being",
its traditional significance was always
positive. Nazi use of its power symbolism made it the most infamously
successful emblem of the 20th century
and the one most altered from its
ancient meaning. The swastika is an
equal-armed cross with the end of
each arm turned at a right-angle to
give it whirling momentum. Pictor-
ially it can suggest a solar wheel with
light trailing from each turning spoke,
and its appearance in many primitive
cults was linked with sun or sky gods,
particularly Indo-Iranian. It can
rotate in either direction. The swastika with the top bar turned to the left –
a Buddhist symbol of the cyclic round
of existence – is sometimes, but not
always, identified with the principle of

male energy and was an emblem used by Charlemagne (*c*.742–*c*.771CE).

The reversed swastika (used by Hitler) was linked with female generative power in upper Mesopotamia and appears on the pubis of the great Semitic goddess Ishtar, equated in the classical world with the Greek Artemis (in Roman myth, Diana). Similarly in China, the reversed swastika is a yin symbol. The swastika's essential meaning of life force, solar power and cyclic regeneration is often extended to signify the Supreme Being, notably in Jainism. It appears on the footprint or breast of the Buddha (unmoving heart of the Wheel of Becoming). It is also a sign of Christ (moving in the world) in catacomb inscriptions, of Vedic and Hindu gods (Agni, Brahma, Surya, Vishnu, Shiva, Ganesha); of Zeus, Helios, Hera and Artemis in Greece; and of Thor, the Scandinavian god of thunder whose hammer may appear in swastika forms suggesting twin lightning bolts. The winged disk on a swastika was used as a symbol of solar energy in Egypt and Babylonia, but the swastika appeared widely elsewhere, on icons or artifacts and with a variety of subsidiary meanings.

Apart from its rotative force, the swastika's other notable graphic feature is that its whirling arms quarter space around a pole or static centre. In Native American symbolism, the swastika was associated with the sacred number four – the four wind gods, the four seasons, or the four cardinal points as in China (where it was the symbol of the "infinite" number 10,000). Its use as a polar symbol survives in the Masonic order. It was a Gnostic secret symbol and the cross of the Manichean Christian sect. The use of the swastika as an emblem of "Aryan" racial purity dates from just before World War I, among anti-Semitic socialist groups in Germany and Austria. The Finnish Air Force adopted it as a military emblem in 1918. Hitler, master of mass psychology, recognized its dynamism as a party emblem and put it on the Nazi banner in August 1920, tilted to give it a bent-legged forward drive. "The effect was as if we had dropped a bomb," he wrote.

Swine *see* **Pig**

Sword

Beyond its obvious aggressive/protective function, an important symbol of authority, justice, decisive judgment, insight, penetrative intellect, phallic power, light, separation and death. One explanation for the unusually rich symbolism of the sword is that the arcane skills of sword-making meant that swords stronger, sharper and better balanced than others were credited with supernatural powers. Hence the many legends of magic swords such as the Arthurian Excalibur, and the frequent appearance of the sword as an emblem of magic. Cults of the sword, particularly in Japan and in religious rituals of the medieval Crusades, gave it a ceremonial as well as a military role, as in the conferring of knighthoods. A sword (in fable drawn from the tail of an eight-headed dragon) is one of the Three Treasures of the Japanese Emperor. In art, the sword is the attribute of Justice, Constancy, Fortitude and Wrath personified – and of St Paul who called the word of God "the sword of the spirit". The two-edged sword is a particular symbol of

Sword: *see*
Alchemy; Cherubim;
Dance; Dragon; Fire,
Flame; Knight; Light;
Phallus; Scales; VIRTUES;
Weapons

From a Navajo Indian sand painting of a swastika.

divine wisdom or truth, notably in Revelation where it protrudes from the mouth of Christ (1:16). Similarly, Buddhism refers to the sword of wisdom cutting through ignorance. Vishnu is shown with a flaming sword of knowledge. The flame-like shape of the two-edged sword also links it with purification, as in alchemy where the sword is an emblem of fire. Purity is implied by the biblical cherubim with flaming swords who guard the way back to Eden (Genesis 3:24). The sword laid between man and woman in bed suggests purity as well as separation. The sword of Damocles, in legend suspended by a hair by Dionysius, tyrant of Syracuse, over the head of an over-ambitious courtier, symbolized the precarious nature of power. As an emblem of justice the sword often appears with the scales. It is carried by the archangel Michael, and appears with retributive significance opposite the lily in paintings of the judgmental Christ. A broken sword symbolizes failure. In Chinese dream symbolism, a woman drawing a sword from water will have a son; a sword falling into water presages a woman's death. Avoidance of death is the symbolism of sword dancing.

Tabernacle

In Hebrew tradition, the earthly throne or dwelling place of God – a sanctuary, originally established by Moses in the wilderness according to precise geometric rules, symbolizing the cosmos and centred upon a Holy of Holies containing the Ark of the Covenant and approached through a series of veiled spaces of increasing sanctity.

Tablet, Table

Linked through its durability with non-mortal or eternal powers, frequently a symbol of communication with them. In the ancient world, law codes, funerary inscriptions and other important documents were inscribed on tablets (sometimes called "tables") of bronze, marble or other metals and stones. Particularly in the Middle East, this led to the idea that divine commandments should be handed down on tablets – as in the Mosaic Tables of the Law. Mesopotamian and Islamic traditions held that tablets of fate or destiny existed on which the future, as well as the past,

was inscribed. Funerary tablets usually symbolized the consecration of tombs to the spirits of the dead. In China they prevented ancestral spirits from wandering. Greek tablets bearing curses on enemies were probably addressed to underworld divinities.

Tamarisk

A resin-giving tree with sacred significance in desert regions, including Mesopotamia, Palestine (where it was possibly a source of manna, as it still is for the Bedouin) and Egypt, where it was associated with the resurrection of the god Osiris. The tamarisk was linked with immortality in China and rain in Japan.

Tambourine

The drum of dancers, associated particularly with orgiastic agricultural fertility rites. Maenads or Bacchantes carry tambourines in the rites of the Greek god Dionysus (in Roman myth, Bacchus). The tambourine's percussive sound, suggesting thunder and rain, made it a fecundity symbol from Africa to Asia and also in

Tabernacle: *see*
Ark; Temple; Throne; Veil

Tablet, Table: *see*
Stone

Tamarisk: *see*
Manna; Resin

Tambourine: *see*
Drum; Rain; Thunder

Tarot: *see*
Cards; Chariot; Clown;
Cup; DEATH; Devils;
Moon; Pentagram, Pentacle;
Star; Sun; Sword; Tower;
VIRTUES; Wand

Central America. In Indian art, it signifies cosmic rhythms in the hand of Shiva, war in the hand of Indra.

Tarot

In occult tradition, a symbol system charting human progress toward spiritual enlightenment or psychic wholeness. The Tarot deck, which drew on the general currency of symbolism at the end of the 14th century, may well have been the origin of modern playing cards' four suits of numbered and court cards. In Tarot, these corresponded to a "minor arcana" of 56 cards (essentially the modern deck

The Fool, the unnumbered card of the Tarot pack, from a 15th-century French deck.

LE·FOU

plus four knights – except that hearts, diamonds, clubs and spades were represented as cups, coins or pentacles, wands and swords); and to this were added 22 Greater Trumps, called the "major arcana", which were later discarded as playing cards but had enough allusive power to become the most poetic medium of Western divination and fortune-telling. Esoteric influences included Cabbalistic lore based on the 22 letters of the Hebrew alphabet, and perhaps some elements of Greco-Egyptian Hermetic lore.

As with all oracular systems, the mystique of the Tarot is based on its interpretative flexibility. The cards of the major arcana have been redesigned many times and have accumulated a vast range of meanings and interpretations. The following skeleton key lists only a handful of traditional associations.

The **Fool** is the only unnumbered card of the major arcana (sometimes alloted zero or XXII) – Everyman, the outsider, the microcosm, the independent seeker. Card I is the **Magician**, **Juggler** or **Minstrel** – skill, the transformable self, the manipulator of human personality, the creative spirit. Card II is the **Archpriestess** – discrimination, moral law, feminine insight. Card III is the **Empress** – security, fecundity, growth, desire. Card IV is the **Emperor** – action, temporal power, virility, leadership. Card V is the **Archpriest** – enlightenment, spiritual energy, the soul, philosophy. Card VI is the **Lover** – union, the choice between love and passion. Card VII is the **Chariot** – success, self-control, vitality. Card VIII is **Justice** – balance, duality, right judgment. Card IX is the **Hermit** – truth, self-sufficiency, morality, solitude. Card X is the

Wheel of Fortune – movement, major change, precarious balance. Card XI is **Strength** – confidence, courage, inner powers. Card XII is the **Hanged Man** – expiation (enforced or voluntary), realignment. Card XIII is **Death** – transition, severance from fleshly desires. Card XIV is **Temperance** – self-control, dilution, the flux of emotional life. Card XV is the **Devil** – trial, self-examination. Card XVI is the **Tower** – misfortune, revelation, emotional release. Card XVII is the **Star** – hope, replenished spiritual energy. Card XVIII is the **Moon** – illusion, the power of imagination. Card XIX is the **Sun** – joy, successful integration. Card XX is the **Judgment** – transformation, the voice of God. Card XXI is the **World** – completion, wholeness, reward.

Tattoo

Usually a symbol of close allegiance to or identification with a social or cultic group. Some tattoos, particularly those depicting animals, were applied as talismans to borrow a specific animal's powers.

Tea

In Zen Buddhism, a ceremonial drink associated with intense meditation, a symbolism supported by a Japanese legend that the first tea plant grew from the eyelids of the meditating Bodhidharma who cut them off to stay awake. Qualities emphasized in the etiquette of the tea ceremony are purity, harmony, tranquillity and the beauty of simplicity.

Teeth

Primordial emblems of aggressive–defensive power. In Greek myth the dragon's teeth sown by Cadmus, a prince of Thebes, were symbols of generative vitality. In reverse, the drawing or loss of teeth is a castration or impotency symbol. The association between teeth and power explains why shamans wear necklaces of animals' teeth.

Temple

In religious architecture, often a symbol of the earthly house of God, the cosmic centre linking underworld, earth and heaven, or the ascending path toward spiritual enlightenment – concepts that have profoundly modified the functional forms of sacred buildings throughout history. In the spirit of the Greek *temenos* ("land set aside as a sacred enclosure"), temples could be as simple as an altar or shrine to a nature divinity sited beside a river, on a mountain top or in a grove of trees. At the other end of the architectural spectrum are the tiered ziggurats, stupas and pagodas of Eastern tradition as well as Central American, the complex mandala forms of Hinduism and the glories of Western temples in the classical, Romanesque, Gothic, Renaissance and baroque periods. Linking all these diverse styles is the attempt to symbolize divine order.

Ten

Inclusiveness, perfection – the mystical number of completion and unity, especially in Jewish tradition; hence the number of the Commandments revealed to Moses by God, summarizing the most important Hebrew religious obligations. In the Pythagorean system, ten was a symbol of the whole of creation, represented by a star of ten points, the holy *tetraktys* – the sum of the first four numbers: 1, 2, 3

Tattoo: *see*
ANIMALS

Teeth: *see*
Castration; Dragon

Temple: *see*
Centre; Mandala;
Mountain; Pagoda; Stupa;
Tabernacle; Ziggurat

Ten: *see*
Hand; NUMBERS; Zodiac

Tetramorphs: *see* CARDINAL POINTS; Eagle; Four; Lion; Ox

Thorn: *see* Acacia; Crown; Goldfinch; Robin; Wreath, Garland

Three: *see* Fleur-de-lis; NUMBERS; Om (Aum); Triad; Triangle; Trident; Trigrams; Trimurti; Trinity; Triskelion

Christt with the Tetramorphs in each corner, from a 12–13th-century manuscript.

and 4. As the number of digits on the human hands, ten was a symbol of completeness even on the simplest level. The Egyptians based their calendar on the decans, 36 bright stars divided by intervals of ten days. Each decan was thought to influence human life – a significant concept in the development of Greek astrology.

A tenth was almost universally the percentage of spoils, property or produce owed to a god or king in the ancient world – the basis of the tithes system. In China, ten was the perfectly balanced number, represented by a cross with a short central bar. As a combination of male and female numerals, ten was sometimes used as a symbol of marriage. The decade symbolizes a turning point in history or a completed cycle in myth, as in the Fall of Troy after a ten-year siege.

Tetramorphs

In some cultures the four-headed guardians of the directions of space – symbolizing in many traditions the universality of divine dominion and a guarantee against the return of primal chaos. The four biblical tetramorphs described in the first chapter of Ezekiel have the heads of a man, lion, ox and eagle. Following the same order, this vision is linked in Christianity with the evangelists Matthew, Mark, Luke and John, and with Christ's incarnation, resurrection, sacrifice and ascension.

Thistle

Retaliation – the symbolism of the thistle as the heraldic emblem of both Scotland and Lorraine. Adam is punished with thistly ground in Genesis. However, like some other spiny plants, the thistle was associated with healing

or talismanic powers and the white-spotted Lady's thistle is linked with the milk of the Virgin Mary. In art, thistles are emblems of martyrdom.

Thorn

Affliction or protection. The thorny acacia appears with both these symbolic meanings in the ancient Middle East – as the attribute of the protective Egyptian goddess Neith and of the mocked Christ with his crown of thorns.

Thread

Continuity in space and time, linkage, destiny – a symbolism linked always with the delicate fabric of human life. In Greek mythology the Three Fates spin, measure and cut the thread of life. In Eastern tradition, two threads woven together symbolized the common destiny of a married couple.

Three

Synthesis, reunion, resolution, creativity, versatility, omniscience, birth and growth – the most positive number not only in symbolism but in religious thought, mythology, legend and folklore where the tradition of "third time lucky" is very old. The Christian doctrine of the Trinity, which enabled a monotheistic God to be worshipped through the Holy Spirit and the person of Christ, is an example of the way in which three can replace one as the symbol of a more versatile and powerful unity. Three-headed or three-fold gods such as the Greek Hecate or the Celtic Brigit had multiple functions or controlled several spheres. The Egyptian god of occult pseudo-sciences, Thoth, was called by the Greeks Hermes Trismegistos: "thrice-greatest Hermes". Religious triads are common – the Hindu Trimurti of Brahma (creator), Vishnu (sustainer) and Shiva (destroyer); the three brothers, Zeus (Jupiter in Roman myth), Poseidon (Neptune) and Hades (Pluto), who controlled the Greek world with their triple attributes, the three-forked lightning, the trident and the three-headed dog Cerberus; the three great Inca deities of sun, moon and storm; the three brothers who controlled the heavens in China. Other mythological and allegorical figures also frequently come in threes, such as the Fates (in both Greek and Norse traditions), the Furies, the Graces, the Harpies, the Gorgons, or the Christian theological virtues of Faith, Hope and Charity. Three is a much repeated number in the New Testament: the three Magi; the three denials of Peter; the three crosses on Golgotha; the Resurrection after three days.

Three was the number of harmony for Pythagoras, of completeness for Aristotle, having an end as well as a beginning and middle. In other traditions, including Taoism, three symbolized strength because it implied a central element. Politically, three was the first number to make possible executive action by a majority, as in the Roman *triumvirates*. In China, it was the auspicious number symbolizing sanctity, loyalty, respect and refinement. It was the number of the Japanese sacred "treasures" – the mirror, sword and jewel. In Buddhism it was the number of holy scriptures, the Tripitaka. In Hinduism, it was the number of letters in the mystic word *Om* (*Aum*), expressing the ternary rhythm of the whole cosmos and of divinity.

Three is, significantly, the number of a family unit, the smallest "tribe". It symbolized the individual body, soul and spirit. In Africa it was the number of maleness (penis and testicles). In sexual relationships, it is an emblem of conflict ("three's a crowd"), the eternal triangle. Otherwise, three is usually seen as a lucky number, possibly because it symbolizes the resolution of a conflict – a decisive action that may lead to success or disaster. In folk tales, wishes are granted in threes. Heroes or heroines are allowed three choices, set three trials or given three chances to succeed. Ritual actions are often performed thrice, as in Islamic daily ablutions, in salutations or in making auguries. The graphic symbol of three is the triangle. Other triform symbols include the triskelion (a form of triple-armed swastika), the trefoil, the Chinese trigram, the trident, the fleur-de-lis, three fishes with a single head (representing the Christian Trinity) and three-legged lunar animals (representing the phases of the moon).

Throne (seat)

Power, stability, splendour. Psychologically, rulers have always projected confidence by seating themselves while others stand. Their thrones, which have become increasingly elaborate throughout history, came to symbolize their authority, so much so that the throne itself became a symbol of glory, as in Buddhist, Hindu and Eastern Orthodox Christian traditions, which sometimes represented the radiant presence of a divinity by depicting an empty throne. The diamond throne is a Buddhist image of the centre. Christ told his Disciples that they would sit upon 12 thrones to judge the 12 tribes of Israel. Steps or a

Throne (seat): *see*
Canopy; Centre; Diamond; JEWELS; Lion; Peacock; Twelve

Thule: *see*
Island; White

Thumb: *see*
Phallus

Thunder: *see*
Axe; Birds; Bull; Bullroarer;
Dragon; Drum; Eagle;
Hammer; Lightning;
Sceptre; Smith; Snake;
Spiral; Word; Zig-zag

Thyrsus: *see*
Fennel; Ivy; Orgy; Pine, Pine
cone; Resin; Rod; Staff; Vine

*The Celtic hero Finn,
gaining knowledge and
power by sucking the
thumb that he had
scalded on the Salmon
of Knowledge. From a
Celtic stone cross.*

dais (elevation) and canopy (heavenly protection) often support the power symbolism of the seat itself. Jewels, precious metals and effigies of solar creatures such as the lion or peacock were popular decorative features. In Egyptian iconography, the goddess Isis is identified with the throne as great mother.

Thule

A classical term for the farthest limit of the known world, hence *Ultima Thule*, often described as a white island (perhaps a reference to Iceland). In legend and symbolism, Thule represents the mystic threshold of the otherworld. Like the Hyperboreans beyond the North Wind, its people were thought to be wiser and longer-living than ordinary mortals.

Thumb

Power – a meaning derived from the thumb's key role in manual skill and gripping strength, and from its phallic symbolism. The downturned thumb was used by Roman emperors to signal that a gladiator should be put to death. In Irish myth the hero Finn sucked his thumb to gain the power of prophecy from the juice of the Salmon of Knowledge, on which he had scalded himlself.

Thunder

Divine might – equated in Semitic and some other traditions with the sounded word of God (lightning represented the written word) – "God thunders wondrously with his voice" (Job 37:5). Thunderbolts (often depicted as jagged arrows of fire hurled from the clouds) are attributes of the most powerful sky gods in many traditions, notably the weapons of the Greek

god, Zeus (in Roman myth, Jupiter). The thunderbolt was a creative–destructive symbol, associated with an impregnating force as well as with chastisement or justice. Thus in Hindu and Buddhist tradition, Indra uses the *vajra*, a thunderbolt in the form of a diamond sceptre, to split the clouds (in Tantric symbolism representing ignorance). The Inca rain god Ilyap'a releases the celestial waters with his thunder sling, symbolism in common with the projectile force usually associated with thunder in the ancient world. In Native North America, the Thunderbird, heard in the mighty concussion of his eagle-wings, is chiefly a protective sky god. Bird symbolism also appears in Siberian mythology. Although predominantly linked elsewhere with male gods such as the Scandinavian Thor, or with divine smiths (often lame), thunder was sometimes associated through its fecundity symbolism with earth or moon goddesses. In Asia, it was linked with the dragon (especially in China), the drum, the rumbling wagon of dead souls and the anger or laughter of the gods. Other associations include the hammer, mallet, chisel, axe, the bellowing bull and bullroarer, rain-linked animals such as the snake, and graphic signs such as the arrowed zig-zag, the fleur-de-lis and the spiral of rolling thunder. Some thunder gods, especially in Japan, were earth as well as sky deities, speaking from the volcano as well as from the clouds.

Thyrsus

The distinctive staff of the Greek god of wine and revelry Dionysus (in Roman myth, Bacchus) and his votaries – a spear-like rod (originally of hollow fennel) tipped with a pine cone or a bunch of grapes and entwined with ivy or vines, symbolizing impregnating and fertilizing power, both sexual and vegetative. Fermented pine resin may have been mixed with wine in Dionysian (Bacchanalian) rites, heightening the significance of the thyrsus as an emblem of orgiastic release.

Tiara

A triple-tiered, beehive-shaped papal crown developed in the 14th century as a non-liturgical headdress symbolizing three aspects of the pope's sovereignty – spiritual authority in the world, temporal authority in Rome, and pre-eminence among other Christian rulers. The modern symbolism of the papal tiara is that the pope is Father of the Church, terrestrial prince and Vicar of Christ.

Tiger

Feline power, ferocity, cruelty, wrath, beauty and speed – a symbol both aggressive and protective, bestial and royal in the traditions of Asia and India, where the tiger largely replaces the lion as the supreme animal image of the great and terrible in nature. William Blake's poem *The Tyger* (1794) takes up the same symbolism of a fearful symmetry, the dangerous force of elemental desire. Like the lion, the tiger can represent both death and life, evil and evil's destruction. Several gods show their power by riding tigers, including Durga in India. More unexpectedly, the god of wealth rides a tiger in China, and here it is also an emblem of gambling or perhaps of its risks (a "tiger" was slang for the lowest hand in poker in the US). The tiger is particularly

linked with military valour and was an emblem of warriors in India. In China, five legendary tigers protected the directions of space: blue in the east, black in the north, red in the south, white in the west and yellow in the centre.

The tiger's protective symbolism also accounts for the stone tigers on graves and doorways in China, and for the ancient custom by which children wear tiger caps. Shiva and his destroyer consort Kali frequently appear in tiger skins in Hindu iconography. Although tigers were rarely seen west of Persia, they are sometimes substituted for leopards as the animals drawing the chariot of the Greek god Dionysus (Bacchus) in Western art. In southeast Asia, the tiger appears as an ancestral figure, and folk tales of ferocious tiger-bodied men and women are known from India to Siberia. The tiger is the third sign of the Chinese Zodiac and personifies Anger in Chinese Buddhism (one of the Three Senseless Animals).

Titans *see* Giants

Toad

In European superstition, a loathsome familiar of witches, suggestive of death and the torments of the damned – a demonic symbolism that stems from the ancient Near East, based perhaps on the toad's toxic secretions. These were used medicinally in China where the toad was a lunar, yin and humid symbol, a rain-bringer and therefore associated with luck and riches. In folklore, a three-legged toad lived in the moon: it was said that a lunar eclipse was the act of the toad swallowing the moon. Rain and fertility symbolism appear in

Tiara: *see*
Crown; Three

Tiger: *see*
ANIMALS; CARDINAL POINTS; Chariot; Leopard; Lion; Zodiac

Toad: *see*
Alchemy; DEATH; Eclipse; JEWELS; LONGEVITY; Moon; Rain; SEVEN DEADLY SINS; Witchcraft

Tongue: *see*
Bell; Fire, Flame; Red;
WISDOM

Tonsure: *see*
Crown; Hair

Torch: *see*
DEATH; Fire, Flame;
LIBERTY; Light; Phallus;
TRUTH; VIRTUES

Mexico and in parts of Africa where the toad is sometimes given the status of a culture hero. Curiously, the toad's link in medieval Europe with darkness and evil, avarice and lust was mixed with birth and rebirth symbolism (through its amphibian transformations) and with the idea of longevity and riches. The notion that the toad, like the snake, had a jewel in its forehead was widespread; the jewel symbolizing happiness. Alchemy associated the toad with the primal elements of earth and water. The "toady" was originally a mountebank's apprentice who pretended to swallow toads so that his master could "cure" him of the ingested poison.

Tongue

Often shown protruding in carvings and paintings, the tongue has a variety of symbolic meanings. As the only internal organ of the body that can be so startlingly displayed, the tongue is a forceful aggressive–defensive symbol. The protruding tongue in Maori carvings and *hakas* (war dances) expresses challenge and defiance (as does everyday tongue-poking). Sexual symbolism is common in primitive art, as in fertility "pole figures" with extended tongues in Borneo. The protective god Bes in Egypt appears with a protruding tongue, often believed to ward off evil. In India, Kali's tongue, similarly extended, symbolizes her consuming power. The fire-god Agni is shown with seven tongues. There is a strong symbolic link between tongues and flames – both red, active, consuming and creative–destructive (through the tongue's powerful role in speech). In the book of Isaiah, the Lord's tongue is "a devouring fire", and in Acts the Apostles receive the gift of languages in the form of cloven tongues "as of fire". The tongue often represents language itself, and also eloquence or wisdom; the Buddha's tongue, for example, is long. In Egyptian funerary art, extended tongues allowed the dead to speak to the gods. Displayed tongues may also have a demonic, carnivorous or frightening symbolism, as in Greek and other stage masks. Some animal effigies with protruding tongues invoke rain.

Tonsure

A hairstyle symbolizing monkish renunciation of the material world. The medieval Christian style of tonsure in which the top of the head was shaved to leave a circle of hair is thought to have commemorated Christ's crown of thorns.

Torch

In the old sense of a burning brand, a symbol of the flame of life, desire and the light of truth, intelligence or the spirit. In art, the Greek Eros (in Roman myth, Cupid), Aphrodite (Venus) and their attendants often carry torches of sexual desire. Burning love is the theme of the "torch singer" and the open secret of the man who "carries a torch" for someone. As a fertility symbol, the flaming torch is usually phallic and male, especially in the ritual of weddings. As a symbol of life it is often carried in art by female mythological figures such as Demeter (Ceres), Persephone (Proserpine) and Hecate, who are all connected with the underworld life, beyond death. The torch is also an attribute of Prometheus, who stole fire for humankind, and Herakles, who used a torch to cauterize the heads of the Hydra in order to kill it. On graves, the flaming torch lights the way for the dead to guide them to the afterworld. Extinguished or reversed, it symbolizes death, as it did in Mithraic ritual. The torch can also symbolize an undying tradition, as in the Olympic ceremonies.

Torii
Literally in Japanese, a "bird perch" – the simplified yoke-shaped gateway to Shinto shrines. Essentially a sun symbol, it is identified as one of the birds in the myth in which birds helped to tempt the sun-goddess Amaterasu from her hiding place, thus depriving the world of light. It also represents the entrance to spiritual light.

Tortoise, Turtle
Strength, patience, endurance, stability, slowness, fecundity, longevity. The tortoise or turtle (members of the same reptile group) is an important and ancient symbol of cosmic order in many traditions, especially those of China. Stone tortoises supporting the pillars of imperial graves allude to the legendary Ao who supported the world on its four legs. Associated with the north, water and winter, the animal also appeared on imperial banners as the Black Warrior. It was protective against fire as well as in war. In Japan, it supported the world mountain, and the marine turtle was the emblem of Kumpira, god of sailors – as it was of Ea, the Sumerian-Semitic Lord of the Deep. With a domed shell on its back and the squarer shell protecting its belly, the tortoise or turtle was widely used as a tripartite cosmic image of the vaulted heaven, the body (humankind) and the earth, underworld or waters. In India, the symbolism of stability was emphasized by the notion that an elephant supported the world by standing on the legs of the cosmic turtle. Alternatively, the cosmic tree is shown growing from the turtle, which is an avatar of the sustainer-god Vishnu. Creator hero symbolism appears again in Native American mythology where the turtle lifts the earth from the deep.

Although mainly a female, lunar and humid symbol, the tortoise is linked both with female and male fertility, as in parts of Africa where the emerging head is seen as penile. As protective emblems, tortoises are a popular household pets there.

Western symbolism is less extensive, best summed up in the *Festina lente* ("Make haste slowly") emblem of Cosimo de' Medici – a turtle with a sail on its back, voyaging slowly but surely. In alchemy, the tortoise symbolizes matter at the beginning of the evolutionary process.

Totem
An animal or other natural object that acts as the identifying symbol of a closely knit clan. In primitive art, the most impressive examples are the giant totem poles of America's northwest coast, which serve almost as heraldic status symbols. The ravens, bears or other animals carved into them represent mythical ancestral spirits in animal guise or symbolize qualities admired by the clan. In initiation rituals, the totem may be a more personal tutelary spirit.

Tower
Ascent, ambition, strength, watchfulness, inaccessibility, chastity. Biblical writers felt that the Tower of Babel (an allusion to the monumental ziggurat at Babylon) carried the axial

Torii: *see*
Birds; Light; Sun

Tortoise, Turtle: *see*
Alchemy; Dome; Elephant; LONGEVITY; Square; Tree

Totem: *see*
ANIMALS; Bear; Initiation; Raven

Tower: *see*
Axis; CHASTITY; Ivory; Ziggurat

Vishnu represented as Kurma the turtle, from a Hindu painting.

Transformation: *see*
Alchemy; Androgyne;
ANIMALS; Blood;
Carnival; Orgy; Soul; Wine

Tree: *see*
Acacia; Almond; Apple;
Ash; Birch; Bo Tree; Cedar;
Cherry; Christmas tree;
CROSS; Cypress; Elder; Fig;
Hawthorn; Hazel; Holly;
Jujube Tree; Larch; Laurel;
Linden, Lime; Maypole;
Mistletoe; Myrtle; Oak;
Olive; Orange; Palm; Peach;
Pear; Pillar; Pine, Pine cone;
Plum; Pomegranate; Poplar;
Sephiroth; Snake; Tamarisk;
Thorn; Walnut; Willow;
Wood; Yew

earth–heaven symbolism of the tower to insolent heights. Tower myths symbolizing human presumption are common in southern Africa too. As emblems of aspiration, towers were retained as status symbols in the architecture of the Loire châteaux long after towers ceased to have a defensive function as donjons. In medieval Christian symbolism, the Virgin Mary was the "Tower of Ivory", both pure and impregnable. In art, the figure of Chastity sometimes appears in a tower, as do many distressed maidens in fairy tales.

Transformation

Transformations of all kinds symbolize liberation from the physical or mortal limitations of nature. Supernatural beings in most mythologies transmogrify at will into animals; winc is transubstantiatcd into blood; Christ is transfigured into a being of light under the eyes of his Apostles, and souls transmigrate into other bodies after death. Cross-dressing (transvestism) symbolizes liberation from the constraints of a single sex, a return to the primal perfection of the androgyne.

Tree

The supreme natural symbol of dynamic growth, seasonal death and regeneration. Many trees are held to be sacred or magic in different cultures (see individual names of trees).

Reverence for the power of trees goes back to primitive beliefs that gods and spirits inhabited them. Animist symbolism of this kind survives in European folklore of the tree-man or Green Man. In fairy tales, trees can either be protective and grant wishes, or appear as frightening, obstructive, even demonic.

As mythologies developed, the idea of a mighty tree that formed a central axis for the flow of divine energy linking the supernatural and natural worlds took symbolic shape in the Tree of Life or cosmic tree, rooted in the waters of the underworld and passing through earth to heaven. This symbol is almost universal. The Tree of Life often becomes a metaphor for the whole of creation. In many traditions it grows on a sacred mountain or in paradise. A fountain of spiritual nourishment may gush from its roots. A snake coiled at its base can represent spiralling energy drawn from the earth; alternatively, the serpent is a destructive symbol. Birds nest in the upper branches, emblems of celestial messengers or souls. Through the Tree of Life, humanity ascends from its lowcr naturc toward spiritual illumination, salvation or release from the cycle of being. Medieval images of Christ crucified on a tree rather than a cross relate to this more ancient symbolism. To be hanged from a tree was the fate of a man cursed, according to Deuteronomy. A tree crucifixion thus heightened the symbolism of salvation through Christ, scapegoat for the sins of the world. The image unifies the Tree of Knowledge (the Fall) with the Tree of Life.

By its very form, the tree is a symbol of evolution, its branches suggesting diversity spreading out from the trunk (unity). In Indian iconography, a tree sprouting from the cosmic egg represents Brahma creating the manifest world. Alternatively, the cosmic tree is reversed to show its roots drawing spiritual strength from the sky and spreading it outward and downward – a favourite image in Cabbalism and other forms of mysticism and magic (also frequently used in drawing genealogical charts). In many traditions, the Tree of Life bears stars, lights, globes or fruit symbolizing the planets, or cycles of the sun or moon. Lunar symbolism is common, the moon drawing up water as sap rises up the tree. The fruit of the Tree of Life can also symbolize immortality – represented in China, for example, by the peach. Many other food-bearing trees appear as Trees of Life – the sycamore fig in Egypt, the almond in Iran, the olive, palm or pomegranate in other Middle-Eastern or Semitic traditions. Their cosmic symbolism seems to have developed out of simpler cults in which the trees were embodiments of the fecund Earth Mother. For this reason, in spite of their phallic verticality, trees are usually feminine in symbolism. Thus, in Egyptian iconography, the sacred fig is identified with the goddess Hathor who is shown in tree form, providing food and drink.

Earth Mother fertility rites were usually centred upon deciduous trees, whose bare winter branches and spring flowering provided apt symbols of the seasonal cycles of death and regeneration. A notable exception was the worship of Attis in Asia Minor and the later Greco-Roman world. The emblematic tree of Attis was a pine, a leading symbol of immortality. His death (by emasculation) and rebirth were celebrated by stripping the pine and winding it in wool – the probable origin of the maypole tradition, a tree-based fertility rite. Dualism in tree symbolism is usually represented by paired trees or trees with divided trunks. In the story of Tristan and Isolde, entwined trees grow from their grave. In the dualist symbolism of the Near East, the Tree of Life is paralleled by a Tree of Death. This is the biblical Tree of the Knowledge of Good and Evil, whose forbidden fruit, when tasted by Eve in the Garden of Eden, brought upon humankind the curse of mortality.

Triad

A group of three, often used in iconography to symbolize closely linked ideas such as body/soul/spirit or divinities sharing functions such as the Fates or Graces in Greek mythology. In Hinduism, the triad Brahma, Vishnu, Shiva symbolizes three aspects of divine power represented by separate gods who are not fused into a single godhead as in the Christian Trinity. Like many Celtic triadic carvings of gods, they can appear as a single three-headed figure. Medieval artists also sometimes portrayed the Trinity in this way until the Church banned such images. The tortoise often appears as a triadic symbol, especially in Taoist art where it is an emblem of earth-man-heaven – a symbolism taken up by the Chinese secret societies known as Triads.

Triangle

One of the most powerful and versatile geometric symbols. The equilateral triangle sitting on its base is a male and solar sign representing divinity, fire, life, the heart, the mountain and ascent, prosperity, harmony and royalty. The reversed triangle – possibly a more ancient sign – is female and lunar, representing the great mother, water, fecundity, rain, heavenly grace. The symbolism of the female pubic triangle and vulva is sometimes made more specific by the addition of a short interior line drawn from the

Triad: *see*
Three; Trimurti; Tortoise, Turtle; Trinity

Triangle: *see*
Alchemy; Eye; Fire, Flame; Halo; Heart; Hexagram; Man; Moon; Mountain; Three; Triad; Trinity; WISDOM; Woman

Trickster: *see*
Coyote; Hare, Rabbit; Raven

Trident: *see*
DEATH; Devils; Lightning;
Three; Trinity

Trigrams: *see*
Three; Yin-yang

bottom point. In China, the triangle appears to be always female. Male and female triangles meeting at their points signify sexual union. Interpenetrating to form a hexagram, they symbolize synthesis, the union of opposites. Horizontally, with bases meeting, two triangles represented the waxing and waning moon. As the simplest plane figure, based on the sacred number three, the triangle was the Pythagorean sign for wisdom, linked with Athene.

In both Judaism and Christianity, the triangle was the sign for God. The God of the Christian Trinity is sometimes represented by an eye within a triangle or by a venerable figure with a triangular halo. Alchemy used upward- and downward-pointing triangles as the signs for fire and water. More generally, linear triangles or triangular-shaped compositions can refer to triads of gods or other three-fold concepts.

Trickster

In mythology and folklore, the anti-hero who relies on cynical quick thinking, cunning and deception rather than moral and physical strength to outwit enemies or achieve aims. Examples include the god Hermes in Greece, the culture-hero Maui in Oceania, and many crafty animal culture heroes such as the Hare, Coyote or Raven in Africa, Asia and Native America.

Tricksters symbolize the important role in evolution of the selfish, subversive, irreverent and shrewd side of human nature.

Trident

Sea power – an emblem of the ancient Minoan civilization (as well as of Britannia ruling the waves). The trident was most famously the authority symbol of Poseidon, Greek god of the sea (Neptune in Roman myth). Its appearance in the hands of some gods of storm supports the view that its prongs represent forked lightning. Others who carry a trident in art include Satan, for whom it serves the same function as the pitchfork, and the figure of Death.

In India the similar *trisula* symbolizes the three aspects of Shiva (creator/sustainer/destroyer), and is a forehead mark of his followers. Its Christian use as a symbol of the Trinity is rare.

Trigrams

Three-line structures of solid (yang) or broken (yin) lines, eight of which (the Pa Kua) form the basis of the great Chinese book of divination, the *I Ching*. They symbolize the Taoist belief that the cosmos is based on a constant flux of complementary forces – the masculine and active yang balancing the female and passive yin. Permutated groups of two trigrams make up the 64 hexagrams of the I

The eight trigrams used in divination, clockwise from top: K'an (the deep); Chen (the arousing); Ken (the still); Tui (the joyous); Li (the clinging); K'un (the receptive); Sun (the gentle); and Ch'ien (the creative).

Ching, the interpretation of which provides a guide to wise action.

Trimurti

Sacred Hindu grouping of Brahma, Vishnu and Shiva, symbolizing the three cycles of manifestation – creation, preservation and destruction. In spite of its similarities with the Christian Trinity, the trimurti is not a three-in-one monotheistic concept. In later Hindu tradition, Shiva can himself represent the three aspects of the trimurti.

Trinity

In Christianity, the three Persons that form the single godhead – God the Father, God the Son and God the Holy Spirit. The doctrine of the Trinity, which reconciled worship of the man-god Christ with monotheism, symbolizes the indivisible essence of a divinity revealing itself in different forms. Figuratively, the Trinity is most directly represented by the figure of God behind and above the crucified Christ with the hovering dove of the Holy Spirit – or by the dove with two enthroned figures. Other symbols include a throne, book and dove (power, intellect, love); three fishes entwined or sharing a single head; three eagles or lions; three suns; a triangle enclosing an eye or with three stars; three overlapping circles or arcs within a circle; a three-leafed clover or three-foil cross.

Triskelion

A three-legged symbol of dynamic energy, somewhat like a swastika but with three instead of four bent limbs rotating in a circle.

As a motif in Celtic art or on Greek coinage and shields, it appears to relate less to solar cycles or lunar phases (one suggested meaning) than to power or physical prowess. It remains an emblem of the Scilly Isles and the Isle of Man.

Trowel

An important initiation symbol in Freemasonry, binding new brothers to the fraternity and to its rules of secrecy. More generally, as the tool used to join building-blocks, it can appear in art as the attribute of the Creator.

Trumpet

Of all musical instruments, the most portentous – a traditional symbol of significant events, momentous news or violent action.

In art, the trumpet is the attribute of Fame personified, and of the seven angels of the Last Judgment. The Romans popularized the shock effect of blowing trumpets before cavalry charges, as well as at important rituals and state ceremonies.

Trumpets announced news brought by heralds and introduced knights in medieval jousting – hence the bragging meaning of "blowing your own trumpet".

TRUTH *see panel on p.212*

Tunnel *see* **Cave; Labyrinth**

Turban

A traditional emblem of the faithful in Islamic countries, particularly linked with personal honour among Sikhs. In some sects and in civil offices, considerable ritual surrounds the style of turban.

The turban, which in Arab countries takes on some of the symbolism of the crown, is closely associated

Trimurti: *see*
Three; Trinity

Trinity: *see*
Book; Circle; Clover;
CROSS; Dove; Eagle; Lion;
Three; Throne; Triangle;
Trimurti

Triskelion: *see*
Swastika

Trowel: *see*
Initiation

Trumpet: *see*
FAME; Knight; Music

Turban: *see*
Crown; Green; Head

TRUTH: see individual
names

TRUTH

A solar virtue, personified in Western art by a female figure who may hold a golden disk or mirror and wear a laurel wreath. In Renaissance paintings she often appears naked or is unveiled by Father Time.

Other symbols of truth include a peach with one leaf (symbolizing the union of heart and tongue), the colours blue, white and gold, the numbers nine and six, weapons such as the sword, and precious metals or jewels, especially gold, jade, silver, diamond, lodestone, onyx and sapphire. Truth is also closely identified with light in general – the day, lightning, the lamp, the lantern and torch. Among other emblems are the acorn, almond, bamboo, bell, crown, cube, globe, heart, ostrich feather, scales, set square, well or spring of water and wine.

Turkey: see
BIRDS

Turquoise: see
Blue; Dragon; Fire, Flame;
Green; JEWELS; Snake;
Sun

Twelve: see
Four; NUMBERS; Solstice;
Three; Year; Zodiac

with the Prophet, whose descendants can wear his sacred colour, green.

Turkey

A traditional thanksgiving food in Mexico long before it acquired the same symbolism in Massachusetts. Native North Americans linked it with female fertility as well as male potency (suggested by its neck-swelling), and the Toltecs with impending rain.

Turquoise

A solar and fire symbol in Mexico, associated with the Aztec fire-god Xiuhtecuhtli, who is shown with turquoise plumes in his youthful aspect as Lord of Turquoise. The stone's blue-green colour suggested to the Aztecs a turquoise serpent linking heaven and earth, sun and fire. In gemstone lore, turquoise is a stone of courage, success, royal protection and the astrological sign Sagittarius.

Turtle see Tortoise

Twelve

The base number of space and time in ancient astronomy, astrology and calendric science, and therefore of considerable symbolic importance, especially in Judeo-Christian tradition where it was the number of the chosen. It represented cosmic organization, zones of celestial influence, and an achieved cycle of time (the 12 calendar months, the 12 hours of day and night, 12 groups of years in China). As the product of the two powerful numbers three and four, it symbolized a union of spiritual and temporal planes. In the Bible, 12 is the number of the sons of Jacob, and therefore of the tribes of Israel, the jewels in the priest's breastplate, major disciples of Christ, fruits of the Tree of Life, gates of the Holy City and stars in the crown of Mary. Twelve was also the number of disciples of Mithras and, for some Muslims, the number of descendants of the prophet Ali. Solar astrology was based upon the movement of the sun through the 12 signs of the Zodiac.

The Greek author Hesiod (fl. c.700BCE) said that there were 12 Titans, and in later Greek tradition 12 gods ruled Olympus. There were also 12 prominent Knights of the Round Table. Calendric symbolism underlies the 12 days of Christmas, a tradition developed from the period of Yuletide and Saturnalia festivity at the December solstice – a day representing each coming month.

Twilight

The half-light of decline and shadowy border of death. In northern Europe, myths of the twilight of the gods – the German Götterdämmerung and the Nordic Ragnarok – symbolize the melancholy ebbing of solar warmth and light in a powerful image of the end of the world and the prelude to a fresh cycle of manifestation. The link between twilight and the west accounts for many myths of gods, heroes or sages disappearing westward, as do Quetzalcoatl in Mexico and Lao-tse in China.

Twins

Harmonious dualism – or dualistic tension. Perhaps the most famous inseparable twins, who act as beneficial guides, are Castor and Polydeuces (Pollux to the Romans) of classical mythology (called the Dioscuri, "sons of god", because their father was, in some accounts, the Greek Zeus, or Jupiter in Roman myth). Another beneficent pair are the Vedic Asvins, born of the sun and the cloud goddess. Both sets represent the positive, powerful aspects of twin symbolism. The Asvins (perhaps symbols of the morning and evening star) work together to usher in the day and night. Castor and Pollux as warriors also symbolize strength in unity – and unity is the motive for their translation to the sky as the constellation Gemini after Castor is killed in battle. Twin disunity is exemplified by Romulus and Remus. The story in which Romulus kills his brother symbolized the dangers of divided responsibility. In some early societies, including China and parts of Africa, twins were ill omens and one or both were left to die. Elsewhere, they were often objects of awe, hence the number of legends in which one or both twins are fathered by divinities. Native American traditions include both twin-heroes and twins with radically different characters. In Iroquois myths, for example, one twin is good, the other evil.

Twins can symbolize other dualities such as spirit–body, action–thought, and perhaps most commonly the duality of light–dark.

Twilight: *see* AFTERWORLDS; CARDINAL POINTS; Darkness; DEATH

Twins: *see* Doubles; Zodiac

Unicorn: *see*
Antelope; BEASTS OF
FABLE; CHASTITY;
CROSS; Horn; Lion;
Mercury; Phallus;
Rhinoceros; Snake; Spear;
Virginity

Umbrella *see* **Parasol**

Unicorn

Chastity, purity, power, virtue – a courtly symbol of sublimated desire and a Christian symbol of the Incarnation. The unicorn is the most ambiguous and poetic of all beasts of fable, usually portrayed in medieval art as a graceful white animal with a single, spirally-twisted horn on its forehead. It has the body, mane and head of a horse (sometimes goat-bearded), an antelope's cloven hoofs and a lion's tail. The Greek physician Ctesias mentions the unicorn's healing powers in his 4th-century-BCE history of Persia and Assyria – an apparent reference to Indian remedies made with powdered rhinoceros horn. Early Christian writers may have associated this healing power with the forehead horns of an animal such as the pale Arabian oryx antelope. According to one theological flight of fancy, the unicorn could purify water poisoned with snake venom by stirring it with its horn in the sign of the cross.

Several other strands are woven into the symbolism of the unicorn in medieval Christian art, notably a pagan tradition that this swift and fierce creature could be captured only by a virgin – an apparent reference to the association between the unicorn and virgin moon goddesses of the hunt such as the Greek Artemis (Diana in Roman myth). The phallic and spear symbolism of the horn, combined with a mythology of purification, made the unicorn an elegant symbol of spiritual penetration – specifically, the mystery of Christ's entry into the virginal womb. This is the allegorical meaning of Gothic miniatures and later tapestries or paintings in which a unicorn lays its head in a woman's lap, attends her in an enclosed garden or rose bower, or is guided toward her by a huntsman (the angel of the Annunciation, Gabriel). In chivalry, the unicorn symbolized the virtue of pure love and the power of a chaste woman to tame and transform the horn of sexual desire. Unicorns draw the chariot of Chastity in Western art.

Although the Western symbolism

of the unicorn is unique, a legendary creature with some similarities is the Ky-lin in China – a yin-yang fertility symbol of wisdom, gentleness and happiness. Its horn or horns (up to five can appear) represent the intellect. In alchemy, the unicorn represents mercury alongside the lion emblem of sulphur. These two animals can represent other dualities, such as sun–moon, and are also popular supporting figures in heraldry. The unicorn, an emblem of Scotland, displaced a Welsh dragon when James VI of Scotland became James I of Scotland and England.

The unicorn in a woman's lap, from The Lady of the Unicorn, *a 15th-century French tapestry.*

Uraeus *see* **Cobra**

Urn
Female and fecundity emblem of water or river gods in art – and of Aquarius in astrology. In Chinese Buddhism a lidded urn is one of eight symbols of good luck and can represent victory over death. This is also the symbolism of an urn with a rising flame, denoting resurrection in Western funerary art.

Urn: *see*
Fire, Flame; Water; Zodiac

VANITY: *see individual names*

Vase: *see* FLOWERS; Foot, Footprint; Lily; Woman

Veil: *see* DEATH; CHASTITY; Light; Tabernacle

VANITY

Conceit is usually allegorized in art as a reclining nude preoccupied with her hair, a mirror symbolizing her self-regarding nature. In the older meaning of futility or emptiness, *vanitas* is a major field for symbolism in Western still lifes. Material possessions such as coins, gold or jewels, and trappings of power such as crowns or sceptres, are shown with symbols of emptiness such as overturned cups or emblems of mortality and evanescence – a skull, clock or hour glass, flowers or a guttering candle. Animals associated with vanity are the ape, the peacock and, less often, the butterfly.

Vase

Often a feminine symbol, particularly in Western art where a vase with a lily refers to the Virgin Mary. In Egyptian funerary art, vases symbolized eternal life. A vase of flowers signifies harmony in Chinese Buddhism, and the vase appears as one of the symbols on the footprint of the Buddha.

Vegetation

In all cultures, a fundamental symbol of the living earth and of the cyclic nature of birth, death and regeneration. Vegetation gods and goddesses were among the earliest divinities, often worshipped as sources of human as well as plant life. Plant–human transformation myths symbolize cosmic unity; the life force animating all things.

Veil

Separation, reticence, protection, modesty, withdrawal, secrecy, sanctity. For nuns, "taking the veil" came to symbolize their separation from the world, although the custom may have originated in the protective veiling of consecrated virgins. The Veil of the Temple screening off the Jewish Holy of Holies marked a division between the material and spiritual planes, earth and heaven. The Disciple Matthew's report that the veil was "rent in two from top to bottom" at

An Indian woman shown lifting her veil in a gesture of the end of innocence, from a costume design.

VICTORY: *see individual names*

Vine: *see* Blood; Corn; Lamb; Tree; Wine

VICTORY

Personified in Western art by the Greek goddess Nike (Roman Victoria) with winged feet and shoulders, sometimes shown crowning warriors, athletes or poets with laurel. Olive, myrtle, ivy or parsley were also victors' wreaths. Other symbols of victory include the triumphal arch, banner, crown, eagle, elephant, falcon, hawk, horse, lance, lion, palm, phoenix, wolf and zigzag sign (the sigrune).

the moment of Christ's death symbolized the Christian view that this event marked a decisive rupture of the old Hebrew Law and a new beginning. In mysticism, the veil is often used as a metaphor for the illusory world of existence – the *maya* of Buddhist tradition. Alternatively, a veil hides ultimate reality, the blinding light of divinity. In Islamic tradition, 70,000 veils of light and darkness hide the face of God. The bridal veil and widow's veil both symbolize states of transition. Death as a mere transition is described as "beyond the veil". Chastity wears a veil in medieval art.

VICTORY *see panel, above right*

VIGILANCE *see panel on p.218*

Vine

One of the oldest symbols of natural fecundity in the ancient Near East – and a still more important symbol of spiritual life and regeneration in both the pagan and Christian worlds. Throughout the Old Testament, the vine is a happy emblem of the fruits of the earth – tantamount to a Tree of Life. The continuing importance of wine in Jewish ritual is based on symbolic links between the vine and God's blessing on a chosen people. The vine was the first plant grown by Noah after the biblical Flood, and in the Book of Exodus a branch with grapes was the first sign that the Israelites had reached the Promised Land. Like earlier agricultural divinities in Mesopotamia, the Greek Dionysus (in Roman myth, Bacchus) was identified with the vine and its fruits. Under the influence of Orphism his cult acquired sacrificial meaning. Christian symbolism is still more specific. "I am the true vine, and my Father is the vinegrower," says Christ in the Gospel of St John (15:1). The vine becomes a spiritual symbol of regeneration and, in the Eucharist, the fermented juice of its grapes is Christ's blood.

Vinous motifs are common in Christian art and architecture, and are

VIGILANCE: *see individual names*

The Egyptian goddess Isis shown holding a vine, from the inside of an ancient coffin lid.

VIGILANCE

Birds, and particularly domestic fowl such as the goose and the cock (rooster), are the most common emblems of vigilance – the symbolism of the cock on church steeples. A popular baroque symbol of vigilance was a crane holding a stone in its mouth. Other emblems include the dog, dragon, griffin, hare, lion and peacock (from the eyes on its tail), carved and painted eye motifs, the lamp and other light sources including the watchful stars.

life emblems in Egypt (linked with the god Osiris). Vines and corn are Eucharistic symbols. A lamb surrounded with thorns and vines is a representative of Christ. Bunches of grapes, redemption symbols in funerary art, are also traditional emblems of hospitality, youthfulness, the Golden Age, the bounty of autumn. Associated with the revels of Bacchus, Silenus and their train, vines can symbolize greed and sottishness.

Violet

In colour symbolism, linked with temperance, moderation, spirituality and repentance, or a transition from active to passive, male to female, life to death. These interpretations are based on the mingling of red (passion, fire or earth) with blue (intellect, water or sky). Christ and Mary wear violet robes in some paintings of Passion scenes. In flower symbolism, the small violet is also associated with modesty or humility – the symbolism of violets in paintings of the Adoration, where they refer both to Mary's chastity and

to the meekness of the Christ Child. Wreaths of violets were remembrance flowers in Rome and were worn at banquets to cool the brow.

Virginity

Spirituality and purity – especially as a chosen state. Vows of virginity by women of marriageable age symbolized their renunciation of worldly desires and dedication to the service of a divinity. In Rome, the virginity of the six maidens who guarded the sacred fire of Vesta guaranteed the purity (and therefore the security) of the fire itself. Virgins of the sun god in Peru similarly ensured flawless attention to his needs. In both traditions, the penalty for backsliding was extremely severe.

Virgin birth added an additional dimension of the supernatural to this symbolism of purity. It suggested a return to the original void in which creation was not an everyday, but an extraordinary event. Hence the number of gods, heroes or sages reputedly sired by gods and born from human virgins, including the Roman twins Romulus and Remus who were abandoned to wolves after their mother was embarrassingly impregnated by the war-god Mars. Of the virgin mother goddesses who preceded Mary, the greatest was Ishtar, the Babylonian and Assyrian personification of the planet Venus. Like other virgin goddesses including Athene and Artemis in Greece, Ishtar was also a warrior goddess, suggesting that virginity was sometimes closely linked with forthright freedom of action. The symbolism of the Virgin Mary as an ideal of motherhood is unique in both its nature and its range. Her attributes in art include the crescent moon (borrowed from Isis as Queen of Heaven), a crown of 12 stars, the dove of the Holy Spirit, the unicorn of chastity, the lily or iris of purity, images of transparency such as crystal and windows, the lamp, clothing of blue, red, violet or grey, the Tree of Life, a flowering branch (the Tree of Jesse), a bridge or ladder, seven swords (Virgin of the Seven Sorrows), and images of enclosure such as the gate, the walled garden, the sealed fountain or the spring. Many of these symbols were taken from the Song of Solomon after Bernard of Clairvaux (1090–1153) interpreted it as an allegory of the relationship between Christ and his virgin mother – especially chapter 4, verse 12, "A garden enclosed is my sister, my spouse; a spring shut up, a fountain sealed."

VIRTUES *see panel on p.220*

Void

A Buddhist and mystic symbol of escape from the round of existence, conceived as the complete absence of ego, emotion or desire – a state of limitless experience and of selfless spiritual revelation.

Volcano

Destructive anger or creative force. In Hawaii the volcano is a symbol of the destroying mother, personified by the goddess Pele whose violent temper is linked with the unpredictable behaviour of the great active crater Kilauea, her home. A female goddess tends the fires of the underworld in Maori myth, and it is from her that the trickster Maui steals fire for humankind. In some versions, the Greek Prometheus steals fire not from heaven but from the divine smith Hephaestus, a

beneficent and creative figure. The volcano was a more sinister symbol in Zoroastrian myth, because trapped in the crater of Mt Demavend, near Tehran, is Ahriman, the spirit of evil, a seminal association of Hell with everlasting fire. More generally, volcanic activity is linked with passion.

Vulture

Now a metaphor for opportunistic greed, but in ancient Egypt a protective symbol. Nekhbet, the great goddess of upper Egypt, was represented as a vulture in her role as guardian of the pharaoh, whose queen wore a vulture headdress. That vultures fiercely guarded their young led to the legend that all vultures were female – and to strained analogies by early Christian writers between the motherly vulture and the Virgin Mary. In ancient Iran, vultures were purifiers, speeding the processes of bodily disintegration and rebirth. Bodies are still laid out for them on Parsee Towers of Silence. Vultures are tutelary spirits in some Indian myths. In Rome, they were sacred to the god Mars and thought to have prophetic powers. They were also associated with old age and were therefore ridden by Saturn.

Vulva

Female generative power – in Western iconography most directly represented by the lozenge. The gate, passage and birth symbolism of the vulva is spiritualized in Christian art as the mandorla. In Tantric Buddhist art, the *yoni* is an important motif, depicted as two adjoining arcs symbolizing the gateway to spiritual rebirth. In Hinduism, the *yoni* can appear as a ring or rings at the base of the lingam dedicated to Shiva as creator.

Violet: *see* Amethyst; Blue; Chastity; FLOWERS; Red; Wreath; Garland

Virginity: *see individual names*

Void: *see* Nirvana

Volcano: *see* AFTERWORLDS; Chimera; Devils; Fire, Flame; Mother; Smith

Vulture: *see* Birds

Vulva: *see* Apple; Lingam; Lozenge; Mandorla; Peach; Pomegranate; Well

VIRTUES: *see*
Anchor; Birds; Blindness;
Bread; Candle; Chalice;
COLOURS; CROSS; Crow;
Dragon; Fire, Flame; Fish;
FLOWERS; Green; Heart;
JEWELS; Lion; Mirror;
Phoenix; Scales; Ship;
Snake; Sword; Tarot; Wine;
and individual names

VIRTUES

Charity Caring love, the greatest of the Pauline virtues, represented in Western art by a young woman. She may hold a bundle of clothes for the naked, food for the hungry, or a flame, candle or flaming heart. Charity can also appear suckling infants or, less often, as a pelican feeding its young – supposedly with its own blood. The chasuble, a vestment representing Christ's robe, can signify Charity. It is one of the five fundamentals of Islam. Other symbols are fruit, the phoenix and the hen.

Faith, after a 16th-century engraving by Lucas van Leyden.

Faith A Pauline virtue, personified in Christian art by a woman with a cross, chalice or candle. She is often shown standing at a font or with her foot on a cube. Other symbols are the colour blue, the emerald and a child.

Fortitude A cardinal virtue, shown in Christian art as a warlike female, wearing nothing more than a helmet and shield and often accompanying a lion or forcing its jaws apart. Other symbols are the camellia, carp, club, pillar and sword.

Hope One of the three Pauline virtues. Hope is shown with an anchor. She may wear on her head a sailing ship (voyaging hopefully), carry a basket of flowers (promise of fruit) or stretch out to a crown. Fish, bread and wine were associated with hope in Hebrew tradition. The crow can appear as hope's symbol, its cry suggesting to the Romans the word "tomorrow" (*cras*).

Justice A cardinal virtue personified in Western art by the confusing figure of a blindfolded woman holding scales of judgment and a sword of power. Baroque artists who added the blindfold intended to show that Justice is unswayed by appearances. Other symbols attributed to justice are the feather, the number four, the globe, jade, mathematical and carpentry instruments, the lion, the sceptre and the thunderbolt. Justice is the eighth card of the major arcana in Tarot.

Prudence Personified in Western art as a woman with a snake or dragon, carrying a mirror; this is prudence in the sense of wisdom rather than caution (the mirror is self-knowledge). Other symbols are the anchor, the compasses, deer and elephants.

Temperence A cardinal virtue represented in Western medieval art by a woman pouring water from one pitcher into another (diluting wine). The water pitcher may appear with a torch (quenching lust). Common attributes of Temperence are a bridle and bit, a clock or a sheathed sword. The amethyst is an ecclesiastical jewel symbolizing temperance and, accordingly, violet is a colour associated with this virtue.

Wall

Beyond its obvious protective function, a symbol of separation. The Wailing Wall in Jerusalem is hallowed by Jews as a relic of the Temple of Herod but also as a symbol of the Diaspora and of those who remain separated from Israel.

Walnut

Like other nut-bearing trees, fertility and wisdom or prophecy – knowledge hidden within the hard outer casing. Walnuts were traditional food at the December solstice, and fertility emblems at Roman weddings. In China they were linked with flirtation.

Wand

An emblem of supernatural powers, less authoritarian than the rod and more specifically associated with sorcery and magical beings. The wand symbolizes ease of transformation.

Washing

An important purification rite, symbolizing an inner rather than outer cleansing – as in the Islamic custom of washing face, hands and feet before thrice-daily worship. In Buddhist initiation ceremonies, novice monks ritually wash away their past lives. By ceremonially washing his hands after his trial of Christ, Pilate sought to absolve himself of any guilt for the Crucifixion.

Wasp

Usually associated with a vitriolic personality, the wasp in some African traditions symbolizes evolution and control over other forms of life. In Mali, the mason wasp was the emblem of a shamanistic élite.

Water

An ancient and universal symbol of purity, fertility and the source of life itself. In all the major cosmologies, life arose from the primordial waters, a female symbol of formless potentiality. In a general sense, water is an emblem of all fluidity in the material world and of the principles of liquid circulation (blood, sap, semen), dissolution, mingling, cohesion, birth and regeneration. The *Rig Veda* sings the

Walnut: *see*
Solstice; Tree

Wand: *see*
Circle; Fairies; Hazel; Rod; Transformation

Water: *see*
Baptism; Dew; ELEMENTS; Flood; Fountain; Lake; Rain; River, Stream; Sea; Spring; Well

Water lily

Watermelon: *see*
Pomegranate

Water symbolism: women bathing in a fountain in the Garden of Youth, after a 15th-century Italian painting.

praises of water as the bringer of all things. The purest waters – especially dew and spring water, but also rain – were thought to have numinous and curative properties as forms of divine grace, gifts of Mother Earth (spring water) or sky gods (rain and dew). Reverence for fresh water as a purifying element is particularly marked in the religious traditions of countries where water was scarce, as Islamic, Jewish, Christian and Indian cleansing or baptism rituals show. Baptism combines the purifying, dissolving and fertilizing aspects of water symbolism: washing away sin, effacing an old life, giving birth to a new one. Flood myths in which a sinful society is destroyed are examples of cleansing and regeneration symbolism.

Water can become a metaphor for spiritual nourishment and salvation, as in the Gospel of St John (4:14) when Christ tells the woman of Samaria: "Those who drink of the water that I will give them, will never be thirsty." The springs flowing from the Tree of Life in paradise are symbols of salvation.

Water is also equated with wisdom, as in the Taoist image of water finding its way around obstacles, the triumph of seeming weakness over strength. In psychology it represents the energy of the unconscious, and also its mysterious depths and perils. Restless water is a Buddhist symbol of the agitated flux of manifestation. By contrast, the transparency of still water symbolizes contemplative perception. In legend and folklore, lakes are two-way mirrors dividing natural and supernatural worlds. Lake and spring divinities, traditionally youthful and prophetic, or else healing, spirits were often propitiated with gifts the origin of throwing coins in fountains and making wishes. The transition symbolism of water accounts for numerous mythologies in which rivers or seas divide the worlds of the living and the dead. Many divinities are water-born or walk on water. In superstition, the purity symbolism of water was so strong that it was thought to reject evil. Hence the custom of identifying witches by hurling women in ponds to see if they floated to the surface.

Water lily *see* **Lily**

Watermelon
In southeast Asia the watermelon shares the fecundity symbolism of the pomegranate because of the number of seeds embedded in the fruit. This is the emblematic meaning of giving seeds to the bride and groom at Vietnamese weddings.

Weapons

Ambiguous symbols of power or the will – aggressive or defensive, oppressive or liberating. In the ancient world, where life was uncertain, few weapons were wholly destructive in their symbolism – apart, perhaps, from the club. Many are linked with truth, aspiration or other virtues, and in myths and legends magical ones are given to heroes. Weapons often became ceremonial emblems of authority or justice. Collectively, weapons usually symbolize warfare in art, and are shown being broken or burned in allegories of peace. A favourite Renaissance theme was the triumph of love over war (or passion), as in Botticelli's *Mars and Venus* (1483) where cupids (the attendants of the love-goddess Venus) play with the sleeping war god's lance.

Weaving

An ancient symbol of cosmic creation, conceived as a continuing process in which temporal events are woven in an ever-changing pattern on a changeless warp. In Japanese mythology, the sun-goddess Amaterasu controls this process in a heavenly Sacred Weaving Hall. The cosmic symbolism of weaving goes back at least to the Babylonian weaver-goddess Ishtar. Counterparts were Neith in Egypt, with her sacred spider, and Athene in Greece. Individual destinies are woven into the pattern as long as the thread is not cut by one of the Fates – the Moirai in Greece, Parcae in Rome, Norns in Scandinavia. Weaving represents cohesion, the constant interplay of the male warp and female weft, as in Chinese thought. In Buddhism, the process symbolizes the weaving of an illusory reality.

Web

The web shares much of the creative symbolism of weaving and of the loom as an image of the structure of cosmic and individual destiny. In particular, the fragile web is an effective Buddhist emblem of *maya* (the world of illusion), the Wheel of Existence and the cycles of time.

Wedding *see* Marriage

Week

An artificial division of time, probably based on the fourfold division of the lunar cycle and the mystical significance of the number seven. This symbolism, enshrined in the Judeo-Christian seven-day week, was strong enough eventually to overcome the previous Roman custom of an eight-day week based on the old interval between market days.

A further influence was the astrological system of seven "planets", which gave their names to the Latin days of the week – the moon, Mars, Mercury, Jupiter, Venus, Saturn and the sun.

Well

Salvation, life, knowledge, truth, purity. In most traditions, but especially Hebrew and Islamic, wells had sacred significance as sources of life. The imagery is specific in the story of how God revealed a desert well to Hagar and her son Ishmael (Genesis 21:9–21). Water rising from the earth symbolized feminine bounty.

In China and elsewhere the well was linked directly with the womb and vagina. Psychologically it is an image of a shaft to the depths of the unconscious. Wishing wells or wells of knowledge, memory, truth or youth,

Weapons: *see*
Arrow; Axe; Bow; Club; Hammer; Knife; Lance; Mace; Net; Spear; Sceptre; Sword; Trident

Weaving: *see*
Loom; Spider; Web

Web: *see*
Spider; Weaving

Week: *see*
PLANETS; Sabbath; Seven

Well: *see*
Spring; Virginity; VIRTUES; Vulva; Water

Whale: *see*
Ark; Belly; Flood;
Initiation; Leviathan;
Moon; Three

Wheel: *see*
Chakra; Chariot; Circle;
Disk; FORTUNE; Light;
Lotus; Moon; Rays; Rose;
Spiral; Sun; Zodiac

*The Buddhist Wheel of
Dharma, from a 7–8th-
century-CE depiction.*

draw on the symbolism of the under-world as a source of magical powers including, in Celtic myths, the power of restoring life to slain warriors.

West *see* CARDINAL POINTS

Whale

An impressive image of the colossal in nature, but also an ancient ark or womb symbol of regeneration, most clearly expressed in the biblical story of the prophet Jonah who was swallowed and regurgitated by a "great fish". Some scholars have seen this as an allegory of the Babylonian captivity and deliverance of the Jews, based on Sumerian-Semitic myths of the chaos-goddess Tiamat. More plausibly, the belly of the whale represents the obscurity of initiation leading to a newly clarified state of life. In the Gospel of St Matthew (12:40) Christ draws a parallel between Jonah's experience and his own impending descent into the earth and resurrection.

Jonah's burial period of three days and three nights suggests the lunar symbolism of the "dark of the moon" followed by its reappearance as a new crescent. Ark symbolism reappears in Islamic texts, and the whale is linked with the idea of initiation in Africa and Polynesia. In southeast Asia there are myths of spiritual heroes delivered by a whale. The whale is often linked with Leviathan. Medieval images of a whale's mouth as the gate of hell were based on fanciful similes in ignorant bestiaries of the day. The great whale in Herman Melville's novel *Moby Dick* (1851) can be interpreted as a symbol of destructive sexual repression.

Wheatsheaf *see* Corn

Wheel

One of the supreme symbols of cosmic momentum – the force that drives the planets and stars – and of ceaseless change and repetition. The Egyptians linked the revolving potter's wheel (the probable origin of the vehicular wheel) with the evolution of mankind itself. Because the first wheels were solid, the earliest wheel motifs were little different from the disks that represented the moon and sun. The wheel may have influenced winged-disk motifs symbolizing the speed of light. The development of a spoked wheel around 2000BCE made the wheel motif conclusively solar, the spokes suggesting the sun's rays as well as whirling momentum (especially when curved, as they are in many carvings). The advent of chariots with their enormous military impact made the wheel a major symbol not only of the sun but of power and dominion generally in Egypt, the Near East, India and Asia. An equally widespread symbolism, especially in Hindu and Buddhist art, linked the turning wheel with the cycles of manifestation, birth, death and rebirth, the Zodiac, time and human destiny.

A motif with two crossing lines inside a circle (known as the wheel cross and later became the gamma cross of Christianity) predates the invention of the wheel and also appears in America where wheels were not used before the arrival of the Spanish. This ideogram appears to be a symbol of totality (the circle) and the divisions of space. Wheel and space symbolism are sometimes hard to disentangle. Confusion can also occur with the three-armed sign of Taranis, the Celtic god of thunder. Gods specifically linked with the wheel are usually solar or all-powerful – Asshur, Shamash and Baal in the Near East; Zeus, Apollo and sometimes Dionysus in Greece; Vishnu-Surya in India. Blazing wheels were once bowled down hills at the June solstice to encourage the sun's chariot to keep rolling over the horizon and reappearing next day. In the extraordinary biblical visions of the prophet Ezekiel, wheels appear again and again as symbols of Jehovah's divine omnipotence, the inexorability of his moral laws, and the undeviating path followed by his angels.

The symbolism of the rotating wheel as an unyielding law of life dominates much of the iconography of Buddhism. The Wheel of Existence carries humanity from one incarnation to another in ceaseless cycles as long as it clings to illusion. Only the Wheel of Law and Doctrine can crush illusion. The Buddha is its unmoving centre. Taoism also uses the axle of the wheel as a symbol of the sage who has reached the still heart of the turning world. Wheel symbolism significantly influenced the choice of the lotus and rose as the dominant symbolic flowers of east and west. The turning *chakra*s that control the flow of spiritual energy in Tantric Buddhism are often shown as lotus wheels. The rose windows of Christian cathedrals are wheel symbols of spiritual evolution. On a less elevated plane, Dame Fortune's wheel is a familiar emblem of the ups and downs of life and the unpredictable aspects of destiny.

Whip, Flail

Power, exorsism, authority – especially judicial authority. In Egypt, the flail, more a threshing tool than a weapon of chastisement, was an emblem of rulership, judgment and also fertility (as an attribute of the icthyphallic wind god, Min). All of this symbolism, including sexual, attaches to the whip. The Roman Lupercalia festival featured young priests running about striking women with thongs to drive out sterility. Christ symbolized his spiritual authority by using a whip to chase money-changers from the Temple. (In art, the whip is also an emblem of Christ's Passion.)

Whipping was a popular medieval means of driving the Devil out of witches, and of mortifying penitents. Kings were symbolically chastised by using a "whipping boy" as a stand-in. Modern use of the whip in Islam is often more symbolic than physically punishing.

Whirlwind

A manifestation of divine power – a symbolism found in the Native American Plains' tribes, as well as in the deserts of the Near East. In the Bible, God speaks to Job from the whirlwind. Indian iconography portrays storm gods, notably Rudra, with braided hair expressing the spiral energy of the typhoon.

The whirlwind, which plucks objects into the air, reverses the symbolism of the whirlpool and is associated with ascent and powers of flight, including the opportunistic flights of witches and demons.

White

The absolute colour of light, and therefore a symbol of purity, truth, innocence and the sacred or divine. Although it has some negative connotations – fear, cowardice, surrender,

Whip, Flail: *see* King; Witchcraft

Whirlwind: *see* Spiral; Wind; Witchcraft

White: *see* AFTERWORLDS; Alchemy; Baptism; Black; DEATH; Dove; Egg; Initiation; Island; Knight; Lily; Marriage; Mercury; Sacrifice

Whore: *see* Mother

Willow: *see* Tree

coldness, blankness and the pallor of death – white is the positive side of the black–white antithesis in all symbol systems. Hence the white knight and the black villain. Its use for mourning garments – traditionally colourless in China, white in Rome and white generally all over Europe for many years – was less emblematic of grief than of initiation to the new life awaiting the dead.

White is almost universally the colour of initiation, the novice or neophyte. The word "candidate" derives from the Latin word meaning "shining white". It is the blameless Christian colour of baptism, confirmation, marriage and other rites of passage. As the colour of spirituality and sanctity, truth and revelation, it was worn by the Druids and other priestly classes in the pagan as well as the Christian world. With the same sacral meaning, white was also the colour of sacrificial victims.

Links between light and joy make white a colour associated with festivals. The white egg symbolizes creation, the white dove peace and the Holy Spirit, the white island paradise, the white lily chastity. White symbolized purity even in China where it was also often associated with treachery, death, autumn and age. Value contrasts between shining and dead whiteness account for some of these apparent ambiguities.

In European folklore, ghosts, vampires and other evil spirits have dead-white faces, as does the Nordic Hel among other death goddesses in mythology. Death is a pale horse. Just as white can symbolize either life or death, it is also associated with both east and west, dawn and evening.

In alchemy, white (the *albedo*) is linked with mercury and the second stage of the Great Work.

Whore

In the Book of Revelation, 17:1, a metaphor for Babylon, "the great whore that sitteth upon many waters". Hebrew hatred of Babylon was in part based on dislike of religious prostitution which, according to the Greek Herodotus (*c*.484–*c*.425BCE), was common at temples of Ishtar (and throughout much of the ancient world). Whether temples used prostitutes as a source of income or for spiritual reasons, the symbolism of the practice was union with the great mother and her fertilizing power.

Willow

For the Jews a tree of lamentation, but in the East a symbol of the springtime of sexual love, feminine grace, the sweet sorrow of parting, resilience and immortality. The willows by the rivers of Babylon where the Hebrews hung their harps and wept remembering Zion (Psalm 137) may not have been the weeping willow, but in legend this species has mourned ever since. It is a Buddhist emblem of meekness and compassion, linked with the Bodhisattva Avalokiteshvara (Guanyin in China).

As a lunar and feminine symbol, the willow is one of the most celebrated of all motifs in Chinese art and decoration. It was a Taoist metaphor for patience and strength in flexibility. In Tibetan tradition, it is the Tree of Life. In Japan the Ainu said it was the backbone of the first man. Painkillers extracted from its bark – and perhaps snake symbolism suggested by supple osiers – may account for its association with health, easy childbirth and other medical and magical benefits in both Asian and Western traditions.

Wind

A poetic image of the animating spirit whose effects can be seen and heard but who remains invisible. Wind, air and breath are closely allied in mystic symbolism, and the idea of the wind as cosmic animator, organizer or support was widespread. Genesis begins with the Spirit of God moving like wind on the face of the deep. The Indo-Iranian wind-god Vayu is cosmic breath. The Aztec wind-god Ehecatl (an aspect of Quetzalcoatl) puffs the sun and moon into motion. The winds also appear as divine messengers and as the forces controlling the directions of space – the origin of the puff-cheeked heads popular with early map-makers. Below the elevated level of this symbolism, individual winds were often personified as violent and unpredictable. In Greek myth, to ensure the hero Odysseus had a calm voyage, Aeolus, master of

The gods of the four winds, from an illustration to Virgil's Aeneid *(1st century BCE).*

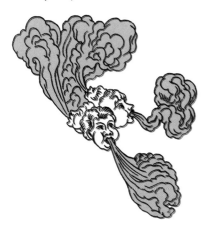

the winds, gave them to him in a bag – which one of his crewmen disastrously opened. Demons were thought to ride violent winds, bringing evil and illness. In China, wind was associated with rumour, a symbolism perhaps derived from hunting and "getting wind of" a scent. Its importance in pollination made it a sexual symbol in China. Generally, wind is a powerful symbol of change, inconstancy, empty bragging and the ephemeral, its dominant meaning in the 20th century.

Wine

Vital force, spiritual blessing, salvation, joy, healing, truth, transformation. Beyond its value as a sociable, nourishing, medicinal drink, the juice of the crushed grape held the mysterious power to change itself into something more potent – and to change those who drank it. This, and the blood colour of red wine, is the basis of its sacramental symbolism. Wine was made in the Near East at least 5,000 years ago and was widely regarded as a divine blessing, proof of the vigour of nature and the beneficial spirit animating it. In Jewish ritual, wine commemorates God's blessing on his people. Islam reserves this blessing for those who have reached paradise – for the Prophet did not condemn wine, only its abuse.

Elsewhere in the Mediterranean world, wine was linked with fertility and life after death (the significance of libations poured on the earth). In the cult of the Greek god Dionysus (in Roman myth, Bacchus) wine was a symbol of ecstatic union with the god himself, and in Orphic rites it was equated with his sacrificial blood. Christianity gave this symbolism new poetic force: "Those who eat my flesh

Wind: *see*
Air; Breath, Breathing; Whirlwind

Wine: *see*
Blood; Grail; Transformation; Vine

Wings: *see*
Angels; Bat; Birds;
Butterfly; Devils; Disk;
Dragon; Fan; Feathers;
Snake; Sun; VIRTUES

Witchcraft: *see*
Black; Broom; Cat; Devils;
Fox; Lamb; Owl; Scapegoat;
SEVEN DEADLY SINS;
Snake; Toad; Wolf

and drink my blood abide in me, and I in them" (John 6:56). Sacramental wine representing the chalice of Christ's redeeming blood is the symbolism of the Eucharist and the Grail. Medieval paintings of Christ standing or kneeling in a wine press refer to the description of him by St Augustine (354–430CE) as "the bunch that has been put under the wine press". Bunches of grapes are funerary emblems of salvation. Alternatively, blood streaming from pressed grapes symbolizes God's wrath, as in Revelation (14:20). A subsidiary symbolism of wine is that it produces truth, either by "opening the heart to reason" in a Rabbinical phrase, or by loosening the tongues of liars and hypocrites. The Bible takes a fairly tolerant view of wine-bibbing as a folly. Noah is shamed rather than condemned for it. "These men are full of new wine," say mockers when the Apostles begin speaking in tongues. However, full wineskins are sometimes emblems of sin.

Wings

Speed, mobility, ascent, sublimation, aspiration, supremacy, liberty, intelligence, inspiration. Although wings are usually elevation or earth-to-heaven emblems, they can also symbolize protection ("taken under the wing"). Wings were often linked with solar deities, adding irony to the Greek myth of Icarus, who, with his father Daedalus, tried to escape the wrath of King Minos of Crete. Icarus fell to his death when the wax on his artificial wings melted as he flew too close to the sun (a real god as opposed to a presumptuous human). In symbolism, wings have to be spiritually earned. The conceited have their wings

clipped or fall in flames like Satan.

Because bird and wing symbolism are closely linked, winged creatures in art can be rapacious and frightening or alternatively angelic, especially those with scaly or bat wings; a sign of Satan. Fairies are more delicately winged like butterflies. The artistic convention of giving angels wings appeared in about the 6th century CE, based on classical images of messenger gods and other winged deities. Apart from angels, souls and personifications of the spirit, such as the dove of the Holy Ghost, others who appear winged in art include the Greek messenger-god Hermes (in Roman myth, Mercury), whose winged sandals and helmet are also worn by the hero Perseus; the god of sleep Hypnos (Somnus) and his son Morpheus; the goddess Nemesis and the Harpies; and the personifications of Fame, History, Peace, Fortune and sometimes Father Time. Winged disks are solar emblems. Winged snakes or dragons combine earth and sky powers.

Winter *see* Seasons

WISDOM *see panel, opposite*

Witchcraft

In western Europe from the 13th to 18th centuries a symbol of the misuse of supernatural powers. Before this time, and in primitive societies generally, witches were feared and distrusted but their services were often sought. Witchcraft became a dangerous occupation when witches were seen not as free agents but as servants of a powerful Devil. This made them the symbolic negative of the priests who served God. Traditions of plural divinities accommodated hag god-

WISDOM

Wisdom is personified in Western art by the Greek goddess Athene (in Roman myth, Minerva) who holds a book and olive branch, and is accompanied by her sacred owl. In medieval paintings, Wisdom also holds a book but often has a snake at her feet. Prudence, as an aspect of wisdom, shares many of the same symbols, especially the snake. Wine and alcohol in general were often linked with wisdom and truth. So was water, especially a spring. Precious metals and jewels were important symbols, especially gold and silver, chrysolite, jade, diamonds, pearls and zircon. Wisdom was linked with the colours gold and blue, the number seven and the triangle. Among other symbols are the caped baboon of Thoth in Egypt, birds generally, the bee, cap, dragon, fool (by inversion), lotus, griffin, hazel, heart, peacock, seven pillars, rat, ring, salt, sceptre, scroll, Greek sphinx, sword, tongue, unicorn and walnut.

desses such as the Hindu Kali as part of a dualistic natural order. By contrast, in monotheistic Christianity, Satan was an error in nature whose followers had to be burnt. At the height of witch-hunting hysteria, "witches" became scapegoats for natural misfortunes such as crop failure, madness or ideas unacceptable to the Church, such as heresy or female lust.

In the ancient world, witches were most closely associated with necromancy. Saul, for example, consulted the witch of Endor who called Samuel from the dead to predict that he would be crushed by the Philistines. Horace described Roman necromancy involving the slaughter of a black lamb. This reverse symbolism is typical of most traditional witching symbols. They include nocturnal animals (such as black cats, and owls); toads; wolves or (in Japan) foxes; goat-like symbols of lust; snakes; poisonous herbs; and such fearful sacrificial offerings as dead babies. Jung saw witches as projections of the dark side of the *anima* or female side of human nature.

Wolf

Ferocity, cunning, greed, cruelty, evil – but also courage, victory, nourishing care. In early pastoral societies, particularly Judeo-Christian and generally in heavily wooded and populated regions of Europe, the wolf is a famous predatory creature in myth, folklore and fairy tale. The big, bad wolf was both a devouring and sexually predatory symbol. Stories of witches turning into wolves and men into werewolves symbolized fears of demonic possession as well as unleashed male violence and sadism. Christian symbolism of sheep as parishioners made the predatory wolf a symbol of the Devil and heresy. Paintings of St Francis of Assisi with a wolf refer to the story that he tamed one. Chinese tradition associated the wolf with rapacity and lechery. In Norse myth, the giant wolf Fenris is a chaos symbol, swallowing the sun at the end of the world. The wolf is a sun-swallower in Celtic myth, too.

Elsewhere, this symbolism is sometimes reversed so that the wolf becomes a triumphal symbol of intelligence through experience and an emblem of warriors. It was sacred to

WISDOM: *see individual names*

Wolf: *see* Devils; Dog; Sheep; Witchcraft

Woman: *see*
individual names

Wood: *see*
Ash; Hawthorn; Hazel; Oak;
Tree; Willow; Yew

Woodpecker: *see*
Birds; Drum; Tree

A bronze statue (6th–5th century
BCE*) showing the Roman twins*
Romulus and Remus, founders of
Rome, suckled by the she-wolf.

Apollo in Greece and to Odin
(Wodan) in Nordic myth. Sacred to
Mars, it was a Roman emblem of
victory if sighted before battle.

The she-wolf suckling Romulus
and Remus (the legendary founders of
Rome) is an image of fierce maternal
care that reappears in the folklore of
India. It may account for the many
stories of wolves as ancestors – of
Genghis Khan for one. Kemal
Atatürk was called "the Grey Wolf".
Turkic wolf symbolism is positive
enough to suggest that it was a
totemic animal in central Asia. In
Mexico and Native America the wolf
was a dancer symbol, associated like
the dog with ghosts and the guidance
of spirits in the afterlife.

Woman
Receptor, carrier, animator, protector
and nourisher of life. This ancient
symbolism dominates the depiction of
women in art, mythology and religion
in all early traditions and is reflected
in the emblems most often associated
with them. These include womb symbols such as the cave, well or fountain;
containers such as the vase, pitcher,
cup, urn, sheath, basket, boat and
boat-shaped lunar crescent; hollows

such as the furrow or valley; fecundity
symbols such as trees and fruits;
specifically sexual images such as the
shell, lozenge or inverted triangle. The
qualities most often associated with
women in traditional symbolism are
soul, intuition, emotion and emotional inconstancy, passivity and the
unconscious, love and purity. In art,
women personify most of the vices
and virtues. They are also strongly
identified with the magic arts, especially divination and prophecy.

Womb *see* **Woman**

Wood
Protection – a symbolism based on
ancient cults of beneficial tree spirits
and on universal traditions in which
the tree is an expression of maternal
nourishment and the life force.

The superstition of touching wood
comes from the supposed magical
powers of ash, hawthorn, hazel, oak
and willow.

In Indian tradition, wood is the primal substance shaping all things –
Brahma. In China it is an emblem of
spring and the east.

Woodpecker
Protection in most traditions, probably from its habit of embedding itself
in "mothering" tree trunks. Like some
other noisy birds it was also credited
with prophetic powers.

It was sacred to the most powerful
classical gods and in legend carried
food to the twins Romulus and
Remus, the legendary founders of
Rome. In ancient India and in some
Native American traditions, its drum-
ming warned of a storm or averted
thunderbolts. For others it was a call
to battle.

Word

In mystic tradition, a symbol of divine creative power. The Hindu notion that the vibration of a sacred primordial sound brought the manifest world into being appears in many traditions. In the book of Genesis, God speaks to create light. The Gospel of St John opens: "In the beginning was the Word, and the Word was with God, and the Word was God." Christ himself is called the logos (Word).

Worm

Dissolution, mortality – a symbolism used in some solemn paintings of grubs on flowers or fruit. More unexpectedly, in the myths of some countries, including Ireland, worms feature as ancestral emblems, taking up the symbolism of larval metamorphosis.

Wreath, Garland

In life, superiority or sanctity; in death, resurrection or immortality. The form of the wreath combines the celestial symbolism of the circle (perfection) and the ring (eternity, continuity, union).

Woven of flowers or leaves and worn on the head, wreaths are living crowns, suggesting both victory and vitality. Their form and position on the crown of the head were so significant in ancient Egypt that they were once worn only by gods or kings. In both classical and Judeo-Christian traditions, wreaths were also originally royal or sacred attributes, often believed to have protective powers. Initiates or followers identified themselves with a particular god by wearing wreaths made from his sacred plant or flower. Sacrifices were garlanded as a means of consecration.

Victors at the ancient Olympic games similarly wore wreaths honouring gods: Zeus by the Olympian olive or Nemean parsley, Poseidon by the Isthmian pine and Apollo by the Pythian laurel wreath.

The plants used in other wreaths are often symbolic. Bridal wreaths of blossom suggest new beginnings, joy and fertility. Funeral wreaths of flowers acknowledge mortality but their ring form implies eternity and the continuity of remembrance.

Wren

In Welsh tradition, the little king of birds, and in Ireland a bird associated with the prophetic powers of Druids. As a versatile songbird, the wren also appears as an emblem of happiness among Native North Americans.

Word: *see* Honey; Om (Aum)

Worm: *see* VANITY

Wreath, Garland: *see* Circle; Crown; FLOWERS; Laurel; Olive; Pine, Pine cone; Ring; Sacrifice; VICTORY

Wren: *see* Birds

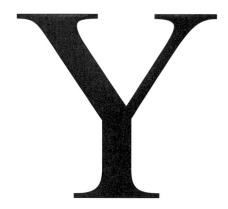

Yellow: *see*
DEATH; COLOURS;
Gold; Sun

Yew: *see*
Bow; Tree; Wand; Wood

Yin-yang: *see*
Androgyne; Birds; Circle;
Earth; FLOWERS; Man;
Mountain; Needle; Tree;
Trigrams; Woman

Yantra *see* **Mandala**

Year
A completed cycle – symbolically of birth, death and regeneration. Hence the traditional significance of New Year as a renewal rather than merely a calendrical marker.

Yellow
Of all primary colours, the most inconsistent in symbolism, swinging from positive to negative according to context and range of hue. Warm yellows share the solar symbolism of gold. In China they were emblems of royalty, merit and the centre. Yellow was the optimistic bridal colour of youth, virginity, happiness and fertility. Yet in the Chinese theatre, yellow make-up was the code for treachery. This symbolism is widespread and explains why Jews (for their supposed "betrayal" of Christ) had to wear yellow in medieval Europe and yellow crosses under Nazism. Links between yellow skin and fear or disease account for yellow corresponding to the colour of cowardice and quaran-

tine. A yellow cross was painted on plague houses. In its negative aspect, yellow is also the colour of dying leaves and overripe fruit. This may account for its wide cultural links with the concept of space linked with death and the afterlife. Yellow has the highest symbolic value in Buddhist countries through its link with the saffron robes of monks. This colour, previously worn by criminals, was chosen by Gautama Buddha as a symbol of his humility and separation from materialist society.

Yew
A tree of immortality, which often seen in English graveyards, and a wood associated with strength, resilience and magical powers (Druid wands as well as bows were made of it). In superstition, yew was lucky to touch but unlucky to bring inside the house because its leaves and seeds are poisonous.

Yin-yang
Unity in duality, symbolized in China by a circle equally divided by a

The yin-yang symbol, encased in an octagram, from an emblem displayed on the park gates outside Bangkok.

backward S-curve into a dark, female half (yin) and bright, male half (yang), each with a small circle of the opposite colour. This simple image is one of balanced dynamism, symbolizing the interdependence of contrary forces and principles in the cosmos. Whereas the perfect androgyne would form an undivided circle, the yin-yang symbol implies that each divided half contains the seed of the other. In the *I Ching* or Book of Changes, a similar interplay of complementary forces is expressed by the alternation of continuous (yin) or broken (yang) lines, even or odd numbers. Creative tension, alternation and fusion between yin and yang generates change and motion, evolution and involution. Yin, which precedes yang, is female, moist, dark, passive, soft, pliable and intuitive, and is associated with the earth, valley, trees and flowers and lunar animals and birds. Yang is masculine, dry, bright, active, hard, inflexible, and rational, and is associated with the sky, mountains and solar animals and birds.

Yoke
Mainly a symbol of oppression and submission. Yoke-shaped structures were used by the Romans to humiliate defeated armies, which had to pass under them, and yokes were a traditional method of shackling slaves on the march.

The older meaning of yoke was "union", the literal meaning of the word *yoga* as a discipline of union with the divine essence. In Christianity, the yoke can symbolize obedience to religious vows.

Yoni *see* Vulva

Yule log
The Celtic and Germanic centrepiece of a 12-day midwinter festival which influenced Christmas and New Year customs. The ritual burning of a sacred oak log symbolized the dying of light at the December solstice and celebrated the warmth of its rebirth.

Yule Log: *see* Christmas tree; Oak; Solstice

Zero: *see*
Egg; NUMBERS; Spiral;
Void

Ziggurat: *see*
Mountain; Pyramid;
SEVEN DEADLY SINS;
Sun; Temple

Zigzag: *see*
Lightning; Runes

Zodiac: *see*
Arrow; Bull; Crab; Goat;
Fish; Lion; Moon; Pitcher;
PLANETS; Ram; Scales;
Scorpion; Star; Sun; Twelve;
Twins; Virginity; Water;
Wheel

Zero

Void, mystery, nothingness, death – but also eternity, the absolute or essence of reality, totality, the cosmic egg or womb, potentiality, the generative interval. Pythagoras saw the sign (known from Babylonia, but mathematically developed mainly in Arabia and India) as containing all things. It was the Tao, the begetter of one. In Mayan glyphs it was represented by the cosmic spiral. The zero is also the power of the decimal multiplier.

Ziggurat

A massive Mesopotamian stepped temple built of brick and forming a symbolic sacred mountain. In Hebrew tradition, the chief ziggurat of Babylon was the Tower of Babel, a derisive symbol of human pride and folly. Spiritually, the ziggurats built between about 2200 and 500BCE represented both human ascension (via the staircases to rising levels) and the hope that the gods to whom they were individually dedicated would descend to the sanctuaries at the top. There are theories that the great Babylonian ziggurat had seven levels, each representing a planet. Ziggurat-like stepped temples in Mesoamerica certainly had planetary significance.

Zigzag

An ancient sign (based on lightning) of power, fertility, heat, energy, battle and death. Once the attribute of storm gods, it was the Sigrune, or rune of victory, in the old Nordic alphabet and was adopted as an emblem of striking force by the Nazi SS, whose insignia was a double zigzag.

Zodiac

A celestial power path – the narrow band of the sky along which the sun apparently travels in the course of a year. The Zodiac is usually symbolized as a circular band or segmented wheel carrying emblems of the constellations within this zone. In astrology, the Zodiac provides the symbolic background for predictions of the mental, physical and emotional make-up of individuals. Based on the grandeur and mystery of the night sky, the Zodiac was one of the most persuasive of all symbol systems.

The Greek word *zoidiakos* meant "a set of creatures", because the ancients are known to have used animals or fabulous beasts to identify the constellations. Before the rudimentary Hellenistic Zodiac of the 2nd century BCE, astrologers were paid to calculate the supposed influence of planetary or star gods on earthly events – especially those affecting rulers. The Greeks blended their own myths with Babylonian and Egyptian star science and the calculations of their best geometers to devise a Zodiac with much richer symbolism and founded on much more accurate and detailed astronomy. Their Zodiac charted the positions of all the visible constellations within a 6° belt each side of the apparent path of the sun (the ecliptic).

The Western Zodiac (like most others) is divided into 12 equal segments, each ruled by the sun, the moon or a planet, and each having a symbolic name and sigil. Each sign is marked by the dates of the sun's passage into and out of its 30° section, beginning with Aries (the ram), on the date when the sun crosses the equator in Northern spring, March 21. Then follows Taurus (the bull); Gemini (the twins); Cancer (the crab); Leo (the lion); Virgo (the virgin); Libra (the scales); Scorpio (the scorpion); Sagittarius (the archer); Capricorn (the goat-fish); Aquarius (the water carrier); Pisces (the fish). Astrologers drew on ancient symbolism, existing science and observations of human nature to allocate qualities and characteristics of all kinds to these signs and suggest polarities and relationships between them as a basis for predicting human personality, and divining the future.

As a whole, the Zodiac symbolizes a persisting belief that the cosmos is a gigantic force field in which everything is interconnected. Mere distance, it suggests, does not prevent powerful celestial bodies influencing human life. To chart the force field relevant to an individual, astrologers traditionally worked from the point at which the ecliptic crossed the dawn horizon at birth. Using the stars as a reference background, they believed that the positions and movements of the sun, moon and planets at this moment formed a pattern that influenced each person's mental and physical make-up. With different emblems and interpretations, but with the same underlying symbolism, the Zodiac appears in all great ancient cultures. Many of the qualities that now seem arbitrarily allocated to individual signs, use a language of symbolism based on deep observation of nature.

The sun is personified in the centre of this redrawing of a 9th-century Zodiac. The signs appear in ecliptic order beginning with Aries in the section above the sun's hand, and then continuing counterclockwise.

Acknowledgments

I should like to thank all those at Duncan Baird who were involved in the production of this book, and Duncan himself for asking me to write it. My thanks go especially to the editors Judy Dean and Mike Darton, and to the designer John Grain. The book owes much to Jane Tresidder and to the London Library.

Index of Supplementary Words

Page numbers indicate a reference in the A–Z dictionary. There may be references in more than one dictionary entry, in captions or in feature boxes, on the same page. Page numbers in **bold** refer to a reference in a feature box only. All cross-references refer to entries in the index.

A

Aaron's rod 11, 48, 171
Aboriginals, Australian **10**, 26, 33, 53, 58, 122, 160, 171
Abraham 114, 148, 167
Achilles 39, 61, 119
Actaeon 63
Adam (biblical) 12, 63, 80, 94, 142, 185, 202
Adonis 67, 172
Aeneas 29, 135
Aeolus 115, 227
Aesculapius 34, 49, 185
Agni 17, 32, **56**, 78, 81, 91, 118, 167, 191, 197, 206
Ahriman **37**, 63, 219
Ahura Mazda 64, 195
Aladdin 40, 119
Alexander III, Pope 170
Alexander the Great 105, 116, 186
Ali 99, 125, 212
Alice in Wonderland 135
Allah 48, 73, 122, 137, 195
Amaterasu 49, 135, 157, 195, 207, 223
ambrosia 22, 45, 104, 132, 169, 187
Amitabha 154
Amun 27, 104–5, 186
Amun-Ra 87, 101, 167
Ananta 48, 184
Andromeda 68

Anger **180**, 205
Anubis 26, 65, 111
Ao 207
Apep 168, 185
Aphrodite 15, 38, **42**, 59, 66, 67, 82, 88, 90, 99, 101, 119, 134, 141, 144, 153, 155, 156, 157, 163, 172, 173, 176, **179**, 188, 196, 206
see also Venus (goddess)
Apollo 29, **42**, 43, 45, 49, 58, 59, 91, 93, 95, 120, 127, 130, **141**, 148, 152, 165, 167, 168, **179**, 181, 186, 195, 196, 225, 230, 231
Aquarius 12, 161, **179**, 215, 235
architecture 15, 40, 47, 50, 66, 123, 152, 160, 164, 201
Ares 28, **42**, 49, 68, 102, 144, 173
see also Mars (god)
Argus 121, 154
Aries 167, **179**, 235
Aristotle 53, 203
Ark of the Covenant 16, 199
art
Buddhist 19
Islamic 15
Taoist 19
temperance 47
see also Christ, in art; Virgin Mary, in art
Artemis 12, 21, 22, 26, 29, 38,

42, 43, 63, 120, 124, 136, 165, 178, 182, 197, 214, 218
see also Diana
Arthurian legend 44, 118, 173, 197, 212
ascension 16, 54, 71, 79, 102, 105, 153, 159, 171, 183, 184
asceticism 22, 96, 97, 142
Ashoka 125
Ashtart (Astarte) 51, 67, 152, 163
Asshur 64, 225
Astarte *see* Ashtart
astrology 138, **162**, 202, 212, 234–5
astronomy 50, 161, 188, 193, 212
Ate 26
Athene 18, 26, 49, 58, 95, 102, 126, 148, 151, 168, 175, 210, 218, 223, **229**
Athens 148
Attis 49, 110, 132, 160, 209
Aurelian, Emperor 187
Aurora *see* Eos
authority 13, 17, 28, 36, 42, 54, 58, 78, 79, 84, 91, 97, 111, 114, 115, 123, 128, 148, 170, 171, 173, 177, 191, 197, 203, 225
Avalokiteshvara 136, 155, 226
Avarice 26, 167, **180**, 206
axial symbolism 18, 45, 66, 139, 149, 153, 159, 161, 170, 193, 195, 207–8

B

Baal 32, 167, 186, 225
Babel, Tower of 207, 234
Babylon 226, 234
Bacchus *see* Dionysus
Balder 135, 187, 195
Bartholdi, Frédéric **122**
Bastet 38
Bato Kannon 105
beauty 15, 33, 35, 38, **85**, 89, 149, 153, 157, 172, 196, 205
Behemoth **23**, 103
Bellerophon **23**, 44, 120
Benares 159
Benu bird 139, 158
Beowulf 68, 186
bereavement 17, **50**, 59, **113**
see also grief
Bernard of Clairvaux 22, 219
Bernini, Gianlorenzo 16
Bes 69, 206
Bethlehem 40, 73, 191
Birth of Venus, The (painting) 177
Black Virgins 26, 61

Blake, William 51, 205
Blue Bird of Happiness, The (play) 25
Book of the Dead **10**
Boreas **179**
Borglum, Gutzon 171
Bosch, Hieronymus 100, 142, 193
Botticelli, Sandro 177, 223
Brahma 73, **85**, 87, 93, 101, 116, 123, 126, 143, 148, 171, 197, 203, 208, 211, 230
Brigit 202
Buddha 19, 24, 27, 38, 61, 64, 66, 74, 76, 80, 81, **83**, 84, **85**, 98, 99, 101, 105, **113**, 122, 125, 126, 143, 152, 153, 155, 159, 160, 167, 172, 181, 185, 191, 193, 195, 197, 206, 216, 225, 232
Busiris 193

C

Cabbalism 146, 172, 178, 188, 200, 208–9
Cadmus 68, 186, 201
calendar 136, 146, 169, 223, 232
Calypso 109
Cancer 53, 148, **179**, 235
Capricorn **23**, 92, **179**, 235
Carravaggio **180**
Carmel, Mt 139
Carthage 160
Cassandra 186
Castor 73, 101, 213
Centaurus 40
Cerberus **23**, 65, 186, 203
Ceres 52, **88**
see also Demeter
Ceridwen 159
Cernunnos 14, 167
Chalchiuhtlicue 127
Charity 82, 88, **220**
Charlemagne 197
Charles V of France 84
Charles V (Holy Roman Emperor) 160
charms
against drowning 39
love 21, 128
Charon **10**, 28
childbirth 39, 71, 192
Chiron 40–41
Chou dynasty 168, 169
Christ 11, 15, 22, 26, 27, 35, 40, 44, 45, 51, 75, 80, **83**, 84, 86, 91, 95, 98, 101, 105, 122, 123, 143–4, 151, 155, 156, 159, 167, 171, 172, 182, 186, 190, 191, 195, 197, 198, 202,

208, 211, 212, 217, 218, 222, 224, 225, 231
in art 29, **56**, **57**, 61, 63, 83, 129, 134, 142, 145, 149, 155, 156, 160, 163, 167, 198, 208, 218, 225, 228
ascension 70, 139, 181
atonement 177
baptism 67
birth 40, 108, 133, 187, 191
blood of 27, 42, 156
Bread of Life 29, 130
crown of thorns 9, 58, 93, 170, 202, 206
crucifixion **56**, 147, **153**, 169, 185
Death 20, 217
divine nature 158
Good Shepherd 59, 65, 118, 181
Humanity 156
and Judgment 92, 176
redeemer 16, 124
resurrection 20, 24, 158, 174
as Saviour 66, 107
Sermon on the Mount 139, 175
tested by Satan 63
see also Messiah
Christmas 35, 45, 103–4, 187, 191, 212, 233
Circe 130, 159
clairvoyance 38, 59, 76, 99
Cleopatra 156
Clovis, king of the Franks 84
Clytemnestra 73
Clytia 102, 130
Coleridge, Samuel Taylor 10, 104
Constantine the Great 45
Conversion of St Paul, The (painting) 180
cosmic egg 72, 93, 125, 193, 208, 234
cosmic tree 16, 20, 24, 25, 35, 73, 154, 207, 208
Courage 12, 15, 21, 36, 38, 48, 54, 100, 105, 108, 111, **113**, 114, 120, 123, 145, 160, 165, 173, 175, 193
Cowardice 79, 99, 106, 225, 232
creation 12, 72–3, 223
Crocodopolis 55
Cronos 36, 38, 40, 120, 149, 173, 182
Ctesias 214
Cúchulainn 160
Cupid 16, 26, 87, 116, 172
see also Eros
curatives 12, 14, 17, 18, 34, 51, 60, 63, 64, 110, 112, **113**, 119,

130, 135, 155, 157, 159, 169, 171, 173, 178, 185, 190, 192, 205, 214, 222, 226, 226–7, 227
Cybele 11, 22, 27, 32, **42**, 91, 124, 132, 138, 140, 147, 148, 160, 192

D

Daedalus 228
Dagda 39, 48, 100
Daikoku 98, 168
Dalai Lama 136, 182
Damocles 198
Danaë 166
Daniel 124
Daphne **43**, 120
David, king of Israel 21, 86, 100, 102
David (sculpture) 98
Day of Atonement 79, 177
Death's Duell (sermon) 24
Deceit 63, 132, 186
Delacroix, Eugène **122**, 158
Delos 165
Delphi 60, 66, 120, 149, 186
see also oracles
Demeter 20, 22, 44, 51, 52, 58, 66, 138, 143, 163, **179**, 206
see also Ceres
destiny *see* fate
destruction 54, 68–9, 76, 103, 109, 111, 115, 122, 123, 138, 140, 151, 167, 168, 190, 193, 194, 205, 219
Devil 30, **37**, 39, 44, 68, 88, 92, 151, 157, 168, 181, 187, 189, 225, 228, 229
see also Lucifer; Satan
dignity 21, 157, 164
Diocletion 181
Diodorus 33
Diogenes 65, 119
Dionysus 32, 33, **42**, 44, 52, 58, 65, 66, 67, 72, 80, 91, 110, 118, 120, 121, 122, 124, 131, 149, 157, 161, 163, 172, 176, **179**, 199, 204, 205, 217, 218, 225, 227
divination 26, 55, 59, 65, 100, 103, 106, 108, 112, **113**, 119, 134, 135, 140, 181, 189, 200–201, 230
divinity 31, 41, 64, 121, 124, 142, 149, 152, 168, 184, 204, 209
Dominicans 65
Donar *see* Thor
Donne, John 24
dreams 12, 144, 163, 187
dress 26, 90, 91, 96, 158, 164

Druids 28, **62**, 72, 79, 85, 135, 147, 157, 226, 231, 232
Dryads 147
Durga 26, 125, 205
Dyck, Anton van 195

E

Ea **23**, **83**, 160, 167, 207
Easter 72, 99
Easter Island sculptures 171
Ecstasy of St Theresa, The (sculpture) 16
Eden 81, 198, 209
El 32
Elephanta 123
Eleusis 22, 107
Elijah 43, 139, 168
Elixir of Life 11, 133, 139, 157
Elizabeth I, Queen 165
Eloquence 22, 104, 145, 182
energy 12, 25, 27, **37**, 80, 108, **113**, 114, 141, 145, 169, 185, 193, 196, 234
Enlil 17
envy **180**
Eos 45, 61
Epona 105
Eros 29, 33, 66, 67, 91, 93, 99, 101, 206
see also Cupid
Essenes 22
Eucharist 27, 42, 52, 72, 106, 217, 218, 227–8
Eurydice 186
Eusebius 45
Eve (biblical) 15, 80, 142, 185, 186, 187, 209
evil eye 76, 80, 90, 106, **113**, 137, 148, **180**
exorcism 131, 154

F

Faerie Queene (epic poem) 165
Faith 203, **220**
Fall, the 15, 142, 187, 208
fate 26, 43, 77, 114, 126, 138, 144, 199, 202, 225
Fates 144, 181, 189, 202, 203, 223
Father Time 182, **212**, 228
Fatima (daughter of Muhammad) 98
Faust, Dr 64, 157
Finn 175, 204
Fisherman's Ring 83, 170
Flora 52, **179**
food 131, 152
forbidden 21, 99, 151, 159
of the gods 15, 22, 64, 104, 140, 187
foolishness 17, 136

foresight 13, 167, 175
fortitude 9, 35, 48, **220**
Fortuna **86**
Francis I (of France) 175
Frazer, J.G. 29, 143, 177
Frederick Barbarossa, Emperor 170
Freemasonry 9, 51, 97, 157, 160, 161, 172, 190, 191, 197, 211
Freud, Sigmund 31, 84, 115
Freya 24, 28, 32, 38, **42**, 77, 79, 106
Freyr 28
Frigg *see* Freya
Fujiyama 139
Furies 203
Fuseli, Henry 106

G

Gabriel (archangel) 15, 114, 123, 214
Gaia 71, 138
Galatea **42**
Ganesha 73, 168, 197
Ganymede 70
Garden of Earthly Delights, The (painting) 100, 193
Garuda 71, 186
Gemini **179**, 213, 235
Genghis Khan 63, 230
gentleness 30, **85**, 93, 118, 164, 215
germination 17, 31, 39, 61, 88, 94, 105, 138, 144
Gilgamesh, Epic of 16, 185
Gluttony 21, 102, 159, **180**
Gnosticism 63, 73, 150, 156, 183, 188, 191, 197
God 16, 48, 87, 144, 149, 210, 211
see also Jehovah
Goethe 157
Golden Age 22, **88**, 103, 218
Golden Bough 29, 135, 177
Golden Calf 32, 34
Gordian knot 116
Götterämmerung 213
Goya, Francisco de 20
Graces 172, 203
Great Serpent Mound 184
Great Spirit 79, 81, 195
Greed 106, 136, 219, 229
grief 13, 97, 109, 226
see also bereavement
Grim Reaper 182, 183
Grünewald, Mathis **57**
Guanyin 19, 155, 226
see also Avalokiteshvara
guardians 43, 58, 65, 69, 103, 106, 124, 135, 151, 185, 188, 191, 194, 219

Index

H

Hachiman 28
Hadad 188, 193
Hades **42**, 59, 102, 143, 151,
   163, 203
Hagar 223
Hamlet (play) 134, 163, 172, 173
Han dynasty 68, 89
Hanuman 15, 136
happiness 9, 19, 48, 52, 69, 73,
   105, 120, 128, 140, 141, 159,
   161, 165, 173, 215, 231, 232
Hathor 52, 80, 104, 209
healing *see* curatives
health 21, 35, 73, 156, 168, 226
hearing 63, 127
Hebe 161
Hecate 54, 55, 65, 100, 137, 138,
   172, 202, 206
Helen of Troy 15, 73
Heliopolis 157–8
Helios 102, 195, 197
hell **10**, 39, 140, 219, 224
Henry VIII 78, 173
Hephaestus 30, **42**, 81, 97,
   118–19, 144, **179**, 184, 219
Hera 27, **42**, 53, 93, 120, 123,
   134, 148, 154, 155, 163, 167,
   192, 197
   see also Juno
Herakles 15, 28, 32, 40, 53, 124,
   134, 147, 160, 163, 170, 186,
   193, 206
Herakles, Pillars of 160
Hercules *see* Herakles
Hermes 34, **42**, 49, 55, 59, 73,
   75, 93, 99, 100, 127, 167, 176,
   179, 181, 185, 192, 202, 210,
   228
   see also Mercury (god)
Herodotus 92, 109, 117, 226
Hesiod 109, 138, 146, 212
Hesperides 15, 67, 149, 186
Hilaria 132
Hine 72, 109
Hiram (King of Tyre) 9
Hobbes, Thomas 121
Holy Spirit 22, 30, 64, 67, 71,
   81, **85**, 175, 202, 211, 226
homeopathy 34, 173, 185
Homer 26, 41, 104
Honour 53, 120
Honshu 68
Hope 103, 177, 203, **220**
Horace 229
Horeb, Mt 139
Horn of Plenty 52, 104
Horus 28, 76, 77, 128, 195
Huitzilopochtli 92, 194
Humility 12, 13, 17, 31, 84, 95,
   98, 106, 115, 118, 140, 149,

155, 232
Hydra **23**, 53
Hypnos 144, 163, 228
Hypocrisy 55, 88, 106, 140, 186

I

Iblis 63
Icarus 228
ignorance 26, 61, 159
ikebana **85**
illumination 22, 35, 42, 48, 58,
   61, 64, 101, **113**, 145, 148,
   150, 168, 171, 177
Imhotep 164
immortality 9, 11, 12, 13, 15, 25,
   29, 33, 40, 42, 45, 47, 53, 59,
   62, 64, 66, 75, 86, 90, 94, 99,
   110, 112, 114, 119, 121, **125**,
   133, 136, 137, 140, 147, 148,
   152, 153, 154, 160, 164, 169,
   176, 177, 181, 192, 199, 226,
   231, 232
Inari 88, 169
incorruptibility 64, 109, 111,
   113, 127, 154, 160, 169, 175
Indra 27, 32, 43, 69, 73, 119,
   154, 167, 184, 204
innocence 44, **85**, 118, 123, 127,
   142, 172, 182, 225
Integrity 64, 170
Isaac 167
Isaiah 118, 178, 179
Isenheim altarpiece **57**
Ishmael 223
Ishtar 82, 102, 124, 137, 152,
   186, 191, 197, 218, 223
Isis 159, 161, 196, 204
Islands of the Blessed 66
Israel 87, 182, 212
Izanagi 134, 154, 169, 188

J

Jacob 118, 212
Jainism 32, 104, **113**, 197
Janus 55, 100, 114, 150
Jason 93
Jehovah 225
   see also God
Jeremiah 178
Jericho 164
Jesus *see* Christ
Jimmu-Tenno 68
Job 63, 225
John the Baptist 67, 104, 118,
   169
Jonah 24, 144, 224
Joseph of Arimathea 94
Joseph (husband of Mary) 123
joy 25, 35, 61, 101, 103, **113**,
   128, 143, 148, 156, 157, 168,
   227

Judas Iscariot 73, 175
Judgment **10**, 176, 182, 225
Julius Caesar, Emperor 93
Julius Caesar (play) 50
Jung, Carl Gustav 21, 33, 34, 42,
   46, 55, **56**, 84, 85, 87, 94, 102,
   113, 129, 140, 144, 185, 188,
   229
Jungle Book, The 21
Juno 116, 147
   see also Hera
Jupiter 86, 122
   see also Zeus
Jupiter (planet) 75, **133**, **162**,
   179
Justice 26, 50, 87, 111, 123, 150,
   176, 177, 190, 197, **220**

K

Kae 109
Kahukara 167
Kali 26, 69, 138, 205, 206, 229
Kama 153, 154
Karnak 118, 188
Keats, John 144
Kemal Atatürk 230
Khepri 177, 195
Kipling, Rudyard 21
Knossos 117
Krishna 22, 27, 122, 130, 141
Kubla Khan (poem) 104
Kumpira 207
Kunlun, World Mountain 139,
   152
Kyoto 89

L

ladder **56**, 100
Lake Moeris 117
Lao-Tse 31, 161, 213
Last Supper, The (painting) 176
Lazarus 24
Leda 73, 196
Lent 72, 79
Leo 124, **179**, 235
Leonardo da Vinci 175–6
Leviathan 121
Liberty (statue) **122**
Liberty Leading the People
   (painting) **122**, 158
Libra 176, **179**, 235
Lightning Bird 25, 122
Lion of Judah 124, 125
locusts 94
lodestone 128
logic 29, 125, 176, 178
Lohengrin (opera) 196
Loki 78, 88
Louis XIV 115
Louis XVI 115
love 15, 30, 36, 66, 67, 86–7, 93,

101, **113**, 123, 137, 138, 141,
   144, 149, 153, 155, 156, 163,
   168, 172, 173, 196, 206, 214,
   223, 226, 230
loyalty 65, 90, 111, 116
Loyola, Ignatius de 101, 107,
   116
Lucifer **37**, 64, 75, **113**
   see also Devil; Satan
luck 15, 17, 20, 28, 43, 49, 54, 73, **83**,
   90, 98, 100, 116, 143, 149,
   156, 157, 160, 169, 173, 181,
   183, 186, 189, 190, 202, 203,
   205, 232
   bad 38, 58, 120, 135, 143, 146,
   156, 170, 232
Lupercalia 225
Lust 15, 17, 20, 28, 43, 48, 49,
   64, 91, 99, 106, 121, 134, 136,
   159, 176, **180**, 206, 229
Lycaeon, Mt 160

M

Ma'at **10**, 79, 150, 176
Macbeth (play) 39
Madonna and Child (altarpiece)
   72
Maeterlinck, Count Maurice 25
Manannan 159
Mandaean sect 141
Mandara, Mt 139
Manicheanism 63, 121, 197
Manitou 99
Manticore **23**
Marduk 124, 143, 161
Mars (god) 93, 105, 172, 218,
   219, 230
   see also Ares
Mars (planet) **133**, **162**, 167, 179
Mars and Venus (painting) 223
Mary, mother of Christ *see*
   Virgin Mary
Maui 72, 81, 210, 219
Maxentius 45
Mecca 47, 59, 159
Medea 39
Medici, Cosimo de 207
medicine *see* curatives
meditation 30, 41, 82, 108, 129,
   201
Medusa 51, 76, 102, 148
meekness 17, 181, 226
melancholia 27, 95
Melville, Herman 224
Memnon 61
Mephistopheles 64, 157
Merchant of Venice, The (play)
   29, 166
Mercury (god) 74, **78**
   see also Hermes
Mercury (planet) **133**, **162**, 179

mermaids **23**, 178
mermen **23**
Merry Wives of Windsor, The
  (play) 151
Meru, Mt 139
messengers 34, 58, 67, 70, 88,
  93, 99, 105, 153, 157, 167,
  168, 195, 208, 227
Messiah 118, 191
  see also Christ
Michael (archangel) **10**, 15–16,
  68, 176, 198
Michelangelo 98
Mictlanteculitli **37**
Midas 17, 158
Midsummer Night's Dream, A
  (play) 17
Milton, John 26
Ming dynasty 94, 155
Minos 117, 134, 186, 228
Mithraism 31, 33, 40, 97, 104,
  171, 192, 207
Mithras 27, 31, 168, 181, 187,
  191, 195, 212
Moby Dick (novel) 224
Moloch 81
monastic communities/orders
  22, 31, 95, 103
Morpheus 163, 228
Moses 20, 32, 33, 43, 86, 122,
  139, 171, 185, 199, 201
mourning *see* bereavement
Muhammad **10**, 86, 140, 163,
  195
  see also Prophet, the
Mycenae 124, 131, 148
Mystic Isles (China) 89, 109

N

Nagas **23**, 48, 185
Nammu 138
Nazism 173, 196, 232, 234
Nebuchadnezzar 150
Nekhbet 219
Nemesis 95, 171, 228
Neptune *see* Poseidon
Newton (painting) 51
Nightingale, Florence 119
Nightmare, The (painting) 106
Nike **217**
Noah 67, 148, 168, 217, 228
Norns 223
Nun 139
nuns 131, 170, 216
Nut 52, 80, 159

O

Obedience 35, 233
Ode to a Nightingale (poem) 144
Odin 28, 86, 102, 105–6, 145,
  160, 168, 195, 230

  see also Wodan
Odysseus 29, 109, 126, 227
Oedipus 55, 58, 188
Olives, Mt of 139
Olympus, Mt 139
oracles 39–40
  see also Delphi
Original Sin 15
  see also sin
Orion 178
Orpheus **83**, 127
Orphism 72, 86, 133, 150, 188,
  217, 227
Osiris 20, 23, 32, 51, 55, 59, 65,
  86, 95, 110, 133, 137, 160,
  161, 176, 179, 187, 191, 192,
  195, 199, 218
Ouranos 38, 182

P

Padma 126
Padmasambhava 127
Pan 64, 91, 169, 176
Pandora's box 29
Paris 15, 158
Pasiphaë 134
Passover bread 118
Patience 13, 17
Patmos 40
Pausanius 40
Pegasus **23**, **78**
Pele 219
Pelias of Iolcus 39
penance 78, 83, 86
Penelope 126
penitence 17, 79, 171
perfection 45, 59, 65, 82, **85**, 92,
  94, 106, 111, 114, 126, 130,
  149, 155, 165, 172, 188, 201
Persephone 17, 20, 49, 143, 163,
  206
Perseus 68, 76, 102, 228
Phaeton 12
pharaoh 48, 93, 164, 181, 185,
  219
Philomela 145
Phrygia 158
Piero della Francesca 72
Piety 12, 63, 123, 192
Pisces **179**, 235
Plato 26, 40, 100
Pliny 79, 99, 135, 156, 175
Plutarch 55, 183
poetry **141**, 196
Polydeuces (Pollux) 73, 101, 213
Pontius Pilate 221
Poseidon 32, **42**, 66, 134, 148,
  203, 210, 231
potency 31, 33, 34, 36, 91, 104,
  122, 135, 141, 147, 171, 188,
  212

poverty 17, 24, 31, 142
power 17, 31, 34, 36, 38, 39, 40,
  41, 47, 64, 98, 104, 105, 111,
  112, 119, 161, 164, 177, 188,
  189, 204, 205, 210, 214, 223,
  225, 234
  divine **23**, 64, 76, 81, 87, 118,
  122, 123, 145, 159, 181, 191,
  193, 202
  judicial 28
  sovereign 73, 91, 97, **113**, 115,
  125, 128, 137, 147, 191, 203
  spiritual 49, 154, 177, 185
  supernatural 68, 171
prayer 35, 37–8, 41, 70, 79, 98,
  107, 115, 171, 184
Priapus 24, 52, 80, 93, 157, 168,
  182
Pride 13, 48, 71, 134, 154, **180**
Prometheus 41, 70, 81, 206, 219
Prophet, the 94, 105, 148, 159,
  212, 227
  see also Muhammad
Proserpine *see* Persephone
Proserpina (painting) 163
prosperity 9, 14, 24, 31, 34, 52,
  54, 73, 80, 83, **88**, 114, 123,
  127, 138, 159, 165, 168, 169,
  181, 209
protection 9, 19, 20, 24, 30, 34,
  36, **37**, 38, 43, 47, 49, 53, 55,
  58, 60, 64, 69, 71, 73, 75, 89,
  95, 97, 98, 101, 105, 106, 109,
  113, 116, 119, 120, 123, 125,
  131, 135, 137, 138, 142, 148,
  153, 157, 164, 167, 169, 170,
  173, 175, 181, 185, 189, 202,
  205, 206, 207, 208, 216, 219,
  221, 228, 230, 231
Proteus 178
Prudence **220**, **229**
Pseudo-Dionysius 13
Psyche 33, 187
Ptah 32
purification 54, 59, 78, 80, 83,
  86, 106, 119, **133**, 150, 159,
  164, 166, 169, 170, 174, 175,
  176, 182, 214, 221
purity 9, 11, 22, 27, 34, 44, 54,
  62, 64, 67, 75, 81, 83, 86, 89,
  91, 92, 100, 104, 106, 107,
  109, 111, **113**, 118, 121, 123,
  127, 129, 130, 134, 139, 142,
  148, 149, 154, 155, 156, 166,
  172, 182, 190, 192, 198, 214,
  218, 221, 222, 223, 225, 230
putti (angels) 13, 31, 52
Pythagoras 82, 87, 104, 129,
  141, 146, 149, 156, 183, 201,
  203, 210, 234
Pythia 120

Q

Qaf 139
quetzal 75, 79, 158
Quetzalcoatl 25, **56**, 75, 79, 82,
  185, 213, 227

R

Ra 22, 32, 48, 64, 77, 92, 147,
  164, 182, 195
Ragnarok 213
Rama 136
Ramadan 79, 118
Ran 144
rebirth 17, 39, 45, 49, 51, 55, 62,
  73, 99, 126, 127, 128, 133,
  135, 136, 138, 143, 147, 149,
  150, 154, 155, 157–8, 160,
  174, 177, **179**, 184, 206, 219,
  233
redemption 16, **57**, 86, 118
regeneration 16, 53, 62, 65, 75,
  80, 84, 99, 136, 150, 181, 208,
  216, 222, 224
reincarnation 22, 145
rejuvenation 39, 64, 86, 185
reliability 48, 170–1
Remus 71, 80, 213, 218, 230
renunciation 17, 31, 59, 95, 97,
  193, 218
resurrection 21, 22, 29, 33, **37**,
  48, 53, 54, 81, 88, 110, 124,
  125, 126, 132, 134, 136, 150,
  152, 158, 163, 172, 177, 181,
  184, 185, 192, 195, 231
retribution 54, 114, 178
revelation, divine 48, 63, 80, 86,
  108, 121, 122, 135
Rhea 138, 149
Richard I, King 125
Rig Veda 221–2
*Rime of the Ancient Mariner,
  The* (poem) 10
Romeo and Juliet (play) 130
Romulus 71, 80, 213, 218, 230
Rossetti, Dante G. 163
royalty 22, 31, 36, 47, 112, **113**,
  123, 153, 154, 164, 173, 194,
  205, 209, 232
Rudra 32, 225
Rushmore, Mt 171

S

Sabazius 79, 163, 187
Safa, Mt 140
sagacity 73, 151
Sagittarius **179**, 212, 235
Sailing to Byzantium (poem) 81
St Alexis 24
St Andrew 171
St Antony of Padua 81, 101
St Augustine 35, 75, 81, 101, 228

Index

St Bartholomew 115
St Bernardino of Siena 107
St Catherine 134
St Francis 229
St George 68, 119
St Helena 142
St James 159, 177, 178
St Jerome 37, 124, 153
St John the Evangelist 29, 39, 40, 70, 144, 202
St Longinus 119
St Luke 151, 202
St Mark 124, 202
St Matthew 18, 202
St Michael *see* Michael (archangel)
St Nicholas 12
St Paul 159, 197
St Paul the Hermit 152
St Peter 49, 114, 144, 159, 171, 181, 182
St Teresa 107
St Theodore 55
St Thomas Aquinas 106, 151
salvation 12, 16, 66, 105, 190, 208, 222, 223, 227, 228
Samson 26, 96, 124, 160
samurai 29, 36, 43, 161
Saqqara 164
Sarasvati 154, 171
Satan 13, 26, 63, 64, 65, 76, 95, 105, 106, 121, 142, 144, 146, 153, 183, 186, 187, 193, 210, 228, 229
see also Devil; Lucifer
Saturn (god) 51, 150, 219
Saturn (planet) 133, 162, 176, 179
Saturnalia 36, 45, 103, 149, 187, 213
Saul, king of Israel 229
scholarship 27, 28, 36, 149, 169
science, Hermetic 12, 15
Scorpio 179, 235
Scylla 23
Sebek 55
Second Coming, The (poem) 63
Seder meal 72
Sekhmet 124
Selene 137
Selket 178
Set 28, 32, 55, 76, 103, 109, 121, 168, 177
Shabuoth 146
Shakespeare, William 17, 29, 39, 50, 109, 130, 134, 151, 163, 166, 172
shamanism 14, 15, 16, 18, 21, 24, 26, 33, 46, 59, 60, 65, 69, 71, 75, 76, 85, 93, 104, 112, 121, 131, 135, 145, 167, 173,

174, 183, 195, 201, 221
Shamash 191, 225
Shen Yeh 24
Shesha 48
Shiva 22, 32, 42, 44, 61, 69, 76, 80, 82, 97, 106, 122, 123, 133, 148, 155, 170, 171, 193, 197, 200, 203, 205, 210, 211, 219
Sigrune 173, 234
Sigurd 68
Sikhs 96, 211
Silenus 108, 218
Silver Age 52, 161, 182
sin 61, 68, 84, 121, 134–5, 150, 164, 176, 177, 187, 228
see also Original Sin
Sin (moon god) 54, 136, 174
Sinai, Mt 86, 122, 139
Skanda 154–5
sleep 37, 144, 163
Sleep of Reason, The (painting) 20
Sloth 159, 180
sobriety 22, 35, 95, 113
solitude 58, 62, 63
Solomon, king of Israel 103, 156, 170
sovereignty 16, 21, 42, 137, 153
Spenser, Edmund 165
spirituality 22, 218
stability 73, 87, 114, 139, 159, 160, 170, 183, 203, 207
sterility 63, 149, 157, 192, 225
strength 15, 73, 82, 90, 98, 103, 104, 109, 114, 123, 151, 159, 168, 170, 185, 192, 207, 213
Styx, river 10, 28
Sufism 96
Sung dynasty 31
Surya 197, 225
Swan Lake (music) 196
Synagogue (in Christian allegory) 26, 58

T

Tablets of the Law 44, 199
Tane 20
Tantrism 30, 41, 126, 127, 133, 153, 167, 204, 219, 225
Taranis 224
Taurus 179, 235
Tchaikovsky, P.I. 196
Temperaments 74, 167
temperance 12, 47, 161, 218, 220
Tempest, The (play) 109
temptation 15, 26, 63, 163, 175, 187
Tezcatlipoca 55, 112
Thanatos 62, 144
Themis 176

Theseus 117, 134
Thetis 39
Thor 9, 21, 24, 28, 32, 42, 43, 91, 97, 167, 186, 197, 204
Thoth 73, 107, 137, 202, 229
Thunderbird 25, 122, 204
Tiamat 23, 68, 144, 178, 224
Tiberius, Emperor 120
Tir nan Og 94, 109
Tiresius 26
Tlaloc 49, 56, 122, 127, 166
Tlaloc, Mt 139
tomb 62
totality 41, 45, 56, 73, 82, 87, 91, 114, 154, 188, 224, 234
Transmigration of Souls 38
treachery 53, 178, 232
Tree of Knowledge 15, 149, 208, 209
Tree of Life 40, 56, 59, 61, 62, 79–80, 86, 87, 137, 148, 152, 170, 178, 179, 190, 208, 209, 212, 217, 222, 226
Tree of Sweet Dew 64
Tristan and Isolde 209
Tritons 23, 51
Troy 15, 147, 157, 202
Tuan mac Cairill 175
Tyger, The (poem) 205

U

Ultima Thule 204
underworld 38, 39, 65, 67, 79, 100, 101, 102, 105, 118, 124, 135, 140, 144, 145, 148, 150, 163, 168, 181, 182, 184, 185, 186, 196, 206, 224
union 18, 116, 130, 135, 164, 165, 182, 190, 210, 226, 233
unity 41, 45, 54, 64, 108, 144, 149, 150, 154, 163, 170, 201, 202, 213, 216, 232
Upanishads 25
Uranus *see* Ouranos

V

Valhalla 10
Valkyries 106
Varuna 28, 83, 128, 195
Vayu 14, 20, 227
Venus (goddess) 73, 94, 172
see also Aphrodite
Venus (planet) 133, 156, 162, 179, 191
Vestal Virgins 218
Virgil 29, 135, 147
virgin birth 11, 218
Virgin Mary 11, 16, 22, 27, 43, 71, 89, 110, 130, 138, 152, 159, 165, 171, 172, 202, 208, 219

in art 25, 29, 33, 36, 52, 67, 71, 85, 89, 94, 96, 109, 123, 127, 129, 134, 137, 143, 167, 187, 191, 212, 214, 216, 218–19
immaculate conception 72, 109
Virgo 75, 179, 235
virility 21, 36, 48, 62, 90, 91, 96–7, 104, 123, 159, 167, 169, 175
Vishnu 22, 27, 28, 48, 51, 55, 64, 71, 73, 80, 83, 105, 113, 123, 125, 126, 143, 148, 153, 178, 184, 197, 198, 202, 207, 211, 225
vows 59, 170, 218, 233

W

Wagner, Richard 196
Walpurgis Night 73
war 58, 113, 168
watchfulness 38, 48, 155
wealth 21, 59, 73, 92, 98, 105, 153, 156, 157, 169, 206
Wheel of Existence 223, 225
Wheel of Life 56, 172
witches 31, 36, 45, 205, 222, 225, 228–9
Wodan 28, 77
see also Odin

X

Xi Wang Mu 154
Xipe Totec 183
Xiuhtecuhtli 212

Y

Yama 31, 65, 135
Yatano-Kagami 135
Yeats, W.B. 63, 81
Yggdrasil 86, 145, 190
Ymir 69
yoga 17, 30, 126, 133, 143, 185, 189, 233
Yom Kippur 79, 177
youth 15, 85, 113, 137, 153, 163, 164, 168, 193, 232

Z

Zeno 9
Zeus 15, 16, 17, 18, 19, 27, 32, 33, 41, 42, 49, 52, 59, 70, 73, 84, 91, 115, 118, 120, 122, 141, 149, 151, 159, 160, 161, 163, 166, 167, 186, 195, 196, 197, 203, 204, 213, 225, 231
see also Jupiter (god)
Zoroastrianism 30, 35, 63, 64, 95, 121, 186, 219
Zoser 164